Evidence-Based

READING INSTRUCTION

PUTTING THE NATIONAL READING PANEL REPORT INTO PRACTICE

Articles From the
International Reading Association

INTERNATIONAL
Reading
Association

800 Barksdale Road, PO Box 8139
Newark, Delaware 19714-8139, USA
www.reading.org

KH

Director of Publications   Joan M. Irwin
Editorial Director, Books and Special Projects   Matthew W. Baker
Senior Editor, Books and Special Projects   Tori M. Bachman
Production Editor   Shannon Benner
Permissions Editor   Janet S. Parrack
Acquisitions and Communications Coordinator   Corinne M. Mooney
Assistant Editor   Charlene M. Nichols
Administrative Assistant   Michele Jester
Editorial Assistant   Tyanna L. Collins
Production Department Manager   Iona Sauscermen
Supervisor, Electronic Publishing   Anette Schütz
Senior Electronic Publishing Specialist   Cheryl J. Strum
Electronic Publishing Specialist   R. Lynn Harrison

Project Editor   Charlene M. Nichols

Library of Congress Cataloging-in-Publication Data
Evidence-based reading instruction : putting the National Reading Panel report into practice.
      p.   cm.
Includes bibliographical references.
   ISBN 0-87207-460-9
1. Reading (Primary)—United States—Case studies.   2. Education, Primary—Activity programs—United States.   I.
National Reading Panel (U.S.)
   LB1525 .E87 2002
   372.4—dc21

2002013040

Eighth Printing, October 2005

11/17/06

Contents

Introduction

On January 8, 2002, President Bush signed into law the No Child Left Behind Act of 2001—the most dramatic reform of the Elementary and Secondary Education Act (ESEA) since it was enacted in 1965. Reading First, part of the No Child Left Behind Act, will provide a billion federal dollars a year for five years to improve the reading achievement of children in high-poverty, low-achieving schools. The law requires that the funds be spent to implement reading instruction based on scientifically based reading research (SBRR) as defined in the act. Each state, upon approval of their application by review panel, will receive funds that are proportional to the number and percentage of children living in poverty. The states will then host competitions among eligible local education agencies (school districts) to determine which districts and schools receive funds. The state will also have a significant amount of funding for statewide professional development that includes teachers in schools that do not receive Reading First funding.

A major requirement of Reading First is that all funds be spent in materials and practices that are supported by SBRR. The act defines SBRR as research that

(A) applies rigorous, systematic, and objective procedures to obtain valid knowledge relevant to reading development, reading instruction, and reading difficulties; and (B) includes research that

(i) employs systematic, empirical methods that draw on observation or experiment;

(ii) involves rigorous data analyses that are adequate to test the stated hypotheses and justify the general conclusions drawn;

(iii) relies on measurements or observational methods that provide valid data across evaluators and observers and across multiple measurements and observations; and

(iv) has been accepted by a peer-reviewed journal or approved by a panel of independent experts through a comparably rigorous, objective, and scientific review. (No Child Left Behind Act of 2001, Sec. 1208)

For more than two years, the National Reading Panel (NRP) reviewed research-based knowledge in reading instruction in order to assess the effectiveness of different approaches used to teach children to read. These findings were presented in the *Report of the National Reading Panel. Teaching Children to Read: An Evidence-Based Assessment of the Scientific Research Literature on Reading and Its Implications for Reading Instruction* (NICHD, 2000). Among the topics the panel addressed were phonemic awareness, phonics, reading fluency, vocabulary development, and comprehension strategies. The Reading First legislation labels these five topics the five essential components, and materials and professional development funded by Reading First must include all five components. The report summarizes scientifically based reading research on each of these topics and presents findings and implications for reading instruction.

This volume uses the report findings and implications as a starting point. For each of the five essential components, recent articles from *The Reading Teacher* are presented that describe instructional practices consistent with the NRP findings. The first five sections of the book summarize the findings related to each of the five essential components in isolation. In each of these sections, the actual findings of the NRP Report are summarized in a box. This is followed by a discussion of the findings and an introduction to each article explaining why it was chosen and how it relates to the findings highlighted.

The sixth section includes articles that employ practices from two or more of the essential elements in an instructional routine. These articles demonstrate how skilled practitioners combine practices across the five essential components as they orchestrate instruction that meets the individual needs of the children they teach.

The book concludes with appendixes that offer the International Reading Association position statement *What Is Evidence-Based Reading Instruction?* and a list of additional resources published by the Association (including the articles cited in the NRP Report).

This collection will be a useful tool for educators as they implement practices consistent with scientifically based reading research and the provisions of Reading First. The articles of-fered here bring descriptive detail to the abstract language of the report, and will help teachers implement excellent reading instruction that will help erase the achievement gap and help make every child a reader.

References

National Institute of Child Health and Human Development. (2000). *Report of the National Reading Panel. Teaching children to read: An evidence-based assessment of the scientific research literature on reading and its implications for reading instruction* (NIH Publication No. 00-4769). Washington, DC: U.S. Government Printing Office.

U.S. Public Law 107-110. 107th Cong., 1st sess., 8 January 2002. No Child Left Behind Act of 2001.

Phonemic Awareness

Phonemic awareness is the ability to hear, identify, and manipulate the individual sounds, or phonemes, in spoken words.

Findings in the National Reading Panel Report

Phonemic awareness can be taught and learned.

Phonemic awareness taught with letters was more effective than phonemic awareness taught without letters.

Teaching one or two phonemic awareness skills was more effective than teaching three or more skills.

Phonemic awareness teaching sessions of about 30 minutes for a total of 5 to 18 hours were most effective.

Computers were effective in teaching phonemic awareness.

Phonemic awareness was most effective with pre-K and K children and children at risk.

Phonemic awareness is an important predictor of early reading achievement. A study by Share, Jorm, Maclean, and Matthews (1984) found that of a variety of measures taken at school entry, phonemic awareness and letter knowledge were the two best predictors of reading achievement at the end of kindergarten and at the end of first grade. Teaching phonemic awareness is important because it helps children understand the alphabetic structure of the English writing system—that is, the basic relationship between letters in written words and sounds in spoken words. It is not easy to distinguish the individual sounds in spoken words because in speech the sounds are not distinct and blend into one another. The point at which one sound ends and another begins is not clear or easy to identify, hence the importance of phonemic awareness training.

Consider the following example: In the word *hat* there are three sounds, /h/, /a/, and /t/, each represented by a single letter. The most common skills taught in phonemic awareness are segmenting—taking the sounds of the word *hat* and breaking them into /h/, /a/, and /t/, and then blending them together to say "hat."

In recent volumes of *The Reading Teacher*, there have been many articles related to phonemic awareness, a sign that the profession recognizes phonemic awareness as important in teaching reading. The first article in this section, "Supporting phonemic awareness development in the classroom," by Hallie Kay Yopp and Ruth Helen Yopp, provides an excellent overview of phonemic awareness instruction. The authors give a clear definition and distinguish phonemic awareness from some terms with which it is frequently confused. They then provide a survey of phonemic awareness instruction and conclude with specific activities for teaching phonemic awareness.

The second article, "Developing a kindergarten phonemic awareness program: An action research project," by Kathleen Reiner, is a report of one teacher's implementation of a phonemic awareness program. The article chronicles Reiner's reasons for teaching phonemic awareness, describes the teaching activities she used, summarizes the data collection, and reports how the data analysis confirmed the value of teaching phonemic awareness and led to changes in her practice.

"Word boxes help children with learning disabilities identify and spell words" by Laurice M. Joseph is included because it gives a detailed description of the use of word boxes, a commonly used activity for teaching phonemic awareness. The author notes that Clay's word boxes are an extension of Elkonin's sound boxes and provides a strong rationale for their use. She then reports the improvement in word identification and spelling of her learning disabled readers after their use of word boxes. She also suggests adaptations for classroom use.

The final article, "Children's books to develop phonemic awareness—for you and parents, too!" by Michael F. Opitz, is included because it provides a list of children's books, specific activities, and a straightforward record-keeping system that teachers can use with parents so that parents' interactions with their children around books can reinforce phonemic awareness skills being taught and learned in the classroom.

Reference

Share, D., Jorm, A., Maclean, R., & Matthews, R. (1984). Sources of individual differences in reading acquisition. *Journal of Educational Psychology, 76*, 1309–1324.

Hallie Kay Yopp
Ruth Helen Yopp

Supporting phonemic awareness development in the classroom

Playful and appealing activities that focus on the sound structure of language support literacy development.

Although it is widely acknowledged that phonemic awareness is important in learning to read, considerable confusion remains about what phonemic awareness is, the role it plays in reading development, and how it should be addressed in classrooms.

Some educators confuse the term *phonemic awareness* with the terms *auditory discrimination*, *phonetics*, or *phonics* and believe that a new label has been invented for an old idea. This is not true. The term *phonemic awareness* refers to a construct relatively new in our understanding of how children become readers. Although related, phonemic awareness is different from auditory discrimination, phonetics, and phonics. The definitions of each of these terms can be found in Figure 1. (See also Harris & Hodges, 1995; Snow, Burns, & Griffin, 1998.) The definition of phonemic awareness, also in Figure 1, is elaborated upon here.

Phonemic awareness is the awareness that the speech stream consists of a sequence of sounds—specifically phonemes, the smallest unit of sound that makes a difference in communication. It is a phoneme that determines the difference between the words *dog* and *hog*, for instance, and between *look* and *lick*. These differences influence meaning. Place these words in sentences ("You dog!" vs. "You hog!" and "Take a look" vs. "Take a lick"), and the power of the phoneme becomes obvious. Individuals who are phonemically aware recognize that the speech stream is a sequence of these small sounds. They can identify the three sounds in the spoken word *fish* (/f/-/i/-/sh/), for example, and

can blend phonemes together to form words (/h/-/o/-/p/ is *hop*). They have the ability to notice, mentally grab ahold of, and manipulate these smallest chunks of speech.

Phonemic awareness may be better understood when placed in the context of two superordinate constructs: phonological awareness and metalinguistics. Phonemic awareness is a type of *phonological awareness*, that is, the awareness of the sound structure of language in general. Phonological awareness refers to a sensitivity to *any size unit of sound*. Thus, the ability to generate and recognize rhyming words, to count syllables, to separate the beginning of a word from its ending (e.g., as in the *st* and *op* in the word *stop*), and to identify each of the phonemes in a word may each be an indication of phonological awareness. Phonemic awareness—a subset of phonological awareness—refers to a sensitivity to and control over the phonemes.

Phonological awareness can, in turn, be placed into the larger context of metalinguistic awareness. Like metacognition, which entails thinking about one's thinking (or cognition), metalinguistic awareness entails thinking about one's language. It refers to one's awareness of and control over one's language in general; it is the ability to focus attention on language in and of itself, independent of meaning (see Hodges & Harris, 1995; Tunmer, Herriman, & Nesdale, 1988; Yaden & Templeton, 1986).

Thus, phonemic awareness is one aspect of phonological awareness which is one component of metalinguistic awareness.

Figure 1
Definition of terms

Term	Definition	Example
Auditory discrimination	The ability to hear likenesses and differences in phonemes and words	Say these sounds: /t/ /p/. Are they the same or different?
Phonetics	The study of the speech sounds that occur in languages, including the way these sounds are articulated	The first sound in *pie* is a bilabial—it is made with the two lips.
Phonics	A way of teaching reading and spelling that stresses symbol-sound relationships (in alphabetic orthographies)	The symbol *m* is used to represent the italicized sounds in the following words: ha*m*, ju*m*p, *m*y.
Phoneme	The smallest unit of speech sounds that makes a difference in communication	The spoken word *fly* consists of three phonemes: /f/-/l/-/ī/. It differs from the word *flea* by one phoneme.
Phonemic awareness	The awareness that spoken language consists of a sequence of phonemes	How many sounds in the spoken word, *dog*? Say all the sounds you hear.

Phonemic awareness and reading

The awareness that the speech stream is made up of a sequence of small units of sound and the ability to manipulate those small units—phonemic awareness—appears to be critical for readers of an alphabetic orthography. Why? Because an alphabetic orthography maps speech to print at the level of the phoneme. In other words, users of an alphabetic written system record the smallest units of sound of their spoken language in print. (Although not a pure alphabetic orthography, English is considered fundamentally alphabetic.) The young child whose writing is shown in Figure 2 clearly is attending to the sounds in her speech stream as she records her ideas.

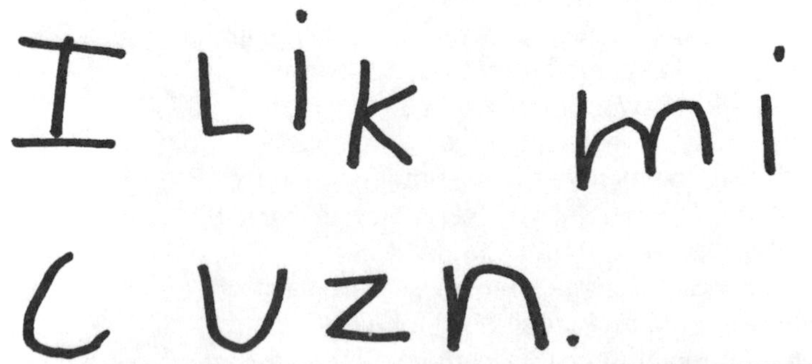

The temporary or inventive spellings seen in Figure 2 reveal much about how the child is thinking about the written system. This child has made the empowering discovery that users of English write down the smallest pieces of the language. In order for a beginning reader to capture the logic of this written system, it appears that he or she must notice that running speech is made up of a sequence of small sounds. Without this insight—without phonemic awareness—the symbol system is arbitrary. The task of dealing with the symbol system, then, can quickly become overwhelming. It is, in short, to one's advantage to be aware of the level of sounds that the written system encodes.

Much has been said about phonemic awareness in the literature in recent years, and many states in the U.S. are addressing phonemic awareness in standards documents and even in legislation governing the funding of professional

Figure 2
A kindergartner's inventive spelling of "I like my cousin"

I LIK mi CUZN.

development activities and the content of teacher training programs. Professional organizations such as the International Reading Association are publishing position statements on phonemic awareness and its role in the teaching of reading (International Reading Association, 1998). Influential documents such as the report of the Committee on the Prevention of Reading Difficulties in Young Children (Snow et al., 1998) recommend that kindergartners have some basic phonemic awareness by the end of their kindergarten year. Moreover, the report asserts that enhancing children's abilities to attend to the sound structure of spoken language should be a *priority* goal in kindergarten classrooms. *Every Child Reading: An Action Plan of the Learning First Alliance* (1998) identifies phonemic awareness as one of the most important foundations of reading success and recommends that its development be addressed in prekindergarten and kindergarten.

School administrators and teachers of young children are anxious to apply recent research findings to practice and are looking for guidance. What does phonemic awareness instruction look like, they ask. How much time should be devoted to it? The purpose of this article is to provide some guidelines for planning phonemic awareness instruction and to share 14 activities that are representative of the type of instruction appropriate for children in preschool, kindergarten, and first-grade classrooms.

Phonemic awareness instruction

What does phonemic awareness instruction look like in the classroom? First, most experts call for phonemic awareness activities that are child appropriate (International Reading Association & the National Association for the Education of Young Children, 1998). Adams and Bruck (1995), for instance, submitted that songs, chants, and word-sound games are ideally suited toward developing young children's sensitivity to the sound structure of language. Beck and Juel (1995) posited that time spent on word play, nursery or Dr. Seuss rhymes, and general exposure to storybooks contribute to phonemic awareness. Mattingly (1984) encouraged classroom teachers to provide their students with linguistic stimulation in the form of storytelling, word games, rhymes, and riddles in order to facilitate phonemic awareness. Yopp (1992), describing developmentally appropriate activities,

argued that phonemic awareness instruction for young children should be playful and engaging, interactive and social, and should stimulate curiosity and experimentation with language.

Second, phonemic awareness instruction should be deliberate and purposeful. Although some teachers have engaged their students in playful language activities for years, they may have done so without knowing the full value of these activities. Any phonemic awareness development that resulted was incidental; it was an unrecognized byproduct of the activities. Yet, Adams and Bruck (1995) emphasized that playful language activities will be most effective in developing phonemic awareness if they are used with that goal in mind. Thus, in addition to being child appropriate, phonemic awareness instruction should be intentional, not incidental (even accidental), in classrooms.

Third, phonemic awareness instruction must be viewed by educators as only one part of a much broader literacy program. Phonemic awareness development is not meaningful in and of itself. It is important only in the context of comprehensive reading instruction. Indeed, Griffith and Olson (1992) argued that phonemic awareness activities will not be helpful unless they can be placed in a context of real reading and writing. Furthermore, teachers must recognize that while sensitivity to the sound basis of language supports literacy development, it is also an outcome of literacy experiences. Therefore, to overemphasize this component of literacy instruction in the initial years of schooling is to limit children's opportunities for more comprehensive literacy development.

In addition to these general guidelines, teachers should consider various dimensions of phonemic awareness instruction when planning and designing learning activities. These include the unit of sound to be emphasized, the type of operation to be performed on those units, and whether the activities are to be strictly oral or include concrete cues such as chips and letters.

Units of sound. As teachers plan phonemic awareness instruction, it will be helpful to consider the sequence displayed in Figure 3. Children appear to be better able to capture and gain control over larger units of sound before smaller units of sound (Stahl & Murray, 1994; Treiman & Zukowski, 1991). Thus, with younger children, such as preschoolers, or older children who have

Figure 3
A sequence for phonemic awareness instruction

Instruction	Example
Activities that focus on rhyme	Let's think of something that rhymes with *cow*. (now)
Activities that focus on syllable units	Clap twice for Harry's name. Har (clap)—ry (clap)
Activities that focus on onset and rime	Say just the first part of *brown*. (/br/)
Activities that focus on phonemes	Let's put these sounds together. /ch/—/ā/—/n/ (chain)

very little sensitivity to the sound structure of language, teachers initially may wish to focus predominantly on rhyme (see Bishop, Yopp, & Yopp, 2000). Then, teachers may engage students in activities that focus on the units of sound within words, the largest unit of which is the syllable. In the word *hopscotch*, for example, there are two syllables: *hop* and *scotch*. Next, instruction might focus on the largest subsyllabic units—the onset and rime. The onset is the part of the syllable that precedes the vowel; the rime is the vowel and any consonants that follow it. The onset in *hop* is /h/ and the rime in *hop* is /op/; the onset in *scotch* is /sk/; the rime in *scotch* is /och/. Some syllables such as *it*, *un*, and *on* have no onset. Finally, attention can be directed to the phoneme. Thus, when planning phonemic awareness instruction the size of the unit of sound to be addressed should be considered, with a general plan to move from larger to smaller units of sound.

Tasks or operations. Another dimension of phonemic awareness instruction is the task or operation the students must perform with sounds. For instance, children may be asked to match sounds, as when they indicate whether two words begin the same (e.g., Do these words begin the same? *fish fight*). They may be asked to isolate sounds (e.g., What is the first/ middle/last sound in *run*?) They may be asked to blend sounds together to form a word (e.g., What word would we have if we put these sounds together? /j/-/u/-/m/-/p/). They may be asked to segment words into their constituent parts (e.g., Tell all the sounds you hear in the word *dog*).

A sampling of tasks is presented in Figure 4, with examples for syllable, onset-rime, and phoneme units. There is evidence to suggest that some tasks may be easier than others (see Adams, 1990; Smith, Simmons, & Kameenui, 1998; Yopp, 1988). For example, matching sounds (especially initial sounds) is one of the easier tasks, and more difficult may be the ability to blend sounds together to form words. The ability to segment spoken words into their constituent parts may be more difficult still. However, the difficulty of the task depends in part upon the number of sounds (fewer sounds are easier than more), which sounds they are (liquids are typically easier than nasals or stops), and their location in the word (middle sounds are more difficult to attend to than initial or final sounds). (See McBride-Chang, 1995, for a discussion.) Therefore, it is much too simplistic to identify a hard-and-fast order in which operations should be presented. Nevertheless, we provide a possible order of what appears to be easier to more difficult operations for many children, given that the same types of sounds, the same number, and the same location are the focus of attention. This information is offered only to support the teacher in making thoughtful decisions about potential sound manipulation activities and is not intended to be prescriptive.

Use of cues. A third dimension of phonemic awareness instruction to consider is the use of cues. Some activities may be strictly oral. These include games, activities, poetry, stories, or songs that demand attention strictly to the spoken language itself. Other activities may make use of some sort of cue or concrete manipulative. Many successful training studies include concrete representations of sounds in order to make mental manipulations more overt (e.g., Ball & Blachman, 1991). For instance, auditory cues are in play when children are asked to clap the number of syllables they hear in a spoken word. Visual cues are

Figure 4
Types of sound manipulation with examples using different linguistic units

	Syllable	Onset-rime	Phoneme
Matching	Do these start the same? *sandwich sandbag* (yes)	Do these start the same? *start stand* (yes)	Do these start the same? *cat kite* (yes)
Isolation	What do you hear at the beginning of *under*? (/un/)	What do you hear at the beginning of *black*? (/bl/)	What do you hear at the beginning of *bug*? (/b/)
Substitution	What word would you have if you changed the /bā/ in *baby* to /may/? (*maybe*)	What word would you have if you changed the /bl/ in *black* to /cr/? (*crack*)	What word would you have if you changed the /ch/ in *chain* to /r/? (*rain*)
Blending	What word would you have if you put these sounds together: /pup/-/py/ (*puppy*)	What word would you have if you put these sounds together: /pl/-/ane/ (*plane*)	What word would you have if you put these sounds together: /p/-/l/-/ā/-/n/ (*plane*)
Segmentation	Tell the parts you hear in this word: *table* (/tā/—/ble/)	Tell the sounds you hear in this word: *spoon* (/sp/—/oon/)	Tell the sounds you you hear in this word: *dog* (/d/-/o/-/g/)
Deletion	Say *napkin* without the /kin/. (*nap*)	Say *grin* without the /gr/. (*in*)	Say *meat* without the /m/. (*eat*)

used when blocks or chips represent sounds. Kinesthetic cues are used when children jump as they repeat sounds. Finally, some activities may incorporate the use of letters as children manipulate and reflect on sounds in speech. In fact, the combination of phonemic awareness activities and letter-sound instruction has been found to be particularly supportive of children's emerging understanding of the alphabetic principle (Bradley & Bryant, 1983; Byrne & Fielding-Barnsley, 1993; Hohn & Ehri, 1983), although the optimal timing of combining these aspects of literacy instruction remains unclear. (Note that once letters are attached to the sound manipulation in phonemic awareness instruction, the activity also becomes a phonics activity. This overlap explains some of the confusion between the terms *phonemic awareness* and *phonics*.)

Time

How much time should be devoted to phonemic awareness instruction? Training programs described in the research literature suggest that relatively modest amounts of time result in increases in phonemic awareness performance (Brady & Moats, 1998; Yopp, 1997). The duration of instruction was anywhere from 10 minutes to 30 minutes per session; in some studies, instruction occurred daily; in other studies the instruction was less frequent, occuring two or three times a week. Training occurred over the course of a minimum of 3 weeks up to 2 years.

We will not recommend a particular amount of time be devoted to phonemic awareness instruction in this article, although we have seen time allocation requirements implemented in a number of school districts across the U.S. Unfortunately, time allocations do not take into account individual differences among learners. It is the *quality* of instruction and the *responsiveness* of the instruction to the individuals in the classroom that should have greater consideration than the amount of time.

We believe that phonemic awareness can be stimulated in many students in large part by providing them with linguistically rich environments—ones in which they are exposed to rich vocabulary, syntactic complexity, and decontextualized language as well as ones in which language itself is explored and experimented with deliberately. In linguistically rich classrooms, phonemic awareness activities will be incorporated intentionally into literature sharing experiences, music experiences, movement experiences, and other experiences throughout the day.

Activities for building sensitivity to sounds of speech

The activities we share here adhere to the general guidelines discussed above: They are playful, they are deliberate in focusing on the sound structure of spoken language, and they can readily be included in a comprehensive reading program. The activities are organized by size of linguistic unit emphasized—rhyme, syllables, onset-rime units, or phonemes. They demand a variety of operations, such as matching, substituting, or segmenting sounds. Some activities are strictly oral; some make use of auditory, visual, or kinesthetic cues to help children attend to sound units; and some include the relationship of letters to the sounds.

Activities that focus on rhyme

1. *The Hungry Thing* (oral)

The Hungry Thing, by Jan Slepian and Ann Seidler, is the story of a creature that asks townspeople for food by pointing to a sign on his chest that says FEED ME. When the townspeople ask what he would like to eat, he responds, "Schmancakes!" The townspeople are flustered and attempt to determine what schmancakes are. After wise men and a cook offer ideas, a little boy declares that "Schmancakes sound like fancakes sound like pancakes to me!" and the townspeople feed him some. The Hungry Thing asks for more and more food and each time the people try to identify what he wants.

The charm of this book is the play with language. Nonsense rhyming words are clues to what the Hungry Thing wishes to eat. The townspeople—and the listener—must think of rhyming foods in order to make sense of the Hungry Thing's requests.

As you read this book aloud, encourage the children to make predictions. The Hungry Thing wants feetloaf. What can that be? Pause before the little boy in the story concludes that "Feetloaf sounds like beetloaf sounds like (pause) meatloaf to me!" Allow the children to make guesses before you read "meatloaf."

After reading the book, pull out a lunchbag and announce how hungry you are. Look into the bag and tell the children what you have for lunch today. "Ah! Mogurt! I love mogurt!" Encourage the children to guess what mogurt is. Once they have figured out that mogurt is yogurt, take it out of the bag to show them and ask them how they knew. Repeat this with three or four other food items you have in the lunchbag.

Next, provide the children with paperbags, paper, and markers (or magazines with photographs of food) so they can create their own lunchbags full of food. After they draw or select and cut out their favorite foods and put them in the bag, have each child sit with a partner and provide "clues" about what his or her bag contains. "I have a piece of nizza." The partner's task is to determine what "nizza" is.

You may also create a center with plastic foods and lunchbags. Children will play with these items, retelling the story and creating rhymes as they have their peers guess what they have in their bags. A copy of the book should be available at the center.

We read this book to a group of 4- and 5-year-olds and discovered how quickly they participate in the story. After reading the Hungry Thing's first request for food, the young audience began to predict each of the other requests upon hearing the nonsense rhyme. When the story was finished, they begged to see what was inside a paperbag that was nearby. When we said that we brought some food and wondered if they could figure out what we had, they grinned with delight. "We have some napes in our lunch today." "Grapes! Grapes!" the children exclaimed. We pulled the grapes from the sack and confirmed their response. Then we said, "Oh, we also have a kanana." "Banana! Banana!" Then we showed the children a stack of paper bags and a tray of plastic foods. We encouraged them to make their own lunches if they wished and to see if others could figure out what they had. The stuffing of bags began in a fury. Bags loaded, the children then moved around the room to seek out one another, parent volunteers, and the teacher. "Look! Look! I have cherries—no, I mean terries!" "I have a pamburger." Children shared their own "lunch" items and guessed one another's lunch items. (See Photo 1.) The bags and plastic foods remained on the table for the day, alongside the book, and children made frequent visits to the center. The book is often requested during story time.

You may also wish to follow a reading of the story with placing a FEED ME sign around your neck. Distribute cards with pictures of foods and begin making requests using nonsense rhymes: "Feed me the nandwich." The child who holds the picture of the food you request (in this case, the sandwich) brings it to you whereupon you pretend to gobble it up. Give volunteers the opportunity to be the Hungry Thing as well.

The Hungry Thing Returns and *The Hungry Things Goes to a Restaurant* are two additional books by the authors that follow the same pattern. Read these at a later time and include menus and food trays at a center so children may engage in play with these items, too. (See Bishop et al., 2000, and Yopp, 1995, for children's books that draw attention to sounds.)

2. Twenty Kids Have Hats (oral)

The book *Ten Cats Have Hats* by Jean Marzollo is a counting book of rhymes: "One bear has a chair, but I have a hat. Two ducks have trucks, but I have a hat." Read the book aloud to the children, and invite predictions. "Five pigs have . . ." The children may respond with *wigs* or *twigs* or *figs*. (Picture clues will allow them to predict the author's rhyme. Because you want the students to attend to the sound clues, you may wish to hide the pictures on the first reading.) Ask the children how they made their guesses. "Why did you guess wigs/twigs/figs?" Children who have not discovered the author's rhyming pattern will hear their peers pointing out the rhyme element. Prompt the children to listen for rhymes as you read further. Continue to encourage predictions.

After sharing the book, create a class big book about students who have hats. Each child selects a number, dictates to an adult a rhyme that follows the pattern in the book, and then illustrates the rhyme. For example, Fatima may be responsible for "one," Kevin may be responsible for "two," and Phyllis may be responsible for

"three." Fatima might say, "One dog has a frog, but I have a hat" and paint or otherwise illustrate one dog with a frog. Then each child paints a picture of himself or herself wearing a hat. Compile the book from one to however many children you have. Teacher Bev Maeda had 20 kindergartners in her multiage class one year. Her students made the book pictured in Photo 2: Twenty Kids Have Hats. After each child's rhyme, insert the author's painting of himself or herself wearing a hat. This student-created book becomes part of the classroom library.

3. "The Ants Go Marching" (oral)

Many songs make use of rhyme. The song "The Ants Go Marching" is an excellent example. Once children catch on to the pattern, they may create their own verses. While marching in a line, children sing the following:

Photo 1

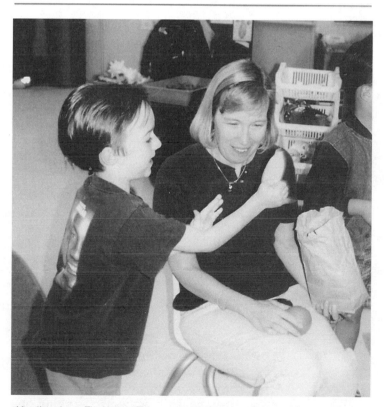

After listening to The Hungry Thing, *preschoolers use plastic foods and paper bags located at a literacy center to create their own lunches. Spontaneous retellings and language play often occur at this time.* Photo by Hallie Kay Yopp

Photo 2

Two pages from one group of kindergartners' version of Ten Cats Have Hats. Photo by Hallie Kay Yopp

The ants go marching one by one,
Hurrah! Hurrah!
The ants go marching one by one,
Hurrah! Hurrah!
The ants go marching one by one,
The little one stops to have some fun,
And they all go down to the ground,
To get out of the sun.
Boom! Boom! Boom!

The song continues with the ants marching two by two, three by three, and so on with any appropriate corresponding rhyme.

We observed kindergartners singing and marching around their classroom to this song. Each time the group sang, "the little one stops to—" a different child proposed a rhyming lyric and everyone mimed the action. Then they all marched lower and lower, bending over, as they "go down to the ground…."

"Down by the Bay" is another song that offers children the opportunity to create their own lyrics. After learning verses such as "Did you ever see a whale with a polka dot tail?" and "Did you ever see llamas eating their pajamas?" children create their own verses such as, "Did you ever see a shark strolling in the park?" We sing "The Corner Grocery Store" with our own young children as we go to the market. The original lyrics include, "There were peas, peas walking on their knees at the store, at the store" and similar silly rhymes. We develop rhymes for the food items on our market lists such as "There was steak, steak, going shake shake at the store, at the store." See Yopp and Yopp (1996) for a collection of songs that draw attention to sounds.

Activities with syllable manipulation

1. "Clap, Clap, Clap Your Hands" (cues)

This popular traditional song is sung in many classrooms across the U.S. Like many songs, it may readily be adapted for language manipulation (Yopp, 1992). In this example, we modify "Clap, clap, clap your hands" to encourage blending syllables. The first two verses below are traditional (there are many more); these are followed by an adaptation.

> Clap, clap, clap your hands,
> Clap your hands together.
> Clap, clap, clap your hands,
> Clap your hands together.
>
> Snap, snap, snap your fingers.
> Snap your fingers together.
> Snap, snap, snap your fingers.
> Snap your fingers together.
>
> Say, say, say these parts.
> Say these parts together.
> Say, say, say these parts,
> Say these parts together:
> Teacher: moun (pause) tain (children respond, "mountain!")
> Teacher: love (pause) ly (children respond, "lovely!")
> Teacher: un (pause) der (children respond, "under!")
> Teacher: tea (pause) cher (children respond, "teacher!")

This example suggests two-syllable words. However, once children are comfortable with the activity, you may include words with three or four syllables.

2. How Many Syllables in a Name? (cues)

Read the story *Tikki Tikki Tembo* by Arlene Mosel about a pair of Chinese brothers, one of whom has a very long name ("Tikki Tikki Tembo No Sa Rembo Chari Bari Ruchi Pip Peri Pembo") and the other of whom has a very short name ("Chang"). After reading and discussing the story, encourage your students to say the two boys' names. Say them again and this time clap with each syllable that is said. Tikki Tikki Tembo's name will have 21 claps. Chang's name will receive one clap.

Then have your students try clapping the syllables in their own names. As a group, say each child's name and clap as you separate the syllables. *Erica* would be said "Er" (with a clap)

-"i" (clap) -"ca" (clap). *Richard* would be said with two claps. Further develop the activity by placing colored pieces of paper in a pocket chart as you say each syllable in a particular child's name. Point to each piece of paper as you say each syllable. Later, let children work at tables to glue the appropriate number of colored pieces on a piece of drawing paper to represent the number of syllables in their names. Encourage them to draw pictures of themselves. Erica, for example, takes three pieces of colored paper from a pile in the center of the table and glues them side by side at the top of a piece of drawing paper. (See Photo 3.) She then draws a picture of herself. Afterwards, children move around the room with their papers in hand and group themselves with others who have the same number of colored pieces glued on the drawing paper. Erica will stand by others who have three colored pieces glued on their papers. As the others in the class listen, ask each child in a group to say his or her name. Encourage all students to say the syllables as each name is slowly said. Comment that they do, indeed, each have the target number of syllables. ("Yes! Jean, Bill, Juan, and Li each have one beat! Let's go to our next group. Let's say their names: Terry, José, Peter, Danny. Do they each have two beats? Yes!" and so on.) Develop a bar graph reflecting the number of students that have a given number of syllables in their names.

As a follow-up activity, you may wish to use clapping when taking attendance for several days, clapping the number of syllables as you call each child's name. And at dismissal time you may clap once and anyone with a one-syllable name may leave. Clap twice and students with two-syllable names may leave, and so on.

Later share the story *Tingo Tango Mango Tree* by Marcia Vaughan in which an iguana is named Sombala Bombala Rombala Roh, a flamingo is named Kokio Lokio Mokio Koh, a parrot is named Dillaby Dallaby Doh, a turtle is named Nanaba Panaba Tanaba Goh, and a bat is named Bitteo Biteo.

3. "Humpty Dumpty" (cues)

This familiar nursery rhyme may be used in a syllable blending activity. Each child should have about five separate cubes of the type that can be snapped together. Recite the nursery rhyme. Tell the children that Humpty Dumpty

Photo 3

Children share their work after representing the number of syllables in their names with pieces of paper and drawing self-portraits. Photo by Hallie Kay Yopp

broke and that you have some broken words, too. Ask them if they can help to put the words back together again. Say the parts of a word (e.g., pop-si-cle) and ask the children to repeat the parts by picking up a cube for each part they say. In this example, they pick up three cubes, one at a time. Then they snap the cubes together, saying each part and then the entire word. Are they able to help Humpty Dumpty? Repeat the process, reciting the poem and then asking the children to put together a new "broken word."

4. Teacher, May We? (cues)

As in the game Mother May I? have your students line up some distance away and face you. Give directions that require children to count the number of syllables in a word such as "You may jump the number of times as there are syllables (some teachers say "beats" or "chunks" for syllables) in the word *bunny*. Students respond, "Teacher, may we?" With your affirmative response, the children say "Bun—ny!" and each child moves two jumps forward. Alter the number of syllables in the cue words you provide (e.g., from one syllable as in *good* up to four—or more—syllables as in *motorcycle*) and

vary the types of movement the students may make (e.g., take small steps, take giant steps, or skip). The first student to reach you may give directions on the next round.

Activities with onset-rime manipulation

1. Mail a Package (oral)

Use a large box or container with a lid to serve as a mailbox. Cut a slit in the lid through which cards can be deposited into the box or container. Give each child a picture card of an object. To ensure familiarity with the objects, ask each child to show his or her card to the class and name the object. The objects should be single-syllable words such as the following: *cup, ring, flag, street, rug, dog, cat, plum, brick*. In this activity, the teacher says the name of an object by segmenting it into its onset and rime components (c-up, r-ing, fl-ag, str-eet, and so on). The child who has the picture of the object named holds the card in the air, blends the sounds to say the word, and brings the card forward to mail. You may wish to recite the following chant prior to each turn.

A package! A package!
What can it be?
A package! A package!
I hope it's for me!

2. Going on a Word Hunt (cues)

Read *We're Going on a Bear Hunt* by Michael Rosen. Then propose to the children that you go on a word hunt. Have children sit on the floor with their feet together and their knees bent up. Everyone slaps their toes, then slaps their knees with the beat of the chant. Keep the rhythm going throughout the chant. The teacher begins and the students echo.

Teacher:	Going	on	a	word	hunt!
	Slap toes	slap knees	slap toes	slap knees	

Students:	Going	on	a	word	hunt!
	Slap toes	slap knees	slap toes	slap knees	

Teacher:	What's	this	word?	
	Slap toes	slap knees	slap toes	slap knees

Students:	What's	this	word?	
	Slap toes	slap knees	slap toes	slap knees

Teacher:	/m/	(pause)	/ap/	(pause)
	slap toes		slap knees	

Students:	/m/	(pause)	/ap/	(pause)
	slap toes		slap knees	

Together:	mmmmmmmmmmmmmmmmap	map!
	slide hands from toes to knee	slap knees

Again, use single-syllable words such as *light, six, man, van, no, zoo, fist*. We also recommend that you use words that begin with continuant sounds so that they may be elongated as hands are sliding from the toes to the knees for the final part of the chant (as in mmmmmmap, above). Continuant sounds include /f/, /l/, /m/, /n/, /r/, /s/, /v/, /w/, /y/, /z/, /th/, /sh/ and vowel sounds. (If you select words that begin with a vowel, such as *it*, there is no onset to separate from the rime. This activity would be used to segment and blend phoneme level units, in that case.)

3. Make a Word (letters)

Select rime units such as *at* to focus upon. Have a card with the letters *at* written on it. In a bag have letter cards that may serve as the onset for this family. A child draws a card from the bag. The class says the sound of the letter drawn, blends it with the *at* and determines whether or not a real word is made. Students give a thumbs up or thumbs down. For instance, a student draws the card *b*. Students say /b/ and blend it with /at/, /b/—/at/: bat. Everyone indicates thumbs up because this is a real word. Someone else draws the letter *g*. Students say /g/—/at/: gat! Thumbs down for this one.

Activities with phoneme manipulation

1. *Cock-a-doodle-moo!* (oral)

In the book *Cock-a-doodle-moo!* by Bernard Most, a rooster wakes up one morning to discover that he cannot crow above a whisper. So the farm animals sleep on. "Z-z-z-cheep," snore the chicks. "Z-z-z-quack," snore the ducks. The rooster tries desperately to teach the cow to "cock-a-doodle-doo" so that she can awaken the farm animals. The cow struggles with this task, substituting phonemes in many ways. She says, "Mock-a-moodle-moo!" and "Rock-a-poodle-moo!" but she just cannot say "cock-a-doodle-doo." When she gets close enough—with "Cock-a-doodle-moo!"—the rooster encourages her to awaken the farm animals. The animals awaken with a laugh: "Oink-ha!" "Quack-ha!" "Meow-ha!" and so on.

In this book, the author engages in phoneme addition and phoneme substitution. As the story is read aloud, children will join in with the phoneme addition, anticipating the "z-z-z" and the "ha" added to the animal sounds. They will enjoy listening to the cow's manipulation of sounds. As you read, talk about what the author is doing in this story to make it so entertaining.

After reading the story, think about farm animals that are not mentioned in the book. How would the author have a goat snore? A sheep snore? How would an awakening horse sound? Reread each of the ways that the cow tried to crow. Have your students think of other ways to say "cock-a-doodle-doo." Encourage as many children to share as possible. (You may wish to write some of their ideas on chart paper or an erasable board, adding letters to the phonemic awareness activity. Write *cock-a-doo-*

dle-doo, erase the initial letters, and replace with letters suggested by the children. Say the new wake-up cry.) Then, think about other sound manipulations. For instance, what if the situation were altered and the pig tried to teach the cow to oink? What might the cow's attempts at oinking sound like?

Place plastic farm animals at a center. Leave the book at the center, too. The children will retell the story and play with sounds as they manipulate the plastic animals. (See Photo 4.)

One of the authors read this story to a small group of preschoolers at a community nursery school. She read through the chicks' snoring, the cows' snoring, and the ducks' snoring. After hearing /zzzzzzz/ read through these pages, 4-year-old Byron interrupted and shouted, "Zzzzack!" (dragging out the initial sound in the name of a fellow student). Byron was attending to the sounds of speech and realized that one of the members of his class had a name that started with the very sound that was being repeated in the story.

2. Find Your Partners (oral)

Using a set of picture cards with which the children are familiar, distribute the cards so that each child has one. Be sure that each card can be matched with another that begins or ends with the same sound or has the same sound in the medial position. For example, if you choose to focus on ending sounds you should select cards such as dog and flag, and hat and nut. Then tell the children that once you give the signal they are each to circulate and find a classmate whose card shares the same sound in the targeted position.

3. Bag Game (cues)

Have a large grocery bag or box that contains many small plastic bags that can be sealed so that objects do not fall out. In each of these smaller bags place one object and the number of interlocking cubes as there are sounds in the name of the object. For instance, one bag might contain a key and two cubes that are connected (representing the two sounds in *key*). Another bag might contain a dime and three cubes that are connected for the three sounds in *dime*. A third bag might contain several nails and four connected cubes for the four sounds in *nails*. To begin the activity, ask a volunteer to draw a small bag from the large grocery bag. The child opens the small bag, pulls out the object and the

Photo 4

A set of farm animals placed at a literacy center with the recently shared book Cock-a-doodle moo! *stimulates further play with sounds and reenactment of the story.* Photo by Hallie Kay Yopp

cubes. He or she names the object and then says the sounds in the object, breaking apart the cubes as he or she speaks each sound. If the child draws a bag that contains a little book, he or she would say, "This is a book. Book." Then, holding up the three connected cubes, the child would break the cubes apart one by one while saying /b/-/oo/-/k/.

4. Scavenger Hunt (letters)

Organize children into teams of about three. Give each team a bag or box that has on it a letter and picture of an object that begins with that letter. For instance, one team receives a bag with the letter *M* on it and a picture of a monkey; another team receives a bag with the letter S on it and a picture of a snake. Children then set off on a scavenger hunt to find objects in the classroom that begin with their target sound. Children with the *B* bag may locate a baby doll in the housekeeping center, a block in the building area, a brush in the painting area, and a book from the library corner. Children with the bag that has the letter *P* written on it may find a pencil, pen, and paper to put in their bag. Give the children enough time and support to be successful, then bring them together to state their target sound and share their objects. Then they may return their objects, trade bags, and repeat the activity.

Comments and cautions

The suggestions shared here represent the type of activities we hope to see young children engaging in with their teachers in preschool, kindergarten, and first-grade classrooms. Some of them also may be used with older children. The activities are playful and appealing while deliberately focusing attention on the sound structure of spoken language. They spring from children's literature, music, or traditional childhood games and therefore are easily incorporated into rich literacy programs. Most of these activities can be modified to focus on a different unit of sound than the one described here. For example, the Bag Game, described here for phoneme manipulation, can be used for syllable manipulation. Mail a Package, suggested for onset-rime level manipulation, can be used with rhymes, syllables, and phonemes as well. Letters easily can be added to most of the activities. Teachers should be flexible with the use of these suggested activities and adapt them for various purposes.

Although we shared a possible sequence of instruction in Figure 4, teachers should avoid rigid adherence to a sequence. It is not the case that teachers should engage exclusively in rhyme activities for weeks before they engage in syllable activities. Likewise, we do not believe that children must "pass" one type of operation (e.g., matching) before having experiences with another (e.g., blending). Phonemic awareness development is not a lockstep process.

We urge teachers to be watchful for children who are not catching on—after multiple exposures—to games and activities such as those presented here. These children may need extra support in phonemic awareness development. It may be helpful to increase the use of concrete objects or other cues to represent sounds and to provide more phonemic awareness instruction that includes familiar letters. Also, by focusing on sounds that can be elongated, teachers are more likely to draw students' attention to those sounds. For example, notice that each of the sounds in the word *safe* can be stretched and thus exaggerated (sssssssss-aaaaaaaaaaa-fffffffff) whereas the initial and final sounds in *get* cannot be stretched (g-eeeeeeee-t). *Get* is a poor choice, then, for an item of reflection in a phonemic awareness activity for a child who is struggling. In addition, using words with fewer phonemes can be helpful; it is easier to manipulate the phonemes in words such as *cat* and *up* (with three and two phonemes, respectively) than in words such as *lips* and *sand* (each having four phonemes).

Our hope is that phonemic awareness instruction becomes a thoughtful, conscious component of early literacy programs. Our concern is that in some classrooms phonemic awareness instruction will replace other crucial areas of instruction. Phonemic awareness supports reading development only if it is part of a broader program that includes—among other things—development of students' vocabulary, syntax, comprehension, strategic reading abilities, decoding strategies, and writing across all content areas.

In sum, we encourage teachers to provide their students with linguistically rich environments in which written and spoken language are used to learn, to communicate, to express ideas, to understand the ideas of others *and* in which language itself is explored and examined—even the smallest parts of language. "Look at the way I write this." "Wasn't that an interesting word?" "My, listen to all the sounds in this word!" "Your two names start alike." "What a sense of humor this author has! Notice the way he plays with words in this section." By providing linguistically rich programs in which both the content and the form of language are examined we are supporting literacy development in the fullest sense.

References

Adams, M.J. (1990). *Beginning to read: Thinking and learning about print*. Cambridge, MA: MIT Press.

Adams, M.J., & Bruck, M. (1995). Resolving the "Great Debate." *American Educator, 8*, 7–20.

Ball, E.W., & Blachman, B.A. (1991). Does phoneme awareness training in kindergarten make a difference in early word recognition and developmental spelling? *Reading Research Quarterly, 24*, 49–66.

Beck, I., & Juel, C. (1995). The role of decoding in learning to read. *American Educator, 8*, 21–25, 39–42.

Bishop, A., Yopp, R.H., & Yopp, H.K. (2000). *Reading for reading: A handbook for parents of preschoolers*. Boston: Allyn & Bacon.

Bradley, L., & Bryant, P.E. (1983). Categorizing sounds and learning to read—A causal connection. *Nature, 301*, 419–421.

Brady, S., & Moats, L. (1998). Buy books, teach reading. *The California Reader, 31*(4), 6–10.

Byrne, B., & Fielding-Barnsley, R. (1993). Evaluation of a program to teach phonemic awareness to young children: A 1-year follow-up. *Journal of Educational Psychology, 85*, 104–111.

Every child reading: An action plan of the Learning First Alliance. (1998, Spring/Summer). *American Educator, 22*, 52–63.

Griffith, P.L., & Olson, M.W. (1992). Phonemic awareness helps beginning readers break the code. *The Reading Teacher, 45*, 516–523.

Harris, T.L., & Hodges, R.E. (1995). *The literacy dictionary: The vocabulary of reading and writing*. Newark, DE: International Reading Association.

Hohn, W., & Ehri, L. (1983). Do alphabet letters help prereaders acquire phonemic segmentation skill? *Journal of Educational Psychology, 75*, 752–762.

International Reading Association. (1998). *Phonemic awareness and the teaching of reading: A position statement*. Newark, DE: Author.

International Reading Association and the National Association for the Education of Young Children. (1998). *Learning to read and write: Developmentally appropriate practices for young children: A joint position statement of the International Reading Association (IRA) and the National Association for the Education of Young Children*. Newark, DE: Author.

Mattingly, I. (1984). Reading, linguistic awareness, and language acquisition. In J. Downing & R. Valtin (Eds.), *Language awareness and learning to read* (pp. 9–25). New York: Springer-Verlag.

McBride-Chang, C. (1995). What is phonological awareness? *Journal of Educational Psychology, 87*, 179–192.

Smith, S.B., Simmons, D.C., & Kameenui, E.J. (1998). Phonological awareness: Research bases. In D.C. Simmons & E.J. Kameenui (Eds.), *What reading research tells us about children with diverse learning needs: Bases and basics* (pp. 61–127). Mahwah, NJ: Erlbaum.

Snow, C.E., Burns, M.S., & Griffin, P. (1998). *Preventing reading difficulties in young children*. Washington, DC: National Academy Press.

Stahl, S.A., & Murray, B.A. (1994). Defining phonological awareness and its relationship to early reading. *Journal of Educational Psychology, 86*, 221–234.

Treiman, R., & Zukowski, A. (1991). Levels of phonological awareness. In S.A. Brady & D.P. Shankweiler (Eds.), *Phonological processes in literacy* (pp. 67–83). Hillsdale, NJ: Erlbaum.

Tunmer, W., Herriman, M. & Nesdale, A. (1988). Metalinguistic abilities and beginning reading. *Reading Research Quarterly, 23*, 134–158.

Yaden, D.B., Jr., & Templeton, S. (Eds.). (1986). *Metalinguistic awareness and beginning literacy: Conceptualizing what it means to read and write*. Portsmouth, NH: Heinemann.

Yopp, H.K. (1988). The validity and reliability of phonemic awareness tests. *Reading Research Quarterly, 23*, 159–177.

Yopp, H.K. (1992). Developing phonemic awareness in young children. *The Reading Teacher, 45*, 696–703.

Yopp, H.K. (1995). Read-aloud books for developing phonemic awareness: An annotated bibliography. *The Reading Teacher, 48*, 538–542.

Yopp, H.K. (November, 1997). *Research developments in phonemic awareness and implications for classroom practice*. Presentation at the Research Institute at the annual meeting of the California Reading Association, San Diego, CA.

Yopp, H.K., & Yopp, R.H. (1996). *Oo-pples and boo-noo-noos: Songs and activities for phonemic awareness*. Orlando, FL: Harcourt Brace School Publishers.

Children's books cited

Marzollo, Jean. (1994). *Ten cats have hats*. New York: Scholastic.

Mosel, Arlene. (1989). *Tikki Tikki Tembo*. New York: Holt.

Most, Bernard. (1996). *Cock-a-doodle-moo!* San Diego: Harcourt Brace.

Rosen, Michael. (1997). *We're going on a bear hunt*. New York: Little Simon.

Slepian, Jan, & Seidler, Ann. (1967). *The Hungry Thing*. New York: Scholastic.

Slepian, Jan, & Seidler, Ann. (1990). *The Hungry Thing returns*. New York: Scholastic.

Slepian, Jan, & Seidler, Ann. (1993). *The Hungry Thing goes to a restaurant*. New York: Scholastic.

Vaughan, Marcia. (1995). *Tingo tango mango tree*. Morristown, NJ: Silver Burdett.

Editors: Beverly J. Bruneau
Kent State University, Kent, Ohio, USA

Editors: Margaret Humadi Genisio
University of Wisconsin–Oshkosh, Wisconsin, USA

Editors: Renee Casbergue
University of New Orleans, New Orleans, Louisiana, USA

Author: Kathleen Reiner
Field Local Schools, Mogadore, Ohio, USA

Developing a kindergarten phonemic awareness program: An action research project

Children enter kindergarten with varying backgrounds and experiences. Many children have been read to regularly since infancy and have had lots of opportunities to draw and talk about their drawings. Their caretakers have pointed out environmental print in grocery stores, while traveling in cars, and in daily excursions. Some children begin their kindergarten year knowing almost all of the 26 letters and sounds of the alphabet. In contrast, other children enter kindergarten having had little or no interactions with storybooks, having done very little drawing and writing, and having little knowledge of the alphabet. Each year I must implement an appropriate literacy curriculum that will help all of my children grow in knowledge, dispositions, and skills (Katz & Chard, 1989) to become capable and confident emergent readers and writers.

For years I followed a commercially prepared "reading readiness and phonics program" organized around a letter of the week. To help maintain the children's interests and develop integrated instruction I worked with my colleagues to develop activities centered around the weekly letter. However, I always felt rushed and limited in what I could do within 1 week. I also began to realize that the weekly program left little time for listening to and responding to poetry, playing with words, and engaging in journal writing. There never seemed to be enough time to do indepth activities when my curriculum was organized in weekly units.

I compounded my time problem when I began to add holistic literacy activities into my daily routine. For example, each morning began with a shared writing activity in which children dictated the morning news, and I also tried to include a daily shared reading of Big Books and poems (Bruneau, 1997). These shared print experiences successfully engaged many of my children, much more so than the weekly letter activities. During the 1995–96 school year I decided to center my curriculum more around stories and poems than weekly letters. However, I believed I needed to document that the children were, indeed, learning letters and related skills specified in our local curriculum.

Working with a university-based colleague, I studied my children's growth in print awareness, alphabet letter knowledge, growth in storybook reading, and growth in invented spelling (Bruneau & Reiner, 1996). Results of this study showed that my children did grow appropriately in alphabet knowledge and enthusiasm and ability for storybook reading. These were program strengths. However, although many children were developing the skill to engage in invented spelling, many children seemed to lack confidence in their ability to write on their own.

I continued my quest for ways to improve my literacy program. I was introduced to the concept of phonemic awareness, the awareness of sounds within our language. Yopp (1992) explained, "In order for children to benefit from formal reading instruction, youngsters must have a certain level of phonemic awareness. Reading instruction, in turn, heightens their awareness of language. Thus phonemic awareness is both a prerequisite and a consequence of learning to read" (p. 697). As I read more, I learned that children could develop phonemic awareness knowledge through various activities such as language play; word play; listening to rhymes, songs, and poetry; and engaging in shared reading of predictable literature.

I realized that phonemic awareness was a valuable piece missing from my literacy curriculum. I began to consider how to implement phonemic awareness activities into my daily routine. As I prepared for the curriculum changes, I continually asked myself (a) What are specific activities I could use? (b) Will phonemic awareness be a predictor of reading success for my students? (c) Am I expecting too much from kindergarten children? and (d) What are the children learning?

Classroom activities

During the winter holiday break, I planned major changes in my daily literacy routines. Previously, the children had written in journals 2 afternoons a week. I decided to move journals to the morning, following a daily phonemic awareness activity. My goal was to immerse my children in language play, rhymes, word play, and rich predictable literature (Bishop & Bishop, 1996).

After the holiday break I started using specific activities to help children become more aware of words and sounds within words. Building on our shared reading of a predictable book, we acted out the story, had the children become the words (see Cunningham, 1995, for more on these activities), clapped syllables, played with rhymes, and read and played with more nursery rhymes. I also used the pocket chart as a basis for children to find words, find missing words, and build sentences from books or nursery rhymes we had read (McCracken & McCracken, 1986). The children seemed to have the most fun sorting words by length and sorting words by letters (Cunningham, 1995).

All of these activities led to the Names Activity (Cunningham, 1995). Daily, I focused on a child's name and used his/her name to help the children look carefully at the letters within words. Once we had counted and named the letters, the class built an ex-

perience chart for that particular child. The children interviewed our "name person." "What is your favorite food?" "How many people are in your family?" "What do you like to do at home?" were typical questions the children asked. As the child answered, I recorded responses on chart paper.

We then counted the letters in the name, looked for little words, and looked for clues to help us read the name. For example, when I selected the name *Luke* from the name basket, T.J. said, "Hey, there is a quiet *e* at the end of his name." And R.J. said, "There are four letters but I only hear three!" After we discussed the charted story, each student wrote the selected child's name on a piece of paper, drew a picture of the focal child, and completed the sentence, "I like _____ because _____." At first I took dictation, but as the weeks progressed the children began to write their own responses. These pages were then bound, and the book was shared with the class before the focal child took it home.

Because I was concerned about what the children were learning (and also simultaneously beginning a graduate course focusing on action research) I decided to keep a daily log of the children's responses to the literacy lessons. For example, on January 15, I recorded the following dialogue on an experience chart after we had studied the name *Katherine.*

Megan: There's a /th/ like the beginning of *thumb.*

T.J.:   Another silent *e*, Mrs. Reiner.

Kathy: You don't really hear the *e* by the *r* either.

Robert: I see the word *in* (and pointed it out using the word finder). (The word finder is a fly swatter with a hole cut out of the middle.)

The children were good observers. However, up to this point in the year they were drawing pictures, writing a few isolated letters, and copying words seen in the classroom. This was typical of what children in my previous classes had accomplished. On January 21, I gave the following directions, "Today, I would like you to write some words that you know and then draw a picture." I was very excited to receive the following responses: "I am omost 6,"

"My mom is butifl," "apl," "bruthr," "Mi hrt is red," "no," "yes," "mom," "dad," names of other children with illustrations, and animal names with illustrations. For the first time, children were confident and enthusiastic as they began writing!

Data collection

As I observed the children participating in various phonemic awareness activities I needed a way to document their progress. I began to keep my own daily teaching journal, but I also wanted some type of progress report to present to the parents. And I was required to collect classroom data as part of my graduate action research requirements. I decided to use the children's daily journal writings to assess their progress. I believed I could gain a vast amount of information from each child's personal writing.

For my own assessment purposes, I kept monthly charts (see the Figure) documenting each child's writing. Once each month I reviewed each child's writing and dated the growth I saw developing. This way I could easily view growth for each month. At the February parent-teacher conferences, I presented every parent with a copy of the journal checklist and explained it to them.

The checklist showed growth from September through February. Most parents were pleased with the information and stated they would encourage writing at home.

For my action research project, I continued to assess and review every child in my class. Twice a month, I used the charts to document each child's progress in daily writing activities. This gave me a good understanding of how each child was developing in alphabet sound knowledge.

Although I charted the information only twice a month, I continued to look at the children's journals and recorded what they were writing in my own notebook. I developed a weekly chart with each child's name and a space to write daily comments. I used this during conferences with children as they completed their daily journal entries. The conferences took time, so again, this led to major changes in my daily

Monthly journal writing checklist

	Uses a picture to write	Uses scribbles or symbols	Isolated letters	Writes words seen around room—copies	Writes words from memory	Spelling—first letter	Attempting to spell words from sounds	Writes phrases	Writes simple sentences

plans. The beginning of a Writers' Workshop will be addressed shortly.

Data analysis

After reviewing my monthly documentation charts, I found that I still did not have a clear picture of what was really happening in my classroom. I could see progress and I noted changes in enthusiasm for writing, but it wasn't until I put the facts together on a large chart that I realized how much growth had taken place. I used my monthly progress chart format to compile class data. I completed a chart for each month, listing every child's name and checking the writing abilities I had documented. In this way I could easily see class progress across the entire year.

From September through November most of the children were still drawing pictures; a few were copying words. The class progressed from 24 children scribbling and drawing pictures in their journals to only 4 children scribbling by the end of January. By April, the class had progressed to 0 scribblers, 1 who drew pictures, 4 who wrote isolated letters, 1 who copied only, 3 who wrote words from memory, 8 who used invented spelling, 2 who wrote phrases, and 6 children who wrote simple sentences! Additionally, I noticed a change in the children's enthusiasm and disposition to read storybooks. Previously there had been little interest in choosing books as a free choice activity. By the year's end, many children were enthusiastically choosing books as a self-selected activity.

Changes in my practice

When I started using phonemic awareness activities in my classroom, I was very apprehensive. I thought the idea was a good one, but I had so few children interested in literacy at the beginning of that year, I wasn't sure if it would work with this particular class. I thought I would try the activities for 2 months. If things were not going well by March 1, I would try another approach. Happily, the phonemic awareness activities worked very well.

As I reflect on changes in my teaching, I find I'm much happier with how I am teaching literacy. I knew the "letter of the week" program was not meeting the needs of all children, especially those children who have not had much previous experience with print. Children with limited print experience typically had difficulty remembering the "letter of the week." Even those children who learned their letters easily were not really interested in reading, rarely choosing to look at books or to try any individual writing beyond copying. The increased enthusiasm the children express for literacy activities has definitely supported the changes in my teaching.

The action research project required me to document children's learning. When I realized that every child had grown as a reader and writer, I became confident of the changes I had made. I had evidence to show that my students' literacy growth exceeded district expectations.

I began this school year with the name game activities I started last year at mid-year. I continue to document the children's growth, which shows me that my students are making good progress. I communicate this growth to parents, who also see children's growth and respond positively to my program changes. I've learned that it is possible to systematically engage kindergarten children in appropriate reading and writing activities. My students are growing as eager and confident readers and writers.

References

Bishop, A., & Bishop, S. (1996). *Teaching phonics, phonemic awareness, and word recognition*. Westminster, CA: Teacher Created Materials.

Bruneau, B. (1997). The literacy pyramid organization of reading/writing activities in a whole language classroom. *The Reading Teacher, 51*, 158 – 160.

Bruneau, B., & Reiner, K. (1996). *Focusing on kindergarten children's literacy development: A tale of two practices*. (ERIC

Document Reproduction Service No. ED 403 547)

Cunningham, P.M. (1995). *Phonics they use: Words for reading and writing*. New York: HarperCollins.

Katz, L.G., & Chard, S.C. (1989). *Engaging children's minds: The project approach*. Newark, NJ: Ablex.

McCracken, R., & McCracken, M. (1986). *Songs, stories, and poetry to teach reading and writing*. Chicago: American Library Association.

Yopp, H. (1992). Developing phonemic awareness in young children. *The Reading Teacher, 45*, 696–703.

Laurice M. Joseph

Word boxes help children with learning disabilities identify and spell words

Instructional approaches that incorporate the interrelationships of phonemic awareness, phonological recoding, and orthographic processing have been proven to be useful for helping young children develop basic word identification and spelling skills (Foorman, Jenkins, & Francis, 1993; Vandervelden & Siegal, 1995). Phonemic awareness involves operating on sounds in words. Phonological recoding refers to recoding letters back into their sound constituents. Orthographic processing involves recognizing visual patterns in words and recalling letter sequences

Word boxes, Clay's (1993) extension of Elkonin's (1963) sound boxes, are designed to help children attend to phonological and orthographic features of words. Word boxes are used not only to help children become aware of sounds in spoken language, but also to help children match sounds to print when identifying and spelling words. Word boxes have been used with first-grade children as part of the comprehensive Reading Recovery program. According to Clay, word boxes are used particularly with children who have difficulty hearing the order of sounds in words. Clay also indicated that word boxes can be useful for helping children attend to orthographic features as they write letters of a word in their proper sequence.

A word box is a drawn rectangle that is divided into sections corresponding to sounds heard in words. A pictorial representation of a word is sometimes placed above the drawn rectangle. Counters are placed below the divided

Word boxes are an innovative approach to word recognition and spelling instruction. The study reported on here examines the use of word boxes with students who have learning disabilities.

sections of the rectangle. As the child articulates each sound in a word slowly she or he simultaneously places the counters in their respective sections of the box. For instance, a child is provided with a word box that is divided into three sections. Above the box is a picture of a cup. As the child articulates the /c/ sound, s/he places the counter in the first divided section of the box. The child places the counter in the next divided section of the box as s/he articulates the /u/ sound and places the counter in the last divided section as the /p/ sound is articulated. Magnetic letters soon replace the counters, and the child is instructed to place magnetic letters into a word box (see Figure 1). Next, the child spells a word by writing the letters in the respective divided sections of a box as she or he hears each sound.

Clay's word boxes employ a scaffolding approach for developing phonemic awareness, word identification, and spelling skills. The

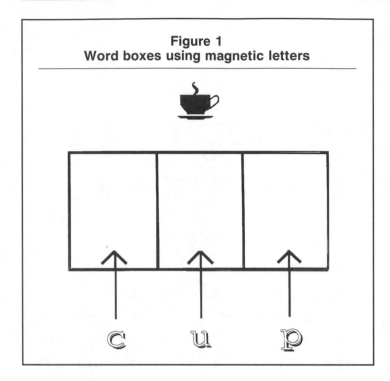

Figure 1
Word boxes using magnetic letters

c   u   p

teacher models the task, shares the task with a child, and gradually guides a child toward completing the task independently with feedback. Carnine, Silbert, and Kameenui (1991) suggested that scaffolds do not exclusively refer to the modeling and corrective feedback provided by a more knowledgeable person, but may be embedded within the task itself. In the case of word boxes, the divided box itself serves as a scaffold in addition to the modeling and feedback provided by the teacher. A supportive structure is created by dividing the box into sections to help children segment each sound heard in words and to help them sequence letter patterns.

Word boxes are considered a plausible approach for developing phonemic awareness, word identification, and spelling (Clay, 1993; Griffith & Olson, 1992; Yopp, 1995) but have not been studied to examine quantifiable changes in children's performance over time. Sound boxes, however, have been combined with other phonemic awareness tasks as part of a comprehensive phonemic awareness training program in empirical investigations (e.g., Ball & Blachman, 1991).

Sound boxes and word boxes have not been studied with second-grade and upper primary-grade children with learning disabilities. Furthermore, word boxes have not been studied to examine simultaneous trends in word identification and spelling performance. Many upper primary-grade children with learning disabilities have difficulty identifying and spelling very basic words, which makes reading and writing connected text cumbersome and/or cognitively demanding (Stanovich, 1994) and, therefore, not enjoyable. Many of these children need systematic instruction applied over time so that they will have sufficient strategies to engage in the process of attacking words. If children are given ample opportunities to engage in the process of decoding unfamiliar words, they are more likely to identify words with ease when they encounter them again (Adams & Henry, 1997).

As a former special education and remedial reading teacher, I decided to examine whether word boxes instruction would be effective for improving word identification and spelling performance of children with learning disabilities. Special education teachers, remedial reading teachers, and general education teachers may find the systematic implementation procedures and ongoing performance monitoring procedures applicable for working with upper primary-grade students who have very basic reading and spelling difficulties.

Implementation of the word boxes study

Participants. I was particularly interested in implementing the word boxes approach with a sample of students with learning disabilities who pose a challenge for their special education teacher because they are so limited in their word identification and spelling skills. Through conversations with their special education teacher and examination of current standardized test results, six urban elementary students who were identified as having a specific learning disability in basic reading skills and receiving resource room instruction for part of each day were selected to participate in this study. All names are pseudonyms. The students were mainstreamed in general education classes for certain subjects. Criteria for diagnosis of a specific learning disability followed state and federal guidelines, including a significant discrepancy between IQ and achievement.

Three second-grade males (Nate, Al, and Harold), two third-grade males (Mark and Sam), and one fourth-grade male (Mick) whose ages ranged from 7 years 9 months to 10 years 2 months (mean = 9 years 8 months) were chosen for the study. Regardless of their diagnostic label, these students essentially demonstrated significant delays in acquiring fundamentals of early literacy skills such as phonological analysis. Current test results revealed that all students performed significantly below average in letter-word identification and pseudoword naming as measured by the Woodcock-Johnson Tests of Achievement–Revised (1990). Spelling test scores derived from the Kaufman Test of Educational Achievement (1983) also reflected significant below average performance. Results from the Test of Phonological Awareness (1994) indicated that the students had not mastered the ability to detect similarities and differences among phonemes in words.

The students' basic word identification and spelling skills were so limited that they demonstrated difficulty with single-syllable words, with consonant-vowel-consonant (CVC) patterns, and consonant blend-vowel-consonant patterns (CCVC). During reading activities in their classrooms, the subjects were observed to have particular difficulties with segmenting and blending sounds in words (phonological analysis) as well as recognizing visual cues and recalling letter sequences in words (orthographic processing).

Literacy instruction in the students' resource room consisted of small-group storybook reading, drill and practice activities involving reading words from a list of sight words, and writing weekly spelling words 10 times each. Other activities included phonic workbook exercises and daily journal writing. Very little if any systematic instruction was observed, especially in facilitating phonological and orthographic processing of words.

Materials. Word identification and spelling quizzes consisted of a list of 10 words that were typed in 24-point font size on white paper. A magnetic board and colored markers were used to draw the divided boxes. Tokens were used as counters; magnetic letters and colored markers were also provided.

Procedures. In order to determine whether the word boxes instructional approach was effective for improving word identification and

spelling performance, I decided to observe quantifiable changes in student performance over time using a multiple baseline design across subjects. A multiple baseline design across subjects is a single-subject research design that permits the instruction to be implemented in a staggered fashion across individual subjects so that changes in performance during instruction sessions are directly comparable to noninstruction (i.e., baseline) conditions. According to McCormick (1995), multiple

---

During reading activities in their classrooms, the students were observed to have particular difficulties with segmenting and blending sounds in words.

---

baseline designs allow one to view ongoing as well as quantifiable changes in performance during the instructional process rather than only at the completion of treatment conditions, as is the case with pretest-posttest designs.

In this study, multiple baseline designs were essentially applied to two groups consisting of three participants in each group. One group consisted of three second-grade students with learning disabilities, and the other group consisted of two third-grade students and one fourth-grade student with learning disabilities.

Baseline. Before the word boxes instruction approach was implemented, word identification and spelling measures were used to obtain students' baseline levels on identifying and spelling words with CVC and CCVC patterns. Word identification and spelling measures consisted of a list of 10 words. Prior to the development of specific quizzes used for each session, 200 words were placed on cards. The cards were shuffled and mixed up, and every 20th word in the stack was chosen to be placed on 10-item probes. This was done separately for word identification and spelling measures so that word identification and spelling quizzes were not completely identical during any one session. All 200 words were similar in type and difficulty level (i.e., a combination of CVC and CCVC patterns). All words contained three to four sounds.

Word boxes instruction sessions. Word boxes instruction consisted of 20-minute daily lessons over approximately 21 sessions. I worked with each student individually to provide ample guidance and feedback. I drew divided boxes that represented sounds heard in a word on a magnetic board. Learning all words with word boxes involved the combined use of counters, magnetic letters, and writing utensils. I initially placed counters underneath the divided box and later replaced the counters with magnetic letters. I demonstrated the task, placing the counters and later magnetic letters into the respective divided sections of the word box as I slowly articulated each sound in a word.

After a few demonstrations, I shared the task by having the student place counters in the divided box while I slowly articulated sounds heard in a word. The student was then asked to slowly articulate sounds in a word while I placed counters in the divided box. The student eventually performed the entire task independently with my feedback. First the student practiced placing the counters. This was followed by placing magnetic letters in the divided word box as words were orally presented and later by writing the letters in the divided word box as he heard each sound in a word.

The word boxes instructional approach was implemented for the first participant in each group once baseline stability was achieved. In order to maintain experimental control, the other students remained in baseline until the first participant demonstrated progress on both word identification and spelling performance quizzes. Once the first participant in each group made progress or reached mastery level, the word boxes approach was implemented with the second student, leaving the third student in baseline until the second student demonstrated progress on daily probes. All subjects were eventually provided with daily instructional lessons with word boxes.

During instructional sessions, 10-item word identification and spelling measures, similar to baseline quizzes, were administered daily after 20 minutes of instruction with the word boxes. The criterion level for successful performance on word identification and spelling probes was set at a minimum score of 90 percent accuracy (9 out of 10 correct responses). The procedures for selecting words for both word identification and spelling measures were the same as those applied during baseline sessions. This permitted me to make direct comparisons between the two conditions.

Maintenance. One month after instruction ended, all subjects were administered 10-item word identification and spelling probes once a week over 10 weeks to determine if students maintained their enhanced performance levels. The weekly measures consisted of words that were similar in type and difficulty level to those that were administered during baseline and instruction conditions.

Transfer. Following the establishment of maintenance levels, students were asked to read short stories that contained the types of words that the participants were taught during instructional sessions. Each student was given one story per week over a 3-week period. Students were also asked to write sentences that were orally dictated once a week over 3 weeks. Each story and dictated sentence task contained a combination of 10 words with either CVC or CCVC patterns. Short stories and dictated sentences tasks were used to evaluate whether the students were able to transfer reading and spelling words to some other context independent of the one that was provided during instruction condition.

Results and discussion

Students' performance scores were calculated for baseline, instruction, maintenance, and transfer phases. All percentages given have been rounded to the nearest whole percentage and are presented in Table 1. Results of each probe for all students are presented on line graphs. Figure 2 shows second-grade students' performance on word identification and spelling probes during baseline, instruction, maintenance, and transfer phases. Figure 3 shows two third-grade students' and one fourth-grade student's performance.

As can be seen from Figures 2 and 3, the word boxes approach was effective for improving and maintaining all students' word identification and spelling skills. All students were able to identify and spell words in another context 1 month after instruction with the word boxes ended.

Table 1

Ranges and average percentages on students' daily word identification and spelling probes during four conditions

Subject	Condition	Word identification		Spelling	
		Range %	Mean %	Range %	Mean %
Nate					
	Baseline	30 – 50	38	10 – 20	15
	Instruction	60 – 100	93	40 – 100	89
	Maintenance	90 – 100	98	90 – 100	91
	Transfer	90 – 100	96	All 80	80
Al					
	Baseline	10 – 60	35	10 – 60	30
	Instruction	70 – 100	95	50 – 100	87
	Maintenance	50 – 90	83	80 – 90	85
	Transfer	80 – 90	86	All 90	90
Harold					
	Baseline	10 – 30	19	0 – 30	11
	Instruction	30 – 100	81	30 – 100	84
	Maintenance	60 – 80	73	70 – 80	76
	Transfer	70 – 80	73	All 80	80
Mark					
	Baseline	60 – 70	62	30 – 40	32
	Instruction	50 – 100	93	30 – 100	87
	Maintenance	90 – 100	99	80 – 90	88
	Transfer	All 100	100	All 80	80
Sam					
	Baseline	40 – 60	52	10 – 50	35
	Instruction	60 – 100	95	60 – 100	87
	Maintenance	80 – 100	91	50 – 100	88
	Transfer	All 100	100	70 – 100	83
Mick					
	Baseline	30 – 50	38	10 – 30	20
	Instruction	30 – 100	74	20 – 100	72
	Maintenance	90 – 100	95	80 – 100	92
	Transfer	70 – 80	73	80 – 90	86

Table 2 presents the number of trials or sessions it took each student to reach a specified criterion score of nine correct responses on word identification and spelling during the instruction condition. For the six students studied, the number of trials or sessions ranged from three to seven with a mean of five trials to reach 9 out of 10 correct responses on word identification. In spelling, trials ranged from four to nine with a mean of approximately six trials to reach the minimum of 9 out of 10 correct.

Informal observations of students during all conditions were noted. Students appeared to have very limited if any strategies for decod-ing and spelling words while they were working on assessments during baseline conditions. A similar pattern that emerged with all students was their difficulty grasping the sequence by which sounds were presented in words. This difficulty with positioning phonemes was even more evident when students were spelling words. Students would often end a word with a letter representing the initial consonant sound in a word and/or leave out the letter representing the middle or vowel sound altogether. This lack of vowel knowledge is characteristic of disabled readers who have not acquired the alphabetic system fully (Ehri & McCormick,

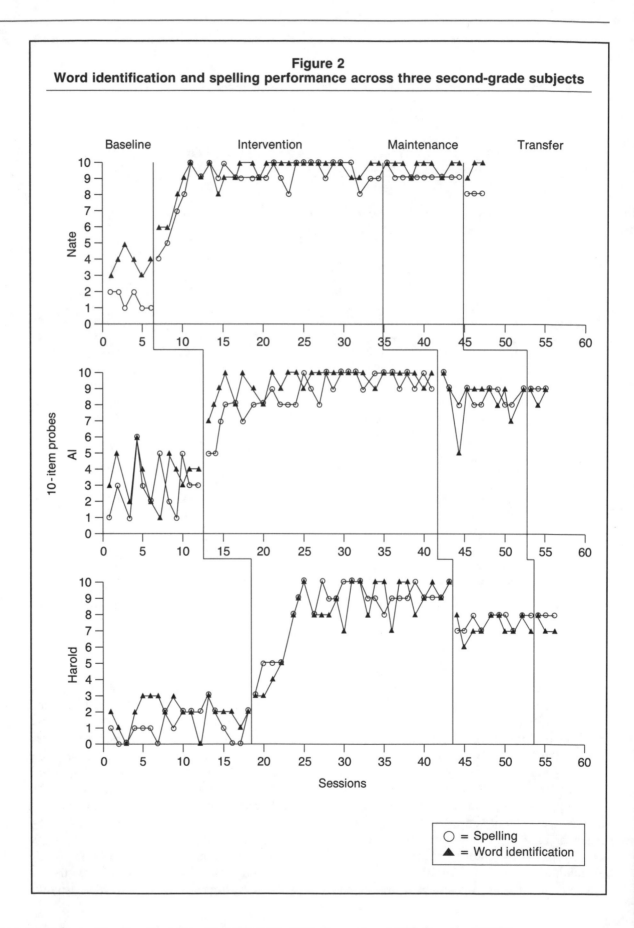

Figure 2
Word identification and spelling performance across three second-grade subjects

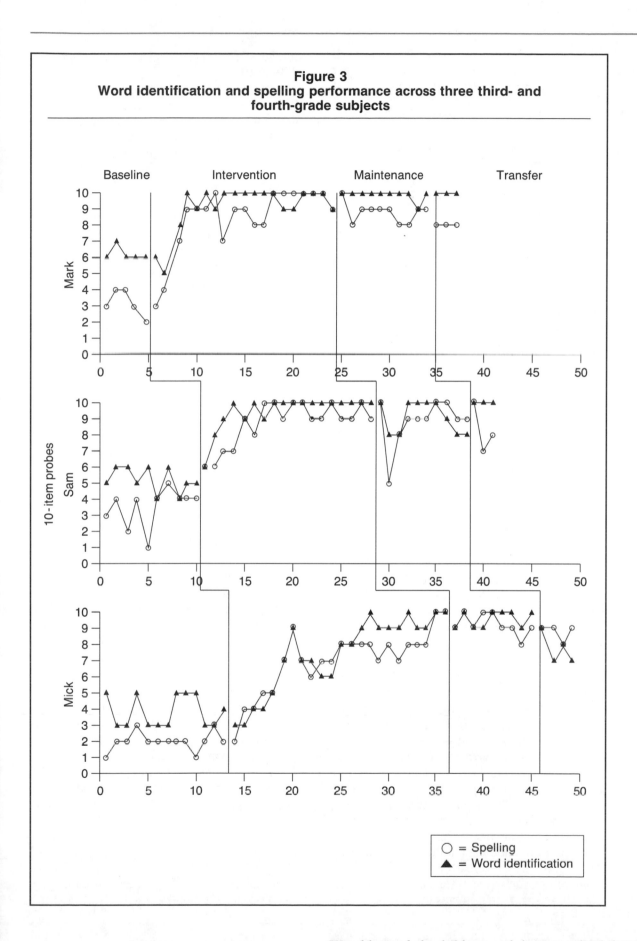

Figure 3
Word identification and spelling performance across three third- and fourth-grade subjects

Table 2

Number of trials it took each student to reach mastery level on word identification and spelling probes during the instruction condition

Subject	Word identification	Spelling
Nate	4	5
Al	3	9
Harold	6	6
Mark	4	4
Sam	3	5
Mick	7	7

1998). Many times the other letters that students wrote did not correspond to the sounds they heard in words.

After several sessions using word boxes, students began to vocalize each letter-sound correspondence in the order in which letters were presented in words before saying the words as a whole. This became evident when students read and spelled words on the assessments as instructional sessions progressed. When words were presented orally during spelling assessment after a 20-minute word boxes lesson, students would orally repeat each sound heard in the words several times before they would spell the entire word. Later, students' vocalizations became subvocalizations (almost whispers) as they attempted to identify and spell words. Students were able to identify and spell words with more ease and automaticity once they internalized phonological and orthographic structures in words.

The word boxes approach was successful in helping children maintain performance levels in identifying and spelling basic words because the supportive structure of the divided boxes first helps children conceptualize each phoneme as a sound segment and later encourages the blending of sounds to make a whole word. According to Busink (1997), children need to become aware of the phonological structure of words, particularly sound segments and blends, so that they are able to benefit from word recognition and spelling instruction. A recent study of a variety of phonological awareness tasks (e.g., rhyme categorization, alliteration categorization, and phonemic segmentation) found that phonemic segmentation was the best predictor of reading and spelling performance (Nation & Hulme, 1997).

Students with reading difficulties not only demonstrate limited phonological skills but also have difficulty grasping orthographic (letter) knowledge about words (Stanovich & West, 1989). In the current study, word boxes also helped students attend to the orthographic features of words. The use of magnetic letters and writing letters in the boxes helped the students process the visual pattern of letters in words. This was especially evident during performance on word identification and spelling probes as students were able to recognize words using visual cues and recall sequences of letters in words.

Adaptations for classroom use

Word boxes provide students with opportunities to operate on the phonological structure of words and grasp orthographic features of words. Word boxes may be used in a variety of language and literacy activities in small- and large-group classroom settings. Operating on phonological structures and attending to orthographic features in words within a meaning-based context may be reinforced by incorporating a combination of word boxes and other word study approaches.

For example, word boxes can be used in combination with learning words by analogy. This can be accomplished through the Word Wall technique described in *Phonics They Use: Words for Reading and Writing* (Cunningham, 1995). Students can construct a Word Wall of words that share similar spelling patterns and draw boxes around each letter or letter combinations that represent sounds heard in words.

After students have ample opportunities to work with a teacher, independent practice using word boxes can be done through reading and writing centers in the classroom. Words can be placed on an audiotape with pauses between each word. As students listen to words slowly articulated on the tape, they can place either counters or magnetic letters and write letters (depending on their developmental levels) in a divided box. A variety of boxes that are divided into three or more sections, depending on the number of phonemes presented in words, can be placed at the table next to the audiotape recorder. Correct responses may be given on the audiotape for self-checking after ample time is given for the student to make a response.

The use of technology can be incorporated with word boxes instruction especially during independent practice sessions. Word boxes and performance monitoring procedures can be created on a computer program. A word can be orally presented, and the student can click on the appropriate boxes presented on the computer screen when he or she hears each sound in a word. Corrective feedback can be given through some form of cueing system embedded in the program.

Word boxes can be instructional tools that reinforce phonological and orthographic awareness while children read and write connected text. Children can be instructed to draw boxes around a letter or letter combinations representing sound units heard in words during contextual reading and writing activities (i.e., reading storybooks and writing stories and daily journal entries).

Word boxes can be used in conjunction with lessons aimed at developing vocabulary. As children learn word meanings, they can draw boxes around morphemic (meaningful) word units, especially segmenting and grasping spelling patterns of words in and out of context.

References

Adams, M.J., & Henry, M.K. (1997). Myths and realities about words and literacy. *School Psychology Review, 26*, 425–436.

Ball, E.W., & Blachman, B.A. (1991). Does phoneme awareness training in kindergarten make a difference in early word recognition and spelling? *Reading Research Quarterly, 26*, 49–66.

Busink, R. (1997). Reading and phonological awareness: What we have learned and how we can use it. *Reading Research and Instruction, 36*, 199–215.

Carnine, D., Silbert, J., & Kameenui, E.J. (1991). *Direct instruction reading.* Columbus, OH: Merrill.

Clay, M. (1993). *Reading Recovery: A guidebook for teachers in training.* Portsmouth, NH: Heinemann.

Cunningham, P.M. (1995). *Phonics they use: Words for reading and writing* (2nd ed.). New York: HarperCollins.

Ehri, L.C., & McCormick, S. (1998). Phases of word learning: Implications for instruction with delayed and disabled readers. *Reading and Writing Quarterly, 14*, 135–163.

Elkonin, D.B. (1963). The psychology of mastery elements of reading. In B. Simon & J. Simon (Eds.), *Educational psychology in the USSR* (pp. 165–179). London: Routledge & Kegan Paul.

Foorman, B.R., Jenkins, L., & Francis, D.J. (1993). Links among segmenting, spelling and reading words in first and second grades. *Reading and Writing, 5*, 1–15.

Griffith, P.L., & Olson, M.W. (1992). Phonemic awareness helps beginning readers break the code. *The Reading Teacher, 45*, 516–523.

McCormick, S. (1995). What is single subject experimental research? In S.B. Neuman & S. McCormick (Eds.), *Single subject experimental research: Applications for literacy* (pp. 1–31). Newark, DE: International Reading Association.

Nation, K., & Hulme, C. (1997). Phonemic segmentation, not onset-rime segmentation, predicts early reading and spelling skills. *Reading Research Quarterly, 32*, 154–167.

Stanovich, K.E. (1994). Romance and reality. *The Reading Teacher, 47*, 280–291.

Stanovich, K.E., & West, R.F. (1989). Exposure to print and orthographic processing. *Reading Research Quarterly, 24*, 402–433.

Vandervelden, M.C., & Siegal, L.S. (1995). Phonological recoding and phoneme awareness in early literacy: A developmental approach. *Reading Research Quarterly, 30*, 854–879.

Yopp, H.K. (1995). A test for assessing phonemic awareness in young children. *The Reading Teacher, 49*, 20–29.

Children's books to develop phonemic awareness—for you and parents, too!

Michael F. Opitz

Phonemic awareness—the awareness that words are composed of sounds—appears to be an important precursor of learning to read (Yopp, 1992). One of the best ways to help children develop it naturally is through the use of children's literature that focuses on some kind of play with the sounds of language (Griffith & Olson, 1992). Rhyme, alliteration, and sound substitution are examples of this language play, and they are used in books in the list. All books have been published within the last 2 years, and the content is suitable for kindergarten and first-grade children. The books can be used by teachers, parents, or both.

What's that? You want to provide parents with more than a list of books? You want to provide them with some specific activities that they can do at home that highlight phonemic awareness? You want to give them a way to keep track of the books they have read and what their children are able to do with words? The letter shown in the box below as well as the accompanying activities and record-keeping form (see boxes on following pages) are designed to help you do just that!

Happy reading!

References

Griffith, P., & Olson, M. (1992). Phonemic awareness helps beginning readers break the code. *The Reading Teacher*, *45*, 516–523.

Yopp, H. (1992). Developing phonemic awareness in young children. *The Reading Teacher*, *45*, 696–703.

Letter to parents

Dear Parents,

One prerequisite for learning to read is being aware that words are composed of individual sounds. This awareness is called *phonemic awareness*. You have already started to help your children to develop this awareness by reading to them. Yes, children who are read to seem to develop phonemic awareness with ease and this awareness helps prepare them for learning to read.

Here's how you can continue to help: While reading just about any book to your children is valuable, books that encourage "playing with sounds" through the use of rhyme, rhythm, and repetition of sounds are especially good for the development of phonemic awareness. I have enclosed a list of books with these characteristics along with a few activities for you to do with these books. I am also enclosing a form for those of you who would like to keep a record of the books you have read and your observations.

As you go about reading these books and doing the activities, remember to:

1. Vary the activities so that you and your children continue to focus on the enjoyment of your story-reading time rather than making it seem like a chore.

2. Focus on what your children can do rather than what they cannot. If they cannot complete an activity, try the idea again at another time with another book.

3. Enjoy the whole read-aloud experience! Doing so will convey the message to your children that reading is a fun and meaningful activity.

Thank you for your willingness to help your children become strong readers by doing these activities. Please call me if you have any questions or if you find some additional books that you think should be put on the booklist. I'm looking forward to hearing from you.

Sincerely,
Your child's teacher

Children's books to develop phonemic awareness

1996 titles

Aylesworth, J. *Wake up little children*. New York: Atheneum. ISBN 0-689-31857-X.
Boynton, S. *Hippos go berserk!* New York: Aladdin. ISBN 0-689-80818-6.
Cowen-Fletcher, J. *Baby angels*. Cambridge, MA: Candlewick. ISBN 1-56402-666-3.
Dijs, C. *Up pop the monsters 1, 2, 3!* New York: Scholastic. ISBN 0-590-84762-7.
Doro, A. *Twin pickle*. New York: Holt. ISBN 0-8050-3802-7.
Edwards, P. *Some smug slug*. New York: HarperCollins. ISBN 0-06-024789-4.
Janovitz, M. *Bowl patrol!* New York: North-South. ISBN 1-55858-636-9.
Hubbard, P. *My crayons talk*. New York: Holt. ISBN 0-8050-3529-X.
Kalan, R. *Moving day*. New York: Greenwillow. ISBN 0-688-13948-5.
Kellogg, S. *Frog jump*. New York: Scholastic. ISBN 0-590-45528-1.
Ketteman, H. *Grandma's cat*. Boston: Houghton Mifflin. ISBN 0-395-73094-5.
Lear, E. *The owl and the pussycat*. New York: Atheneum. ISBN 0-689-81032-6.
Loomis, C. *Rush hour*. Boston: Houghton Mifflin. ISBN 0-395-69129-X.
MacDonald, A. *Cousin Ruth's tooth*. Boston: Houghton Mifflin. ISBN 0-395-71253-X.
Martin, B. *"Fire! Fire!" said Mrs. McGuire*. San Diego, CA: Harcourt. ISBN 0-15-227562-2.
Martin, M. *From Anne to Zach*. Honesdale, PA: Boyds Mills. ISBN 1-56397-573-4.
McBratney, S. *The caterpillow fight*. Cambridge, MA: Candlewick. ISBN 1-56402-804-6.
Most, B. *Cock-a-doodle-moo!* San Diego, CA: Harcourt. ISBN 0-15-201252-4.
Peters, L. *October smiled back*. New York: Holt. ISBN 0-8050-1776-3.
Reasoner, C. *Color crunch!* Los Angeles: Price Stern Sloan. ISBN 0-8431-3936-6.
Reiser, L. *Beach feet*. New York: Greenwillow. ISBN 0-688-14400-4.
Roberts, B. *Camel caravan*. New York: Tambourine. ISBN 0-688-13939-6.
Rotner, S. *Action alphabet*. New York: Atheneum. ISBN 0-689-80086-X.
Seuss, Dr. *My many colored days*. New York: Knopf. ISBN 0-679-87597-2.
Sturges, P. *What's that sound, wooly bear?* Boston: Little, Brown. ISBN 0-316-82021-0.
Tucker, S. *1 2 3 count with me*. New York: Simon & Schuster. ISBN 0-689-80828-3.
Yee, W. *Mrs. Brown went to town*. Boston: Houghton Mifflin. ISBN 0-395-75282-5.

1997 titles

Andrews, S. *Rattlebone rock*. New York: Harper Trophy. ISBN 0-06-443484-2.
Calmenson, S. *Engine, engine, number nine*. New York: Hyperion. ISBN 0-7868-2127-2.
Carlson, N. *ABC I like me!* New York: Viking. ISBN 0-670-87458-2.
Carlstrom, N. *Better not get wet, Jesse bear*. New York: Aladdin. ISBN 0-689-81055-5.
Carlstrom, N. *Raven and River*. Boston: Little, Brown. ISBN 0-316-12894-5.
Ellwand, D. *Emma's elephant*. New York: Dutton. ISBN 0-525-45792-5.
Grover, M. *The accidental zucchini*. San Diego, CA: Harcourt. ISBN 0-15-201545-0.
Hamanaka, S. *The hokey pokey*. New York: Simon & Schuster. ISBN 0-689-80519-5.
Harris, P. *Mouse creeps*. New York: Dial. ISBN 0-8037-2183-8.
Jonas, A. *Watch William walk*. New York: Greenwillow. ISBN 0-688-14172-2.
Katz, B. *Truck talk*. New York: Scholastic. ISBN 0-590-6928-X.
Kessler, C. *Konte Chameleon: Fine, fine, fine*. Honesdale, PA: Boyds Mills. ISBN 1-56397-181-X.
Kirk, D. *Miss Spider's tea party*. New York: Scholastic. ISBN 0-590-06519-X.
Knowles, S. *Edwina the emu*. New York: Harper Trophy. ISBN 0-06-443483-4.
Lavis, S. *Cock-a-doodle-doo*. New York: Lodestar. ISBN 0-525-67542-6.
Lundgren, M. *We sing the city*. New York: Clarion. ISBN 0-395-68188-X.
Mallett, D. *Inch by inch*. New York: Harper Trophy. ISBN 0-06-443481-8.
Martin, B. *The wizard*. San Diego, CA: Harcourt. ISBN 0-15-201568-X.
Masurel, C. *No, no, Titus*. New York: North-South. ISBN 1-55858-725-X.
McDonnell, F. *A B C*. Cambridge, MA: Candlewick. ISBN 0-7636-0118-7.
Medearis, A. *Rum-a-tum-tum*. New York: Holiday House. ISBN 0-8234-1143-5.
Miller, M. *Whose hat?* New York: Mulberry. ISBN 0-688-15279-1.
Mora, P. *Uno, dos, tres; One, two, three*. New York: Clarion. ISBN 0-395-67294-5.
Most, B. *Moo-ha*. San Diego, CA: Harcourt. ISBN 0-15-201248-6.
Most, B. *Oink-ha*. San Diego, CA: Harcourt. ISBN 0-15-201249-4.
Murphy, C. *Alphabet magic*. New York: Simon & Schuster. ISBN 0-689-81286-8.
Nichols, G. *Asana and the animals*. Cambridge, MA: Candlewick. ISBN 0-7636-0145-4.
Noll, S. *Surprise!* New York: Greenwillow. ISBN 0-688-15170-1.
Parker, V. *Bearobics*. New York: Viking. ISBN 0-670-87034-X.
Paulsen, G. *Work song*. San Diego, CA: Harcourt. ISBN 0-15-200980-9.

(continued)

Children's books to develop phonemic awareness (cont'd.)

Pomeroy, D. *Wildflower A B C*. San Diego, CA: Harcourt. ISBN 0-15-201041-6.
Ruelle, K. *The book of baths*. San Diego, CA: Harcourt. ISBN 0-15-201003-3.
Ruelle, K. *The book of bedtimes*. San Diego, CA: Harcourt. ISBN 0-15-201001-7.
Ruelle, K. *The book of breakfasts*. San Diego, CA: Harcourt. ISBN 0-15-201064-5.
Ryan, P. *A pinky is a baby mouse*. New York: Hyperion. ISBN 0-7868-2190-6.
Shappie, T. *Where is your nose?* New York: Scholastic. ISBN 0-590-87727-5.
Sierra, J. *Counting crocodiles*. San Diego, CA: Harcourt. ISBN 0-15-200192-1.
Siomades, L. *A place to bloom*. Honesdale, PA: Boyds Mills. ISBN 1-56397-656-0.
Taylor, L. *Can I be good?* San Diego, CA: Harcourt. ISBN 0-15-201552-3.
Testa, F. *A long trip to Z*. San Diego, CA: Harcourt. ISBN 0-15-201610-4.
Wegman, W. *ABC*. New York: Hyperion. ISBN 1-56282-696-4.
Wellington, M. *Night house, bright house*. New York: Dutton. ISBN 0-525-45491-8.

Ideas for using the books to develop book enjoyment and phonemic awareness

1. Read the book to your children for enjoyment.

2. Read the book and stop when you come to a rhyming word. Ask your child to state which word might fit. For example, after reading the first few pages of *Bowl Patrol!* you might read the word *stop* and pause to see if your child fills in the rhyming word *drop*.

3. Ask your child to tell you another word that begins with the same sound as the given word. For example, when reading *Watch William Walk*, ask for additional words that begin with the same sound as *William*.

4. Tell or ask your child what the author is doing with the words. When reading *Camel Caravan*, for example, you might say something like, "The author is changing the first part in some of these words. She then uses the word three times. Can you hear it?" If you want to determine if your child noticed on his or her own, you might say something like, "What's the author doing with some of these words?"

5. Allow for spontaneous responses. Your child may chime in with words, want to dramatize some or all of the story, or create another similar story. All of these responses are appropriate and will further help your child sense that reading is a pleasurable activity.

Parents' phonemic awareness observation record

Child's name_____

Date	Title of book	States words that rhyme; states other rhyming words	Hears and states sound at the start of a word	States another word that begins with the same sound as a given word	Other observations

Phonics

> *Phonics is the understanding that there is a predictable relationship between phonemes, the sounds of spoken language, and graphemes, the letters and spelling that represent those sounds in written language.*

Findings in the National Reading Panel Report

Systematic phonics instruction (i.e., synthetic, larger unit, and miscellaneous phonics as defined in the report) made a more significant contribution to children's growth in reading than did alternative programs providing unsystematic or no phonics instruction.

Specific systematic phonics programs (synthetic and larger unit programs) were all more effective than non–phonics programs, and they did not appear to differ significantly from one another in their effectiveness.

Systematic phonics instruction was effective when delivered through tutoring, through small groups, and through teaching classes of students.

Systematic phonics instruction produced the biggest impact on growth in reading when it began in kindergarten or first grade before children had learned to read independently.

Systematic phonics instruction was significantly more effective than unsystematic or no phonics instruction in helping prevent reading difficulties among at-risk students and in helping to remediate reading difficulties in disabled readers. No conclusion was drawn in the case of low achieving readers because it was unclear why systematic phonics produced little growth in their reading and whether the finding is even reliable.

Phonics involves learning letter-sound correspondences and learning how to apply this knowledge in reading. There are many different approaches to teaching phonics, and the National Reading Panel (NRP) focused on systematic—as opposed to unsystematic or no phonics—instruction. Systematic phonics is distinguished from unsystematic or no phonics by delineating a planned, sequential set of phonics elements and teaching them systematically. The phonics elements taught include both consonants and vowels.

There are many different types of systematic phonics approaches. The NRP Report mentions synthetic phonics, analytic phonics, embedded phonics, analogy phonics, onset-rime phonics, phonics through spelling, and phonics in context approaches. The basic finding was that systematic phonics is more effective than unsystematic or no phonics instruction. The panel did not find differences in effectiveness for the different types of systematic phonics. The panel did determine that it is essential for a planned sequence (including consonants and vowels) to be taught explicitly.

In searching past volumes of *The Reading Teacher*, articles that focused explicitly on teaching a sequence of phonic elements could not be found. However, one of the successful systematic phonics approaches from the NRP Report was published in another Association journal, *Reading Research Quarterly*. "An assessment of Early Steps: A program for early intervention of reading problems," by Carol M. Santa and Torleiv Høien, has been included in this volume because the program is well described and exemplifies the way systematic phonics can be integrated into a balanced program.

In addition, Steven A. Stahl's classic article "Saying the 'p' word: Nine guidelines for exemplary phonics instruction" has been included. This article was selected because it gives an excellent overview of phonics instruction, and is consistent with the NRP's findings because it includes a number of the methodologies listed as systematic. One point that is not emphasized is the use of a planned sequence of elements. Stahl addresses this issue by commenting that in many basals the patterns taught in the phonics lessons appear infrequently in the text, leading students to believe that phonics is unrelated to the task of reading. He suggests that teachers using a basal might rearrange the phonics lessons so that a more appropriate element is taught with each story. Although no particular sequence of phonic elements has been demonstrated to be more effective than any other, the use of a planned sequence is more effective than random order.

"Strategies used for phonics instruction in early childhood classrooms," by Lesley Mandel Morrow and Diane H. Tracey, provides a description of actual phonics instruction observed in preschool through grade 2 classrooms. The authors report a change in the type of instruction used between preschool and kindergarten and first and second grades. Direct explicit instruction of phonics increased dramatically in the first and second grades. The descriptions of direct instruction in the article will be helpful for clarifying the range of instruction that is explicit. The focus on a specific sequence is not obvious in the descriptions but is there implicitly as most of the teachers in these grades were using commercial materials that included a specific sequence of phonic elements, one of the key characteristics of systematic phonics instruction.

The article "Building practical knowledge of letter-sound correspondences: A beginner's Word Wall and beyond" by Janiel M. Wagstaff shows how Word Walls can be used to reinforce the teaching of initial phonics lessons. The Word Wall in itself would not qualify as systematic teaching of phonics. It is included here, however, to show how a particular strategy in elementary classrooms can be used as part of systematic phonics instruction if the implementation is guided by the use of a specific sequence of phonic elements. The use of sequence does not mean that all children need to be taught each phonic element. Some children may already know a particular element. Diagnostic information should be used to determine which children know which sounds and which need to have direct instruction in particular elements in the sequence.

Carol M. Santa
Kalispell School District, Kalispell, Montana, USA

Torleiv Høien
Dyslexia Research Foundation, Stavanger, Norway

An assessment of Early Steps: A program for early intervention of reading problems

For the last decade there has been a renewed focus on improving the instruction of children at risk for not learning to read well. Unfortunately, most of the instructional programs have produced disappointing results (Walmsley & Allington, 1995). Some even complicate the process for the struggling reader by offering approaches to reading that are philosophically different from those offered in the classroom. Therefore, most poor readers never catch up with their peers in reading and writing abilities, and the gap between low and high readers broadens as children progress through the grades (Stanovich, 1986).

As a consequence, both researchers and teachers are eagerly asking what can be done to help. One way is to focus on early intervention before children acquire a sense of failure and while the gap between those who are succeeding and those who are having difficulty is relatively narrow. By far the best known and most successful of these early intervention programs is Reading Recovery (for a review, see Wasik & Slavin, 1993).

While Reading Recovery has demonstrated effects with first-grade reading achievement (Clay, 1985; Lyons, Pinnell, Short, & Young, 1986; Pinnell, Huck, & DeFord, 1986; Pinnell, Lyons, DeFord, Bryk, & Seltzer, 1994; Pinnell, Lyons, Young, & DeFord, 1987), the program has also run into some practical as well as some methodological criticisms (Center, Wheldall, Freeman, Outhred, & McNaught, 1995; Chapman & Tunmer, 1991; Hiebert, 1994; Nicolson, 1989; Shanahan, 1987). A critical question deals with issues about the low-progress students in Reading Recovery. Why is it that children with severe reading difficulties often complete the number of designated lessons without learning to read? While no program can be expected to be successful with all children, it is nonetheless interesting to speculate as to why a program such as Reading Recovery seems to be less effective for children with the most severe reading difficulties.

One possibility is that severely reading-disabled children need more explicit instruction in phonological analysis for acquiring reading skills (for review, see Adams, 1990; Hulme & Snowling, 1994; Lundberg & Høien, 1991; Share & Stanovich, 1995). With Reading Recovery, children are assumed to acquire skills in word recognition through reading connected text and through writing. The program does not include explicit phonemic awareness training. Rather, the phonemic component is emphasized in the context of writing. The child says and writes letters that he or she hears, and phonological analysis skills are assumed to arise incidentally in the process of reading text and in writing (Clay, 1985).

Iversen and Tunmer (1993) examined the phonological issue directly in an investigation in which they compared the standard Reading Recovery program with a version including more explicit phonemic awareness instruction. Children who participated in either of the Reading Recovery programs performed as well or better than comparison groups composed of average-achieving first graders. However, the children with phonemic awareness training needed statistically significantly fewer lessons for discontinuation than children in the standard Reading Recovery Program. These results probably indicate that the children selected for Reading Recovery are deficient in the phonological domain and that attention placed on the systematic development of the phonological component leads to more rapid progress.

The results from the Iversen and Tunmer (1993) study clearly showed the beneficial effect on reading development when the Reading Recovery program is supplemented with more explicit phonological instruction. This feature is characteristic of the Early Steps reading program examined in the present study. The Reading Recovery program with the modification suggested by Iversen and Tunmer (1993) seemed to represent a significant step in the direction of a powerful preventive and remedial program for children at risk, but it is a very expensive program (Bell, 1995). We therefore looked for a program combining the beneficial component of the Iversen and Tunmer modification with a reasonable cost of implementation.

Early Steps

Early Steps, originally developed by Darrell Morris (Morris, Shaw, & Perney, 1990; Santa, 1998), is a little-known one-to-one tutorial program quite similar in philosophy to Reading Recovery. We begin by describing some general parameters used by school personnel in Kalispell, Montana, USA, for making the decision to implement Early Steps. Then, we empirically examine whether or not the intervention worked as intended.

We sought an early intervention program that represented a *balanced approach* to reading, one that was neither too phonologically based nor too whole language based (Pressley, Rankin, & Yokoi, 1996). Moreover, we wanted a program that would blend philosophically with instructional programs already in place within the district. Ideally the program would engage children in *reading and rereading connected text*, involve them in *daily writing*, and assist them in *acquiring phonological skills* and *applying phonological strategies* for solving their own word recognition problems. Let us now briefly examine each of these features.

Elements of an early intervention program

Given that a child's reading performance improves as a function of the amount of time spent reading (Anderson, Wilson, & Fielding, 1988), we sought a program where children would spend at least half of their instructional time reading. This reading should occur with real books where children gain a sense of accomplishment and pleasure from reading literature (Tunnell & Jacobs, 1989).

We also emphasized the importance of *instructional level* and *pacing*. Children must have an opportunity to read books on the level where they can profit most from instruction (Morris, in press), but they must also progress to increasingly more advanced levels. Children learn most effectively in situations where they are challenged, but not overwhelmed (Gambrell, Wilson, & Gantt, 1981). Therefore, we wanted a program where teachers paced children through increasingly challenging reading selections.

In addition to reading increasingly challenging texts, our students should have daily experiences in rereading familiar text for fluency. They need to experience what it means to be a good reader. The effectiveness of these repeated reading experiences has a long history in reading research (Samuels, 1979). Researchers consistently find that repeated readings help students understand and remember more, lead to increased speed and accuracy, and improve students' oral reading expression. Practice with rereading selections also leads to increased speed, accuracy, and comprehension in new, unpracticed selections (for a review, see Dowhower, 1994).

We sought an early intervention program that included daily writing. Reading and writing are reciprocal processes, and when used together they advance the child's literacy development (Winsor & Pearson, 1992). Practitioners have long known that children have more success reading texts they have written themselves and learning sight words based on their own experiences (Stauffer, 1969).

Encouraging children to write using the letter sounds they hear provides them with a concrete way to apply hypotheses about letter-sound correspondences (Calfee, 1991). Clarke (1988) compared the effectiveness of invented spelling versus an emphasis on correct spelling in first-grade classrooms. The children using invented spelling were superior to others on measures of decoding at the end of the year. Interestingly enough, the effect was most striking with children initially identified as most at risk.

Based on the extensive literature about phonological processing, we also wanted an intervention program with explicit instruction in phonemic analysis. A large body of research indicates that such instruction is important in beginning reading instruction (for a review, see Adams, 1990). Moreover, severely reading-disabled children in particular need explicit instruction in phonological analysis for acquiring reading skills (Lundberg & Høien, 1989; Stanovich, 1991).

In addition, we wanted a program that helped children learn strategies for solving their own word identification problems. Past research indicates that knowledge of strategies assists children with reading comprehension tasks (Palincsar & Ransom, 1988; Paris, Wasik, & Turner, 1991; Peters & Graves, 1987; Whitehead, 1986). When children have been shown how, when, and why to use various cognitive strategies, their reading performance improves. Similarly, with word identification tasks, children who have explicit instruction in strategies for applying what they know about letter-sound correspondences progress more quickly in learning to read than children who have not received strategy instruction (Share & Stanovich, 1995). Even when children have learned many individual instances of letter-sound correspondences, we cannot assume that they grasp the rule that allows them to generalize (Cunningham, 1990).

Program selection

When applying these parameters to intervention programs currently available to schools, we narrowed the field to two possibilities: Reading Recovery and Early Steps. Both programs met our selection criteria. They are one-to-one tutorials offering balanced instruction. Children spend most of their time reading. They write daily and apply phonological processing strategies in word recognition. Despite the similarities between the two programs, there were two important differences. Early Steps allows for explicit instruction in phonological analysis, and it is less expensive.

With Early Steps, children apply their phonological knowledge in daily sentence writing as they work out words in their writing. In addition, a specific portion of the lesson is set aside strictly for word study, where children systematically focus on increasingly complex levels of phonological problems. The program also takes into account newer reading research demonstrating the utility of using orthographic units on onset-rime level and analogy strategies when teaching word recognition (Goswami, 1997; Moustafa, 1995; Peterson & Haines, 1992). Moustafa (1995) found that the onset-rime analogy explanation accounted for first graders' correct recoding of pseudowords better than a phoneme blending explanation. Peterson and Haines (1992) investigated the effect of teaching kindergarten children orthographic analogies based on onset and rime units. They found the analogy training specifically based on onset-rime units an effective method to assist children as they moved into reading.

Pragmatically, Reading Recovery had less potential than Early Steps for deep implementation within our district. When investigating the possibility of adopting Reading Recovery, we realized that our district could not afford to train more than one or two teachers. With such minimal impact, Reading Recovery had little potential for becoming deeply rooted in our district. This was not the case with Early Steps. For the same amount of money needed for training two or three teachers in Reading Recovery, we could train all of the first grade teachers and Title I tutors in two elementary schools. There were also fewer constraints for program adoption. We were able

to do the staff development on site as a graduate class sponsored by Title I funds and the University of Montana.

Thus, Early Steps seemed like a better choice for our school district than Reading Recovery. We could train more teachers at less cost and serve more children. The program also had a systematic phonological component. Given that we decided to implement Early Steps rather than the better known and more thoroughly researched Reading Recovery Program, it became even more essential to examine program effects.

Darrell Morris initially developed the Howard Street Tutoring Program, an after-school tutoring program for low-reading second graders in Chicago (Morris et al., 1990). He then expanded the Howard Street model into an early intervention program for first graders (Early Steps), and he has subsequently assisted a small number of schools in North Carolina, New York, and Illinois with implementing the program. While each of these districts that have implemented the program offer personal testimonials of success, there are no clear data about the effectiveness of Early Steps as an early intervention model. We needed to know whether or not the program was effective for our students before spreading it throughout the district.

Therefore, we designed this study to answer some important questions. First of all, did Early Steps help at-risk first graders learn to read? Are children in the program reading better than comparable children in a Title I program already in place in the district? If so, do these effects hold over time? How are children who participated in the program in Grade 1 performing in second grade? Moreover, do different effects occur as a function of the risk level of children entering the program? Is a relatively expensive one-to-one tutorial model like Early Steps necessary for all children classified as at risk for not learning to read, or do some at-risk children learn just as well in a more traditional small-group setting? Finally, we anticipated that our data might help clarify some of the factors leading to the improved reading performance of at-risk children. For example, could these data offer any insights about how the phonological processing instruction in Early Steps might influence children's reading development? With these questions in mind, we began the investigation.

Method

Participants and setting

Schools

Four neighborhood schools in Kalispell, Montana, USA, were selected to participate in the study—two experimental and two control schools. The children came from lower middle class Caucasian families with similar socioeconomic backgrounds. All four schools qualified for Title I funding, with an equivalent number of students in each school eligible for free or reduced-price lunch. Children from all four schools performed similarly according to comparisons of achievement data. For the last 5 years there was no appreciable difference in average achievement of children attending the four schools as indicated by both district-developed and standardized assessments of all fourth-grade students, carried out as part of a district-wide assessment program.

The Kalispell district advocates an instructional philosophy by which children spend extensive time reading and writing in school. Children in both experimental and control classrooms have a 2-hour language arts block in the morning. After opening calendar activities, they participate in language arts activities focusing on a cross-curricular theme. This might be the shared reading of a Big Book, the development of a language experience story, or small-group reading of class trade books. These reading activities are generally followed by a writing period in which children develop stories patterned from class books or individually selected little books.

The children also have from 20 to 30 minutes each day for individual reading from classroom libraries of books leveled by difficulty. Teachers continually assess children, using running records to ensure that individual children are reading books on an appropriate instructional level. Children have their own Reader's Portfolio where they keep a checklist of books read. Children are also expected to read at home.

During the language arts block, children participate in a daily 10- to 15-minute word study that includes both phonics and spelling. Each week the teacher lists words on a chart that focus on specific phonics elements (e.g., short-vowel words like *cat, fat, mat, pat*). On Monday the children read the chart and talk about the common patterns. Over the next several days, they reread the word lists and practice writing them as part of daily slate spellings. In addition, the teacher dictates a sentence each day for the children to write in their sentence books. The sentence contains words having the specific phonics elements featured that week. Throughout this word study progression the teachers assess the students' understanding of the word elements by asking individual children to read words containing the featured phonic element. They also assess through spell checks and writing tasks. Children having difficulty with specific elements are taken aside individually or in small groups for extra help.

Teachers

All first-grade teachers and Title I tutors teaching in the experimental and control schools participated in the study. The first-grade teachers in both conditions were all highly experienced. Two first-grade teachers (one

teaching an experimental class, the other a control) had master's degrees. All of the other first-grade teachers participating in the study had taught first grade in the district for at least 5 years. The Title I tutors in each school were all certified teachers. One of the tutors in the experimental group had only taught for 1 year; the others in both the experimental and control groups had at least 4 years of teaching experience as Title I tutors.

Participant selection

During the first 3 weeks of school the first-grade teachers observed and informally evaluated their students' early reading behaviors. The teachers then listed the children in the lower half of their classes who seemed least ready for formal reading instruction. During the fourth week of September the children in the lower half of each first-grade class were then evaluated more thoroughly using the Early Reading Screening Instrument (Morris, 1992). This screening instrument focuses on four reading-related abilities: letter knowledge, concept-of-word in text, spelling, and word recognition. Teachers, who had received training in both administering and scoring the assessment, gave the instrument to children in both the experimental and control schools. The selection of students was based on the results of four different literacy tasks.

The evaluation of *letter knowledge* included three parts: identification of upper-case letters, identification of lower-case letters, and letter production. The examiner first pointed to a random list of upper-case letters and asked the child to name them. The examiner followed the same procedure with the lower-case letters. Then, the examiner dictated the letter names in random order and the child wrote them. Three subscores were computed: upper-case letter recognition (0–26), lower-case letter recognition (0–26), and production (0–26), giving a maximum score of 78. Internal-reliability estimate on this measure for this sample was $r = .97$ (Cronbach's alpha).

The assessment of *concept-of-word in text* involved the examiner and child taking turns reading and pointing to sentences in two early emergent books, *Katie* in Morris (1992), and *My Home* written by June Melser and published by the Wright Group (1990). The examiner read, and finger-pointed a sentence and then asked the child to read and finger-point the same sentence. The examiner noted whether or not the child pointed to each word correctly when reading. Next, the examiner pointed to a word in the sentence the child had just read and asked the child to identify it. Two subscores measuring concept-of-word were used: (a) reading accurately and finger-pointing, and (b) identifying a specific word in the sentence. A total score was obtained by adding these two subscores, giving a maximum of 16 points. The Cronbach's alpha reliability was $r = .88$.

A 12-word *spelling test* was also administered. The examiner began by demonstrating how to spell two practice words by saying each word slowly and by writing down the letters heard. If the child gave the wrong letters or failed to respond, the examiner provided corrective feedback until the practice words were spelled correctly. The child was asked to follow the same procedure to spell the 12 words on the test. One point was given for each phoneme represented adequately. Phonemes represented out of order were not awarded points. Students could receive a maximum of 3 or 4 points per word yielding a total possible score of 42 (Morris, 1992). For this sample of subjects, the internal reliability estimate was $r = 0.92$ (Cronbach's alpha) ($n = 123$). Two persons independently scored the spelling results. Interrater reliability for this measure was $r(123) = .99$, $p < .001$. The scoring system and spelling words used are presented in Appendix A.

The assessment of *word recognition* contained two different word sets, 10 easily decodable words and 10 common sight words with more complex grapheme-phoneme correspondences (see Appendix B). The child received 1 point for each word pronounced correctly, yielding a maximum score of 20. Extensive floor effect and restriction of range make it impossible to estimate a reliability coefficient.

The test scores on the different tasks were transformed to standard scores (z-scores), and a combined score for each child was computed. The children from each experimental and control class were ranked from highest to lowest, and the 20% in each class with the lowest combined scores were selected to participate as experimental or control subjects in the study.

Students

Of this group of 49 children, the selection criterion yielded 23 children (14 boys and 9 girls) in the experimental group, and 26 children (16 boys and 10 girls) in the control group. The mean age in the experimental group was 79.8 months ($SD = 3.4$ months), and 80.2 months ($SD = 3.4$ months) in the control group. Table 1 presents the means and standard deviations for each test of the two groups.

The 49 children participating in the study came from a similar lower to middle class background. They all attended their neighborhood schools. None of them had participated in any school program the summer before or after the intervention. No summer school programs were sponsored by the school district.

There were no statistically significant differences in mean performance between the two groups in letter knowledge [$t = -1.785$, $p = ns$], concept-of-word [$t = (123) 0.838$, $p = ns$], spelling [$t = -0.678$, $p = ns$], or word recognition [$t = 0.652$, $p = ns$]. These findings were confirmed by the results obtained on the nonparametric Mann-Whitney U test. Therefore, we can conclude that the

Table 1 Descriptive statistics on the pretests: September 1994

Variable	n	M	SD	Minimum	Median	Maximum
Letter knowledge						
All	49	59.7	11.7	35.0	63.0	76.0
Experimental	23	57.1	12.4	35.0	54.0	76.0
Control	26	62.0	10.8	40.0	65.5	76.0
Concept-of-word in text						
All	49	7.8	3.2	1.0	8.0	15.0
Experimental	23	8.3	3.1	3.0	8.0	15.0
Control	26	7.3	3.2	1.0	7.5	13.0
Spelling task 1						
All	49	13.0	7.5	0.0	12.0	31.0
Experimental	23	12.5	7.3	0.0	11.0	31.0
Control	26	13.4	7.8	0.0	16.0	24.0
Word recognition task 1						
All	49	0.3	1.0	0.0	0.0	6.0
Experimental	23	0.4	1.4	0.0	0.0	6.0
Control	26	0.2	0.5	0.0	0.0	2.0
Total pretest score						
All	49	15.7	4.3	5.8	15.3	29.5
Experimental	23	15.6	4.4	4.4	14.4	29.5
Control	26	15.8	4.2	5.8	16.6	21.9

experimental and control group children were not statistically different based on pretest measures.

On one of the pretests, word recognition task 1, a clear floor effect was observed. Only a few of the children in either of the groups had acquired any word recognition ability at this stage of development. Most received a score of zero. On the other pretests, however, a more normal distribution of scores was obtained, especially on spelling task 1.

Materials

Posttests

A postintervention assessment was done in late May during the last 2 weeks of school. To assess spelling and reading abilities, three tests were employed: a spelling test, a word recognition test, and a passage reading test.

Spelling task 2. This test consisted of 15 words. Twelve of the words were identical to those administered in the pretest. The posttest scoring rubric was slightly modified to account for both phonemic and orthographic properties of the children's spelling (Morris & Perney, 1984, see Appendix C). The maximum score was 75. The internal-reliability estimate for this sample was $r = .94$ (Cronbach's alpha), and the interrater reliability was $r = .99$, $p < .001$.

Word recognition task 2. Each child read a list of 40 words frequently found in first- and second-grade reading materials (see Appendix D). One point was given for each word read correctly. If the child was unable to read a word after about 5 seconds, the examiner moved on to the next word. Testing continued until the child failed to respond correctly to 7 consecutive words. One point was given for each word read correctly, yielding a maximum score of 40. The internal-reliability estimate on this measure for this sample was $r = .93$ (Cronbach's alpha).

Passage reading task 1. In this test the children read up to six passages progressing in difficulty as shown in Table 2. Books were leveled previously by Darrell Morris and teachers participating in the Early Steps program. Factors such as predictability, the amount of print on each page, picture support, and difficulty of vocabulary were taken into consideration for determining book levels. The book levels represent an approximation of reading levels. It is also worth noting that the leveling does not represent equal levels of difficulty. For example, the difference in difficulty between levels 4 and 6 was greater than between levels 1 and 3. Also included was a zero level representing students who were unable to meet the criteria for reading level 1 books. The children read 100-word passages from each book. They began reading at level 1 and progressed as far as they could. Some reached the maximum, level 6.

Table 2 Reading levels

Level	Reading level
0	Pre-emergent — first month of Grade 1
1	Emergent — second/third month of Grade 1
2	Late emergent — fourth/fifth month of Grade 1
3	Primer — middle of Grade 1
4	First reader — end of Grade 1
5	Early Grade 2
6	Middle Grade 2

While the child read, the examiner kept track of time and made a running record of errors. The child progressed to more difficult selections until either his or her reading rate or percentage of word recognition errors reached the cut-off criteria. The cut-off criteria were 10% errors in word recognition or a reading rate of less than 30 words per minute. The following oral reading miscues were counted as errors: substitutions, insertions, omissions, and teacher help. Self-corrections were not counted as errors. Including reading rate as one of the criteria provided some control for reading fluency. The performance index was the passage reading level obtained. For this sample of participants, the internal reliability was $r = .87$ (Cronbach's alpha). Two persons evaluated each child's performance by using the reading levels described in Table 2. Interrater reliability was $r(49) = .96$, $p < .001$.

A *follow-up assessment* was performed again in the fall (September, Grade 2) among the experimental and control group children to determine the stability of the effects and to measure the generalizability of results using standardized measures. The children were given the Woodcock Reading Mastery Test (WRMT-Revised, Form G) by a school psychologist. Word recognition, nonword reading, and passage reading were assessed by the subtests Word Identification (task 3), Word Attack (task 4), and Passage reading (task 5) in the Woodcock Reading Mastery Tests.

WRMT: Word Identification task 3. The Word Identification task contains 106 words arranged in order of difficulty, which the child reads aloud. The examiner followed the directions for test administration as outlined in the test manual. For an answer to be scored correctly, the child had to read the word within about 5 seconds. The testing continued until the child failed to respond correctly to 10 consecutive words. The score represented the total number of words read correctly, with a maximum score of 106. According to the test manual the split-half reliability coefficient (Spearman-Brown corrected) is $r = .98$ ($N = 602$). Raw scores on the odd and even items were used in the split-half coefficient calculations. The same procedure was also used when calculating the reliability coefficient on the nonword reading and passage comprehension test.

WRMT: Word Attack task 4. Phonological decoding was assessed by the WRMT-R Word Attack subtest. This subtest requires the child to read aloud phonetically regular nonsense words beginning with monosyllabic words of two to four letters and progressing to multisyllabic words. All participants began the Word Attack test with a demonstration item and two practice items along with corrective feedback. The test was discontinued if the child offered no response or an incorrect response to 10 items in a row. The performance index used was the number of nonsense syllables correctly pronounced, yielding a maximum score of 45. The manual-reported split-half reliability coefficient (Spearman-Brown corrected) is $r = .94$.

WRMT: Passage reading task 5. The Woodcock passage comprehension test is a cloze assessment evaluating the reader's ability to read a two- or three-sentence passage and to identify a key word missing from the passage. Some of the easier passages have accompanying pictures. To complete the item the child must understand the sentence with the blank as well as the other sentences in the selection. A correct response indicates that the child has comprehended the entire selection. Before beginning the test, the examiner told the child to read each passage silently and then to figure out the words deleted in the text. The test continued until the child made six consecutive errors. The performance index used was the total number of correctly inserted words, giving a maximum score of 68. The split-half reliability coefficient (Spearman-Brown corrected) reported in the test manual is $r = .94$.

Procedure

The intervention took place between September and May during the 1994–95 academic year. All of the first-grade teachers (six teachers) and the Title I tutors (four tutors) from the two experimental schools participated in the intervention. Additional Early Steps teachers were the Language Arts Coordinator and an elementary school principal from one of the experimental schools. The principal tutored one child, and the Language Arts Coordinator tutored two children. Each first-grade teacher tutored one child for 30 minutes during his or her daily planning periods. During this planning time a parent volunteer or classroom assistant read aloud to the rest of the children. The teacher took the child to the Title I room for the tutoring sessions. The Title I tutors taught from three to four children in the Early Steps program. They tutored each child individually for 30 minutes in the Title I room.

During the intervention all teacher participants took part in an intensive inservice training program for implementing Early Steps. This included a graduate class taught jointly by the first author and Darrell Morris. The class met weekly for the first month of school and then once a month for the rest of the year. Darrell Morris also trained the Language Arts Coordinator to be the on-site teacher trainer. He visited the project five times during the school year. During these visits he observed and provided feedback on tutoring sessions and led the graduate class. The teachers were observed once per month by the Language Arts Coordinator and given feedback about their teaching.

None of the classroom teachers or Title I tutors from the two control schools participated in the Early Steps inservice program. However, they did attend two inservice training sessions, one in the fall and one midyear, given by an outside consultant. These sessions primarily focused on guided reading strategies designed for small-group instruction. In addition to these district-sponsored workshops, the tutors also attended several sessions at the state Title I conference. Several also attended regional and national IRA conferences.

Experimental group instruction

The 30-minute lessons were fast paced and intensive. The Early Steps lesson contained four basic parts: rereading familiar books, word study, writing, and introduction of a new book.

The program emphasizes real *book reading*. The first 8 to 10 minutes of the lesson are spent in rereading the series of leveled books the child had read in previous lessons.

The next 5 to 6 minutes of the lesson involves *word study*, where the tutor takes the child through a series of letter and/or word sorts depending on the child's alphabetic and phonemic knowledge. Word study assists poor readers to acquire phonological processing skills, to develop sight vocabulary, and to obtain effective metacognitive strategies when identifying unfamiliar words in reading and when spelling unfamiliar words. We also hypothesized that the most at-risk children would need help with phonological processing skills (phonological awareness and phonological recoding), and that their progress in reading would be strongly related to the development of these skills. The aim of the word study instruction is to make children aware that words with common sounds often share spelling patterns. The assumption is that children will learn to read more quickly if they see how the visual patterns and the sounds shared by different words are related (Iversen & Tunmer, 1993).

This portion of the lesson takes the child from letter knowledge to consonant sounds and then through the most common word patterns in English. For many children the first weeks of lessons involved learning how to name and write the letters. Once children demonstrated knowledge of the alphabet, they next practiced discriminating initial consonant sounds by sorting picture cards representing different initial letters. After students could discriminate the sounds with pictures, they learned the names of the initial letters corresponding to the sounds of the picture names. Next, they progressed to word sorting, where they simultaneously examined visual and auditory patterns. The children started with word families (rhyming patterns) and then progressed through short- and then long-vowel patterns.

The typical word sorting exercise involves three patterns with four words in each pattern. The three words (header words) across the top must be known words, each representing one of the three families. If the child does not know the three header words as sight words, the tutor teaches them to the child. The tutor will often draw small pictures on header cards in case the child forgets the words.

The teacher places the three words horizontally on the table and the remaining cards in a pile. After the teacher demonstrates the task, the child takes the cards and sorts each one into the appropriate column and then reads the words. After the child becomes somewhat adept with a particular sort, the teacher reinforces knowledge through spelling checks and games. An example of a successful word sorting task is given below:

hat	*man*	*cap*
rat	fan	map
cat	pan	lap
sat	can	tap

It is logical that the initial focus of word sorts is on phonograms. Phonograms are the common elements in word families (e.g., the letter sequence -at in hat, rat, sat, and fat). These patterns not only strengthen the child's beginning consonant awareness but also direct the child's attention to the medial vowel and ending consonants.

There appear to be two major advantages to using phonograms in the beginning stages of reading instruction. First, the use of phonograms enables children to take advantage of the intrasyllabic units of onset and rime. Onset is the initial consonant or consonant cluster, and rime is the vowel and any following consonants. Research has indicated that awareness of onsets and rimes precedes the development of full-blown phonological awareness (Goswami & Bryant, 1990). Because onsets and rimes are relatively accessible to beginning readers, and because onsets often contain single phonemes, an initial focus on word families may greatly facilitate the process of learning to isolate and recognize individual phonemes (Treiman, 1992). A second major advantage is that the complexity of vowel generalization is greatly reduced. Vowel sounds are generally quite sta-ble in the rhyme phonograms that appear in beginning reading materials.

Once students had learned to read and write the short-vowel word families, they began the short-vowel sorts where words no longer rhyme but occur in consonant-vowel-consonant (CVC) patterns:

can	*pig*	*hot*
hat	sit	top
lap	win	job
bag	lip	stop

As the child progressed through the short-vowel patterns and then the long-vowel patterns, the teacher continued to reinforce the child's knowledge with spelling games and with reading the words in randomized lists. (For more information on word sorts, see Morris, 1992. Appendix E has a complete list of words used for word sorting.)

The emphasis was also on developing *metacognitive knowledge and strategies* for reading and writing. The instruction focuses not only on making children more aware that words fall into visual and phonological groups, but also on helping them apply knowledge gained from the word study to the reading and writing portions of the lesson. For example, if a child had difficulty figuring out a word containing the CVC pattern while reading connected text, the teacher would remind the student to use information from a particular letter sound and word sort, as well as contextual clues, to figure out the word. Similarly, during sentence writing, the teacher would prompt the child to include phonological information gained from word sorting to writing. For example, if the student left out a short vowel in a CVC word, the teacher would remind the reader about the word sort containing this element.

During book reading both at the beginning and end of the lesson, tutors encouraged students *to become aware of reading strategies*. For example, when a child came to an unknown word while reading the tutor might offer prompts such as the following:

1. What can you do to figure out that word by yourself? What are some strategies that might help you?

2. Read that line again. What does the word start with?

3. I think that word is similar to some words that we have done in the word sorts. What word pattern do you know that might help you?

4. Read through the sentence. Leave the word out. What word makes sense there?

The wisdom of including strategy instruction with every aspect of the lesson is well supported by research. Metacognitive instruction not only influences children's understanding of text (Paris, Wasik, & Turner, 1991), but also clearly improves word recognition strategies.

Cunningham (1990) found that encouraging children to reflect upon the application and usefulness of phonemic awareness during reading helped them later to apply these skills during their own reading.

For the next 5 to 8 minutes the child *writes* a sentence from his or her own experience. After a short discussion, the child begins writing, saying aloud each word as he or she writes. The teacher encourages the child to write down the letter sounds he or she hears. The teacher assists by calling attention to specific letter sounds and words. After writing, the child rereads the sentence. Then, the tutor rewrites it on a sentence strip. After the child reads the sentence again, the tutor cuts it apart for the child to put together and reread. Encouraging children to write using the letters they hear is a powerful way to teach phonemic awareness (Calfee, 1991). Early writing involves hearing the sequential sounds in a word and relating each sound to the letter. For example, in writing the word *mad*, a child must first separate the word into sequential sounds (/m/a/d/) and then produce the spelling that corresponds to these sounds (*mad*).

The fourth step in the lesson is the *introduction of a new book* that the child is expected to read without much help the next day. The book is often at a slightly more advanced level than the books the child had previously read. Before reading, the teacher and child discuss the book as they look at the pictures and talk about the vocabulary. The teacher helps the child build a frame of meaning prior to reading the text. This new book then becomes the third book that the child rereads at the beginning of the next day's lesson.

During book reading, one of the most challenging tasks for the tutors was coaching children to figure out words on their own and allowing time for children to correct their own reading errors. If children have little opportunity to correct their own errors, they have little chance of employing strategies essential for independence. The issues of wait time and coaching came up frequently with teachers taking the Early Steps training.

Control group instruction

The children in the control group received daily help with reading in addition to regular classroom instruction. This instruction, primarily involving the reading of books, was based on the notion that slow-progress children need additional reading practice in addition to the language arts instruction occurring in the classroom. Given that a child's reading performance improves as a function of the amount of time spent reading (Anderson et al., 1988), this approach seemed theoretically sound.

Children met in small groups of two to four children in pull-out situations or in the corner of the classroom. During these daily 30-minute sessions, the children read and reread books used in classroom lessons as well as additional small books and selections from a variety of basal anthologies. The children were grouped so that they were reading on approximately the same level of difficulty. Thus, the emphasis on book reading was similar in the experimental and control groups.

During these guided reading lessons, the teacher constantly monitored and evaluated the children to ensure that the books were neither too difficult nor too easy. While the lesson changed as the children developed in reading skills, it basically contained four parts: book introduction, first reading, second reading, and rereading.

The teacher began the lesson by introducing a new story. Together, the group did a walk-through of the book in which they examined the pictures and talked about what was happening on each page. During this introduction the tutor used in the discussion any words in the book that might be unfamiliar to the children and pointed out any words that the children might not know. After walking through the book, the tutor would often reread each page followed by the children chorally reading the same page. Following the choral reading of the book, the children would then mumble read the whole book themselves with the teacher assisting. After the introduction of the new book, the children would next reread in pairs. This would be followed by the students rereading other familiar books alone or in pairs. The tutors carefully selected books so that the children read progressively more difficult books that corresponded as closely as possible to their reading levels.

As the children progressed, the teacher varied the amount of support, particularly when introducing the story and modeling reading. The idea was for students to do as much as they could for themselves.

The small-group lessons did not include a systematic word study program. When children met a word they did not know in their reading, the tutor made a note of it or simply reminded the children to use clues such as the initial letter, vowel pattern, or context. Practically the entire 30-minute session was spent in reading.

Results

Postintervention evaluation

All 49 at-risk children originally selected for the program were included in the analysis. Table 3 shows the descriptive statistics for each of the three postintervention tests.

Gender differences in all dependent variables were examined, and no statistically significant differences were found. Therefore, the gender variable was not included in the subsequent analyses.

Spelling task 2

A *t*-test analysis showed that the postintervention spelling performance in the experimental group (M = 59.6, SD = 5.95) was statistically significantly higher than in the control group (M = 53.7, SD = 12.4), t (47) = 2.067, p < .05.

However, it could be the case that individual variation before intervention took place had biased the results. As mentioned earlier, this study did not employ a random assignment of subjects to the two treatment groups. In such cases the use of analysis of covariance (ANCOVA) can help reduce potential bias, but it is important to first ascertain which preintervention factors make a statistically significant contribution to the variance in the dependent variable.

Therefore, a regression analysis was performed with spelling as the dependent variable and with the four preintervention tests (letter knowledge, concept-of-word, spelling, and word recognition) as predictors. To avoid bias due to treatment effects among the experimental students, only the participants in the control group were included in the regression analysis. The results revealed that only preintervention spelling statistically contributed significantly to the variation in the dependent variables.

Before analyzing the data with analysis of covariance (ANCOVA), we also addressed the homogeneity of slopes assumption, which is a major condition for a valid application of ANCOVA. No statistically significant interaction was found between the covariate and the treatment groups, thereby justifying the application of ANCOVA. In the subsequent analyses of covariance, we always tested for the assumption of homogeneity.

The first ANCOVA was performed with spelling task 2 as dependent variable, with group as independent factor, and with spelling 1 as covariate. The ANCOVA revealed a statistically significant group effect [F (1,46) = 5.172, p = .05] and thereby confirmed the results of the *t*-test analysis.

It might be that the treatment effect could be even stronger for children at the lowest achievement level. In order to locate the treatment effect more precisely, the children were classified into two categories depending on their scores on the preintervention spelling test. The children scoring 12 points (the median value in the total sample) or below on spelling were categorized as high-risk children. This cutoff yielded 13 children in the experimental group and 12 children in the control group. Those scoring higher than 12 points were categorized as low-risk children. Ten children in the experimental group and 14 in the control group were classified in this category. These risk categories were employed in all subsequent analyses because spelling was the only preintervention task that statistically contributed significantly to explain variance in all dependent variables.

An ANCOVA was performed with spelling task 2 as dependent variable, group and risk category as independent factors, and with spelling task 1 as covariate. The analysis confirmed our expectation. In addition to a main group effect [F (1,44) = 5.997, p ≤ .05], the ANCOVA revealed a clear group by risk category interaction [F (1,44) = 6.057, p ≤ .05]. The posthoc comparison (Tukey's honestly signficant difference test) demonstrated that the high-risk experimental group children outperformed the high-risk controls [t (44) = 12.591, p < .01], whereas no statistically significant difference was found in mean values between the low-risk experimentals and controls [t (44) = 0.597, p = *ns*]. The means, adjusted for initial differences in spelling, are displayed in Table 4.

Table 3 Descriptive statistics on the posttests: May 1995

Variable	n	M	SD	Minimum	Median	Maximum
Spelling task 2						
All	49	56.5	10.3	7.0	57.0	74.0
Experimental	23	59.6	5.9	49.0	59.0	74.0
Control	26	53.7	12.4	7.0	55.5	67.0
Word recognition task 2						
All	49	26.3	7.8	9.0	28.0	38.0
Experimental	23	29.8	5.7	16.0	31.0	38.0
Control	26	23.2	8.2	9.0	24.0	37.0
Passage reading task 1						
All	49	3.0	1.4	0.0	3.0	6.0
Experimental	23	3.6	1.3	0.0	4.0	6.0
Control	26	2.6	1.4	0.0	2.5	6.0

Although the experimental group statistically scored significantly higher in spelling than the control group, a closer look at the figures in Table 4 clearly demonstrates that the group difference is solely caused by the progress made by the high-risk experimental group children.

Word recognition task 2

A *t*-test analysis showed that the children in the experimental group statistically scored significantly higher on postintervention word recognition ($M = 29.8$, $SD = 5.8$) than did the control group children ($M = 23.2$, $SD = 8.2$), [$t (47) = 3.233$; $p \leq .005$].

An ANCOVA was run with word recognition task 2 as the dependent variable, group and risk category as independent factors, and with spelling task 1 and letter knowledge as covariates. The rationale for choosing these two preintervention tests as covariates was based on the result of a regression analysis. The ANCOVA revealed a substantial group effect [$F (1,43) = 11.915$, $p \leq .001$], and posthoc comparisons (Tukey's HSD test) showed that the experimental group significantly outperformed the control group [$t (43) = 6.714$, $p \leq .001$].

Again, it is worth noting the statistically significant group-by-risk interaction [$F (1,43) = 6.413$, $p \leq .02$]. Posthoc comparisons confirmed that the high-risk children in the experimental group scored substantially higher in word recognition than the high-risk control group children [$t (43) = 11.640$, $p < .001$], whereas no statistically significant difference was found between the low-risk groups [$t (43) = 1.789$, $p = ns$]. We also noticed that the high-risk experimental subjects scored higher than the low-risk experimental subjects. Table 5 displays the adjusted means.

Passage reading task 1

The experimental group children averaged considerably higher in text reading than did the control group children ($M = 3.6$; $SD = 1.3$ versus $M = 2.6$; $SD = 1.4$), giving a statistically significant mean difference between the groups
[$t (47) = 2.523$, $p = .05$].

An ANCOVA was performed with passage reading task 1 as the dependent variable, group and risk category as independent factors, and with spelling task 1 as the covariate. The rationale for using this task as covariate was based on the result of the regression analysis that showed that the preintervention spelling task was the only variable that in a statistical way significantly predicted variance in passage reading.

Again, the ANCOVA revealed a statistically significant group effect [$F (1,43) = 9.804$, $p \leq .005$] and a statistically significant group by risk category interaction [$F (1,43) = 11.372$, $p < .002$]. The posthoc comparison test showed that the experimental group statistically significantly outperformed the control group [$t (44) = 10.026$, $p < .005$], but again the most substantial mean difference was found between the high-risk experimental and the high-risk control group children [$t (44) = 2.174$, $p < .001$].

Table 4   Adjusted means on spelling task 2

	Experimental		Control		
	n	*M*	*n*	*M*	*t*
All	23	59.3	26	53.3	−5.997*
High risk	13	62.6	12	50.0	−12.591**
Low risk	10	56.0	14	56.6	*ns*

* $p < .05$; ** $p < .01$

Table 5   Adjusted means on word recognition task 2

	Experimental		Control		
	n	*M*	*n*	*M*	*t*
All	23	29.7	26	22.9	−6.715*
High risk	13	30.8	12	19.2	−11.640**
Low risk	10	28.5	14	26.7	*ns*

* $p < .05$; ** $p = .001$

Table 6 Adjusted means on passage reading task 1

	Experimental		Control		
	n	*M*	*n*	*M*	*t*
All	23	3.58	26	2.46	−10.026*
High risk	13	3.87	12	1.55	−2.174**
Low risk	10	3.29	14	3.37	*ns*

* $p = .005$; ** $p = .001$

Table 7 Descriptive statistics on the follow-up tests: September 1995

Variable	*n*	*M*	*SD*	Minimum	Median	Maximum
Word identification task 3						
All	41	36.1	9.8	21.0	35.0	66.0
Experimental	19	39.1	10.6	21.0	38.0	66.0
Control	22	33.6	8.4	21.0	32.5	54.0
Word attack task 4 (nonword reading)						
All	41	16.3	7.7	2.0	15.0	33.0
Experimental	19	20.5	6.8	10.0	20.0	33.0
Control	22	12.7	6.5	2.0	11.5	27.0
Passage reading task 5						
All	41	18.7	6.1	10.0	17.0	33.0
Experimental	19	21.3	6.3	13.0	20.0	33.0
Control	22	16.3	5.0	10.0	16.0	26.0

No statistically significant difference was found between the two low-risk categories [$t(44) = 0.122$, $p = ns$]. Table 6 displays the adjusted means.

Perhaps even more telling than these averages is the fact that 52% of the experimental group children (12 out of 23) were reading at level 4, 5, or 6 by the end of the year. Only 4 experimental group children completed the year reading at levels 1 or 2. These results were dramatically different from the control group children, where only 24% (6 out of 25) completed the year at levels 4, 5, or 6. Ten control group children completed the year at level one.

In summary, the experimental group statistically significantly outperformed the control group on all postintervention tests. However, the differences between experimental and control students reflect the progress by the high-risk experimental group children on all postintervention tests.

Follow-up evaluation

The follow-up testing served two purposes. It allowed us to validate the results on the postintervention tasks with a standardized reading assessment (Woodcock Reading Mastery Test), and it yielded information about the stability of the results across time.

The results on the three follow-up tests are shown in Table 7.

Four participants from the experimental group and 4 from the control group did not participate in the follow-up assessment because they moved to other school districts. The mean values of these students, however, did not deviate statistically significantly from the average.

For each of the follow-up tests, regression analyses were performed with preintervention tests as predictors. Again, statistically, only the spelling task contributed significantly in explaining the variance in the dependent variables, and consequently the preintervention spelling scores were used as covariate in the follow-up study.

Word recognition task 3 (Woodcock Reading Mastery–Word Identification)

While the follow-up test was different from the word recognition test used at postintervention, the Pearson correlation between the two different forms was .71 ($p \leq .001$), which demonstrated that the two tests were fairly equivalent. An ANCOVA was run with Word recognition task 3 as dependent variable, group and risk category as dependent factors, and with spelling task 1 as covariate. Again, a main group effect was found [$F(1,36)$ = 4.842, $p \leq .05$], with the experimental group scoring statistically significantly higher [$t(36) = 6.209$, $p \leq .05$] than the control group. Additionally, the analysis revealed a clear group-by-risk interaction [$F(1,36) = .058$, $p \leq .05$], and again the posthoc comparison test proved that the high-risk experimental group children statistically significantly outperformed the high-risk control group subjects [$t(36) = 13.125$, $p < .01$]. Thus, the follow-up results confirmed the results obtained on the postintervention word recognition test. The adjusted means are given in Table 8.

Nonword reading (Woodcock Reading Mastery–Word Attack)

The correlation between word recognition task 2 and nonword reading was .82 ($p \leq .001$). An ANCOVA was run with nonword scores as dependent variable, with group and risk category as independent variables, and with spelling task 1 as covariate. Not surprisingly, the posthoc comparison analysis showed that the experimental group children still outperformed the control group children [$F(1,36) = 14.757$, $p < .001$], but no overall effect was found for the group-by-risk-category interaction [$F(1,36) = 1.173$, $p = ns$].

According to Wilkinson, Hill, Welna, and Birkenbeuel (1992), posthoc comparison procedures like Tukey's HSD test are also designed to maintain the over-all protection level. Therefore, to get more information about a possible difference between high-risk and low-risk groups, the Tukey's HSD test was applied. The mean values are displayed in Table 9.

The difference obtained between the experimental and the control group was quite impressive considering that neither group was exposed to any nonword reading activities as part of the intervention program [$t(36) = 8.318$, $p \leq .005$]. Even more impressive was the result obtained among high-risk experimental group children as compared with the high-risk controls [$t(36) = 10.550$, $p \leq .001$].

Passage reading task 2 (Woodcock Reading Mastery)

The follow-up assessment included a standardized passage comprehension task instead of the more informal passage reading test employed in the postintervention assessment. The Pearson correlation between the results on the two tests was .80 ($p \leq .001$). The high and statistically significant correlation between the results on these two tasks shows that the more informal passage reading task can be used as a valid measurement of reading comprehension.

An ANCOVA was run with group and high risk as independent variables and with phonemic awareness (spelling) as the covariate. Statistically significant effects were found for group [$F(1,36) = 10.341$, $p \leq .005$], but again no overall statistically significant group-by-risk-category interaction was found [$F(1,36) = 3.317$, $p = .08$]. The adjusted mean scores are displayed in Table 10.

Table 8 Adjusted means on word recognition task 3

	Experimental		Control		
	n	M	n	M	t
All	19	38.7	22	32.8	2.02*
High risk	12	39.2	9	26.1	3.79**
Low risk	7	37.2	13	37.1	ns

* $p < .05$, ** $p < .005$

Table 9 Adjusted means on nonword reading

	Experimental		Control		
	n	M	n	M	t
All	19	20.5	22	12.2	−8.318**
High risk	12	20.2	9	9.8	−10.550***
Low risk	7	20.8	13	14.7	ns

** $p < .005$; *** $p < .001$

Table 10 Adjusted means on passage reading task 2

	Experimental		Control		
	n	M	n	M	t
All	19	21.4	22	15.7	−5.678**
High risk	12	20.9	9	12.0	−8.879**
Low risk	7	21.9	13	19.4	ns

** $p < .005$

Table 11 Effect sizes on the posttests and follow-up tests for the Early Steps and control students

Measures	Posttests		Follow-up tests	
	All[1]	High risk[2]	All[3]	High risk[4]
Spelling	0.5	1.0	*	*
Word recognition	0.7	1.4	0.7	1.6
Nonword reading	*	*	1.2	1.5
Passage reading	0.7	1.0	1.0	1.8

[1]Posttests: Early Steps ($n = 23$); Control ($n = 26$). [2]High risk: Early Steps ($n = 13$); Control ($n = 12$). [3]Follow-up: Early Steps ($n = 19$); Control ($n = 22$). [4]High risk: Early Steps ($n = 12$); Control ($n = 9$).
* Data are not available.

The posthoc comparison revealed a statistically significant difference in performance between the experimental group and the control group [$t(36) = 5.678$, $p \leq .005$], and between the high-risk experimental subjects and high-risk control participants [$t(36) = 8.879$, $p \leq .005$].

In the study we also calculated the effect sizes (ES), and the figures are displayed in Table 11.

Effect sizes use the means and standard deviations of the control group to compute standard scores, and effect sizes are commonly used when comparing the impact of different instructional programs (Center et al., 1995). In our study, the results yielded positive, though moderate, effect sizes in favor of the experimental group on all the three posttests, with values varying from 0.5 to 0.7. This pattern was also confirmed by the results on the follow-up tests. However, the effect sizes became even more substantial when comparing the two high-risk groups. The values in favor of the high-risk experimental group children varied from 1.0 to 1.8. Most remarkable was the high effect size on nonword reading ($ES = 1.5$) and on reading comprehension ($ES = 1.8$).

Discussion

Our data clearly show that Early Steps led to accelerated growth, particularly for children most at risk for not learning to read. Moreover, these results were substantiated on a variety of dependent measures and were maintained over the summer after students had completed the program. The experimental group children were reading better than their control group counterparts at the beginning of Grade 2. Therefore, the data provided an answer to our overall question of program effectiveness. The program did improve the experimental group children's spelling, sight word abilities, and passage reading compared to the control group children.

Even though the main effect of group occurred on all dependent variables, it is interesting to note that most of the effect can be accounted for by differences between the high-risk experimental and control group children. The program was clearly most effective with high-risk children. The low-risk children in the control group did almost as well on most measures as the low-risk experimental group children. Why did these differential effects occur?

Let us begin with some speculations about the low-risk children. While low-risk experimental group children did better on the standardized reading comprehension and nonword measure, they performed similarly to the low-risk control group children on all other dependent variables. It appears as if the small-group Title I instruction worked quite effectively for children less at risk for not learning to read. Recall that the control group children spent most of their 30-minute lesson reading books. In fact, they actually spent from 10 to 15 minutes more per day reading than the experimental group children. While some word study and writing occurred incidentally in these small-group lessons, neither of these components was an integral part of their daily lesson. We have long known the importance of the practice effect in reading. Perhaps the extra time each day for reading books on an appropriate level of difficulty may be enough to accelerate the performance of most children less at risk.

Why then did the high-risk experimental group children perform so much better than the high-risk controls? These results cannot be explained by outliers or by regression towards the mean. Students with extremely low preintervention scores would be expected to have a higher score on the next test by the mere operation of chance. Therefore, before running each analysis we tested for outliers using leverage and studentized residuals. *T*-test analyses showed no statistically significant mean differences in preintervention spelling performance between the two high-risk groups. When comparing the results obtained by high-risk and low-risk control group children, it became clear that a possible regression effect did not lower the performance gap between high-risk and low-risk performers. Consequently, we do not consider the regression effect to be an important factor when trying to explain the progress found among the high-risk experimental group children, because there is no reason to expect that the regression effect would have a different impact on high-risk experimental than on high-risk control group children.

Neither can the beneficial effect solely be explained by the one-to-one tutoring. If so, we would also expect the low-risk experimental group children to outperform the group-instructed, low-risk control group children. As mentioned, the data did not support this expectation. Although research can document that one-to-one tutoring yields better results than working in groups (Vellutino et al., 1996), the one-to-one approach in itself is obviously not sufficient (Pinnell et al., 1994).

Another hypothesis might be that the tutors were unconsciously giving high-risk children more attention and perhaps more systematic and well-structured instruction. Although we cannot neglect the possibility that such factors might have a beneficial impact on learning to read, the substantial discrepancy between high-risk and low-risk experimental group children cannot solely be explained by variations in attention and instructional procedures. If so, a similar tendency should also occur when comparing the results between high-risk and low-risk control group children.

The differences between the high-risk groups must be a function of program components. Small-group extended reading was clearly not as effective for these children as were the strategies implemented in Early Steps. High-risk children seemed to need the additional help

with phonological processing through word sorting and writing. This is in accordance with earlier research demonstrating that children at risk benefit the most from phonological awareness training (Iversen & Tunmer, 1993; Lundberg, 1994). It is worthwhile to note that the high-risk children performed better than the low-risk controls in every word level measure: spelling, sight vocabulary (both word recognition tasks 1 and 2), and nonword reading. The Early Steps program seems to be particularly strong in teaching children phonological processing skills.

Although spelling tasks were part of incidental instruction in the small-group Title I program and in the regular classroom instruction, Early Steps offered a more comprehensive and systematic approach for enhancing phonemic awareness. This seems particularly beneficial to high-risk readers. The students wrote words and sentences. Before writing the words, they segmented them into constituent phonemes and used this strategy when writing. It makes sense that encouraging children to write using invented spelling assists them in becoming better decoders. Clarke (1988) compared the effectiveness of invented spelling versus an emphasis on correct spelling in first-grade classrooms. The children using invented spelling were superior to others on measures of decoding at the end of the year. However, the effect was most striking with children initially identified as most at risk.

The program also emphasized identification of initial sounds by sorting picture cards representing different beginning letters, and it provided explicit instruction in letter-sound and sound-letter correspondences, which assists children in internalizing common spelling patterns. Children not only sorted and read words according to specific patterns but also practiced spelling them. We assumed that all these tasks increase phonemic awareness and also benefit spelling (Lundberg, Frost, & Petersen, 1988).

Every aspect of the Early Steps lesson undoubtedly promoted word recognition performance. The children had opportunities to acquire sight vocabulary by reading and rereading books. In the beginning the books were very predictable, thus allowing children to encounter the same words several times. The sentence writing also assisted children in acquiring sight vocabulary. After writing, the teacher rewrote the sentence on a sentence strip, and the child practiced reading the sentence several times before cutting it apart and putting it together again. All of these activities reinforced word knowledge, and this kind of repetition seemed particularly important for high-risk children.

Additionally, the Early Steps program seems to increase word recognition by incorporating word-study tasks with direct attention to letter patterns and their phonological equivalents. In particular, word sorting focuses on common spelling patterns in word families, thereby increasing awareness of orthographic structures and providing children with a useful metacognitive strategy when dealing with unfamiliar words. Treiman (1985, 1986) found that dividing syllables into their onsets (initial consonants) and rimes (remaining vowel stems) was easier and more natural than dividing at other points in the syllable. Moreover, Goswami and Bryant (1990) argued that a possible explanation of the link between rhyming and reading was that the ability to recognize rhyming words may form the basis for noticing that these words often share common spelling. A child who can hear that *sand* and *hand* rhyme will likely recognize that the spelling pattern at the end of these words is the same, and this insight guides him or her in recognizing an unfamiliar word following the same pattern (*land*). This analogy awareness is exactly what the Early Steps program fosters in the word-sort tasks. Having explicit instruction in analogies seemed particularly important for the high-risk children. These results are consistent with conclusions that have been drawn in earlier research (Goswami, 1986, 1988, 1997; Treiman, 1985, 1992).

Probably one of the most intriguing findings occurred with the nonword reading, because it was a task far removed from the instructional strategies offered in either condition or in the regular classroom. Yet Early Steps children, particularly the high-risk children, did far better than their control counterparts on this task. Given that nonword reading is among the purest measures of phonological competency, these performance differences mark the experimental group children as more adept with phonological skills (Share & Stanovich, 1995).

Why then does the Early Steps program seem to have such a powerful impact on nonword reading ability? We hypothesize that progress in nonword ability is a consequence of the strong emphasis in the program on phonemic awareness and word study. These results might in part explain the experimental group's consistently superior performance on both of the word recognition assessments (Word recognition task 1 and Word recognition task 2) because efficient word recognition depends on proficient phonological decoding ability (Lundberg & Høien, 1996; Rack, Hulme, Snowling, & Wightman, 1994).

Phonological skills are important not only when learning to decode and recognize words but also in the process of text comprehension. The reader's ability to efficiently activate phonological codes for support of working memory is assumed to be critical also in text comprehension (Crain, Shankweiler, Macaruso, & Bar-Shalom, 1990; Yuill & Oakhill, 1991). During reading, sequences of words must be held in a temporary storage buffer while the comprehension processes integrate them into a meaningful conceptual structure that can be stored in long-term memory (Baddeley, 1986). Without automaticity and speed in word recognition, much of the child's energy and attention focuses on figuring out the word rather than understanding the text (Adams, 1990; Goswami & Bryant, 1990; Just & Carpenter, 1987; Stanovich, 1991). Moreover, the emphasis on reading fluency and on reading progressively more difficult books appears to be especially important for the high-risk children.

When considering the results of this study, we must take into consideration the limits of our experimental paradigm. The constraints of the district prevented the random assignment of conditions, students, and teachers. All of these factors restrict the generalizability of results.

Ideally, we would have liked to follow the reading development of the experimental and control group children over a 2- to 3-year period. However, given these data demonstrating the effectiveness of the program for the most at-risk students, teachers and administrators in Kalispell schools felt it would be unethical for the low children in the control group not to have the benefit of Early Steps. We cannot keep effective programs from the very children who need them the most. Therefore, in the fall of Grade 2, the lowest second-grade readers from the control group participated in Early Steps. Several of the experimental group children also continued in the program for part of Grade 2.

It is also difficult to tease out effects related to one-to-one tutorials. While we have some evidence that the results of this study cannot be explained solely by the fact that Early Steps was a one-to-one tutorial, it would be worthwhile to test this question in a cleaner design, for example, comparing the efficiency of the Early Steps program with a control program also using one-to-one tutoring. Another focus of further study might be to investigate whether or not Early Steps instruction would work as well for high-risk readers within small groups as in a one-to-one setting.

Conclusion

Even within the limits of this study, we can conclude that Early Steps made a difference for our children. The reasons seem clear. It represents a balanced program that incorporates key features of effective reading instruction (Spiegel, 1995). It takes place early, before children develop ineffective literacy habits and devastating psychological problems about their own learning inadequacies. It also provides children with the opportunity to make accelerated progress. Children spend time reading books rather than with fragmented texts and isolated drills. The time spent reading is also with books that match the child's own instructional level. Students also progress through levels of books that become progressively more difficult.

The program also incorporates principles of direct instruction with teacher explanations and demonstrations followed by the gradual release of responsibility to the child.

Coupled with every aspect of instruction is a focus on metacognitive strategies. Students learn to monitor their own performance and to apply comprehension strategies (prediction, meaning checks) and word recognition strategies (picture clues, word-sort patterns, single letters) for identifying and solving their own reading problems.

Early Steps also includes a sequential program of word study in which children learn to apply knowledge of letters and word parts in a purposeful manner. Incorporating systematic word study that directs children's attention to letter patterns and phonological equivalents is an essential component of early intervention programs, particularly for high-risk children.

Finally, writing occurs daily. Children write about their own experiences. Moreover, writing is particularly important in a beginning reading program where children apply segmentation of speech sounds and invented spelling to enhance phonemic awareness.

Furthermore, knowing that Early Steps made the most difference with high-risk children gave us insight as to the best use of educational resources. We also know that Early Steps or any other program will not fix everybody by the end of Grade 1. Some children will need additional help in Grades 2 and 3.

In conclusion, these data assist us in making more informed decisions about the best allocation of funds. Reserving Early Steps instruction for children most at risk makes sense, given that our traditional Title I program seems to work quite effectively for children less at risk for reading failure.

REFERENCES

ADAMS, M.J. (1990). *Beginning to read: Thinking and learning about print.* Cambridge, MA: MIT Press.

ANDERSON, R.C., WILSON, P.T., & FIELDING, L.G. (1988). Growth in reading and how children spend their time outside of school. *Reading Research Quarterly, 23,* 285–303.

BADDELEY, A.D. (1986). *Working memory.* Oxford, England: Oxford University Press.

BELL, J.A. (1995). *Promising practices and programs for improving students' achievement.* Sacramento, CA: California Department of Education.

CALFEE, R. (1991). Decoding and spelling. What to teach, when to teach it, how to teach it. *Psychological Science, 2,* 83–85.

CENTER, Y., WHELDALL, K., FREEMAN, L., OUTHRED, L., & MCNAUGHT, M. (1995). An experimental evaluation of Reading Recovery. *Reading Research Quarterly, 30,* 240–263.

CHAPMAN, Y., & TUNMER, W. (1991). Recovering Reading Recovery. *Australia and New Zealand Journal of Developmental Disabilities, 17,* 59–71.

CLARKE, L.E. (1988). Invented spelling versus traditional spelling in first graders' writings: Effects of learning to spell and read. *Research in the Teaching of English, 22,* 281–309.

CLAY, M.M. (1985). *The early detection of complex behavior.* Auckland, New Zealand: Heinemann.

CRAIN, S., SHANKWEILER, D., MACARUSO, P., & BAR-SHALOM, E. (1990). Working memory and comprehension of spoken sentences: Investigations of children with reading disorders. In G. Vallar & T. Shallice (Eds.), *Neuropsychological impairments of short-term memory*

(pp. 477–508). Cambridge, England: Cambridge University Press.

CUNNINGHAM, A. (1990). Explicit versus implicit instruction in phonemic awareness. *Journal of Experimental Child Psychology, 50,* 429–444.

DOWHOWER, S.L. (1994). Repeated reading revisited: Research into practice. *Reading and Writing Quarterly: Overcoming Learning Difficulties, 10,* 343–358.

GAMBRELL, L.B., WILSON, R.M., & GANTT, W.N. (1981). Classroom observation of task attending behaviors of good and poor readers. *Journal of Educational Research, 74,* 400–404.

GOSWAMI, U. (1986). Children's use of analogy in learning to read: A developmental study. *Journal of Experimental Child Psychology, 42,* 73–83.

GOSWAMI, U. (1988). Orthographic analogies and reading development. *Quarterly Journal of Experimental Psychology, 40A,* 239–268.

GOSWAMI, U. (1997, November). *Orthographic processing in normal readers.* Paper presented at the conference on Dyslexia: Advances in Theory and Practices, Dyslexia Research Foundation and Center for Reading Research, Stavanger, Norway.

GOSWAMI, U., & BRYANT, P. (1990). *Phonological skills and learning to read.* Hillsdale, NJ: Erlbaum.

HIEBERT, E.H. (1994). Reading Recovery in the United States: What difference does it make to an age cohort? *Educational Researcher, 23*(9) 15–25.

HULME, C., & SNOWLING, M. (1994). *Reading development and dyslexia.* London: Whurr.

IVERSEN, S., & TUNMER, W. (1993). Phonological processing skills and the Reading Recovery program. *Journal of Educational Psychology, 8,* 112–126.

JUST, M.A., & CARPENTER, P.A. (1987). *The psychology of reading and language comprehension.* Needham Heights, MA: Allyn & Bacon.

LUNDBERG, I. (1994). Reading difficulties can be predicted and prevented: A Scandinavian perspective on phonological awareness and reading. In C. Hulme & M. Snowling (Eds.), *Reading development and dyslexia* (pp. 180–199). London: Whurr.

LUNDBERG, I., FROST, J., & PETERSEN, O.P. (1988). Effects of an extensive program for stimulating phonological awareness in preschool children. *Reading Research Quarterly, 23,* 263–284.

LUNDBERG, I., & HØIEN, T. (1989). Phonemic deficits in developmental dyslexia. *Irish Journal of Psychology, 10,* 579–592.

LUNDBERG, I., & HØIEN, T. (1991). Initial enabling knowledge and skills in reading acquisition: Print awareness and phonological segmentation. In D.E. Sawyer & B. Fox (Eds.), *Phonological awareness: The evolution of a concept* (pp. 73–95). New York: Springer-Verlag.

LUNDBERG, I., & HØIEN, T. (1996). Levels of approaching reading and its difficulties. In B. Ericson & J. Rönnberg (Eds.), *Reading disabilities and its treatment* (pp. 11–33). Linköping, Sweden: Linköping University.

LYONS, C.A., PINNELL, G.S., SHORT, K., & YOUNG, P. (1986). *The Ohio Reading Recovery Project,* Vol. 4, pilot year, 1985–86. Columbus, OH: Ohio State University.

MORRIS, D. (1992). *Case studies in teaching beginning readers: The Howard Street tutoring manual.* Boone, NC: Fieldstream.

MORRIS, D. (in press). The role of clinical training in teaching of reading. In P. Mosenthal & D. Evensen (Eds.), *Reconsidering the role of the reading clinic in a new age of literacy.* Greenwich, CT: JAI Press.

MORRIS, D., & PERNEY, J. (1984). Developmental spelling as a predictor of first grade reading achievement. *Elementary School Journal, 84,* 441–457.

MORRIS, D., SHAW, B., & PERNEY, J. (1990). Helping low readers in grades 2 and 3: An after-school volunteer tutoring program. *Elementary School Journal, 91,* 133–150.

MOUSTAFA, M. (1995). Children's productive phonological recoding. *Reading Research Quarterly, 30,* 464–476.

NICHOLSON, T. (1989). A comment on Reading Recovery. *New Zealand Journal of Educational Studies, 24,* 95–97.

PALINCSAR, A.S., & RANSOM, K. (1988). From mystery spot to the thoughtful spot: The introduction of metacognitive strategies. *The Reading Teacher, 41*, 784–789.

PARIS, S.G., WASIK, B., & TURNER, J.C. (1991). The development of strategic readers. In R. Barr, M. Kamil, P. Mosenthal, & D. Pearson (Eds.), *Handbook of reading research: Vol. 2* (pp. 609–640). White Plains, NY: Longman.

PETERS, E., & GRAVES, A.W. (1987). Special focus: Effective instruction in reading. Improving comprehension skills. *Teaching Exceptional Children, 19*, 63–65.

PETERSON, M.E., & HAINES, L.P. (1992). Orthographic analogy training with kindergarten children: Effects on analogy use, phonemic segmentation, and letter-sound knowledge. *Journal of Reading Behavior, 24*, 109–127.

PINNELL, G.S., HUCK, C.S., & DEFORD, D.E. (1986). *The Reading Recovery Project in Columbus, Ohio*, Vol. 5, year 1, 1985–86. Columbus, OH: Ohio State University.

PINNELL, G.S., LYONS, C.A., DEFORD, D.E., BRYK, A.S., & SELTZER, M. (1994). Comparing instructional models for the literacy education of high-risk first graders. *Reading Research Quarterly, 29*, 8–39.

PINNELL, G.S., LYONS, C.A., YOUNG, P., & DEFORD, D.E. (1987). *The Reading Recovery Project in Columbus, Ohio*, Vol. 6, year 2, 1986–87. Columbus, OH: Ohio State University.

PRESSLEY, M., RANKIN, J., & YOKOI, L. (1996). A survey of instructional practices of outstanding primary-level literacy teachers. *Elementary School Journal, 96*, 363–384.

RACK, J., HULME, C., SNOWLING, M., & WIGHTMAN, J. (1994). The role of phonology in young children learning to read words: The direct mapping hypothesis. *Journal of Experimental Child Psychology, 57*, 42–71.

SAMUELS, S.J. (1979). The method of repeated readings. *The Reading Teacher, 17*, 403–408.

SANTA, C.M. (1998). *Early Steps: Learning from a reader.* Kalispell, MT: Scott.

SHANAHAN, T. (1987). Review of early detection of reading difficulties. *Journal of Reading Behavior, 19*, 117–119.

SHARE, D.L., & STANOVICH, K.E. (1995). Cognitive processes in early reading development: Accommodating individual differences into a model of acquisition. *Issues in Education: Contributions from Educational Psychology, 1*, 1-57.

SPIEGEL, D.L. (1995). A comparison of traditional remedial programs and Reading Recovery: Guidelines for success for all programs. *The Reading Teacher, 49*, 86–96.

STANOVICH, K.E. (1986). Matthew effects in reading: Some consequences of individual differences in the acquisition of literacy. *Reading Research Quarterly, 21*, 360–406.

STANOVICH, K.E. (1991). Changing models of reading and reading acquisition. In L. Riben & C.A. Perfetti (Eds.), *Learning to read: Basic research and its implications* (pp. 19–31). Hillsdale, NJ: Erlbaum.

STAUFFER, R. (1969). *Directing reading maturity as a cognitive process.* New York: Harper & Row.

TREIMAN, R. (1985). Onsets and rimes as units of spoken syllables: Evidence from children. *Journal of Experimental Child Psychology, 39*, 161–181.

TREIMAN, R. (1986). The division between onsets and rimes in English syllables. *Journal of Memory and Language, 25*, 476–491.

TREIMAN, R. (1992). The role of intrasyllabic units in learning to read and spell. In P.G. Gough, L.C. Ehri, & R. Treiman (Eds.), *Reading acquisition* (pp. 65–106). Hillsdale, NJ: Erlbaum.

TUNNELL, M., & JACOBS, J. (1989). Using real books: Research findings on literature based reading instruction. *The Reading Teacher, 42*, 470–477.

VELLUTINO, F.R., SCANLON, D.M., SIPAY, E.R., SMALL, S.G., PRATT, A., CHEN, R., & DENCKLA, M.B. (1996). Cognitive profiles of difficult-to-remediate and readily remediated poor readers: Early intervention as a vehicle for distinguishing between cognitive and experiential deficits as basic causes of specific reading disability. *Journal of Educational Psychology, 88*, 601–638.

WALMSLEY, S., & ALLINGTON, R. (1995). Redefining and reforming instructional support programs for at-risk students. In R. Allington & S. Walmsley (Eds.), *No quick fix: Rethinking literacy programs in America's elementary schools* (pp. 19–44). Newark, DE: International Reading Association.

WASIK, B.A., & SLAVIN, R.E. (1993). Preventing early reading failure with one tutoring: A review of five programs. *Reading Research Quarterly, 28*, 179–200.

WHITEHEAD, D. (1986). What shall we teach children to help them comprehend? *Australian Journal of Reading, 9*, 59–69.

WILKINSON, L., HILL, M.J., WELNA, J.P., & BIRKENBEUEL, G.K. (1992). *SYSTAT for Windows: Statistics.* Evanston, IL: SYSTAT.

WINSOR, P.J., & PEARSON, P.D. (1992). *Children at risk: Their phonemic awareness development in holistic instruction.* Urbana, IL: University of Illinois at Urbana-Champaign, Center for the Study of Reading.

YUILL, N., & OAKHILL, J. (1991). *Children's problems in text comprehension: An experimental investigation.* Cambridge, England: Cambridge University Press.

APPENDIX A
Scoring system for spelling (pretest)

	Scores for sample spellings			
	1 point	2 points	3 points	4 points
1. Back	b, bn	bc, bk ba, bae	bak, bac bake, back	
2. Feet	f, fa	ft, fe fot	fet, feat fete, feet	
3. Step	s, c soe	st, cp sa, se	stp, sdp sap, cep	stap sdap step
4. Junk	j, g	jk, gc go, ju	jok, goc juk, gnk	jonc gunk
5. Picking	p, po	pk, pc Pe, pn	pec, pek pkn, pen	pekn picen
6. Mail	m, me	ml, ma mao	mal, maol male, mail	
7. Side	s, c st	sd, cd sa, si	sid, cid sade, sod	
8. Chin	g, j h	gn, hn	gen, hen chen, chin	
9. Dress	d, g, j	js, gs jos	jas, des jrs, drs dess, gas	dras jres dres
10. Peeked	p pk	pt, pe pek, peet	pet, pct peked peekt	pect
11. Lamp	l	lp, la, lop	lap, lapc lmp	lampc (must have nasal *m*) lamp
12. Road	r, w	rd, ro	rod, roed rode, road	

Total possible: 42 points.
Explanation of spelling scores:
1. The number of phonemes represented in a spelling is considered (fet for *feet* and lap for *lamp* = 3 points, but ft and lp = 2 points).
2. The sequencing of phonemes is considered (again, fet or lap = 3 points, but fte or lpa = 2 points; p for *peeked* = 1 point, but t for *peeked* = 0 points).
3. Appropriate consonant substitutions are allowed (jr for dr in *dress*, c for s in *step*, h or even j for ch in *chin*).
4. Appropriate vowel substitutions are allowed (a for short *e* in *step* and *dress*; e for short *i* in *picking* and *chin*, and o for short *u* in *junk*).

APPENDIX B
The Early Reading Screening Instrument:
Word Recognition

Basal words	Decodable words
1. is	1. cap
2. come	2. net
3. good	3. win
4. here	4. bug
5. like	5. fat
6. and	6. mop
7. mother	7. led
8. make	8. dig
9. work	9. job
10. day	10. mud

APPENDIX C
Spelling Scoring System for Early Steps for the end of the year

Correct spelling = 5 points

Scores for sample spellings

	1 point	2 points	3 points	4 points
1. Back	b	bk, bc	bak, bac bake	backe
2. Feet	v, f	ft	fet	feat, fete
3. Step	c, s	sp, se, sa st, setp, stp	sap, set cap, ctep stap	stepe
4. Junk	g, j	gc, jk, jo gu, jike	guc, juc, joc juke, gok gnk, gonk	gunk (must have *n*) gunc, junke
5. Picking	p	pc, pg, pn pcn, peke pek, pne, pen	peking piknig pekn, pekin	piking pikig
6. Mail	m	ml, ma mial	mal, mall mel	male, maill, maile
7. Side	s, c	sd, sed	sid, sod sode, sade sad	sied, siad
8. Chin	c, j, g h, t	cn, ci, ce cind, thei	cin, gin, hin hen, thin chen	chine
9. Dress	d, g, j rs	ds, js, drs gs gras, gres jas, das	des, gas dais, drres	dres, dresse
10. Peeked	p	pk, pikt, pe pen, peet peke, pct pit, pkt	pcct, pckd pekt, peekt	peked peaced
11. Lamp	l	lp, la, lm	lap, lam, lape lmp	lampe (must have nasal *m*)
12. Road	r, w	rd, ro, rodt wd, romd	rod, wod	rode, rood roid, roed

(continued)

		Scores for sample spellings		
	1 point	2 points	3 points	4 points
13. Plant	p	pt	pat, plat plate	plante (must have nasal *n*)
14. Short	s	sh, chort shrt, sot	shot, shotse sorte, sort	shorte
15. Grabbed	g	gab, grad gd, gb	gabd, grabd	grabed

Total possible score: 75 points

Explanation of spelling scores:

For all words:
1. Left-right reversals (b-d) count as correct, up-down reversals (m-w) as incorrect.
2. Beginning consonant or appropriate substitution = 1 point.
3. Beginning and ending consonant or appropriate substitution = 2 points.
4. Beginning consonant and correct vowel or appropriate substitutions = 2 points.
5. Beginning consonant, medial vowel, and final consonant (or appropriate substitutions) = 3 points.
6. Two vowels together in middle of word; first vowel is correct or substitution is appropriate (e.g., dais for *dress* = 3 points).
7. Long vowel is marked and all consonants are correct including blends and digraphs (e.g., fete or feat for *feet*) = 4 points (first vowel must be correct).
8. Point deducted for extraneous consonants at the end of a word (e.g., cind for *chin* = 2 points).
9. Point deducted for missing beginning consonant (e.g., rs for dress = 1 point).
10. Point deducted for letters out of order (e.g., tsap for *step* = 2 points).

Words with suffixes
1. Must have vowel (or appropriate substitution), beginning and ending consonants of the baseword, and the suffix must be represented by an appropriate letter (e.g., pekn for *picking*) = 3 points. (But peck for *picking* = 2 points.)
2. Must have correct vowel, correct consonants including blends and digraphs, marker vowel, and correct spelling for suffix (ed, ing) = 4 points.

APPENDIX D

Word recognition task 2
1. cat
2. is
3. like
4. old
5. your
6. said
7. big
8. not
9. back
10. sun
11. bird
12. saw
13. feet
14. lake
15. hid
16. about
17. rain
18. how
19. window
20. mother
21. leg
22. black
23. smile
24. dark
25. couldn't
26. because
27. shout
28. glass
29. paint
30. children
31. table
32. stand
33. gate
34. spill
35. pull
36. prize
37. shoot
38. wrote
39. able
40. change

APPENDIX E
Word families

cat	man	cap	back		hit	big	win	sick		hot	too	sock	look		pet	red	tell	hen		cut	bug	run	duck
mat	can	lap	tack		sit	fig	tin	kick		pot	pop	rock	book		net	led	sell	pen		nut	hug	gun	luck
sat	van	nap	rack		fit	wig	pin	lick		lot	cop	lock	took		set	bed	fell	men		but	dug	fun	suck
pat	ran	tap	sack		pit	dig	kin	pick		not	hop	block	cook		met	fed	well	ten		hut	rug	sun	stuck
rat	fan	map	pack		kit	pig	fin	tick		got	mop	clock	hook		wet	shed	bell	then		shut	jug	spun	truck
flat	pan	sap	black		bit	twig	thin	trick		dot	stop	knock	shook		let	sled	shell	when			slug	bun	tuck
hat	plan	clap	track		knit		chin	brick		spot	drop				jet		smell				mug		buck
	tan		snap	snack			spin	stick			chop				get		yell				plug		cluck
							skin	thick															

Short vowels

bad	pet	pig	top	bug
hat	bed	win	hot	cup
ran	let	hit	job	nut
map	red	lip	mom	fun
mad	web	kid	hop	cut
back	tell	his	fox	bus
had	less	sick	doll	but
has	sell	this	rock	luck
that	then	ship	chop	shut
clap	when	with	stop	truck
glad	sled	swim	drop	must

Vowel patterns - a

cat	lake	park	rain	day	fall	?
ran	race	car	mail	say	ball	was
dad	tape	hard	wait	may	tall	have
hat	page	barn	pain	way	call	what
cab	same	jar	tail	pay	wall	saw
map	make	card	chain	clay	hall	want
jam	name	far	paint	stay	mall	
flat	take	part	maid	play	small	
clap	gave	farm	sail	tray		
back	trade	harm	paid	stray		
trap	shake	dart	stain			
that	made	start				
	cake	shark				
	cage	sharp				

Vowel patterns - i

hit	ride	right	girl	wild	by
lip	nice	night	dirt	mind	my
win	bike	light	bird	find	fly
big	five	might	sir	child	cry
kick	mile	bright	first	climb	sky
hid	side	high	firm	kind	eye
pin	drive	fight	shirt	mild	bye
trip	mine		birth	blind	buy
swim	dime		third		
fit	wise				
chin	shine				
this	slide				
	life				
	white				

Vowel patterns - o

top	rope	boat	for	book	told	go		moon	boil
job	note	road	corn	good	cold	no		roof	coin
pot	hole	soap	fork	look	colt	so		pool	soil
mom	nose	coal	foot	stood	gold			boot	point
dot	coke	load	born	hook	post			tool	noise
drop	hope	loaf	fort	brook	folk			shoot	spoil
jog	bone	soak	horn	wood	sold			tooth	voice
lock	code	coach	pork		hold			broom	
stop	woke	toast	torn		ghost				
bomb	stone	float							boy
shock	spoke	cloak							toy
	close								

Vowel patterns - e

pet	feet	meat	he	head	herd	?
red	deep	team	we	lead	germ	been
beg	meet	lead	she	dead	clerk	these
get	feel	mean	me	bread	nerve	the
bell	free	peak	be	deaf	serve	were
less	green	clean		breath	learn	great
nest	seed	beat		spread	pearl	
left	need	dream		sweat		
ten	queen	beach				
step	jeep	leaf				
sled	bleed	wheat				
	sweet					

Vowel patterns - u

bug	cute	blue	hurt	knew	fruit
cup	rule	true	burn	grew	suit
bus	use	glue	curl	new	juice
fun	rude	clue	fur	few	
rug	tune		turn	chew	
club	huge		purr	screw	
sun	June		nurse	flew	
mud	fuse		curve		
drum	flute				

Steven A. Stahl

Saying the "p" word: Nine guidelines for exemplary phonics instruction

Phonics, like beauty, is in the eye of the beholder. For many people, "phonics" implies stacks of worksheets, with bored children mindlessly filling in the blanks. For some people, "phonics" implies children barking at print, often in unison, meaningless strings of letter sounds to be blended into works. For some people, "phonics" implies lists of skills that must be mastered, each with its own criterion-referenced test, which must be passed or the teacher is "in for it." For some people, "phonics" somehow contrasts with "meaning," implying that concentrating on phonics means that one must ignore the meaning of the text. For others, "phonics" is the solution to the reading problem, as Flesch (1955) argued and others have concurred (see Republican Party National Steering Committee, 1990), that if we just teach children the sounds of the letters, all else will fall into place.

Because "phonics" can be so many things, some people treat it as a dirty word, others as the salvation of reading. It is neither. With these strong feelings, though, extreme views have been allowed to predominate, seemingly forcing out any middle position that allows for the importance of systematic attention to decoding in the context of a program stressing comprehension and interpretation of quality literature and expository text. The truth is that some attention to the relationships between spelling patterns and their pronunciations is characteristic of all types of reading programs, including whole language. As Newman and Church (1990) explain:

> No one can read without taking into account the graphophonemic cues of written language. As readers all of us use information about the way words are written to help us make sense of what we're reading.... Whole language teachers do teach phonics but not as something separate from actual reading and writing.... Readers use graphophonic cues; whole language teachers help students orchestrate their use for reading and writing. (pp. 20–21)

"Phonics" merely refers to various approaches designed to teach children about the orthographic code of the language and the relationships of spelling patterns to sound patterns. These approaches can range from direct instruction approaches through instruction that is embedded in the reading of literature. There is no requirement that phonics instruction use worksheets, that it involve having children bark at print, that it be taught as a set of discrete skills mastered in isolation, or that it preclude paying attention to the meaning of texts.

In this article, I want to discuss some principles about what effective phonics instruction should contain and describe some successful programs that meet these criteria.

Why teach phonics at all?

The reading field has been racked by vociferous debates about the importance of teaching phonics, when it is to be taught, and how it is to be taught. The interested reader can get a flavor of this debate by reviewing such sources as Adams (1990), Chall (1983a, 1989), Carbo (1988), and so on. To rehash these arguments would not be useful.

The fact is that all students, regardless of they type of instruction they receive, learn about letter-sound correspondences as part of learning to read. There are a number of models of children's initial word learning showing similar stages of development (e.g., Chall,

---

Some attention to the relationships between spelling patterns and their pronunciations is characteristic of all types of reading programs, including whole language.

1983b; Firth, 1985; Lomax & McGee, 1987; McCormick & Mason, 1986). Frith, for example, suggests that children go through three stages as they learn about words. The first stage is *logographic* in which words are learned as whole units, sometimes embedded in a logo, such as a stop sign. This is followed by an *alphabetic* stage, in which children use individual letters and sounds to identify words. The last stage is *orthographic* in which children begin to see patterns in words, and use these patterns to identify words without sounding them out. One can see children go through these stages and begin to see words orthographically by the end of the first grade. Following the orthographic stage children grow in their ability to recognize words automatically, without having to think consciously about word structure or spelling patterns.

These stages in the development of word recognition take place while children are learning about how print functions (what a written "word" is, directionality, punctuation, etc.), that it can signify meanings, about the nature of stories, and all of the other learnings that go on in emergent literacy (see Teale, 1987). Learning about words goes hand in hand with other learnings about reading and writing.

All children appear to go through these stages on their way to becoming successful readers. Some will learn to decode on their own, without any instruction. Others will need some degree of instruction, ranging from some pointing out of common spelling patterns to intense and systematic instruction to help them through the alphabetic and orthographic stages. I want to outline some components of what exemplary instruction might look like. These components could be found in classrooms based on the shared reading of literature, as in a whole language philosophy, or in classrooms in which the basal reader is used as the core text.

Exemplary phonics instruction...

1. *Builds on a child's rich concepts about how print functions.* The major source of the debates on phonics is whether one should go from part to whole (begin by teaching letters and sounds and blend those into words) or from whole to part (begin with words and analyze those into letters). Actually, there should be no debate. Letter-sound instruction makes no sense to a child who does not have an overall conception of what reading is about, how print functions, what stories are, and so on, so it must build on a child's concept of the whole process of reading.

A good analogy is baseball. For a person learning to play baseball, batting practice is an important part of learning how to play the game. However, imagine a person who has never seen a baseball game. Making that person do nothing but batting practice may lead to the misconception that baseball is about standing at the plate and repeatedly swinging at the ball. That person would miss the purpose of baseball and would think it a boring way to spend an afternoon.

Adams (1990) points out that children from homes that are successful in preparing children for literacy have a rich idea of what "reading" is before they get to school. They are read to, play with letters on the refrigerator door, discuss print with their parents, and so on. Other children may have had only minimal or no exposure to print prior to school. The differences may add up to 1,000 hours or more of exposure to print.

For the child who has had that 1,000 hours or more, phonics instruction is grounded in his or her experiences with words. Such a child may not need extensive phonics instruction. Good phonics instruction should help make sense of patterns noticed within words. Just "mentioning" the patterns might suffice. However, for the child with little or no exposure, phonics instruction would be an abstract and artificial task until the child has additional meaningful encounters with print.

To develop this base of experience with reading, one might begin reading in kindergarten with activities such as sharing books with children, writing down their dictated stories, and engaging them in authentic reading and writing tasks. Predictable books work especially well for beginning word recognition (Bridge, Winograd, & Haley, 1983). Stahl and Miller (1989) found that whole language programs appeared to work effectively in kindergarten. Their effectiveness, however, diminished in first grade, where more structured, code-emphasis approaches seemed to produce better results. In short, children benefited from the experiences with reading that a whole language program gives early on, but, once they had that exposure, they benefit from more systematic study.

2. *Builds on a foundation of phonemic awareness*. Phonemic awareness is not phonics. Phonemic awareness is awareness of sounds in *spoken* words; phonics is the relation between letters and sounds in *written* words. Phonemic awareness is an important precursor to success in reading. One study (Juel, 1988) found that children who were in the bottom fourth of their group in phonemic awareness in first grade remained in the bottom fourth of their class in reading four years later.

An example is Heather, a child I saw in our clinic. As part of an overall reading assessment, I gave Heather a task involving removing a phoneme from a spoken word. For example, I had Heather say *meat* and then repeat it without saying the /m/ sound (*eat*). When Heather said *chicken* after some hesitation, I was taken aback. When I had her say *coat* with the /k/ sound, she said *jacket*. Looking over the tasks we did together, it appeared that she viewed words only in terms of their meaning. For her, a little less than *meat* was *chicken*, a little less than *coat* was *jacket*.

For most communication, focusing on meaning is necessary. But for learning to read,

especially learning about sound-symbol relationships, it is desirable to view words in terms of the sounds they contain. Only by understanding that spoken words contain phonemes

---

Letter-sound instruction makes no sense to a child who does not have an overall conception of what reading is about.

---

can one learn the relationships between letters and sounds. The alternative is learning each word as a logograph, as in Chinese. This is possible, up to a certain limit, but does not use the alphabetic nature of our language to its best advantage.

Heather was a bright child, and this was her only difficulty, but she was having specific difficulties learning to decode. Other children like Heather, or children with more complex difficulties, are going to have similar problems. We worked for a short period of time on teaching her to reflect on sounds in spoken words, and, with about 6 weeks of instruction, she took off and became an excellent reader. The moral is that phonemic awareness is easily taught, but absence of it leads to reading difficulties.

3. *Is clear and direct*. Good teachers explain what they mean very clearly. Yet, some phonics instruction seems to be excessively ambiguous.

Some of this ambiguity comes from trying to solve the problem of pronouncing single phonemes. One cannot pronounce the sounds represented by many of the consonants in isolation. For example, the sound made by *b* cannot be spoken by itself, without adding a vowel (such as /buh/).

To avoid having the teacher add the vowel to the consonant sound, however, some basals have come up with some terribly circuitous routes. For example, a phonics lesson from a current basal program begins with a teacher presenting a picture of a key word, such as *bear*, pronouncing the key word and two or three words with a shared phonic element (such as *boat*, *ball*, and *bed*). The teacher is to point out that the sound at the beginning of each is spelled with a *B*. The teacher might then say some other words and ask if they, too, have the same sound. Next, written words are introduced and may be read by the whole class or by individuals. After this brief lesson, students might complete two worksheets, which both involve circling pictures of items that start with *b* and one which includes copying upper- and lowercase *b*'s.

In this lesson, (a) nowhere is the teacher supposed to attempt to say what sound the *b* is supposed to represent and (b) nowhere is the teacher directed to tell the children that these relationships have anything to do with reading words in text. For a child with little phonemic awareness, the instructions, which require that the child segment the initial phoneme from a word, would be very confusing. Children such as Heather view the word *bear* not as a combination of sounds or letters, but identical to its meaning. For that child, the question of what *bear* begins with does not make sense, because it is seen as a whole meaning unit, not as a series of sounds that has a beginning and an end.

Some of this confusion could be alleviated if the teacher dealt with written words. A more direct approach is to show the word *bear*, in the context of a story or in isolation, and pointing out that it begins with the letter *b*, and that the letter *b* makes the /b/ sound. This approach goes right to the basic concept, that a letter in a word represents a particular phoneme, involving fewer extraneous concepts. Going the other direction, showing the letter *b* and then showing words such as *bear* that begin with that letter, would also be clear. Each of these should be followed having children practice reading *words* that contain the letter *b*, rather than pictures. Children learn to read by reading words, in stories or in lists. This can be done in small groups or with pairs of children reading with each other independently. Circling pictures, coloring, cutting, and pasting, and so on wastes a lot of time.

4. *Is integrated into a total reading program.* Phonics instruction, no matter how useful it is, should never dominate reading instruction. I know of no research to guide us in deciding how much time should be spent on decoding instruction, but my rule of thumb is that at least half of the time devoted to reading (and probably more) should be spent reading connected text—stories, poems, plays, trade books, and so on. No more that 25% of the time (and possibly less) should be spent on phonics instruction and practice.

Unfortunately, I have seen too many schools in which one day the members of the reading group do the green pages (the skills instruction), the next day they read the story, and the third day they do the blue pages. The result is that, on most days, children are not reading text. Certainly, in these classes, children are going to view "reading" as filling out workbook pages, since this is what they do most of the time. Instead, they should read some text daily, preferably a complete story, with phonics instruction integrated into the text reading.

In many basals, the patterns taught in the phonics lessons appear infrequently in the text, leading students to believe that phonics is somehow unrelated to the task of reading (Adams, 1990). What is taught should be directly usable in children's reading. Juel and Roper/Schneider (1985) found that children were better able to use their phonics knowledge, for both decoding and comprehension, when the texts they read contained a higher percentage of words that conformed to the patterns they were taught. It is best to teach elements that can be used with stories the children are going to read. Teachers using a basal might rearrange the phonics lessons so that a more appropriate element is taught with each story.

Teachers using trade books might choose elements from the books they plan to use, and either preteach them or integrate the instruction into the lesson. A good procedure for doing this is described by Trachtenburg (1990). She suggests beginning by reading a quality children's story (such as *Angus and the Cat*, cited in Trachtenburg, 1990), providing instruction in a high utility phonic element appearing in that story (short *a* in this case), and using that element to help read another book (such as *The Cat in the Hat* or *Who Took the Farmer's Hat?*). Trachtenburg (1990) provides a list of trade books that contain high percentages of common phonic elements.

Reading Recovery is another example of how phonics instruction can be integrated into a total reading program. Reading Recovery lessons differ depending on the child's needs, but a typical lesson begins with the rereading of a familiar book, followed by the taking of a "running record" on a book introduced the previous session (see Pinnell, Fried, & Estice, 1990, for details). The phonics instruction occurs in the middle of the lesson and could involve direct work in phonemic awareness, letter-sound correspondences using children's spelling or magnetic letters, or even lists of words. The teacher chooses a pattern with which the child had difficulty. The "phonics" instruction is a relatively small component of the total Reading Recovery program, but it is an important one.

5. *Focuses on reading words, not learning rules.* When competent adults read, they do not refer to a set of rules that they store in their heads. Instead, as Adams (1990) points out, they recognize new words by comparing them or spelling patterns within them to words they already know. When an unknown word such as *Minatory* is encountered, it is not read by figuring out whether the first syllable is open or closed. Instead most people that I have asked usually say the first syllable says /min/ as in *minute* or *miniature*, comparing it to a pattern in a word they already know how to pronounce. Effective decoders see words not in terms of phonics rules, but in terms of patterns of letters that are used to aid in identification.

Effective phonics instruction helps children do this, by first drawing their attention to the order of letters in words, forcing them to examine common patterns in English through sounding out words, and showing similarities between words. As an interim step, rules can be useful in helping children see patterns. Some rules, such as the silent *e* rule, points out common patterns in English. However, rules are not useful enough to be taught as absolutes. Clymer (1963) found that only 45% of the commonly taught phonics rules worked as much as 75% of the time.

A good guideline might be that rules might be pointed out, as a way of highlighting a particular spelling pattern, but children should not be asked to memorize or recite them. And, when rules are pointed out, they should be discussed as tentative, with exceptions given at the same time as conforming patterns. Finally, only rules with reasonable utility should be used. Teaching children that *ough* has six sounds is a waste of everyone's time.

6. *May include onsets and rimes.* An alternative to teaching rules is using onsets and rimes. Treiman (1985) has found that breaking down syllables into onsets (or the part of the syllable before the vowel) and rimes (the part from the vowel onward) is useful to describe how we process syllables in oral language. Teaching onsets and rimes may be useful in written language as well.

Adams (1990) points out that letter-sound correspondences are more stable when one looks at rimes than when letters are looked at in isolation. For example, *ea* taken alone is thought of as irregular. However, it is very regular in all rimes, except *-ead* (bead vs. bread), *-eaf* (sheaf vs. deaf), and *-ear* (hear vs. bear). The rime *-ean*, for example, nearly always has the long *e* sound. Of the 286 phonograms that appear in primary grade texts, 95% of them were pronounced the same in every word in which they appeared (Adams, 1990).

In addition, nearly 500 words can be derived from the following 37 rimes:

-ack	-ain	-ake	-ale	-all	-ame
-an	-ank	-ap	-ash	-at	-ate
-aw	-ay	-eat	-ell	-est	-ice
-ick	-ide	-ight	-ill	-in	-ine
-ing	-ink	-ip	-ir	-ock	-oke
-op	-or	-ore	-uck	-ug	-ump
-unk					

Rime-based instruction is used in a number of successful reading programs. In one such program, children are taught to compare an unknown word to already known words and to use context to confirm their predictions (Gaskins et al., 1988). For example, when encountering *wheat* in a sentence, such as *The little red hen gathered the wheat*, a student might be taught to compare it to *meat* and say "If m-e-a-t is *meat* then this is *wheat*." The student would then cross-check the pronunciation by seeing if *wheat* made sense in the sentence. This approach is comprehension oriented in that students are focused on the comprehension of sentences and stories, but it does teach decoding effectively (see also Cunningham, 1991).

7. *May include invented spelling practice.* It has been suggested that when children work out their invented spellings, they are learning phonic principles, but learning them "naturally." For this reason, many whole language advocates suggest that practice in writing with invented spelling might be a good substitute for direct phonics instruction. Practice with invented spelling does improve children's awareness of phonemes, which, as discussed

earlier, is an important precursor to learning to decode.

However, there is very little research on the effects of invented spelling. That research is positive, but I know of only one study that directly addresses the question. Clarke (1989) found that children who were encouraged to invent spelling and given additional time for writing journals were significantly better at decoding and comprehension than children in a traditional spelling program. However, the classes she studied used a synthetic phonics program as their core reading program. These results may not transfer to a whole language program or even to a more eclectic basal program. An evaluation of the Writing-to-Read program, a computer-based program incorporating writing, found that it had little effect on children's reading abilities (Slavin, 1991).

We need not wait for the research needed to evaluate the use of invented spelling. Writing stories and journal entries using invented spelling does not seem to hurt one's reading or spelling abilities and may help them, and it certainly improves children's writing.

The purpose of phonics instruction is not that children learn to sound out words.

---

8. *Develops independent word recognition strategies, focusing attention on the internal structure of words.* The object of phonics instruction is to get children to notice orthographic patterns in words. Effective strategies, whether they involve having a child sound a word out letter by letter, find a word that shares the same rime as an unknown word, or spell out the word through invented or practiced spelling, all force the child to look closely at patterns in words. It is through the learning of these patterns that children learn to recognize words efficiently.

Good phonics instruction should help children through the stages described earlier as quickly as possible. Beginning with bookhandling experiences, story book reading and "Big Books," and other features of a whole language kindergarten support children at the logographic state. Frith (1985) suggests that writing and

spelling may aid in the development of alphabetic knowledge. This can be built upon with some direct instruction of letters and sounds, and showing students how to use that knowledge to unlock words in text. Sounding words out also forces children to examine the internal structure of words, ad does rime-based instruction. These can help children make the transition to the orthographic stage. In the next stage, the child develops automatic word recognition skills, or the ability to recognize words without conscious attention.

9. *Develops automatic word recognition skills so that students can devote their attention to comprehension, not words.* The purpose of phonics instruction is not that children learn to sound out words. The purpose is that they learn to recognize words, quickly and automatically, so that they can turn their attention to comprehension of the text. If children are devoting too much energy sounding out words, they will not be able to direct enough of their attention to comprehension (Samuels, 1988).

We know that children develop automatic word recognition skills through practicing reading words. We know that reading words in context does improve children's recognition of words, and improvement which transfers to improved comprehension. There is some question about whether reading words in isolation necessarily results in improved comprehension. Fleisher, Jenkins, and Pany (1979–1980) found that increasing word recognition speed in isolation did not result in improved comprehension; Blanchard (1981) found that it did. Either way, there is ample evidence that practice reading words in text, either repeated readings of the same text (Samuels, 1988) or just reading of connected text in general (Taylor & Nosbush, 1983), improves children's comprehension.

Good phonics instruction is also over relatively quickly. Anderson, Hiebert, Wilkinson, and Scott (1985) recommends that phonics instruction be completed by the end of the second grade. This may even be too long. Stretching phonics instruction out too long, or spending time on teaching the arcane aspects of phonics —the schwa, the silent *k*, assigning accent to polysyllabic words—is at best a waste of time. Once a child begins to use orthographic patterns in recognizing words and recognizes words at an easy, fluent pace, it is time to move away from phonics instruction and to spend even more time reading and writing text.

The "politics" of phonics

Given that all children do need to learn about the relationships between spelling patterns and pronunciations on route to becoming a successful reader, why all the fuss about phonics?

Part of the reason is that there is confusion about what phonics instruction is. A teacher pointing out the "short *a*" words during the reading of a Big Book in a whole language classroom is doing something different from a teacher telling her class that the short sound of the letter *a* is /a/ and having them blend in unison 12 words that contain that sound, yet both might be effective phonics instruction. The differences are not only in practice but in philosophy.

In discussions on this issue, the philosophical differences seem to predominate. These exaggerated differences often find people arguing that "phonics" proponents oppose the use of literature and writing in the primary grades, which is clearly false, or that "whole language" people oppose any sort of direct teaching, also clearly false. The truth is that here are commonalities that can be found in effective practices of widely differing philosophies, some of which are reflected in the nine guidelines discussed here.

In this article, I have proposed some characteristics of exemplary phonics instruction. Such instruction is very different from what I see in many classrooms. But because phonics is often taught badly is no reason to stop attempting to teach it well. Quality phonics instruction should be a part of a reading program, integrated and relevant to the reading and writing of actual texts, based on and building upon children's experiences with texts. Such phonics instruction can and should be built into all beginning reading programs.

References

Adams, M.J., (1990). *Beginning to read: Thinking and learning about print*. Cambridge, MA: M.I.T. Press.

Anderson, R.C., Hiebert, E.F., Wilkinson, I.A.G., & Scott, J. (1985). *Becoming a nation of readers*. Champaign, IL: National Academy of Education and Center for the Study of Reading.

Blanchard, J.S. (1981). A comprehension strategy for disabled readers in the middle school. *Journal of Reading, 24*, 331–336.

Bridge, C.A., Winograd, P.N., & Haley, D. (1983). Using predictable materials vs. preprimers to teach beginning sight words. *The Reading Teacher, 36*, 884–891.

Carbo, M. (1998). Debunking the great phonics myth. *Phi Delta Kappan, 70*, 226–240.

Chall, J.S. (1983a). *Learning to read: The great debate* (revised, with a new foreword). New York, NY: McGraw-Hill.

Chall, J.S., (1983b). *Stages of reading development*. New York: McGraw-Hill.

Chall, J.S. (1989). Learning to read: The great debate twenty years later. A response to "Debunking the great phonics myth." *Phi Delta Kappan, 71*, 521–538.

Clarke, L.K. (1989). Encouraging invented spelling in first graders' writing: Effects on learning to spell and read. *Research in the Teaching of English, 22*, 281–309.

Clymer, T. (1963). The utility of phonic generalizations in the primary grades. *The Reading Teacher, 16*, 252–258.

Cunningham, P.M. (1991). *Phonics they use*. New York: HarperCollins.

Fleisher, L.S., Jenkins, J.R., & Pany, D. (1979–1980). Effects on poor readers' comprehension of training in rapid decoding. *Reading Research Quarterly, 15*, 30–48.

Flesch, R. (1955). *Why Johnny can't read*. New York: Harper & Row.

Frith, U. (1985). Beneath the surface of developmental dyslexia. In K.E. Patterson, K.C. Marshall, & M. Coltheart (Eds.), *Surface dyslexia: Neuropsychological and cognitive studies of phonological reading*. Hillsdale, NJ: Erlbaum.

Gaskins, I.W., Downer, M.A., Anderson, R.C., Cunningham, P.M., Gaskins, R.W., Schommer, M., & The Teachers of Benchmark School. (1988). A metacognitive approach to phonics: Using what you know to decode what you don't know. *Remedial and Special Education, 9*, 36–41.

Juel, C. (1988). Learning to read and write: A longitudinal study of fifty-four children from first through fourth grade. *Journal of Educational Psychology, 80*, 437–447.

Juel, C., & Roper/Schneider, D. (1985). The influence of basal readers on first grade reading. *Reading Research Quarterly, 20*, 134–152.

Lomax, R.G., & McGee, L.M. (1987). Young children's concepts about print and reading: Toward a model of reading acquisition. *Reading Research Quarterly, 22*, 237–256.

McCormick, C.E., & Mason, J.M. (1986). Intervention procedures for increasing preschool children's interest in and knowledge about reading. In W.H. Teale & E. Sulzby (Eds.), *Emergent literacy: Writing and reading* (pp. 90–115). Norwood, NJ: Ablex.

Newman, J.M., & Church, S.M. (1990). Commentary: Myths of whole language. *The Reading Teacher, 44*, 20–27.

Pinnell, G.S., Fried, M.D., & Estice, R.M. (1990). Reading Recovery: Learning how to make a difference. *The Reading Teacher, 43*, 282–295.

Republican Party National Steering Committee. (1990). *Position paper on teaching children to read*. Washington, DC: Author.

Samuels, S.J. (1988). Decoding and automaticity: Helping poor readers become automatic at word recognition. *The Reading Teacher, 41*, 756–760.

Slavin, R.E. (1991). Reading effects of IBM's "Writing to Read" program: A review of evaluations. *Educational Evaluation and Policy Analysis, 13*, 1–11.

Stahl, S.A., & Miller, P.D. (1989). Whole language and language experience approaches for beginning reading: A quantitative research synthesis. *Review of Educational Research, 59*, 87–116.

Taylor, B.M., & Nosbush, L. (1983). Oral reading for meaning: A technique for improving word identification skills. *The Reading Teacher, 37*, 234–237.

Teale, W.H. (1987). Emergent literacy: Reading and writing development in early childhood. In J.E. Readence & R.S. Baldwin (Ed.), *Research in literacy: Merging perspectives, Thirty-sixth yearbook of the National Reading Conference* (pp. 45–74). Rochester, NY: National Reading Conference.

Trachtenburg, P. (1990). Using children's literature to enhance phonics instruction. *The Reading Teacher, 43*, 648–653.

Treiman, R. (1985). Onsets and rimes as units of spoken syllables: Evidence from children. *Journal of Experimental Child Psychology, 39*, 161–181.

Lesley Mandel Morrow
Diane H. Tracey

Strategies used for phonics instruction in early childhood classrooms

Determining the role of phonics in the reading instruction program is an issue that has been with us for many years. Questions that have been a constant source of concern are as follows: "At what age should we start teaching phonics?" "How much time should be spent on instruction?" "What rules should be taught?" "What strategies for teaching are the most effective?" and "Should we teach phonics at all?" In this article we describe how phonics is taught in a number of early childhood classrooms. The results of these extensive observations tell us how teachers in these classrooms are dealing with some of the questions just raised.

What do we know about phonics instruction?

Historically, one of the most impassioned arguments in education has been the role of phonics instruction in early reading. According to educational historian Nila Banton Smith (1965), phonics was first introduced to reading instruction in the U.S. in the 1790s through the inclusion of phonetically organized word lists in Noah Webster's now famous Blue Back Spellers (Webster, 1798). These word lists supplemented the alphabetic method of early reading in which children learned the names of letters, learned how to spell syllables, and then memorized passages of content that had been used since the early 1600s. In the mid-1800s, however, reading instruction again took a turn with the introduction of the word method, in

Phonics instruction in early childhood classrooms was examined. Observations indicated a change in the type of instruction used between preschool and kindergarten and first and second grades.

which children learned to read and memorize entire words rather than analyze words according to their sounds. According to Smith (1965), since the introduction of the word method, the field of reading has been embroiled in a controversy surrounding the superiority of either a phonetic approach or a whole-word approach to early reading instruction. This debate has given rise to major research initiatives such as "The Great Debate" (Chall, 1967) and "The First Grade Studies" (Bond & Dykstra, 1967), which found no definitively superior method. Most recently a commissioned report of phonics instruction resulted in the publication of *Beginning to Read* (Adams, 1990), which found that while phonics knowledge is essential for children's success with reading and writing, children must also be taught to read for purpose and meaning.

Given the importance of phonics knowledge in early reading, the current debate in the area can no longer be whether or not this type of instruction is important, but rather which approaches to teaching phonic relationships are most effective. Advocates of whole language suggest that phonics should be taught in the context of reading and writing activities and not be isolated. Materials such as worksheets and flashcards are considered inappropriate. Instead, the teaching of skills emerges naturally from activities in which the class is engaged (Goodman, 1990; Harste, 1994). Others, however, contest that teaching phonics only through naturally occurring activities in context is not systematic enough and leaves a lot to chance. These writers argue that most children need some direct, systematic sound-symbol instruction to learn to read (Adams, 1990; Stahl, Suttles, & Pagnucco, 1993).

Alternately, a third position has been set forth concerning a "middle-of-the-road" approach to literacy instruction. There is talk about "Centering" literacy instruction (Pearson, 1995), a "Combination Approach" (McIntyre & Pressley, 1996), or "The Radical Middle" (Morrow, 1995). These approaches suggest the integration of the best strategies from different theories representing both whole language and explicit approaches (Pressley & Woloshyn, 1995). With this combined approach, phonics instruction can include both functional and in-context experiences, as well as explicit, systematic instruction. The combined approach also emphasizes the selection of instructional strategies that are most appropriate for individual children.

Purpose of the project

The debate continues as to how much phonics instruction is ideal and which approaches to teaching these skills are most effective (Adams, 1990). In this article, we do not discuss the superiority of one type of phonics instruction or another. Rather, the purpose of the present study was to examine classroom teachers' actual practices when teaching phonics. The information obtained can inform teachers about the methods their colleagues practice in classrooms and educational researchers about the impact of their debates, research, and theories upon classroom strategies. We also raise questions for further research.

A description of the project

Students enrolled in a teacher education program at a northeastern U.S. university were trained to observe and record incidents of phonics instruction. Phonics lessons were defined as instruction that focused on the association of speech sounds with printed symbols (Burns, Roe, & Ross, 1992). The student observers were told to record, in as much detail as possible, all incidents of instruction in phonics, including actual dialogue, that occurred during their classroom visits. Consequently, more than one incident could be recorded in an observation of a classroom. If instruction related to phonics did not occur during an observation, that was also recorded. The observations took place in 76 classrooms: 29 preschool classrooms, 20 kindergartens, 13 first grades, and 14 second grades. During a 4-month period, each room was observed every third week for the entire school day, 6 visits per room, for a total of 456 visits. The classrooms were located in districts of varied socioeconomic (SES) levels and mixed racial and ethnic backgrounds. Some classrooms were located in urban, low-SES, and racially diverse communities, while others were situated in more middle-class, homogeneous, suburban areas. Although the classroom teachers were informed that the student observers would be taking notes about classroom practices, they did not know the focus of the note-taking. At the conclusion of the data-collection period, the teachers were interviewed regarding how they taught phonics and the importance they placed on it in literacy instruction. Teachers' comments were compared with the recorded observations of their actual practices.

After completion, all observations were read and categorized. The categories that emerged are as follows:

Explicit instruction is the systematic, sequential presentation of phonics skills using isolated, direct instructional strategies. Explicit instruction, as it was most often used in these classrooms, involved the use of worksheets that tested knowledge in phonics. The following description of a phonics lesson that Mrs. M. carried out with her first-grade class represents what we are calling explicit instruction:

Mrs. M: Today we will be learning a new digraph. Who can tell me what a digraph is?

Raul: A digraph is two letters together that make a different sound.

Mrs. M.: That's excellent, Raul. Two letters that work together to make a new sound. We've already learned that the *sh* digraph makes the sound /shhh/. Today we'll be learning the *ch* digraph. *ch* makes the sound /ch/ch/ch/ like in the words *children*, *chicken*, and *church* [she writes these words on the board]. Everyone say the /ch/ sound with me. Good. Now everyone read these /ch/ words [*children*, *chicken*, *church*]. Now I'm going to show you some picture cards. When I show you each card, I want you to raise your hand if you think the picture shows something that begins with the *ch* sound. Ready? Here we go.

Contextual instruction includes learning within meaningful or functional contexts. Incidents of such instruction can happen spontaneously when the teacher or a child points out a phonic element. Contextual instruction can occur in activities such as the morning message, language experience charts, storybook reading, or anytime when the teacher or child notices phonic elements within a text and discusses them as they arise. The following episode, which took place in a kindergarten classroom, demonstrates how this teacher took advantage of a spontaneous situation to create a phonics learning experience in context.

Because her class had finished putting on a show for their grandparents, Mrs. M. thought it would be a good idea if they wrote a thank-you note to the music teacher who assisted them with the performance. The note was composed by the students with the teacher's help. She wrote the note on the board and sounded out each word to help the students with spelling. After they finished writing, Mrs. M. read the entire note and also had the students read the note aloud.

Mrs. M.: How should we start this letter?

Student: Dear Mr. Miller.

Mrs. M.: Very good. [as she writes] "Dear Mr. Miller" has three words. *Dear* is the first word, *Mr.* is the second word, and *Miller* is the third word. Boys and girls, I just realized that my name and Mr. Miller's name both begin with the letter *M*. Let's say these *M* words together, Mr. Miller, Mrs. Martinez.

Combined approach is the term we are using for phonics instruction in which both explicit instruction and contextual experiences are used. The teacher plans for phonics instruction by providing meaningful settings for learning with explicit strategies. The following description of Mrs. S. and her kindergarten class illustrates what we call a combined approach.

Mrs. S.'s class was learning about animals. She planned to focus on the consonant *p* during the unit since the letter appeared frequently in texts and discussions about animals. She read the book *The Pet Show* (Keats, 1972), and children noticed the letter *p* in the book title as well as in *Peter Rabbit* (Potter, 1903) and *Petunia* (Duvoisin, 1950). Today Mrs. S. read *Katy No-Pockets* (Payne, 1972), which is about a kangaroo in need of a pocket. After the story, she put on an apron full of pockets. In each pocket were little animal figures. Each of the animal's names began with the letter *p*, such as a pig, puppy, peacock, and a panda bear. Children were given a chance to take the figures out of Mrs. S.'s pockets and name them. She wrote these words on a chart entitled *Animal Names Beginning with P*. Mrs. S. gave out worksheets showing pictures of the animals that had been in her pockets, which children identified by writing the letter *p* in a space provided. She asked the children to look around the room for things beginning with the letter *p* to list on their worksheets and place in the pockets of her apron.

Grade-level differences

A total of 722 observations of phonics instruction were recorded from the 76 classrooms. We grouped the first- and second-grade observations together because we had fewer rooms at those levels.

Table 1 shows the percentage of lessons observed that included phonics instruction for the different grade levels. As can be observed, contextual phonics instruction was most prevalent in the preschool years and decreased in frequency as children matured. In contrast, explicit instruction was observed least frequently at the preschool level and increased as children matured. In short, instruction was most often context based for younger children and explicit for older children. Finally, a combined approach was infrequently observed for all children.

Preschool teachers engaged their children in contextual experiences related to phonics more often than did teachers at other grade levels.

An examination of the phonics instruction observed across the grade levels suggests that preschool teachers in this study engaged children in contextual experiences related to phonics more often than did teachers at other grade levels. There was more dialogue at this level compared to other levels, and children were more involved through verbal interaction and hands-on projects. Teachers at the preschool level appeared to be concerned with making learning fun, and many lessons were done in a way that directly related to the children's lives. In contrast to the other grade levels, in preschool many of the references to phonic relationships appeared more spontaneous than planned. The following episode illustrates phonics instruction that was coded as contextual and that was found most often in preschool.

The teacher and student were using rubber stamps with different letters and pictures on them to stamp onto paper. The teacher picked up a letter and said, "Look, Frankie, this letter makes the /j/ sound. It is the letter *j*.

It makes the /j/ sound. Do you hear this sound in my name?"

The child replied (after saying the teacher's name aloud), "Joyce. Yeah, I hear it at the beginning, right?"

The teacher said, "Great! How about this?" (She takes the letter *f* stamp and stamps it on the paper.)

Frankie excitedly replied, "Hey, that is for Frankie!"

The teacher stopped and said, "Yes, /f/ is the sound that the letter *f* makes in *Frankie*."

In contrast, the observations of kindergartens revealed mostly explicit instruction. Literacy lessons were teacher directed with a set of discrete skills that were taught sequentially (Dahl & Freppon, 1995). The phonics lesson that follows typifies those most often observed in kindergarten.

The teacher showed the children some cards of items that began with the letter *g*. She said, "Here is a gopher. Here are a man and a woman next to their garden. Not a boy but a ...?" A student then called out "girl!". The teacher replied, "Right, girl.../g/g/g/" (making the /g/ sound). She then went on, "This is a picture of some grass, and it is *green*." She then proceeded to write the upper and lower case *g* on the board and told the students to go back to their seats for a worksheet.

In first and second grades, 67% of the phonics lessons were categorized as explicit. The following episode illustrates a typical first- or second-grade phonics lesson.

Ms. G. had written the following words on a chart:

Word families
ame—name, game, fame, same
ide—ride, side, hide, slide

She told the children that these were word families, because the ends of the words had the same letters. They read the two family letter combinations *ame* and *ide* out loud as well as the words that followed. Ms. G. distributed a worksheet and said, "Cut and paste the words that end in *ide* on the left side of your page and those that end in *ame* on the right side. Place different letters at the beginning of the word families to form new words. It is okay if they aren't real words."

A small percentage of teachers at all levels used a combined approach; that is, strate-

Table 1
Percent and types of phonics instruction observed in early childhood classrooms

	Preschool	Kindergarten	Grades 1 and 2
Contextual	72%	33%	21%
Explicit	19%	56%	67%
Combined approach	9%	11%	12%

N = 29 Preschool
N = 20 Kindergarten
N = 27 Grades 1 and 2
N = 76 Total number of classrooms

gies within a broad meaningful context that were planned and included some explicit experiences as well. The following example illustrates the use of a combined approach in a second-grade classroom.

Ms. D. had been teaching word families to her class. She began this lesson by reading *Goodnight Moon* (Brown, 1947) and told the children to listen for all the word families they heard. At the conclusion of the story, the students recalled families of words from the story, and Ms. D. recorded them on the chalkboard. The children were given a worksheet that provided practice in building words from different combinations of word families. After Ms. D. was assured that the children understood the concept, she gave them an opportunity to apply what they had learned in a meaningful context. She gave pairs of students a sheet with the story *Goodnight Moon* typed on it. The students' job was to write their own version of the story using the original as a model. Ms. D. helped them brainstorm word families to use in place of the ones they heard in the story. The students then chose the word families they wanted. Samantha and Katie's story illustrates what they learned from Ms. D.'s lesson:

> Our word family story based on *Goodnight Moon*
> In the big red room, there was a big red boom
> And a giant pink pest, and a giant pink vest,
> There were three big crickets, sitting on tickets,
> And two big frogs, sitting on logs.
> There were three gold fish, swimming in a dish
> And a bowl full of jello, and a bird that said "hello"
> Goodnight room, goodnight boom; Goodnight pest, goodnight vest;

> Goodnight crickets, goodnight tickets; Goodnight frogs, sitting on logs;
> Goodnight fish, swimming in a dish;
> Goodnight bowl full of jello, goodnight bird that said "hello."

Interview responses across grade levels

Teachers were interviewed about the strategies they used to teach phonics and the importance they placed on phonics in literacy instruction. The results from these interviews are presented in Table 2.

Teachers reported using more phonics instruction as grade levels increased, as well as more commercially prepared materials. Worksheets were the materials used most by teachers in kindergarten and first and second grades. Less than 50% of the preschool teachers reported that they taught phonics while 100% of the kindergarten and all but one of the first- and second-grade teachers reported they did.

Preschool teachers seemed to engage their students in more experiences with phonics than they reported. For example, we observed phonics instruction in 82% of our preschool observations, yet only 47% of the teachers reported teaching phonics relationships. The observed incidents of preschool instruction were mostly in context and spontaneous.

Generally, however, teachers behaved in the ways they reported. For example, teachers placed different emphases on the ways in which phonics were taught throughout the grade levels. Preschool teachers reported that their phonics instruction was handled in a variety of ways and in settings that occurred naturally in the

Table 2
Survey of teachers' responses about teaching phonics

1. Do you teach phonics?

	Yes	No
Preschool	13	16
Kindergarten	20	0
Grades 1 and 2	26	1

2. Do you use commercially published materials to teach phonics?

	Yes	No
Preschool	10	19
Kindergarten	15	5
Grades 1 and 2	22	5

3. Do you teach phonics without commercially published materials?

	Yes	No
Kindergarten	11	9
Grades 1 and 2	25	2

4. How important do you think the skills of phonics are to learning to read and write compared to other skills?

	Most important	Moderately important	Not very important
Preschool	4	9	16
Kindergarten	9	6	5
Grades 1 and 2	11	14	2
Total	25	36	6

N = 29 Preschool
N = 20 Kindergarten
N = 27 Grades 1 and 2
N = 76 Total number of teachers

children's daily experiences at school. These teachers said that they taught phonics to "encourage correct speech," "introduce children to letter-sound relationships," and to "help non-English speakers." Kindergarten, first-grade and second-grade teachers reported that they taught phonics for the following reasons: "It is part of the curriculum," "It is on the standardized tests," "It is a requirement of the reading program," and "It is necessary to help children read and write independently."

Discussion

The results of this study indicated that the high percentage of spontaneous, contextual activities used to teach phonic relationships in the preschool classrooms dropped off dramatically when children entered kindergarten and the primary grades where instructional experiences were mostly explicit. Furthermore, phonics instruction observed throughout the grades tended to be either contextual or explicit, with only a few incidents of what we defined as a combined approach. The use of commercial materials increased dramatically when children entered kindergarten and increased further in first and second grade. Finally, the interviews with teachers indicated that the way in which they described teaching in these areas was fairly consistent with their actual classroom practices.

One explanation for the finding that phonics instruction became more explicit and less contextual as children progressed through the grades is that first- and second-grade teachers may feel more compelled to follow a set curriculum that uses an explicit approach. In contrast, since preschool teachers are not often overseen by the state or a school board and are not likely to be concerned with standardized test performances, they may also feel less pressure to teach through traditional modes. Additionally, since there aren't as many manuals for preschool teachers to follow, these educators may make up their own activities and materials and take advantage of spontaneous, contextual experiences to strengthen knowledge of phonics. Another possible explanation is that preschool teachers use more such experiences and fewer explicit activities because their educational backgrounds foster developmentally appropriate practices, which encourage contextual learning for young children.

A second finding in the study was some possible misconceptions among classroom teachers regarding phonics instruction. Preschool teachers reported that they did not teach phonics often, when in fact, according to our observations, they taught phonic relationships frequently. Perhaps these teachers were under the impression that only explicit teaching, relying heavily on the use of worksheets, can be considered phonics instruction and that contextual experiences, in which they frequently engaged, would not be considered instruction in phonics. If this is the case, the misconceptions regarding what does and what does not constitute phonics instruction need to be clarified for educators.

The third finding in this study was that the combined approach to teaching was observed infrequently; that is, few teachers used contextual experiences along with explicit instruction. This finding has several possible interpretations: (a) Teachers may not be aware of what a combined approach is, (b) they may be making conscious decisions not to implement such strategies in favor of exclusively contextual or explicit ones, or (c) they are not making conscious decisions regarding the ways in which they teach phonics. Another explanation is that it may be more difficult to design combined lessons. The question of why teachers did not use combined lessons to teach phonics often is worthy of further study, especially at a time when the concept of combined instruction is being discussed by many literacy researchers.

Conclusions

Current research indicates that a strong foundation in letter-sound relationships is important to success with reading and writing development (Adams, 1990; Symons, Woloshyn, & Pressley, 1994). However, we have not yet determined the relative impact of explicit, contextual, and combined instruction on children's reading achievement. Studies to determine which strategies are best are necessary for future research. While this is a meaningful research direction, and intervention studies in this area are needed, it may be some time before we know the importance of these distinctions for children's learning. In the meantime, based on the results of this investigation, we suggest that teachers make a conscious effort to examine and reflect upon the strategies they use for teaching phonics in order to select the best type of experiences for the children they teach. We also suggest that those in charge of teacher preparation programs and staff development in schools provide careful study in this area. We believe that the integration of enhanced knowledge and increased self-reflection will lead to improved learning for children.

Authors' note

The authors would like to acknowledge Michelle Kazanowsky for the work she did in helping to analyze the data for this investigation.

References

Adams, M.J. (1990). *Beginning to read: Thinking and learning about print.* Cambridge, MA: MIT Press.

Bond, G., & Dykstra, R. (1967). The cooperative research program in first-grade reading instruction. *Reading Research Quarterly, 2,* 5–141.

Burns, P.C., Roe, B.D., & Ross, E.P. (1992). *Teaching reading in today's elementary school.* Boston: Houghton Mifflin.

Chall, J.S. (1967). *Learning to read: The great debate.* New York: McGraw-Hill.

Dahl, K.L., & Freppon, P.A. (1995). A comparison of inner-city children's interpretations of reading and writing instruction in skills-based and whole language classrooms. *Reading Research Quarterly, 30,* 50–74.

Goodman, K.S. (1990). Whole language research: Foundations and development. *Elementary School Journal, 90,* 208–221.

Harste, J. (1994). New questions, different inquiries. In C. Braun (Moderator), *Whole language: The debate* (pp. 143–154). Bloomington, IN: ERIC Clearinghouse on Reading, English and Communication.

McIntyre, E., & Pressley, M. (1996). *Strategies and skills in whole language: An introduction to balanced teaching.* Boston: Christopher-Gordon.

Morrow, L.M. (1995, November). *Approaching the radical middle in literacy instruction.* Paper presented at the National Reading Conference, New Orleans, LA.

Pearson, P.D. (1995, November). *Reclaiming one center: A reading curriculum for all students and all teachers.* Presentation at the meeting of the California Reading Association, Anaheim, CA.

Pressley, M., & Woloshyn, V. (1995). *Cognitive strategy instruction that really improves children's academic performance* (2nd ed.). Cambridge, MA: Brookline Books.

Smith, N.B. (1965). *American reading instruction.* Newark, DE: International Reading Association.

Stahl, S.A., Suttles, C.W., & Pagnucco, J.R. (1993, April). *The effects of traditional and process literacy instruction on first graders' reading and writing achievement and orientation toward reading.* Paper presented at the meeting of the American Educational Research Association, San Francisco, CA.

Symons, S., Woloshyn, V., & Pressley, M. (Eds.). (1994). The scientific evaluation of the whole language approach to literacy development [Special issue]. *Educational Psychologist, 29*(4).

Webster, N. (1798). *The American spelling book.* Boston: Isaiah Thomas and Ebenezer Andrews.

Children's literature references

Brown, M.W. (1947). *Goodnight moon.* New York: Harper.
Duvoisin, R. (1950). *Petunia.* New York: Knopf.
Keats, E.J. (1972). *The pet show.* New York: Macmillan.
Payne, E. (1972). *Katy no-pockets.* Boston: Houghton Mifflin.
Potter, B. (1903). *Peter Rabbit.* New York: Scholastic.

Janiel M. Wagstaff

Building practical knowledge of letter-sound correspondences: A beginner's Word Wall and beyond

"Teacher, I can't do it." Ezzie's wide eyes were eager to learn, yet teary with frustration, as the pencil wobbled awkwardly in her little fingers. I looked around the room on that first day of kindergarten to see others struggling to steady their pencils too. Before the week was over, I realized the challenge that lay ahead: Few of my students could identify letters or numbers, most had little book knowledge, none could write their names, and, like Ezzie, some had rarely had opportunities to put pencil to paper. They were beginning literacy learners in the truest sense. Where would I start teaching them what they needed to know?

My school district had an answer: Letter of the Week. I could introduce a letter and sound on Monday for my students to practice throughout the week. Bulletin boards, science, social studies, and other curricula would revolve around that letter. Using this curriculum, I might have the alphabet covered three fourths of the way through the school year. Not only did this seem painfully slow, but the approach focuses on letters and sounds in isolation. Would my students be able to understand and apply this letter-sound knowledge?

This article discusses the development of self-monitoring and searching behaviors in beginning readers.

The case against Letter of the Week

I had read *Becoming A Nation of Readers* (Anderson, Hiebert, Scott, & Wilkinson, 1985), where the Commission on Reading characterizes exemplary reading instruction as varied and fast-paced. In *No Quick Fix: Rethinking Literacy Programs in America's Elementary Schools* (1995), Richard Allington makes a case for picking up the pace of instruction: "designing schools that offer instruction that accelerates development early, in kindergarten and first grade, must become our priority" (p. 8). For Ezzie and her classmates, who enter school with few literacy experiences, the slow pace of programs like Letter of the Week is a serious disadvantage.

In addition to the problem of pacing, Letter of the Week instruction allows letters and sounds to be introduced without connection to meaningful reading and writing. Too often, reading time is spent practicing letters and sounds in isolation or completing paper-and-pencil tasks related to the latest letter. Activities like these may leave learners with no understanding of how to apply letter-sound knowledge. Stahl (1992) relates this deficit to baseball.

> For a person learning to play baseball, batting practice is an important part of learning how to play the game. However, imagine a person who has never seen a baseball game. Making that person do nothing but batting practice may lead to the misconception that baseball is about standing at the plate and repeatedly swinging at the ball. That person would miss the purpose of baseball and would think it a boring way to spend an afternoon. (p. 620)

Yes, knowledge of letters and sounds, along with phonemic awareness, has been shown to be of utmost importance in learning to read (Adams, 1990). But a decontextualized, Letter of the Week curriculum is not the best way to help students develop that knowledge.

Yet, in some classrooms, Letter of the Week is the only reading instruction children receive. Although some educators still argue that kindergarten should serve solely a social purpose and that formal reading instruction should start in Grade 1, there is much support for kindergarten curricula that include phonemic awareness activities, the development of letter-sound correspondence knowledge, and purposeful reading and writing (Adams, 1990; Button, Johnson, & Furgerson, 1996; Clay, 1991; Fountas & Pinnell, 1996; McGill-Franzen, 1992; Richgels, Poremba, & McGee, 1996). Such activities are certainly promoted by findings from emergent literacy research that children begin learning literacy very early as they interact in a literate environment. In accord with this principle, Teale and Sulzby (1989) suggest daily reading and writing as a natural part of the early childhood curriculum. In New Zealand, where the literacy rate is the highest in the world, there is no debate about when literacy instruction should begin. Time is not wasted on "reading readiness"; rather, it is filled with rich literacy instruction and balanced with a variety of reading and writing activities, beginning on every child's 5th birthday (Smith & Elley, 1994).

If not Letter of the Week, what?

Even though Ezzie entered school with little book experience, she did have life experiences she could talk about. So did her classmates. It was logical to start with these stories as the basis for communicating on paper. I began writing workshop with a minilesson emphasizing that I would accept anything from scribble marks to drawings and letter-like forms, as long as students "got something down on paper." It worked. My children began writing in journals daily. They put down scribbles, drawings, and letter-like forms. Following writing time, they shared their stories with one another, and a community began to develop.

Through shared reading of simple predictable books, I began modeling what readers do: where to begin reading; left to right progression; the difference between letters, words, and spaces; and one-to-one correspondence. I thought aloud about using initial letters and other cues to read words, and I read aloud frequently. Students began independent emergent storybook readings as they reread familiar stories based on our shared reading (Holdaway, 1979). They often checked these books out to read at home, and Ezzie led in number of checkouts.

Feeling we were off to a successful start, I thought of how I might extend these foundational lessons. My students were beginning to get a sense of letters, sounds, and their purposes as I gave them feedback on their writing and called attention to print during reading. Next, I wanted to keep track of our known and developing letter-sound correspondences. I immediately thought of building a Word Wall (Cunningham, 1995), so students would have a permanent reference to use while reading and writing.

In my years of teaching second grade, the Word Wall was an important classroom feature. I learned the technique from Pat Cunningham's book, *Phonics They Use: Words for Reading and Writing* (1995). In second grade, we built the Word Wall with key words containing useful chunks or rimes. These chunks, such as *ake* in *cake* and *art* in *dart*, help students read and write unknown words by analogy to words they already know rather than sounding out letter-by-letter or using phonetic rules. For example, using the key words *cake* and *dart*, students may more easily read or write words like *rake*, *cart*, *snowflake*, and *starting*. For a full description of building and using a Word Wall with chunks to facilitate students' reading and writing, see Wagstaff (1994; in preparation), Brown, Sinatra, and Wagstaff (1996), Cunningham (1995), Downer and Gaskins (1991), and Gaskins, Gaskins, and Gaskins (1991).

Given the needs of my kindergartners, it did not make sense developmentally to begin building a Word Wall with chunks. These students needed work in phonemic awareness and recognizing letters, letter names, and beginning consonant sounds. In second grade, we selected our Word Wall words from the context of humorous poetry. Since I had experienced great success with this method, I immersed my kindergartners in familiar rhymes, poems, and chants as a means of building a different type of Word Wall: an ABC Wall.

Building a beginner's Word Wall: The ABC Wall

Our first familiar rhyme was "Jack and Jill." After reading, reciting, and dramatizing the nursery rhyme, we selected *Jack*, *water*, and *pail* as first key words for our ABC Wall. I emphasized the beginning sound of each word, helping students hear and say the sound and notice how they made the sound with their mouths and tongues. We then practiced writing the first letter in each word and evaluated other words for like beginnings. After "playing" with words and sounds for a short time, we reread the whole rhyme, putting the words back into a meaningful context. During the

week, I heard Ezzie quietly reciting it to herself in a sing-song voice while working at her desk. This delighted me. "Jack and Jill" was revisited throughout the week in repeated shared readings.

Through shared reading of simple predictable books, I began modeling what readers do.

We worked with the new letter-sound correspondences for one week through varied word play activities, then added them to the ABC Wall. The words were boldly written on different colored construction paper, carefully cut along letter boundaries (for an additional visual cue), and stapled on the Wall with an accompanying illustration (see Figure 1). Once on the Wall, the key words served as references for reading and writing new words all year long.

Note that 3 weeks would have been required to cover the three letter-sound correspondences from "Jack and Jill" in a Letter of the Week classroom. Using an ABC Wall as described here doubles or triples the pace of instruction. Two instructional emphases help students feel comfortable with this pace. First, their letter-sound knowledge is reinforced through appropriate word play. Second, daily reading and writing activities allow students to continuously use their growing knowledge in purposeful ways.

Word play

Word play activities are designed to build students' phonemic awareness and knowledge of letters and sounds. Each activity is fast-paced and short in duration, which maximizes the use of class time for reading and writing connected text. Given the ABC Wall word *Jack*, for example, I tell students the word begins with the letter *j* and this letter will be seen and heard in a lot of words like *jam*, *jacket*, and *jelly*. Students are asked to respond positively (i.e., with thumbs up) to words I say that begin with the same sound as the ABC Wall word, or negatively (thumbs down) to words

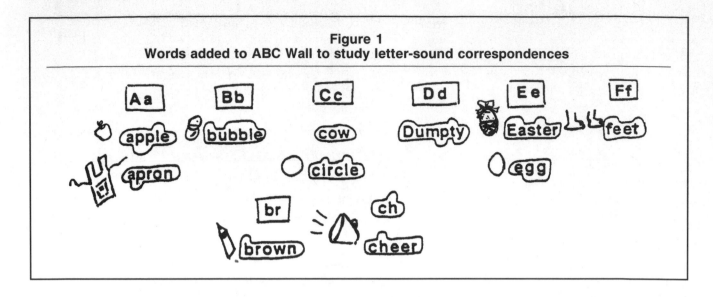

Figure 1
Words added to ABC Wall to study letter-sound correspondences

beginning with a different sound. We then practice writing capital *J* and lower case *j* in the air, on dry erase boards, and on scratch paper. I ask students to volunteer words that begin with *j*. We listen to volunteers and decide if the word offered does indeed begin with *j*. We may make *j* words with magnetic letters or add *j* words to a chart through interactive writing (Button et al., 1996).

We proceed in the same fashion with other key words, letters, and sounds (i.e., *water* and *pail*). During reading workshop, students may be asked to hunt for words that begin with *j, w,* and *p* and add them to letter charts or write them on index cards. Later, these words can be sorted for beginning letters or other salient features.

As we read and reread the familiar rhyme, chant, or poem from a large chart during the week, we review and apply our knowledge. We read chorally, working on one-to-one correspondences, concepts of print, and fluency as commonly done with shared reading. Students volunteer to identify words on the ABC Wall and other known words by placing an index finger in front and behind the word on the shared reading poster. By Wednesday, the students are very familiar with the rhyme due to our repeated readings. I give each student a copy of the rhyme to illustrate and put in their "favorites folders." Students pair up and read from their folders, using pointers to work on one-to-one correspondences. Rereading familiar material like this is a critical part of building beginners' confidence and fluency.

The ability to hear and manipulate sounds in spoken words is an important phonemic awareness component. This capacity facilitates writing development since children must hear sounds in order to represent them with letters. During a repeated reading of our rhyme, we sometimes substitute sounds in words as one way to build this ability. For example, with "Jack and Jill" we may substitute /p/ for some of the words, reading, "Pack and Pill went up the pill to petch a pail of pater," etc. This type of oral language play reinforces the sounds represented on the ABC Wall.

At the end of the week, I place the chart with the rhyme on an easel, chart stand, or affix it to a classroom wall. The chart remains visible so students may choose to revisit it during reading workshop time. As the next week begins, a new rhyme, poem, or chant is selected, and two or three new key words are highlighted for the ABC Wall.

Applying learning in varied contexts

I want my students to apply their growing knowledge of letter-sound correspondences in meaningful reading and writing contexts. One such opportunity occurs during the morning message (Routman, 1991). Before reading the message with students, I encourage them to read as much as they can. We talk about their attempts, how they are able to identify words, and what parts of the message are particularly troubling. One strategy we work on is making associations to key words on the ABC Wall to figure out unknown words. For example, Ezzie reported, I see *p* like in *pail*" at the beginning of the word *paint* in the morning message sentence, "In art, we will paint." This sparked a discussion:

Teacher: How does knowing the word *pail* help you figure out this word?
Students: It starts with the same letter.
Teacher: So, if you know *pail*, (orally stretching and segmenting the word) /p/—-ail, you know the beginning sound is /p/. What else will help here?
Students: Think of what makes sense.
Teacher: Yes, (rereading from the message) "In art, we will /p/---." What makes sense and fits there?
Students: Paint!
Teacher: So, using what you know helps you figure out what you don't know. That's why we build and use our ABC Wall.

Discussion like this, initiated within a meaningful context, encourages students to use the ABC Wall in purposeful ways and to derive meaning using all three cueing systems (semantic, syntactic, and graphophonic). Records from student conferences indicate that children use the Wall during independent reading. Ezzie recently commented, "I know [read] some words because they start like words on the Wall."

The ABC Wall is referenced regularly during daily writing. As a minilesson, I often think aloud as I write a story in my journal or in the context of modeled writing. I might say something like, "Snydley, my cat, jumped in the garbage can again last night. I am writing the word *jumped* in my story. First, I hear /j/, just like the word *Jack*. I must need to start the word *jumped* with the letter *j*." As I write aloud and elicit help from students, I review stretching and segmenting words orally and making associations to key words on the ABC Wall. Letter-sound correspondences not yet represented on the Wall are also briefly introduced. This type of modeling naturally carries over to writing workshop. My anecdotal records have frequent accounts demonstrating students' use of the ABC Wall. For example, as Philip wrote about his family trip to the beach, Ezzie helped by referencing the key word *bubble*. "*Beach* starts like *bubble*. You need a *b*." Students use this strategy independently as well, recording initial, final, and medial sounds with increasing accuracy and understanding throughout the year.

The same kind of activity takes place as the students and I work cooperatively to write the daily news (Routman, 1991). Once students share happenings in their lives and we choose one to record for the day, I elicit their help in deciding which letters are needed to spell the words in the news. Volunteers come forward and share the writing task. During activities like these, I make a point of asking students how they know which letter(s) is needed for a sound in the word we are writing. I want them to be able to describe their strategy use and share it with others. In one debriefing session, Lena shared her strategy, "If you don't know how to write a word, you can look up [on the ABC Wall] to find a word that sounds the same."

Other Word Wall possibilities

Once the ABC Wall is built, key words that begin with common digraphs like *sh*, *th*, and *ch* may be added. As students demonstrate facility with identifying and utilizing letters and sounds, similar methods may be used to build a Word Wall with common rimes (Wagstaff, 1994; Wagstaff & Sinatra, 1995). By the third and fourth school quarters many kindergartners are ready to use more than initial and final sounds to decode and spell. Thus, it becomes appropriate to demonstrate and reinforce looking for the chunks in words to assist students in moving beyond a letter-by-letter strategy. I focus my students' attention on simple, frequent rimes like *an*, *at*, *ell*, *it*, *op*, and *ug*, again, taken from rhymes, poems, and chants. We create a separate Chunking Wall with key words containing these chunks (see Figure 2). The chunks, like the letter-sound correspondences, are learned, reinforced, and applied through short word play sessions and meaningful literacy activities.

During the first months of school, many first-grade teachers review the alphabet and basic letter-sound correspondences. Building an ABC Wall from the context of shared reading or writing is an appropriate way to revisit what first-grade students know and to create a classroom reference for use throughout the year. Depending on students' needs and abilities, an ABC Wall may be built more quickly than recommended here for kindergarten. From this starting point, classes may move into building a Chunking Wall.

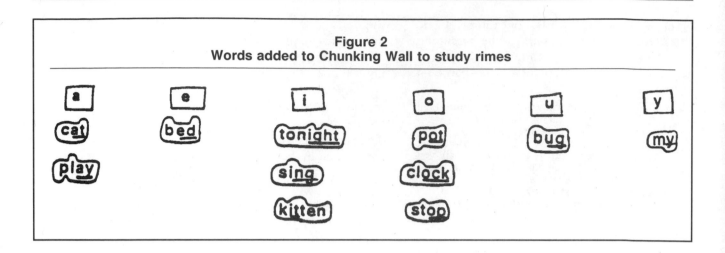

Figure 2
Words added to Chunking Wall to study rimes

Concluding remarks

I chose the course of action summarized here to advance my students' phonemic awareness, letter-sound knowledge, and facility with reading and writing. As I look around my classroom, I am surrounded by proof of lessons learned. This morning's daily news proudly boasts, in a variety of 5-year-olds' handwriting samples, "Last night Ralph's hamster had four babies. They look like pink jelly beans." On my desk is a pile of checkout papers, crowded with names of motivated readers and titles of favorite books. A stand holds today's poem, "Little Bo Peep has lost her sheep...." I study the ever-growing walls of words around us. They are reflections of learning proudly constructed with ownership shared between students and teacher.

Ezzie writes in her journal. She scans the Word Wall until she finds the letters she needs, then resumes writing. Her grasp on the pencil is secure. And the fears of the first day of kindergarten are a faded memory.

References

Adams, M. (1990). *Beginning to read: Thinking and learning about print*. Cambridge, MA: MIT Press.

Allington, R.L. (1995). Literacy lessons in the elementary schools: Yesterday, today, and tomorrow. In R.L. Allington & S.A. Walmsley (Eds.), *No quick fix: Rethinking literacy programs in America's elementary schools* (pp. 1–15). New York: Teachers College Press.

Anderson, R.C., Hiebert, E.H., Scott, J.A., & Wilkinson, I.A.G. (1985). *Becoming a nation of readers: The report of the Commission on Reading*. Washington, DC: National Institute of Education.

Brown, K.J., Sinatra, G.M., & Wagstaff, J.M. (1996). Exploring the potential of analogy instruction to support students' spelling development. *The Elementary School Journal, 97,* 81–99.

Button, K., Johnson, M.J., & Furgerson, P. (1996). Interactive writing in a primary classroom. *The Reading Teacher, 49,* 446–454.

Clay, M.M. (1991). *Becoming literate: The construction of inner control*. Portsmouth, NH: Heinemann.

Cunningham, P. (1995). *Phonics they use: Words for reading and writing* (2nd ed.). New York: HarperCollins.

Downer, M.A., & Gaskins, I.W. (1991). *Benchmark word identification/vocabulary development program*. Media, PA: Benchmark Press.

Fountas, I.C., & Pinnell, G.S. (1996). *Guided reading: Good first teaching for all children*. Portsmouth, NH: Heinemann.

Gaskins, R.W., Gaskins, J.C., & Gaskins, I.W. (1991). A decoding program for poor readers—and the rest of the class, too! *Language Arts, 68,* 213–225.

Holdaway, D. (1979). *The foundations of literacy*. Sydney: Ashton Scholastic.

McGill-Franzen, A. (1992). Early literacy: What does "developmentally appropriate" mean? *The Reading Teacher, 46,* 56–58.

Richgels, D.J., Poremba, K.J., & McGee, L.M. (1996). Kindergartners talk about print: Phonemic awareness in meaningful contexts. *The Reading Teacher, 49,* 632–642.

Routman, R. (1991). *Invitations: Changing as teachers and learners K–12*. Portsmouth, NH: Heinemann.

Smith, J.W.A., & Elley, W.B. (1994). *Learning to read in New Zealand*. Katonah, NY: Richard C. Owen.

Stahl, S.A. (1992). Saying the "p" word: Nine guidelines for exemplary phonics instruction. *The Reading Teacher, 45,* 618–626.

Teale, W.H., & Sulzby, E. (1989). Emergent literacy: New perspectives. In D.S. Strickland & L.M. Morrow (Eds.), *Emerging literacy: Young children learn to read and write* (pp. 1–15). Newark, DE: International Reading Association.

Wagstaff, J.M. (1994). *Phonics that work! New strategies for the reading/writing classroom*. New York: Scholastic.

Wagstaff, J.M. (in preparation). *Working word walls: A book of integrated literacy lessons*.

Wagstaff, J.M., & Sinatra, G.M. (1995). Promoting efficient and independent word recognition: A new strategy for readers and writers. *Balanced Reading Instruction, 2,* 27–37.

Reading Fluency

> *Fluency is reading with speed, accuracy, and proper expression without conscious attention.*

Findings in the National Reading Panel Report

Repeated and monitored oral reading had a significant positive impact on word recognition, fluency, and comprehension.

Fluency instruction was appropriate for children in grades 2 through high school, particularly for struggling readers.

Fluency instruction was equally effective for good and poor readers.

There was no evidence to support the effectiveness of encouraging independent and recreational reading, as for example in sustained silent reading programs.

Fluency has been called the neglected reading skill (Allington, 1983). Until recently, teachers and researchers assumed that fluency would follow accurate word identification, so efforts were focused on word identification. In general it was possible to teach struggling readers to identify words. However, accurate word identification was not necessarily accompanied by fluent word identification. For many struggling readers, word identification remained a slow and laborious process requiring significant conscious attention. In recent years the need to be fluent as well as accurate in word identification has received more attention.

The NRP Report lists several procedures that are included in repeated reading, the first major category of fluency instruction the panel focused on—repeated reading, neurological impress, radio reading, paired reading, and a variety of similar techniques. The panel also investigated formal efforts to increase the amounts of independent or recreational reading that children had, including sustained silent reading programs. There was evidence that fluency instruction in the first category was effective; however, there was insufficient evidence to draw a conclusion about the effectiveness of encouraging independent and recreational reading. Because the one uncontested belief in the field is that children who read more read better, the lack of research is not surprising. It probably has not occurred to researchers to test the hypothesis because it is such a widely held assumption and there is such a broad evidence base in correlational studies (see Anderson, Wilson, & Fielding, 1988).

The first article in this section, "The method of repeated readings," by S. Jay Samuels, is included here because it is the seminal article in this area and one that readers frequently request. It has had a profound impact in the field of reading instruction. The article provides a clear description of the procedures involved in repeated reading and sample data for a mentally retarded student reading five different passages. The effectiveness of repeated reading has been replicated with many different types of students of different abilities and ages. The concluding sentence, "the theoretical and empirical evidence leads us to believe that the method of repeated readings deserves to be more widely used as a technique for building fluency in reading," is strongly supported by the NRP Report.

"Speed does matter in reading," by Timothy V. Rasinski, gives a good explanation of the need for fluency and provides an overview of a number of techniques and procedures that teachers can use with dysfluent readers to improve their fluency. The author ends the article with a caveat, "Do not ignore reading rate."

"'I never thought I could be a star': A Readers Theatre ticket to fluency," by Miriam Martinez, Nancy L. Roser, and Susan Strecker, gives a more in-depth description of one of the techniques recommended by Rasinski—Readers Theatre. It provides an overview of the procedures, describes a weekly routine for implementation, and includes a list of books that are good prospects for Readers Theatre.

The final article in this section is "Be a good detective: Solve the case of oral reading fluency," by Meribethe Richards. The article again provides a sound rationale for fluency instruction and describes another set of activities for fluency instruction. The final section deals with the relationships between fluency and comprehension.

References

Allington, R.L. (1983). Fluency: The neglected goal. *The Reading Teacher, 36,* 556–561.

Anderson, R.C., Wilson, P.T., & Fielding, L. (1988). Growth in reading and how children spend their time outside of school. *Reading Research Quarterly, 23,* 285–303.

S. Jay Samuels

Originally published in *RT* in January 1979
(Volume 32)

The method of repeated readings

A true reading classic, S. Jay Samuels's "The Method of Repeated Readings" has had a profound impact on the field of reading instruction. In this article, he explained a deceptively simple yet powerful technique called Repeated Reading. The theoretical rationale and research he described was a natural extension of his earlier work in the 1970s toward a model of information processing in reading (LaBerge & Samuels, 1974; Samuels, 1976). The Repeated Reading technique was based on his automaticity theory, which suggests fluent readers are those who decode text automatically, leaving attention free for comprehension.

The article initiated (and in some cases was the forerunner of) a new line of research in the 1980s and 1990s on this and other multiple reading techniques emphasizing practice and repetition. Instructionally, Repeated Reading has been amazingly enduring, influencing educational practice for nearly 2 decades. The technique has been broadly adaptable, working for all stances and philosophies, from holistic to interactive to skill-based reading instruction; widely applicable, helping both regular and special needs students and young children and adults become better readers; and extremely effective, increasing word recognition, fluency, and comprehension. Strong evidence, from numerous studies done since the article was published, suggests that repeated reading, in all its simplicity, works!

Perhaps more important than the technique itself, Samuels's article called the attention of scholars and practitioners to an even bigger issue—fluency. As a result, we have a growing body of knowledge addressing the importance of fluency, fluency techniques, and the many ways fluency can be nurtured in the classroom. Since its publication, Samuels's seminal article has been cited in hundreds of books and journals. With it, Samuels has made a lasting mark on both reading research and classroom instructional practice.

Sarah Dowhower
Miami University
Oxford, Ohio, USA

References
LaBerge, D., & Samuels, S.J. (1974). Toward a theory of automatic information processing in reading. *Cognitive Psychology, 6*, 293–323.
Samuels, S.J. (1976). Automatic decoding and reading comprehension. *Language Arts, 53*, 323–325.

A mentally retarded elementary school student asks for a stopwatch for his birthday so that he can keep track of his gains in reading speed with each rereading of short paragraphs he has selected. An adult with a history of reading failure continues to reread a passage after her tutor has left because for the first time she is reading with fluency. In a junior high school remedial reading classroom, a group of students wearing earphones is rereading a story while simultaneously listening to it on a tape recorder.

These situations share a little known and easily used technique called the method of repeated readings. Some teachers are familiar with this technique and have used it, but it is so useful for building reading fluency that it deserves to be more widely known and used.

It is important to point out that repeated reading is not a method for teaching all beginning reading skills. Rather, it is intended as a supplement in a developmental reading program. While the method is particularly suitable for students with special learning problems, it is useful for normal children as well.

While we were researching this method at the University of Minnesota, unknown to us Carol Chomsky at Harvard University was using similar techniques with poor readers and was getting similar good results. With regard to the effectiveness of this method, she (Chomsky 1978) states, "The procedure proved to be facilitating for slow and halting readers, increasing fluency rapidly and with apparent ease. Successive stories required fewer listenings to reach fluency.... The work provided in addition a heightened sense of confidence and motivation. Within several months the children become far more willing and able to undertake reading new material on their own."

What is the procedure?

The method consists of rereading a short, meaningful passage several times until a satisfactory level of fluency is reached. Then the procedure is repeated with a new passage.

For example, in one of our earlier studies, children who had been experiencing great difficulty in learning to read were instructed to select easy stories which were of interest to them. Then, depending on the reading skill of the student, short selections (50–200 words) from these stories were marked off for practice.

The student read the short selection to an assistant, who recorded the reading speed and number of word recognition errors on a graph, as shown in the Figure. The student then returned to his/her seat and practiced reading the selection while the next student read to the assistant. When the first student's turn came again, the procedure was repeated until an 85-word-per-minute criterion rate was reached. Then the student went on to the next passage.

The accompanying Figure shows the progress made by one student on reading speed and word recognition accuracy on five separate passages. These passages began at tests 1, 8, 15, 21, and 25. As reading speed increased, word recognition errors decreased. As the student continued to use this technique, the initial speed of reading each new selection was faster than initial speed on the previous selection. Also, the number of rereadings required to reach the criterion reading speed decreased as the student continued the technique.

The fact that starting rates were faster with each new selection and fewer rereadings were necessary to reach goals indicates transfer of training and a general improvement in reading fluency. Although this figure shows the progress of one individual, the charts for other students were quite similar.

Since the main purpose of repeated reading is to build fluency, it is important to be able to define fluency in ways which are observable and measurable. In the Minnesota research, fluency was separated into two components—accuracy of word recognition and reading speed. While both components are important, for purposes of building fluency, speed was emphasized.

Why emphasize speed over accuracy? There appears to be a trade-off between accuracy and speed. If 100% word recognition accuracy is required before the student can move on to a new passage, the student becomes fearful of making a mistake, and consequently the pace of reading slows down. In fact, if we overemphasize accuracy, we tend to impede fluency. Therefore, for purposes of building fluency, speed rather than accuracy should be stressed.

Repeated readings can be done either with or without audio support. If audio support is used, the student reads the passage silently while listening to the tape recorded narration

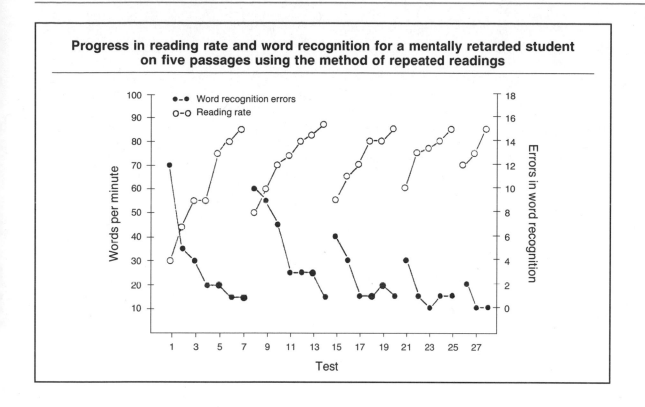

Progress in reading rate and word recognition for a mentally retarded student on five passages using the method of repeated readings

over earphones. After a number of rereadings, the audio support is no longer necessary and the student reads the story without help.

There are additional factors to consider regarding the use of repeated readings. So that students will understand why rereading is done, we have involved them in a discussion of how athletes develop skill at their sports. This discussion brings out the fact that athletes spend considerable time practicing basic skills until they develop speed and smoothness at their activity. Repeated readings uses this same type of practice.

Some teachers who are considering using repeated readings are concerned that the method will lead to student boredom. On the contrary, we found that the students were excited by the gains they made in fluency. Similarly, Amarel (1978) has found that beginning readers are very interested in working at the skills necessary for helping them to comprehend text.

While it is not essential that each student keep an individual reading record of the type in the Figure, we found it to be an excellent motivating device. Without the graph, gains can at times go unnoticed. The graph provides visible proof of progress. Of course, a tape

recording can show improvement from an early to a later reading and is useful for showing gains in fluency to students and their parents.

What about comprehension?

Teachers may wonder what role comprehension plays in the rereading method. Repeated reading is a meaningful task in that the students are reading interesting material in context. Comprehension may be poor with the first reading of the text, but with each additional rereading, the student is better able to comprehend because the decoding barrier to comprehension is gradually overcome. As less attention is required for decoding, more attention becomes available for comprehension. Thus rereading both builds fluency and enhances comprehension. One additional technique for building comprehension is to ask the student a different comprehension question with each rereading of the story.

The amount of material to be read depends on the student's skill. Generally the passage should be short. At Minnesota our early experimental work was done with mentally retarded students without audio support. These students had extremely poor reading skills, and we started them on passages of about 50 words. As they gained in reading skills, the length of the passages increased to 200 words.

In other studies, students of average intelligence who were word-by-word readers were given passages of about 200 words. These passages usually came from a book the student had selected, which was broken into short passages. Once mastery on one short passage was reached, the next short section of the book was used for practice. By breaking a longer story into parts and mastering one part at a time before moving on, the student experiences relatively frequent successes.

Other students in the class, teacher aides, and parents can be used to help with repeated readings. They can listen to students read, record word recognition errors and time, and help with words the students need to learn. In other words, while the teacher is giving directed reading instruction to one group of students, other students, either on their own or with the aid of others, can be practicing repeated readings.

Theoretical rationale

The rereading method emerged largely from the teaching implications of the theory of automatic information processing in reading (LaBerge & Samuels, 1974). According to automaticity theory, a fluent reader decodes text automatically—that is, without attention—thus leaving attention free to be used for comprehension. Beginning readers, on the other hand, are nonautomatic in their decoding since attention is required. Because the beginning reader's attention is on decoding, it is not immediately available for comprehension, thus making the process of deriving meaning more difficult and slower.

In approaching the problem of how teachers can help students develop fluent reading skills, we traced the development of word recognition skill through its three levels. The first level is what may be called the non-accurate stage. The student has great difficulty in recognizing words, even when a reasonable amount of time is provided.

The next level is the accuracy stage. The student is able to recognize printed words with accuracy but attention is required. When listening to the oral reading of a student who is at the accuracy stage, one notes that the reading is rather slow and halting, without expres-sion, and despite high word recognition accuracy, there may be poor comprehension.

The third and most advanced level is what we call the automatic stage. At the automatic stage, the student is able to recognize the printed words without attention. The oral reading of a student at the automatic stage is characterized by a rate which approximates or may even be faster than speaking rate, the reading is with expression, and if the material is familiar, the student should be able to comprehend while reading aloud.

Currently we do not have tests suitable for classroom use which would tell us if a student is at the automaticity stage, so we have to settle for what may be called indicators of automaticity. Fortunately, several research studies suggest that speed of response may be used as an indicator of automaticity (LaBerge, 1973; Perfetti & Lesgold, n.d.; McCormick & Samuels, 1976).

Teachers can do two things to help students achieve automaticity in word recognition. They can give instruction on how to recognize words at the accuracy level. Second, they can provide the time and the motivation so that the student will practice these word recognition skills until they become automatic. One important function of repeated reading is that it provides the practice needed to become automatic.

Several other questions had to be dealt with in the development of the project. Are there activities in which extremely high levels of performance are required? If there are such activities, are the methods of training different from those used in teaching reading? The answers to these questions led directly to the development of repeated reading.

Compare with music, sports

Two general areas in which high levels of performance are required come immediately to mind: sports and music. In sports such as football, soccer, boxing, and wrestling, moves must be made rapidly and automatically.

Musicianship is somewhat different from sports but bears many similarities to reading. The musician is faced with a text comprised of notes. The goal is not just the mechanical rendition of sounds indicated by the notes, but rather the rendering of those printed notes with fluency and expression. Decoding must be done automatically so that the mind of the musician is free to play the score with emotion and feeling.

When comparing the methods used to train athletes and musicians to those used in reading, one notes an important difference. Both in athletics and music, the beginning student is given a small unit of activity and this unit is practiced over and over until it is mastered. At the risk of overgeneralizing, in contrast, we in reading are often too eager to have children cover a year's work in a year's time, so that some children, especially those having difficulty with reading, are moved too rapidly through a book, never having mastered a single page. What repeated readings does is to give the student the opportunity to master the material before moving on.

Leaving the theoretical side of repeated reading, let us examine how versions of this method were used in early schooling. In 17th-century America and Europe, the books used for reading instruction frequently contained familiar material, some of which the student could recite from memory but could not read. For example, hornbooks, used in 17th-century America, introduced reading through the use of prayers and verses already familiar to the children (Meyer, 1957, p. 34). Common prayers were also included in *The New England Primer* (Ford, 1899, p. 13).

Another text used frequently for teaching reading was the catechism (Littlefield, 1904, p. 106). Young Puritans memorized the catechism at home, and later at school reading was taught by having them read from the catechism. In Europe, school was often taught by the local priest, who integrated memorization of the catechism with reading.

Small (1914, p. 366) reports the Bible was one of the most popular texts. In a religious age, many of the Bible stories were already familiar to the young children. The teacher would then have skilled readers repeatedly read the same Bible passage orally until the less skilled had learned the words

In each of the cases mentioned, the children were introduced to reading with material which was known to them, and they read the material a number of times until they were able to read the words with some degree of fluency.

Recent reports of methods used by Heckelman (1969) and Hollingsworth (1970) superficially resemble repeated reading. Their "listening while reading" technique attempts to increase reading fluency in slow readers. However, their students read new material at each listening session instead of concentrating on a particular passage until mastery was reached.

Recent studies using repeated reading have produced interesting results. Gonzales and Elijah (1975) had students who were at the third grade reading level read the same passage twice. The researchers found that the second reading had 3.3% fewer errors than the first reading. This improvement was equivalent to the second reading's being at the instructional level of difficulty whereas the first reading was at the frustration level.

In another study, Terry (1974) had college students read *Reader's Digest* stories typed in mirror-image print. She reported that while the first reading was painfully slow with poor comprehension for most students, both speed and accuracy improved following several readings. After a week of repeated reading practice using a new story each day, the comprehension rate was as high as it was for stories typed in regular print.

It should be pointed out in closing that a carefully designed empirical study of repeated readings (Dahl & Samuels, n.d.) was done with elementary school children who were the poorest readers in the school but who were of normal intelligence. When repeated readings were used as an adjunct to regular instruction, significant gains were made over the control group in both comprehension and reading speed.

The theoretical and empirical evidence in this article leads us to believe that the method of repeated readings deserves to be more widely used as a technique for building fluency in reading.

Author notes

I was very pleased to learn that my article on repeated reading, published almost 20 years ago, is being reissued. Since its publication, I have kept a literature search on this topic and have learned the following from the almost 200 studies on the topic:

1. The original finding has been replicated; that is, a high degree of accuracy and speed develops on the practiced text. We can give accuracy and speed another name if we wish—fluency.

2. There is transfer of fluency to other portions of the text, even the parts that were not specifically practiced. Some have even reported improvements in comprehension.

3. Repeated reading is the most universally used remedial reading technique to help poor readers achieve reading skill.

4. Repeated reading is now widely used to teach reading in foreign languages.

SJS

References

Amarel, M. (1978). Educational Testing Service reading study. *Institute for Research in Teaching: Notes and News, 5,* 2–3.

Chomsky, C. (1978). When you still can't read in third grade: After decoding, what? In S.J. Samuels (Ed.), *What research has to say about reading instruction* (pp. 13–30). Newark, DE: International Reading Association.

Dahl, P.R., & Samuels, S.J. (n.d.). *A mastery based experimental program for teaching poor readers high speed word recognition skills.* Unpublished manuscript.

Ford, P.L. (1899). *The New England primer.* New York: Dodd, Mead.

Gonzales, P.G., & Elijah, D.V. (1975). Rereading: Effect on error patterns and performance levels on the IRI. *The Reading Teacher, 28,* 647–652.

Heckelman, R.G. (1969). A neurological impress method of reading instruction. *Academic Therapy, 44,* 277–282.

Hollingsworth, P.M. (1970). An experiment with the impress method of teaching reading. *The Reading Teacher, 24,* 112–114.

LaBerge, D. (1973). Attention and the measurement of perceptual learning. *Memory and Cognition, 1,* 268–276.

LaBerge, D., & Samuels, S.J. (1974). Toward a theory of automatic information processing in reading. *Cognitive Psychology, 6,* 293–323.

Littlefield, G.E. (1904). *Early schools and schoolbooks of New England.* Boston: The Club of Odd Volumes.

McCormick, C., & Samuels, S.J. (1976). *Word recognition by second graders: The unit of perception and interrelationships among accuracy, latency and comprehension* (Research Rep. No. 102). Minneapolis, MN: Research, Development and Demonstration Center in Education of Handicapped Children, University of Minnesota.

Meyer, A.E. (1957). *An educational history of the American people.* New York: McGraw-Hill.

Perfetti, C., & Lesgold, A. (n.d.). *Coding and comprehension in skilled reading.* Unpublished manuscript, University of Pittsburgh, PA.

Small, W.H. (1914). *Early New England schools.* Boston: Ginn.

Terry, P. (1974). *The effect of orthographic transformations upon speed and accuracy of semantic categorization.* Unpublished doctoral dissertation, University of Minnesota, Minneapolis.

Timothy V. Rasinski

Speed does matter in reading

Reading rate can be a tool for assessing students' performance. Authentic instructional activities can then be woven into the reading program.

As a director of a university diagnostic reading clinic, I see children of all ages who, for one reason or another, are making poor progress in learning to read. Our job in the reading clinic is to determine the nature and source of the child's reading problem and suggest (and implement) instructional interventions for helping the child improve. Often the children we see in our clinic demonstrate remarkable strengths. Many have excellent vocabularies; they know the meanings of many words. Others manage to read with few errors in word recognition. Still others often demonstrate high levels of comprehension, even when their oral reading of a passage is marked by a large number of uncorrected word recognition errors. One of the most common manifestations of reading problems in the children we see, however, is slow, disfluent, or what we have come to call inefficient reading. Even when these children have adequate comprehension of a passage, their reading is often characterized by slow, labored, inexpressive, and unenthusiastic rendering of a passage.

Wondering if this manifestation of slow reading among struggling readers is present in readers other than those seen in our reading clinic, my colleague Nancy Padak and I examined all the children in Grades 2 through 5 referred for Title I reading services by their teachers in the Akron, Ohio public schools—over 600 students (Rasinski & Padak, 1998). We asked these children to read a passage at their assigned grade level and one below their grade placement us-

ing standard informal reading inventory procedures. What we found surprised us.

The informal reading inventory criteria showed that students' comprehension and word recognition were, on average, at their frustration level—but they were near the threshold for instructional-level reading. In other words, comprehension and word recognition were poor, but it wouldn't take much improvement to move their performance to an instructional level. Reading rate, however, was a different story. When reading passages at their grade level, these students, who their teachers identified as struggling readers, read at a rate that was approximately 60% of their instructional level reading rate; for a passage below their grade level the rate was 50% (Rasinski, 1999). Clearly reading rate, or speed, was a significant factor in classroom teachers' perceptions of their students' proficiency or lack of proficiency in reading.

Excessively slow, disfluent reading leads to less overall reading

It is interesting and, to me, somewhat ironic that slow and labored reading rate may be a reason teachers see fit to recommend certain of their students for supplementary reading services such as Title I. Often when I speak with teachers about reading fluency I mention that reading rate may be an indicator of fluent or disfluent reading. This frequently results in concern expressed by some in the audience that reading rate or reading speed should not be considered a significant factor in reading. This concern is often expressed in a comment like this: "As long as students understand what they read, as long as they are making meaning out of the text, reading rate should not matter." While I certainly and absolutely agree that understanding what is read is the end game for reading, reading rate, or speed, cannot be ignored either as an indicator of reading fluency or, more precisely, as evidence of excessively slow processing of text. The simple fact that slow reading requires readers to invest considerably greater amounts of time in the reading task than classmates who are reading at a rate appropriate for their grade level should be a major cause for concern for all teachers.

Most of us would agree that reading progress is determined to a large extent by the amount of reading one does (Anderson, Wilson, & Fielding, 1988; Postlethwaite & Ross, 1992). Slow readers, however, by definition, read fewer words per given amount of time than readers who read at more normal rates. Thus, just to keep up with their classmates in the amount of reading done, these slower readers have to invest considerably more time and energy in their reading.

Indeed, data from the 1992 National Assessment of Educational Progress (NAEP) (Pinnell et al., 1995) demonstrate a relationship between reading rate and fluency and self-selected reading in and out of school. The most fluent readers tended to be self-motivated, while less fluent readers were less likely to read in class or out of school. While the causal nature of this relationship has not been empirically established, it seems reasonable to assume that fluency in reading leads to greater reading and greater reading leads to gains in fluency—fluency and reading volume are cause and consequence of one another. (See Stanovich, 1985, for a more complete description of this phenomenon he termed the Matthew effect.)

Excessively slow, disfluent reading is associated with poor comprehension

Moreover, for most children, slow reading is associated with poor comprehension and poor overall reading performance. Research dating back over 60 years suggests that faster readers tend to have better comprehension over what is read and tend to be, overall, more proficient readers (Carver, 1990, Pinnell et al., 1995). The

1992 NAEP study found that 15% of all fourth graders (one out of seven) read "no faster than 74 words per minute...a pace at which it would be difficult to keep track of ideas as they are developing within the sentence and across the page" (Pinnell et al., 1995, p. 42). Indeed, the same 1992 NAEP study found that holistic ratings of reading fluency as well as fourth graders' reading rates were associated with overall reading proficiency (Pinnell et al., 1995; White, 1995). Slow, disfluent reading, then, is linked with poor comprehension. This leads to students reading less, which in turn results in their making slower progress in reading than students who read at a more normal rate for their age or grade placement.

Excessively slow reading leads to reading frustration

Even at the classroom instruction level, slow reading has negative consequences. Imagine yourself as a fifth-grade student who is assigned to read a 12-page chapter in a social studies book in school. Imagine also that you are a disfluent or inefficient reader. You read at 58 words per minute (the average reading rate when reading grade level material of fifth graders referred for Title I support, Rasinski & Padak, 1998), or about half the rate of your classmates. You begin reading as best you can. Like most students, you are well aware of what is happening around you. You are about halfway through the passage, and you notice that many of your classmates have finished reading—they are done and you still have six pages to read. What do you do? Do you pretend to have completed the assignment even though you haven't read or comprehended the entire passage? Or, do you continue reading knowing that by doing so you will be broadcasting your lack of reading proficiency and making your classmates wait on you? Neither solution is very palatable, yet the problem is all too common.

Even if an assignment were made for home reading, the 60-minute reading assignment for most students would become 2 hours of reading for you. Checking out of the reading club may be just around the corner. You may become a 9-year-old (one out of eight as reported by the NAEP) who claims never or hardly ever to read for fun. And if you don't read, chances are your progress in reading will continue to decelerate. Clearly, excessively slow and disfluent reading is an indicator of concern.

Helping slow readers

How do we help slow readers? Does slow inefficient reading require putting students into some sort of special regimen or treatment for increasing reading rate? Absolutely not. For most readers, a slow reading rate, one that lacks flow or fluency, suggests that the student is an inefficient reader. Although the student may have some success in decoding words, it is far from a smooth, automatic, and efficient process—the kind that requires little investment of attention or cognitive energy. The slow reader has to devote so much time and attention to decoding that overall reading pace is significantly reduced; moreover, cognitive resources that could have been used for comprehension must be reallocated to word recognition (LaBerge & Samuels, 1974). As a result, comprehension suffers. Slow, disfluent reading may also be associated with a lack of sensitivity to meaningful phrasing and syntax (how words are ordered and organized in sentences within a passage) that also helps the reader construct the meaning of text (Schreiber, 1980).

Improving students' word recognition efficiency and helping readers develop greater sensitivity to the syntactic nature of the text will result in more efficient reading and improved reading rate or fluency. But again, this does not have to be achieved through isolated skills practice or boring drills. Reading rate, efficiency, or fluency can be developed through instructional activities such as repeated readings, especially authentic ways, such as practicing poetry or scripts for later performance, and supported reading when it is done in activities where the reader reads an authentic text but is supported by a more fluent partner.

One key to nurturing fluent reading is finding the appropriate text for the reader to read. Texts that are too difficult, overly dense with unfamiliar vocabulary and concepts, can make any otherwise fluent reader disfluent (if you don't believe this, try reading aloud an unfamiliar legal document or a selection from a textbook on nuclear physics). Thus, it is important that we find texts that are well within the reader's independent-instructional range in order to promote fluency. Short, highly predictable selections that are meant to be read aloud and with expression, such as rhyming poetry, are ideal for reading fluency instruction.

Poetry and reading fluency are an excellent match in nearly any classroom and for all students. Integrating poetry into the reading curriculum is a great way to promote fluent reading through repeated reading of readable and intriguing texts. However, despite the wonderful potential of poetry to explore language, it is one of the most often neglected components of the language arts curriculum (Denman, 1988; Perfect, 1999). Turning poetry into a performance, which it is meant to be (Graves, 1992; Perfect, 1999), and turning away from too much critical analysis, can give poetry its rightful place in the reading-language arts curriculum. Moreover, when poetry performance is fostered in the classroom, reading fluency is also nurtured as students attempt to make their oral interpretations just right—and this means repeated readings, but in a very natural and purposeful way.

In some classrooms I have visited, teachers simply select a day for a poetry party. Several days prior to the event, students select a poem to learn from one of the poetry books and anthologies in the teacher's personal collection or from a library, or they compose their own poem. Over the next several days students practice reading their poems, usually from a variety of perspectives, in preparation for the poetry party.

When the poetry party day finally arrives, the overhead lights in the classroom are dimmed, a lamp on the teacher's desk is turned on, hot apple cider and popcorn are served, and students take turns performing their poems for their classmates and other visitors. Students' expressive and interpretive readings of their poems are responded to with warm applause (or, harkening back to a previous generation, with the snapping of fingers). I'll never forget the cold, snowy day in January when a fourth grader gave a heartfelt rendition of *The Cremation of Sam McGee* (Service, 1907/1986). I can still feel the shivers it sent down my spine.

Readers Theatre is another very natural and authentic way to promote repeated readings. Readers Theatre does not rely on costumes, movement, props, or scenery to express meaning—just the performers and their voices as they face their audience with script in hand. For students to perform a Readers Theatre script in a meaningful and engaging manner, they need to practice the script beforehand. Students love to perform for an audience when they are given sufficient opportunities to rehearse the script. In a 10-week implementation of Readers Theatre in which small groups of second-grade students were introduced to, practiced, and performed a new script each week, students made significant gains in reading rate and overall reading achievement as measured by an informal reading inventory (Martinez, Roser, & Strecker, 1999). Through the repeated readings inherent in preparation for Readers Theatre, students made an average rate gain of 17 words per minute, about the gain that could be expected in an entire year (Rasinski, 1999), while students engaged in more traditional reading activities made less than half the gain the Readers Theatre students experienced. In addition to its application in classroom settings, Rinehart (1999) found that Readers Theatre was a particularly effective and motivating approach for students experiencing reading difficulties.

Paired reading (Topping, 1987), echo reading, choral reading, and reading with talking books are ways to provide support for less fluent readers. Topping (1987), for example, found that paired reading could significantly accelerate students' reading fluency and overall proficiency. In our university reading clinic we ask parents of struggling readers to engage in a form of paired reading with their children for 10 to 15

Teachers need to be aware of children's needs and plan accordingly with instruction that meets those needs.

---

minutes each evening. In our version of paired reading, parents read a brief poem or passage to their children. This is followed by the parent and child reading the text together several times. Finally, the child reads the text to the parent; the parent responds to the child's reading with enthusiastic and authentic praise for a job well done. We have found that children who engage in this form of paired reading make significant

gains (in as little as 5 weeks) over children who receive clinical tutoring without the parental paired reading support (Rasinski, 1995). Similar types of paired and supported reading done in the classroom with less fluent readers have been found to result in improvements in reading rate and overall reading achievement (Rasinski, Padak, Linek, & Sturtevant, 1994).

Buddy reading is another excellent example of how teachers can create complex instructional scenarios that are engaging, authentic, and lead to gains in fluency. Let's look at a third grader who is having trouble reading. We know that repeated readings lead to fluency gains (Samuels, 1979). We also know that supported reading in the form of paired reading will also lead to gains in fluency, word recognition, and comprehension (Topping, 1987). This child's third-grade teacher, cognizant of his struggle with fluency, decides, with the child's permission, to pair this third grader with a second grader who is also having difficulty in reading. The third grader will meet with the second grader twice a week and read with her a passage from one of the second grader's textbooks for about 20 minutes. In anticipation of each meeting, the third grader needs to practice the assigned passage (which will be somewhat easier for the third grader to read because it is at a difficulty level appropriate for the second grader) so that he can read it with accuracy and expression with his partner. This may require two or three or more readings of the passage. Yet the third grader does so enthusiastically, for he has a real reason to practice.

When the partners read, first the third grader reads the passage to his partner, then they read it together once or twice, and then, if time allows, the second grader reads it while the partner follows along and provides support and encouragement. The practice is natural and the outcome is clear. Through repeated readings of somewhat easier texts the third grader makes significant strides in his reading fluency and overall reading. The second grader, with the additional modeled and paired reading support, makes significant gains in her reading as well.

The opportunities to create authentic and engaging reading instruction that meets the needs of all readers, but especially inefficient and disfluent readers, are enormous. Creative and informed teachers have been designing reading instruction that meets the needs of their students for years. We need to empower all teachers to do the same. Teachers need to be aware of children's needs and plan accordingly with instruction that meets those needs. Slow, disfluent reading is one indication of a problem for a significant number of young readers.

The goal in fluency instruction is not fast reading, although that often happens to be a byproduct of the instruction, but fluent and meaning-filled reading. To this end I have found that reading to students is a wonderful way to model the connection between fluent reading and meaningful reading. Often I will read to students in as meaningful and expressive a voice as possible. Then, after I have read the selection and discussed its meaning with students, I will draw their attention to my reading of the passage. I will ask them to remember how I read the passage and how my expressiveness affected their understanding. "What did that long pause in my reading make you think? What happened when I read this part in a soft voice? How did my reading this section fast and loud affect how you understood this part of the story? And when I read these words very slow and deliberately, what did that do for for you?" Sometimes I will read a poem or text from various points of view: as if I am angry, as if I am calm, or as if I am nervous. Then I will discuss with students how the expression I embedded in the words helped to communicate to the listener my own point of view. This sort of reading and discussion helps students develop a metacognitive understanding that the meaning of a passage is not carried only in the words, but also in the way the words are presented to the reader. It also provides a model for students' own meaningful, expressive, and contextualized reading, whether orally to an audience or silently with that inner voice that is heard only by the reader.

Reading to students and discussing the nature of the reading allows us to focus on the flexible attitude readers need to bring to the reading act. Fluent and understandable reading, not fast reading, is the goal of our instruction. Fluent reading is often quick paced, but not always. Sometimes, especially with difficult, technical, expository, or unfamiliar content texts, readers need to slow down and process texts more deliberately. Reading these more challenging passages to students and discussing their understanding helps students realize that a truly fluent reader is one who is able to adjust his or her reading rate according to the challenge posed by the text and the information the reader needs to get from the text.

Do not ignore reading rate

I do not wish to take anything away from comprehension as the desired and ultimate result of reading and reading instruction. Rather, the point I am hoping to make is that we need to take the notion of slow, inefficient, disfluent reading seriously. Even with adequate comprehension, slow and labored reading will turn any school or recreational reading assignment into a marathon of frustration for nearly any student.

A slow reading rate may be symptomatic of inefficient word recognition or lack of sensitivity to the phrase—the natural unit of meaning in reading. But these problems can be addressed through authentic and engaging instructional activities and routines that can be woven seamlessly into the regular reading curriculum and that are appropriate for all students, not just those identified as disfluent. As reading teachers, diagnosticians, and specialists, we need to be aware of the importance of reading rate as a diagnostic indicator and to use reading rate as one of many tools for assessing students' overall reading performance. To ignore reading rate when assessing children's reading and designing appropriate instruction may do a major disservice to many readers who struggle with reading.

References

Anderson, R.C., Wilson, P.T., & Fielding, L.G. (1988). Growth in reading and how children spend their time outside of school. *Reading Research Quarterly, 23,* 285–303.

Carver, R.P. (1990). *Reading rate: A review of research and theory.* San Diego, CA: Academic Press.

Denman, G.A. (1988). *When you've made it your own...: Teaching poetry to young people.* Portsmouth, NH: Heinemann.

Graves, D.H. (1992). *The reading/writing teacher's companion: Explore poetry.* Portsmouth, NH: Heinemann.

LaBerge, D., & Samuels, S.J. (1974). Toward a theory of automatic information processing in reading. *Cognitive Psychology, 6,* 293–323.

Martinez, M., Roser, N., & Strecker, S. (1999). "I never thought I could be a star": A Readers Theatre ticket to fluency. *The Reading Teacher, 52,* 326–334.

Perfect, K.A. (1999). Rhyme and reason: Poetry for the heart and head. *The Reading Teacher, 52,* 728–737.

Pinnell, G.S., Pikulski, J.J., Wixson, K.K., Campbell, J.R., Gough, P.B., & Beatty, A.S. (1995). *Listening to children read aloud.* Washington, DC: U.S. Department of Education, National Center for Education Statistics.

Postlethwaite, T.N., & Ross, K.N. (1992). *Effective schools in reading*. The Hague: International Association for the Evaluation of Educational Achievement.

Rasinski, T.V. (1995). Fast Start: A parent involvement reading program for primary grade students. In W. Linek & E. Sturtevant (Eds.), *Generations of literacy: The 17th yearbook of the College Reading Association* (pp. 301–312). Harrisonburg, VA: College Reading Association.

Rasinski, T.V. (1999). Exploring a method for estimating independent, instructional, and frustration reading rates. *Reading Psychology: An International Quarterly, 20*, 61–69

Rasinski, T.V., & Padak, N. (1998). How elementary students referred for compensatory reading instruction perform on school-based measures of word recognition, fluency, and comprehension. *Reading Psychology: An International Quarterly, 19*, 185–216.

Rasinski, T.V., Padak, N., Linek, W.L., & Sturtevant, E. (1994). Effects of fluency development on urban second-grade readers. *Journal of Educational Research, 87*, 158–165.

Rinehart, S. (1999). "Don't think for a minute that I'm getting up there": Opportunities for readers' theater in a tutorial for children with reading problems. *Reading Psychology: An International Quarterly, 20*, 71–89.

Samuels, S.J. (1979). The method of repeated readings. *The Reading Teacher, 32*, 403–408.

Schreiber, P.A. (1980). On the acquisition of reading fluency. *Journal of Reading Behavior, 12*, 177–186.

Service, R. (1986). *The cremation of Sam McGee*. New York: Greenwillow. (Original work published 1907)

Stanovich, K.E. (1985). Matthew effects in reading: Some consequences of individual differences in the acquisition of literacy. *Reading Research Quarterly, 21*, 360–407.

Topping, K. (1987). Paired Reading: A powerful technique for parent use. *The Reading Teacher, 40*, 608–614.

White, S. (1995). *Listening to children read aloud: Oral fluency*. Washington, DC: U.S. Office of Education, Office of Educational Research and Improvement.

Miriam Martinez
Nancy L. Roser
Susan Strecker

"I never thought I could be a star": A Readers Theatre ticket to fluency

Five second graders make their way, scripts in hand, to the front of the classroom. They giggle with anticipation as they turn their backs to the audience. "Ladies and gentlemen," their teacher announces, "The Readers Theatre of Room 313 proudly presents an adaptation of Edward Marshall's *Fox in Love!*" Five performers turn on cue, and Juanita begins: "Well, wait until the girls hear about this!" She reads saucily, and the narrator's words follow to explain that Raisin (played by Juanita) has just seen her boyfriend, Fox, with another girl. The second-grade audience frowns disapprovingly; the performance promises to be yet another success for the repertory group. As always, Fox's cunning is trumped, and laughter and applause close the reading.

Readers Theatre is a great way to develop children's meaningful and fluent reading. Here's the story of two classrooms that took Readers Theatre to new heights.

Engaged and fluent reading performances, like the one in which Juanita participated, came from children who weeks before read haltingly and without confidence. For 10 weeks, their language arts instruction included daily Readers Theatre experiences aimed toward increasing the children's oral reading fluency. Because their practices were "rehearsals," rereadings were both purposeful and fun. At the end of the 10 weeks, these second graders had made reading gains that were significantly greater than students in comparison classrooms.

As many teachers know, Readers Theatre is an interpretive reading activity in which readers use their voices to bring characters to life.

Unlike conventional theater, Readers Theatre requires no sets, costumes, props, or memorized lines. Rather, the performer's goal is to read a script aloud effectively, enabling the audience to visualize the action. Besides the characters, the narrator has a special role in Readers Theatre. Narrators provide the cementing details and explanations that may be found in the original text's narration, descriptions, or even illustrations. Although we realized Readers Theatre has been used to encourage students' appreciation of literature and eagerness to read, we were interested in the influence of Readers Theatre on the fluency of second-grade students who need more practice to make their hesitant reading more fluid.

Readers Theatre is an interpretive activity in which readers use their voices to bring characters to life. Photo by Susan Strecker

Defining fluency

Although most teachers have fluency as one of their goals for children's reading, they frequently find it a struggle to explain what fluency is. As one teacher observed, "I don't know how to define it, but I know it when I hear it." Others offer explanations that are logical, yet incomplete: "Fluency is reading at a good pace." "Fluent reading is reading without errors." "It's reading with expression."

Even investigators who have looked closely at oral reading fluency don't seem to agree. Some have inspected rate (e.g., Chomsky, 1976; Dahl & Samuels, 1974). Some have broadened the lens to include accuracy as well as rate in their inspections of fluency (e.g., LaBerge & Samuels, 1979). Still others have looked at phrasing (e.g., Schreiber, 1980) or the use of prosodic features such as pitch, stress, pauses, and expressiveness (e.g., Dowhower, 1987; Herman, 1985). We considered each of these indicators when we inspected fluency. If demonstration of fluency depends upon appropriate rate, accuracy, phrasing, and expression, we

wondered whether Readers Theatre had potential to orchestrate all these fluency components.

What fluency instruction looks like

There are both logical arguments and observational evidence that Readers Theatre can support instruction in reading fluency. That is, the individual instructional features of Readers Theatre have already been associated with growth in fluency both in studies and teachers' testimonies.

Access to manageable materials. Students who are becoming fluent readers need manageable texts in which to practice (Allington, 1983; Rasinski, 1989; Zutell & Rasinski, 1991). The reading selection itself is an important element in building fluency. First, it's important to choose texts for Readers Theatre that are within the reader's reach. By definition, text within a reader's instructional range reduces word recognition demands and allows for more rapid reading. As rate increases, the reader is able to devote more attention to meaning and the interpretation of meaning through phrasing and expressiveness. That is, accuracy, rate, phrasing, and expressiveness are all depressed when the text is too difficult.

Second, work within the world of oral interpretation suggests that stories with certain features are more easily adapted to Readers Theatre. Stories with straightforward plots that present characters grappling with dilemmas requiring thought and talk can easily be turned into scripts. For example, a strong script is likely to result from a story like Marc Brown's *Arthur Babysits* in which the main character grapples with an ethical dilemma. By contrast, a story like Alexei Tolstoy's *The Great Big Enormous Turnip* with sprawling, boisterous action begs for enactment; it almost demands that children form a chain to pull up that turnip rather than read the story from stools at the front of the room.

Third, Readers Theatre can also build on children's enthusiasm for series books. Feitelson, Kita, and Goldstein (1986) found that familiar story characters and settings are more easily grasped and better understood by young children. Similarly, if children meet the same characters in script after script, those characters become much like friends who have shared many different experiences. They can anticipate those recurring characters' reactions—even to new situations. When it's time to step into those characters' shoes, the children's portrayals of the characters become increasingly believable.

Effective reading models. To know what fluent reading "sounds like," students need to hear effective models (e.g., Bear & Cathey, 1989; Eldredge, 1990; Hoffman, 1987). Sometimes teachers request, "Read that again with expression," but children don't always know what expressive reading is. By listening to good models of fluent reading, students can hear how a reader's voice makes text make sense. That understanding, more than exaggerated voice inflection, is the basis for expressiveness. When teachers read aloud the stories on which Readers Theatre scripts are based, teachers guide students into the sounds and meanings of those stories.

Rereadings. Students who have opportunities for repeatedly reading the same texts become fluent (e.g., Dahl & Samuels, 1974; Dowhower, 1987; Reutzel & Hollingsworth, 1993). Teachers have understood for a long time that reading stories repeatedly improves

fluency (as in Samuels, 1979). Chall (1983) argues that children at about second-grade level *choose* to read repeatedly for the sheer joy of becoming proficient. No longer glued to print, they "take off" in reading. People who observe

---

By listening to good models of fluent reading, students can hear how a reader's voice makes text make sense.

---

these readers note their love of riddles and jokes and almost any kind of text that lends itself to being read aloud often. Hickman (1979) found that second and third graders were far less likely to want to talk about stories than younger or older children because they were so intent on practicing their craft. As 7-year-old Erin explained it, "It's like getting the training wheels off your bicycle. You just ride and ride and ride. Now I got reading. I just read and read and read."

Instructional support and feedback. Students who receive instruction and feedback are more likely to develop reading fluency (Koskinen & Blum, 1986; Rasinski, 1989). Students can gain insights into how to become more fluent readers by talking with their teachers and peers about how good readers sound. Immature readers sometimes describe good reading as "knowing every word" or "reading fast." With guidance, they come to understand that good oral reading also involves bringing the text to life by producing a defensible interpretation. Guidance can occur informally as teacher and children talk about a just-completed performance, or it can be a more planned demonstration of a strategy that fluent readers use.

Into the classroom with Readers Theatre

Given what we understood about fluency instruction, we introduced an instructional model for 30-minute daily sessions in Readers Theatre. The two second-grade classes that participated in the project were in inner-city school districts. One class was composed of Hispanic children of low socioeconomic status; the other was an ethnically mixed group from varying socioeconomic backgrounds.

Choosing the texts. Because the children in each classroom were at a range of reading levels, we looked for books of varying difficulty level, so that each child could meet with text within his or her instructional range. We looked for a body of works—a series—with interesting characters who meet ponderable dilemmas to ensure that children would come to know the characters well and thoroughly. We wanted texts that would provide a sufficient number (four or five) of recurring roles. In addition, we sought humorous texts.

For the lower level readers in the two classes, we chose Marshall's Fox series (for example, *Fox on Stage, Fox in Love*). The mid-range readers read scripts based on Marc Brown's Arthur series. We didn't find a series that seemed a perfect fit with the upper level readers in the two classrooms, so we chose, instead, a set of related books—tongue-in-cheek fairy tales written or illustrated by James Marshall (e.g., *Hansel and Gretel, Cinderella*). We knew this meant that the best second-grade readers in these classes wouldn't be meeting the same characters repeatedly (as would the other students), but the books they read were stylistically similar and the tales themselves were familiar ones. As soon as the groups were formed, they became three "repertory companies" and carried that designation throughout the project.

Preparing the scripts. The books were recast as Readers Theatre scripts with only these changes: Brief narration was added when nec-essary to describe story action revealed only by an illustration. Long narrations were sometimes divided into two speaking parts (Narrators 1 and 2). A portion of a script appears in Figure 1.

For every book we made two copies of each script for each child. The first copy was carried home so that each child could practice each of the speaking parts throughout the week. The second script, the "at-school" copy, had each character's speaking parts highlighted with neon markers. Teachers collected these second copies at the end of each day's practice session. During the week's rehearsals, children would pass along both the script and the role they had just read. Once the performance day's role was decided upon, however, they held on to the script with their own lines highlighted.

Organizing the repertory groups. The three repertory groups were organized in each classroom and each group read scripts based on texts written at appropriate levels of difficulty. Like real repertory companies, the players faced the challenge of regularly rehearsing new material (in this case, each week). The groups had a practice routine, and each player was asked to take on different roles each week. In some instances, a player even had to take on more than one part in a production. Again, like real repertory groups, the players knew they were rehearsing for a real audience. The companies staked their rehearsal areas in the corners of the classrooms. Their weekly instructional and performance routines are described in the sections that follow.

The weekly routine. Every Monday morning, the children looked forward to hearing their teacher read three new stories aloud. These were the stories on which the week's Readers Theatre scripts would be based. Because the teacher had practiced each story, as each was read aloud, the teacher made a special effort to interpret it in ways that would bring the story to life. After the second graders talked about the content and meaning of the stories, the teacher presented a minilesson designed to demonstrate and make explicit some aspect of fluent reading. For example, one lesson focused on why and when a good reader might need to slow down or speed up. In another, students discussed how a reader uses the circumstances a character faces to decide how

---

Figure 1
Script for *Fox on Stage*

Narrator:	Fox wanted a part in the class play.
Miss Moon:	We must be fair.
Narrator:	The teacher put everyone's name into a shoebox.
Miss Moon:	Let's see who will play the pretty princess.
Narrator:	She drew out the first name.
Miss Moon:	The pretty princess will be played by Carmen.
Carmen:	Oh, goody!
Miss Moon:	And now for the part of the mean dragon.
Narrator:	Fox held his breath.

to convey that character's feelings. As a result of those lessons, when Maria played the role of Arthur in Marc Brown's *Arthur Meets the President*, her interpretation of Arthur's speech at the White House began slowly and painfully, "Good afternoon, Mr. President. When I think…about…what…I…can…do…to…make America…great…ah, ah, ah…." Maria explained her slow reading: "I know Arthur is embarrassed. He can't remember what he wants to say. Everyone is looking at him. Arthur hates that. His words are stuck."

Following the minilesson, the teacher distributed copies of the three scripts to the repertory groups. The students practiced reading the scripts either independently or with a buddy. At the end of the session, the children were encouraged to take their copy of the script home to do more practicing that night and through the week.

On Tuesday, the students gathered in their respective repertory groups. The teacher passed out the second set of scripts to each group. On this set, specific parts were highlighted in color. Children practiced reading as a "company" for the first time. When they finished, the children passed their scripts to the left so that each ended up with a new script and a new role to practice. Rehearsal began again. The teacher circulated among the three groups, coaching and providing feedback. Coaching sounded like this:

- "Remember that D.W. just rode her bike for the first time. How do you think she might sound?"
- "Could you read that again and pause for the comma? Let's see if it makes more sense."
- "I noticed how you 'punched' the word *never* in that sentence. That really helps the listener get the meaning."

Feedback also came from other players and felt much like the collaboration found in Author's Chair: "Here's what I liked about the way Jazz read Arthur's part…" Scripts continued to be read and passed until the end of the session.

Wednesday's routines were exactly like Tuesday's. That is, students rehearsed by reading the highlighted part and then exchanging scripts to practice another role. In the final 5 minutes of the session, signaled by the teacher, students in each repertory company learned to negotiate and quickly determine roles for Friday's audience performance. The teacher encouraged the children to pay special attention to their performance role when they practiced their at-home copy of the script.

The anticipation of an audience is what made reading practice seem like a dress rehearsal.

On Thursday, students spent the session working together reading and rereading their performance roles in preparation for the next day's production. During the final few minutes, students sometimes made character labels and discussed where each would stand during Readers Theatre performance.

By Friday, each performer was ready, having, on average, read the script or the story 15–20 times. Every week each repertory group performed before a live audience. The audience varied; some weeks the repertory groups read in other classrooms. Parents were sometimes invited for the performance. The principal, school librarian, or counselor were frequently in the audience. At other times, the class itself served as audience, as one repertory company read in front of the other two groups. There was great anticipation as to who the week's audience would be. The children themselves made lots of eager suggestions. "The audience effect was important," explained Ms. Carter, one of the teachers who participated in the study. "The anticipation of an audience is what made reading practice seem like a dress rehearsal."

As for "classroom management," the children settled fairly rapidly into the routines of their repertory group. At first, there were some warm exchanges about coveted roles, even though teachers made it clear that everyone would play every role, and that continuing roles would be rotated. Manuscript passing, role assignment, and turn-taking soon became routine. Like the procedures for Author's Chair, the routines for repertory groups (see Figure 2) became automatic, so that the focus

---

**Figure 2
A 5-day instructional plan for Readers Theatre**

Pre Day 1   Teacher chooses stories and develops scripts for each text.

Day 1
- Teacher models fluency by reading aloud the stories on which the week's scripts are based.
- Teacher offers a brief minilesson that presents explicit explanation of some aspect of fluency.
- The teacher and students discuss each of the three stories.
- Students begin to practice reading personal copies of scripts, reading all the parts independently.
- Teacher encourages students to take these unmarked scripts home for further practice.

Day 2
- Students gather in repertory groups. Teacher provides scripts for each group with specific parts highlighted.
- Students read the script, taking a different part with each reading.
- Teacher circulates among the three repertory groups, coaching and providing feedback.

Day 3
- Procedures are the same as for Day 2.
- During the final 5 minutes, students within each repertory group negotiate and assign roles for Day 5's performance.
- Teacher encourages children to pay special attention to their newly assigned performance role when practicing at home.

Day 4
- Students read and reread the parts to which they are assigned within their repertory groups.
- During the final 10 minutes, students make character labels and discuss where each will stand during the performance.

Day 5
- Repertory groups "perform," reading before an audience.

---

moved toward smoothing the performance, as well as on enjoyment and showmanship.

What children gained from Readers Theatre

We made pre- and postassessments of students' oral readings of unrehearsed stories from the same or similar series we had used in the repertory groups. Over the 10-week project, nearly all of the children posted gains in their rate of reading. Some of these gains were dramatic. For example, Victoria read her pre-project text at 74 words per minute. By the end of the project, she read at 125 words per minute. Similarly, Rebecca's rate grew from 40 to 88 words per minute. Overall, there was an average rate increase of 17 words per minute for these second graders, while two similar classes of second graders who had the series books in their classroom libraries, but no Readers Theatre, gained an average of 6.9 words per minute. Even so, Readers Theatre experiences didn't affect the rate of every child. We puzzled over Patricia, for example, whose rate

stayed exactly the same over the 10-week period. Hasbrouck and Tindal (1992) hold that 78 words per minute is an expected rate for second graders. Given that standard, 76% of our group fell below at the outset, yet at the end of 10 weeks, 75% had approached or exceeded the standard.

Gains in accuracy told us less. That may be because the materials "fit" the students at the outset. Each student's accuracy was already at an acceptable—or instructional—level. They got better, but there was little room to show accuracy growth in these texts. There were also gains in reading levels on the Informal Reading Inventories administered prior to the beginning of the project and at the project's end. For the children for whom all data were available, 9 gained two grade levels, and 14 gained one grade level. Only 5 children showed no reading level gain. Across the hall, in the two comparison classrooms, 3 children gained two grade levels; 13 gained one grade level, and 12 showed no gain in reading level.

We used a 5-point scale to rate students' fluidity, phrasing, and expressiveness of oral reading on the pre- and postassessments. This analysis documented improvement for all but 4 of the children. The remaining children improved in at least one facet of oral reading fluency, with most improving in two or even three facets. In comparison groups, 10 of the 28 children showed no improvement in oral reading fluency. The children who did show growth typically did so in only one facet of fluency (e.g., phrasing).

Readers Theatre seemed especially well suited to helping children go "inside" the story, experiencing the thoughts and feelings of the characters. As we observed in the two classrooms, we witnessed many instances of this. Sometimes a teacher probe assisted students in contemplating the meaning of a scene: "How is James Marshall's *Goldilocks* different from other Goldilocks? How can the voice of Goldilocks give the audience a clue to that difference?" At other times students themselves initiated discussion regarding oral interpretation that delved into comprehension on a deep level, as evidenced in this interaction about *Hansel and Gretel* (Marshall, 1990).

> Vicky: Your voice is too sweet. I don't think Gretel would talk nice to her stepmother.
>
> Jessica: That's what I'm doing. Gretel is being *too* sweet because she can't stand her. I want it to sound like phony, not like I'm really trying to be nice.

As expected, we found that the series books promoted familiarity with characters' personae. For example, Arthur's friend Francine was interpreted as a know-it-all smarty pants every week, regardless of the performer. Children also learned to expect certain types of story situations to occur in the series books. Leaving the classroom one Friday afternoon, Daniel called back, "I can't wait to see what trouble Fox gets in next week!" Such expectations for story can serve as a solid basis for interpreting future stories through Readers Theatre.

The teachers, Ms. Carter and Mr. Meneses, also attended to their students' enthusiasm for Readers Theatre. Reading practice as "rehearsal" proved to be a motivational method to encourage repeated readings. The "lure of performance" (Busching, 1981, p. 34) offered an incentive for returning to the text again and again, as students worked to bring the written words to life for Friday's audience. Ms. Carter explained the pervading influence of the scripts

---

Books for use in Readers Theatre

Easy books

Alphin, E.M. (1996). *A bear for Miguel*. Ill. J. Sandin. New York: HarperCollins.

Byars, B. (1994). *The Golly sisters ride again*. Ill. S. Truesdell. New York: HarperCollins.

Byars, B. (1996). *My brother, Ant*. Ill. M. Simont. New York: Viking.

Byars, B. (1997). *Ant plays bear*. Ill. M. Simont. New York: Viking.

Eastman, P.D. (1960). *Are you my mother?* New York: Random House.

Fox, M. (1987). *Hattie and the fox*. Ill. P. Mullins. New York: Bradbury.

Kraus, R. (1970). *Whose mouse are you?* Ill. J. Aruego. New York: Aladdin.

Marshall, E. (1981). *Three by the sea*. Ill. J. Marshall. New York: Puffin.

Marshall, E. (1986). *Three up a tree*. Ill. J. Marshall. New York: Puffin.

Marshall, E. (1994). *Fox in love*. Ill. J. Marshall. New York: Puffin.

Marshall, J. (1993). *Fox on stage*. New York: Puffin.

Minarik, E.H. (1957). *Little Bear*. Ill. M. Sendak. New York: Harper & Row.

Wiseman, B. (1959). *Morris the moose*. New York: HarperTrophy.

Books for average readers

Brown, M. (1991). *Arthur meets the president*. Boston: Little, Brown.

Brown, M. (1992). *Arthur babysits*. Boston: Little, Brown.

Champion, J. (1993). *Emily and Alice*. Ill. S. Stevenson. San Diego, CA: Harcourt Brace.

Champion, J. (1995). *Emily and Alice again*. Ill. S. Stevenson. San Diego, CA: Harcourt Brace.

Hall, D. (1994). *I am the dog, I am the cat*. Ill. B. Moser. New York: Dial.

Johnson, A. (1989). *Tell me a story, Mama*. Ill. D. Soman. New York: Orchard.

Marshall, J. (1986). *Wings: A tale of two chickens*. New York: Viking.

Mazer, A. (1991). *The salamander room*. Ill. S. Johnson. New York: Knopf.

Naylor, P.R. (1992). *King of the playground*. Ill. N.L. Malone. New York: Atheneum.

Schotter, R., & Schotter, R. (1994). *There's a dragon about: A winter's revel*. Ill. R.W. Alley. New York: Orchard.

Stevens, J. (1995). *Tops and bottoms*. San Diego, CA: Harcourt Brace.

Wood, A. (1988). *The horrible holidays*. Ill. R.K. Hoffman. New York: Dial.

Challenging books

Ehlert, L. (1992). *Moon rope/Un lazo a la luna*. San Diego, CA: Harcourt Brace Jovanovich.

Karlin, B. (1992). *Cinderella*. Ill. J. Marshall. Boston: Little, Brown.

Kimmel, E.A. (1992). *Anansi goes fishing*. Ill. J. Stevens. New York: Holiday House.

Kimmel, E.A. (1994). *Anansi and the talking melon*. Ill. J. Stevens. New York: Holiday House.

(continued)

in classroom life: "They read those [original] books during their reading time. They wrote about the books and their own plays based on the same characters. They wrote story extensions of the scripts. They also invited their parents to attend performances and repeatedly asked, 'Is it time for Readers Theatre?'" We found further evidence of the motivational power of Readers Theatre in the students' writing journals. Omar wrote, "Readers theater is the funnest reading I've ever did before!" Lucia wrote, "I never thought I could be a star, but I was the BEST reader today."

Conclusions

Readers Theatre seems to offer teachers a way to incorporate repeated readings within a meaningful and purposeful context. Creating opportunities for students to perform before an audience requires multiple readings of the text in order to achieve the fluency needed for the performance, and that practice works. Ms. Carter summarized the benefits: "I see two reasons why Readers Theatre helped my students so much. The first is comprehension that results from having to become the characters and understand their feelings, and the second is the repetition and practice." Encouraging appropriate oral interpretation not only assists students with their expressiveness, but also sharpens their insights into the literature for themselves and their listeners. As Coger (1963) states, "The study of the written page becomes fun, and reading it aloud deepens the reader's understanding of the text, for in read-ing it aloud the readers experience the writing more deeply" (p. 322).

Preparing a reading for an audience is a powerful incentive for reading practice. We observed the energy of students performing for a new audience. We observed changes in levels of confidence that a well-rehearsed effort produces. We also observed the changes in popularity of the books in the classroom library, and students who were content to just "read and read and read." They never seemed to tire of perfecting their craft.

Readers Theatre, then, offers a reason for children to read repeatedly in appropriate materials. It provides a vehicle for direct explanation, feedback, and effective modeling. Perhaps due to the interplay of these influences, we found that Readers Theatre promoted oral reading fluency, as children explored and interpreted the meanings of literature (with joy)!

Authors' note

We would like to thank Claire Carter and Ed Meneses for sharing their insights about Readers Theatre.

Books for use in Readers Theatre (continued)

Kroll, V. (1994). *The seasons and someone*. Ill. T. Kiuchi. San Diego, CA: Harcourt Brace.

Marshall, J. (1988). *George and Martha round and round*. Boston: Houghton Mifflin.

Marshall, J. (1990). *Hansel and Gretel*. New York: Dial.

Martin, B., Jr, & Archambault, J. (1985). *The ghost-eye tree*. Ill. T. Rand. New York: Henry Holt.

Mora, P. (1994). *Pablo's tree*. Ill. C. Lang. New York: Macmillan.

Noble, T.H. (1980). *The day Jimmy's boa ate the wash*. Ill. S. Kellogg. New York: Puffin.

Noble, T.H. (1984). *Jimmy's boa bounces back*. Ill. S. Kellogg. New York: Dial.

Temple, F. (1994). *Tiger soup*. New York: Orchard.

References

Allington, R.L. (1983). Fluency: The neglected goal. *The Reading Teacher, 36*, 556–561.

Bear, D., & Cathey, S. (1989, November). *Writing and reading fluency and orthographic awareness*. Paper presented at the meeting of the National Reading Conference, Tucson, AZ.

Busching, B. (1981). Readers' theater: An education for language and life. *Language Arts, 58*, 330–338.

Chall, J.S. (1983). *Stages of reading development*. New York: McGraw-Hill.

Chomsky, C. (1976). After decoding: What? *Language Arts, 53*, 374–390.

Coger, L.I. (1963). Theatre for oral interpreters. *Speech Teacher, 12*, 322–330.

Dahl, P.R., & Samuels, S.J. (1974). *A mastery based experimental program for teaching poor readers high speed word recognition skills*. Unpublished manuscript, University of Minnesota, Minneapolis.

Dowhower, S.L. (1987). Effect of repeated reading on second grade transitional readers' fluency and comprehension. *Reading Research Quarterly, 22*, 389–406.

Eldredge, J.L. (1990). *An experiment using a group assisted repeated reading strategy with poor readers*. Unpublished manuscript, Brigham Young University, Provo, UT. (ERIC Document Reproduction Service No. ED 314 721)

Feitelson, D., Kita, B., & Goldstein, Z. (1986). Effects of listening to series stories on first graders' comprehension and use of language. *Research in the Teaching of English, 20*, 339–356.

Hasbrouck, J.E., & Tindal, G. (1992). Curriculum-based oral reading fluency norms for students in grades 2 through 5. *Teaching Exceptional Children, 24*, 41–44.

Herman, P.A. (1985). The effect of repeated readings on reading rate, speech pauses, and word recognition accuracy. *Reading Research Quarterly, 20*, 553–564.

Hickman, J.G. (1979). *Response to literature in a school environment, grades K–5*. Unpublished doctoral dissertation, The Ohio State University, Columbus.

Hoffman, J.V. (1987). Rethinking the role of oral reading in basal instruction. *Elementary School Journal, 87*, 367–374.

Koskinen, P.A., & Blum, I.H. (1986). Paired repeated reading: A classroom strategy for developing fluent reading. *The Reading Teacher, 40*, 70–75.

LaBerge, D., & Samuels, S.J. (1979). Toward a theory of automatic information processing in reading. *Cognitive Psychology, 6*, 293–323.

Rasinski, T.V. (1989). Fluency for everyone: Incorporating fluency instruction in the classroom. *The Reading Teacher, 42*, 690–693.

Reutzel, D.R., & Hollingsworth, P.M. (1993). Effects of fluency training on second graders' reading comprehension. *Journal of Educational Research, 86*, 325–331.

Samuels, S.J. (1979). The method of repeated reading. *The Reading Teacher, 32*, 403–408.

Schreiber, P.A. (1980). On the acquisition of reading fluency. *Journal of Reading Behavior, 12*, 177–186.

Zutell, J., & Rasinski, T. (1991). Training teachers to attend to their students' oral reading fluency. *Theory Into Practice, 30*, 212–217.

Children's books cited

Brown, M. (1991). *Arthur meets the president*. Boston: Little, Brown.

Brown, M. (1992). *Arthur babysits*. Boston: Little, Brown.

Karlin, B. (1992). *Cinderella*. Ill. J. Marshall. Boston: Little, Brown.

Marshall, E. (1994). *Fox in love*. Ill. J. Marshall. New York: Puffin.

Marshall, J. (1990). *Hansel and Gretel*. New York: Dial.

Marshall, J. (1993). *Fox on stage*. New York: Puffin.

Tolstoy, A. (1968). *The great big enormous turnip*. London: Piccolo.

Meribethe Richards

Be a good detective: Solve the case of oral reading fluency

How can teachers help students become fluent oral readers? Here are clues.

A good mystery is characterized by an elusive suspect, complex clues, and a final trap to capture the culprit. For today's reading teacher, tracking the role of fluency in reading instruction is similar to solving a good mystery. In order to confidently improve and assess students' oral reading fluency, teachers are required to become good detectives and follow the clues to fluency's true nature.

Before trying to solve this complex case, good detectives must understand what they are looking for and why it is important. What is oral reading fluency? For successful readers, it is the ability to project the natural pitch, stress, and juncture of the spoken word on written text, automatically and at a natural rate. Is oral reading fluency a critical aspect of reading performance and instruction? Current research states a definitive "yes."

Nathan and Stanovich (1991) suggested that fluency "may be almost a necessary condition for good comprehension and enjoyable reading experiences" (p. 176). Furthermore, because good readers are also fluent oral readers, it is to an instructor's advantage to discover how fluency contributes to good reading. For if the goal of reading instruction is to help children interact meaningfully with a variety of texts, they must be competent in word recognition, read at a suitable rate, and understand how to project the phrasing and expression of the spoken word upon the written word (Zutell & Rasinski, 1991). Understanding the way good readers use these elements of fluent reading to comprehend text is necessary for authentic reading instruction and assessment to take place.

At this point, it is also important to distinguish oral reading fluency from the fluency of silent readers. Since the early 20th century, fluent silent reading has generally been accepted as the ultimate goal of reading instruction (Stayter & Allington, 1991). Despite this emphasis on silent reading, Taylor and Connor (1982) suggested three reasons that oral reading remains an essential aspect of reading instruction, especially in the primary grades. First, it appears that "young children need to hear themselves read" (p. 442). A second reason students read orally is the necessity of receiving feedback from adult readers in order to monitor reading progress. Finally, Taylor and Connor stated that "through oral reading, children can show off an acquired skill" (p. 442) that is valued by society. The purpose of this article is to discover methods of improving students' oral reading fluency because oral reading is an integral aspect of learning to read.

If oral reading fluency is an important element in reading instruction, it is puzzling that teachers should be expected to solve this case on their own. There seem to be several reasons fluency is a mystery to today's teachers. Bear (1991) suggested that fluency instruction may have been lost in the debate between phonics and whole language. This focus on methods rather than an "integrated, developmental model" of reading has led teachers to overlook the importance of incorporating fluency instruction in their reading program (p. 156). In an informal survey of currently used reading methods texts, Dowhower (1991) found that fluency is mentioned briefly, if at all, in these texts. Because future teachers are simply not taught to attend to fluency, it is hard to expect them to incorporate fluency in their instruction. Zutell and Rasinski (1991) supported this finding, mentioning that reading teachers tend to focus on word recognition, vocabulary development, and comprehension because these are the goals of most basal reading series. Fluency is considered an "outcome" of the goals "rather than a contributing factor" (p. 211). Fluency simply is not a stressed aspect of reading instruction.

Rate, recognition, and phrasing

When teachers first begin to solve the case of fluency, they quickly uncover two of the three important clues, namely reading rate and automatic word recognition. Many teachers believe fluency can be tracked through just these aspects of good oral reading. However, according to Lipson and Wixson (1977), fluency does not depend solely on reading rate. They explained that reading rate is the speed at which oral or silent reading takes place. To be mathematically specific, it is the number of words in a passage multiplied by 60, and then divided by the number of seconds taken by a specific individual to read a particular passage (Stieglitz, 1992, p. 57).

While reading rate is a clue to fluency's complex character, teachers should not be satisfied with such a simple definition of fluency. As well, teachers should not mistake automatic word recognition for fluency. Allington (1983) explained, "This interpretation [of fluency], commonly accepted by teachers unfortunately often leads to further instruction in letters, sounds or words in isolation" for nonfluent readers (p. 557). This bottom-up effort to improve how quickly children recognize words is not detrimental to their reading, but it does not necessarily lead to fluent oral reading.

While many teachers can mistake fluency for reading rate or automatic word recognition, some teachers may conclude that their nonfluent readers need to simply read with more expression. There are still others who may be misled entirely by the idea that children who read nonfluently are weak readers in all other elements of reading, including comprehension. Zutell and Rasinski (1991) asked future teachers to define fluent oral reading and in response

were given the following descriptions: "accurate word recognition, fast word recognition, quick reading, reading with expression, paying attention to punctuation, and using appropriate intonation" (p. 212). However, these assessments of students' oral reading ability indicate poor understanding of the interactive characteristics of fluency's true nature.

Actually, most teachers are fairly good detectives in that they naturally recognize two of the three clues to fluency, the importance of reading rate and automatic word recognition. Zutell and Rasinski (1991) described the rate aspect of fluency as "pace" and automatic word recognition as "smoothness" on their Multidimensional Fluency Scale (p. 215). The third element on this scale is phrasing. Dowhower (1991) described this final clue to fluency's character. She explained that the element of prosody, commonly referred as "reading with expression," is "the ability to read in expressive rhythmic and melodic patterns" (p. 166).

Prosody is the ability to read a text orally using appropriate pitch, stress, and juncture; to project the natural intonation and phrasing of the spoken word upon the written text. Prosodic cues are the structure of text and language, which help students identify the correct pitch, stress, and juncture to be assigned a given text. Unfortunately, students may have difficulty identifying prosodic cues when reading orally because written text lacks definitive signs as to what constitutes the natural phrasing (Allington, 1983). Students are expected to automatically use this syntactic knowledge when reading orally, yet teachers spend little or no time instructing students in this skill. For good readers, this lack of instruction is not a problem. For poor readers, it can lead to "unrewarding reading experiences that lead to less involvement in reading-related activities" (Nathan & Stanovich, 1991, p. 177).

Once teachers have identified the three clues that interact for fluent oral reading, it is necessary to decide how to trap the suspect in the reading classroom in order to provide students with positive, rewarding reading experiences. How do teachers instruct children to become fluent oral readers? In order to select and facilitate the best method of fluency instruction for individual children and individual classrooms, teachers should examine the evidence that suggests why some students are more fluent readers than others.

Allington (1983) described six hypotheses: First, children who have models of fluent oral reading at home learn that fluent reading is the goal when reading aloud. Second, successful readers are often encouraged to focus on the elements of expression while poor readers are asked to focus solely on word recognition, phonics, and other skills in isolation. Third, readers who demonstrate fluent oral reading are given more opportunities to read and therefore further develop this skill. Fourth, readers who read fluently are often reading texts at their instructional level, if not independent level; those readers who lack fluency are often reading texts that are too difficult, in other words at their frustration level. Fifth, good fluent readers have more time to read silently, time in which they "reread sentences in an attempt to understand phrases and experiment with intonation, juncture and stress" (p. 558). Finally, good fluent readers understand that the ultimate goal is not solely accuracy but also meaningful expression.

Methods for capturing fluency

There are various means currently being researched and practiced in order to capture fluency for today's students. These methods for developing fluency include modeling, repeated reading, paired oral reading, the Oral Recitation Lesson, and choral reading. A brief look at each method will help teachers decide how best to capture fluency in their classroom.

Modeling. As Allington (1983) pointed out, good fluent readers have good models at home who have helped them identify fluency as the goal of oral reading. Teachers can model fluent oral reading in the classroom as well. This may be happening already as they read daily to their students from picture books, chapter books, newspapers, language experience charts, and poetry selections. Older students who have mastered a specific text can model fluent oral reading for younger students. Each of these model readings should be uninterrupted because the objective is to demonstrate the phrase-like quality of oral reading. Teachers need to model oral reading fluency for their students struggling with this element of reading. Zutell and Rasinski (1991) pointed out that "poor readers only have other poor readers as models" due to the organization of most reading groups (p. 216). It is im-

portant for every student to listen to effective fluent oral reading during reading instruction.

Repeated readings. Another means of incorporating fluency training in the classroom is through repeated readings. Dowhower (1989) explained the benefits of repeated reading and several methods for implementing this practice in the classroom. Repeated reading increases rate and accuracy, which then transfers to new texts. Repeated reading also helps children to further understand the phrasing of the text. Finally, repeated reading may also lead to increased comprehension of the selected text as a result of multiple exposure. This increased comprehension also transfers to new text "when the stories are at the same reading level and accuracy and speed have also increased" (p. 504). Bearing this evidence in mind, teachers should carefully consider incorporating at least one method of repeated reading in their classrooms.

There are three ways to provide repeated reading experiences for students in the classroom. A teacher can use direct instruction, an independent learning approach, or cooperative repeated reading. In direct instruction, the teacher models fluent reading of the selected passage, and then discusses new vocabulary and content. Then the class practices the text as a whole group, focusing on the prosodic features of the text; finally, the students practice independently. Dowhower (1989) suggested a goal of "75 WPM [words per minute] and 98% accuracy with good expression" (p. 505). Teachers who decide to implement repeated reading as an independent choice provide a special place in the classroom where children can practice reading orally. An assisted method can be used where a tape recorder, book, and tape of the book are used simultaneously as the child reads orally. Dowhower described the last method of encouraging repeated reading in the classroom as "cooperative repeated reading" (1989, p. 506). It is similar to the method of paired oral reading, which will be described later in this article.

Shared reading is a method of whole-group reading instruction that lends itself to the incorporation of direct instruction in oral reading fluency through repeated readings. Big Books are an excellent text format for these shared reading lessons. Many teachers use a lesson plan that includes five repeated readings of the same text, one reading for each day of the week. For the first reading, the teacher simply models a fluent reading of the text during a directed reading activity, which includes making predictions, establishing purpose, and discussing the events of the text, specifically in relation to the students' personal experiences. The teacher uses the subsequent readings, or repeated readings, to develop oral reading fluency as well as comprehension, sight word vocabulary, and word recognition skills. The teacher should emphasize volume changes, character emotion, and phrasing as aspects of fluent oral reading. During these repeated readings, the teacher not only models fluency but also allows students to practice reading the text as well. Finally, the students are provided with an individual copy of the text for further practice. This further practice is repeated reading by independent choice. It is appropriate to place these books in the class library or another area in the room designated for repeated reading of texts that the class has read initially during shared reading.

Paired oral readings. Rasinski and Zutell (1990) suggested two methods for developing fluency. The first method, paired oral reading, developed by Koskinen and Blum (1984), requires students to work as pairs. Passages are selected and read silently by each student. Then, the students take turns reading the passage three times orally, in succession, to the other student. The listening student takes on the role of teacher giving suggestions and positive feedback to the partner.

By way of introduction, the teacher can model paired reading for the class. The teacher begins by selecting a volunteer who is comfortable reading a short passage before the class. To demonstrate paired reading, the teacher and student sit side by side, shoulder to shoulder, both holding the book between them. Partners make predictions based on the title and pictures. Then the partners decide together who will begin reading. If one of the readers encounters difficulty, he or she asks the partner for help. When modeling paired reading initially, the teacher should pretend to experience difficulty to demonstrate how students should help their partners. If the reading is particularly difficult for one of the partners, they can decide to read the story simultaneously. After the partners have read together, the first reader asks a question about the text and makes a nice comment about the partner's reading. The second reader reciprocates with a question and comment. After the teacher and student have modeled paired oral

reading, the class can brainstorm questions and comments they might address to one another during paired reading. For example, questions might include eliciting opinions about the main character or asking for a prediction about upcoming events in the story. Comments might compliment the partner for independently deciphering unknown words or reading characters' dialogue with appropriate emotion.

After paired reading has been modeled, it can be used in a variety of instances in the classroom. Students might choose a partner after small-group reading instruction in order to practice a new text. Poetry, especially poems introduced through the Oral Recitation Lesson described next, can be collected in a notebook and used for paired reading throughout the school year. After a shared reading experience, specifically with books in a Big Book format, individual books of the same text can be used for paired reading.

The Oral Recitation Lesson (ORL). This method is similar to using repeated reading as a component of direct instruction. Children are introduced to the text with comprehension as the focus of instruction. After the teacher selects a text and models a fluent oral reading of the text, she or he chooses a strategy of discussion focusing on comprehension. However, the teacher does not end the lesson at this point but continues with a discussion of the prosodic elements found within the specific text. Students are then asked to practice the text as a group as well as individually. The final stage of the ORL is performance. Students are asked to read a portion of the text for an audience. A variety of texts could be adapted for this type of lesson including poetry and nursery rhymes for younger children and fairy tales and plays for upper elementary students.

To begin the Oral Recitation Lesson, the teacher selects a text that lends itself to performance. For example, texts with dialogue that is already present or that can be written in a shared writing activity are useful for this method of oral reading fluency development. Stories that require simple props for reenactment are also appropriate. The initial reading of the text should model fluent oral reading for the students. After the second reading, the teacher selects a strategy to further develop the students' understanding of the text. Strategies such as sequencing or summarizing the events of the story, creating a story map, using a graph or table to organize information presented in the story, and comparing and contrasting the story to another familiar text can be used to help the students construct meaning from the text. Only after a discussion of the meaning of the text does the teacher discuss the prosodic elements of the text.

The discussion of the prosodic elements is very text specific. Teachers should focus on helping students read the text using language patterns that they would use if they were talking. For example, in the story *Who Said Red?* by Mary Serfozo, a little boy is looking for his red kite. His sister, who is helping him, keeps asking him the color of his kite. In the story, the repeated refrain, "No, I said red," is printed in all capital letters. In an examination of the prosodic elements of this text, the teacher would discuss how the capitalized words are a reflection of the little boy's feelings. The students should practice the dialogue, reading it as if they were talking. Other prosodic features for discussion might include distinguishing between question and statement voices; understanding the character's expressed emotion, such as anger, sadness, joy, or disgust; and reading longer phrases with appropriate pauses.

The final aspect of the Oral Recitation Lesson includes performance of the text. For *Who Said Red?* the text can be divided into the sister's dialogue and the little boy's repeated response. The class can read the sister's part while one volunteer can be chosen to be the little boy. In addition to stories, nursery rhymes are particularly easy to perform because they usually require simple props. For example, a stool, plastic bowl and spoon are all that is needed for "Little Miss Muffet," from *Brian Wildsmith's Mother Goose.* After modeling a fluent oral reading of the text and teaching a comprehension lesson, the teacher selects students to act out the rhyme while the rest of the class reads it from individual copies of the text. Young children love to read the text, when upon the pronouncement of the word *away*, they can watch one of their classmates scream and toss the bowl and spoon into the air. If there are enough props, students can be grouped so that individual students read independently while the other students in the group act out the text. Of course, students should rotate their roles so that each student has the opportunity to read and act.

Choral reading. A final suggestion for incorporating fluency training in the regular read-ing classroom includes the use of poetry in choral reading lessons. Miccinati (1985) explained that "through choral reading, children learn to enjoy listening and responding to sound, stress, duration, and pitch" (p. 207). These are the prosodic cues necessary for fluent oral reading to take place. As children develop their skills in detecting prosodic features of a specific selection, their abilities to identify patterns of syntax also develop. Poetry can be read by the class in unison, a line per child, or by groups, or students can simply learn and analyze the prosodic features of a refrain. All these methods lend themselves to fluent oral reading practice.

For choral reading of poetry, it is helpful to write the poem on chart paper or provide each student with an individual copy of the text. If the text is on chart paper, adding an illustration to develop meaning for the students is helpful. For the poem "September" from Maurice Sendak's *Chicken Soup With Rice*, a picture of a child riding a crocodile down a river of chicken soup organizes the nonsense of the poem. Developing a simple motion to match the meaning of each phrase also helps the students read the poem with fluency. If each student has a copy of the selection, the poem can be used for paired oral reading as well. Repeated reading of the poetry can be encouraged by allowing the students to take home their individual copies.

In addition to the regular reading classroom, fluency instruction can also be incorporated in the individualized reading lesson. DeFord (1991) proposed that fluency should and can be a goal for poor readers who require individualized instruction. The Reading Recovery lesson as developed by Marie Clay (see DeFord, 1991) provides ample time for modeling and instruction in the prosodic features of not one but several texts. This would occur at the beginning of the lesson when children engage in repeated reading of familiar texts. During these readings, teachers have the opportunity to work on natural phrasing as well as rate and automatic word recognition.

DeFord (1991) suggested three methods to increase oral reading fluency when the student rereads familiar texts at the beginning of the lesson. The teacher can break the text into phrases, asking the child to read each phrase smoothly, emphasizing that "a phrase is read as a unit" (p. 209). The teacher and the student can read the familiar text together, the teacher setting the pace of the reading and modeling appropriate phrasing. The teacher can also choose to move a marker under the text to increase the rate of the reading.

Integrating fluency and comprehension

There are two suggestions for selecting text that will encourage fluent oral reading when implementing all of these methods (Zutell & Rasinski, 1991). First, teachers should use texts at an instructional level, if not an independent level, when the purpose of instruction is fluency training. Second, teachers should choose texts that model natural language patterns. This precludes most basal readers because "the word difficulty and sentence length controls built into beginning basal series and high interest-low vocabulary materials often interfere with the predictability inherent in natural language, so that the texts themselves inhibit fluent oral reading" (1991, p. 216). Hoffman and Isaacs (1991) recommended text with a predictable structure. Texts with a rhyming pattern, repeating refrain, or cumulative episodes are considered different types of predictable text. If fluency is to be developed, not only appropriate methods but also appropriate materials must be used.

Finally, it is important to remember that while students can be trained to read fluently, this instruction should not ignore, and does not preclude, comprehension of the text. Good detectives will seek to help children understand contextual clues as well as syntactic clues. The Oral Recitation Lesson especially lends itself to integrating these two goals. It prescribes comprehending the text before asking students to read the text fluently. The use of poetry for fluency instruction also demands the incorporation of comprehension instruction. When poetry is read aloud, it is the comprehension of the author's meaning that allows the reader to competently express the phrasing, rhythm, and rhyme of the text. Otherwise, it becomes a fluent "singsong" that deprives the reader and the audience of the poem's inherent joy and meaning.

Many teachers evaluate their students' oral reading fluency without a complete understanding of the three interactive aspects of this reading component. If assessment is going to take place in this area, teachers should make sure students receive instruction in oral reading fluency. Many methods of instruction have recently been developed in order to make this possible. Fluency may be elusive, but not necessarily unattainable. Fortunately, there are many ways to help today's students capture fluency and achieve success in oral reading.

References

Allington, R.L. (1983). Fluency: The neglected reading goal. *The Reading Teacher, 36,* 556–561.

Bear, D.R. (1991). "Learning to fasten the seat of my union suit without looking around": The synchrony of literacy development. *Theory Into Practice, 30,* 149–157.

DeFord, D.E. (1991). Fluency in initial reading instruction: A Reading Recovery lesson. *Theory Into Practice, 30,* 201–210.

Dowhower, S.L. (1989). Repeated reading: Research into practice. *The Reading Teacher, 42,* 502–507.

Dowhower, S.L. (1991). Speaking of prosody: Fluency's unattended bedfellow. *Theory Into Practice, 30,* 165–173.

Hoffman, J.V., & Isaacs, M.E. (1991). Developing fluency through restructuring the task of guided oral reading. *Theory Into Practice, 30,* 185–194.

Koskinen, P.A., & Blum, I.H. (1984). Paired repeated reading: A classroom strategy for developing fluent reading. *The Reading Teacher, 40,* 70–75.

Lipson, M.Y., & Wixson, K.K. (1997). *Assessment and instruction of reading and writing disability.* New York: Longman.

Miccinati, J.L. (1985). Using prosodic cues to teach oral reading fluency. *The Reading Teacher, 39,* 206–211.

Nathan, R.G., & Stanovich, K.E. (1991). The causes and consequences of differences in reading fluency. *Theory Into Practice, 30,* 176–184.

Rasinski, T.V., & Zutell, J.B. (1990). Making a place for fluency instruction in the regular reading curriculum. *Reading Research and Instruction, 29*(2), 85–91.

Stayter, F.Z., & Allington, R.L. (1991). Fluency and the understanding of texts. *Theory Into Practice, 30,* 143–148.

Stieglitz, E.L. (1992). *The Stieglitz informal reading inventory.* Boston: Allyn & Bacon.

Taylor, N.E., & Connor, U. (1982). Silent vs. oral reading: The rational instructional use of both processes. *The Reading Teacher, 35,* 440–443.

Zutell, J., & Rasinski, T.V. (1991). Training teachers to attend to their students' oral reading fluency. *Theory Into Practice, 30,* 211–217.

Children's books cited

Sendak, Maurice. (1962). *Chicken soup with rice.* New York: HarperCollins.

Serfozo, Mary. (1988). *Who said red?* New York: Simon & Schuster.

Wildsmith, Brian. (1964). Little Miss Muffet. *Brian Wildsmith's Mother Goose.* New York: Franklin Watts.

Vocabulary Development

> *Vocabulary is stored information about the meanings and pronunciations of words necessary for communication.*

Findings in the National Reading Panel Report

Children learned the meanings of most words indirectly, through everyday experiences with oral and written language.

Some vocabulary, particularly technical and very subject-specific words, was learned through direct instruction.

Quality vocabulary instruction led to gains in reading comprehension.

The following were found to be effective: keyword method, incidental learning, repeated exposure, preteaching of vocabulary, restructuring reading materials, context method.

Vocabulary development has a long history of study in relation to reading. There are five types of vocabulary:

- Listening vocabulary—the words needed to understand what is heard

- Speaking vocabulary—the words used when speaking

- Reading vocabulary—the words needed to understand what is read

- Writing vocabulary—the words used in writing

- Sight vocabulary—those words that can be identified without explicit decoding during reading

The NRP Report notes that the importance of vocabulary in reading achievement has been recognized for more than half a century. Many studies have shown that reading ability and vocabulary size are related. Early descriptions of reading comprehension viewed reading as consisting of two skills, word knowledge, or vocabulary, and reasoning in reading (Davis, 1944).

In early reading the reader translates the relatively unfamiliar words in print into more familiar speech forms of the words. If readers recognize and have meanings stored for the spoken forms (i.e., the word is in their speaking vocabulary), they gradually add such words to their reading vocabulary. Later in reading development, readers are able to add both pronunciations and meanings for words encountered first in print rather than in speech to their reading vocabulary.

Despite the fact that there are strong correlations between vocabulary size and reading achievement, it has been difficult to demonstrate that teaching vocabulary improves reading comprehension. The difficulty is probably related to the fact that vocabulary is learned both directly and indirectly. Estimates of how many words elementary children learn per year vary, but an estimate of over 2,000 words per year is quite reasonable (Nagy & Scott, 2000). Direct teaching of vocabulary cannot possibly account for the learning of so many words; however, research has shown that teaching of particular vocabulary such as technical words and words central to understanding narrative text can improve reading comprehension. It is clear, as the NRP Report specifically states, "vocabulary should be taught both directly and indirectly" (p. 4-27).

The first article in this section, "Vocabulary instruction in a balanced reading program," by William H. Rupley, John W. Logan, and William D. Nichols, provides an explanation of indirect vocabulary learning and presents a number of techniques for direct instruction of vocabulary. The article highlights concept wheel/circle, semantic word map, webbing, concept of definition, and semantic feature analysis.

The remaining four articles in this section are brief descriptions of particular vocabulary instructional strategies. "Word detectives," by Dodie Ainslie, addresses incidental learning of vocabulary and provides a strategy to encourage incidental learning. The strategy immerses children in reading while encouraging them to find out the meaning of unknown words. "Said Webs: Remedy for tired words," by Kathryn L. Laframboise, is an instructional technique specifically directed at developing synonyms for the overused word *said*. "Vocabulary anchors: Building conceptual connections with young readers," by Rod Winters, draws from strategies developed by upper grade content area teachers to help elementary teachers with strategies for dealing with technical vocabulary in informational prose. The final article, "Fun with vocabulary," by Janet Towell, uses a vocabulary acrostic to introduce enjoyable and effective strategies and activities for vocabulary instruction.

References

Davis, F.B. (1944). Fundamental factors in reading comprehension. *Psychometrika, 9*, 185–197.

Nagy, W.E., & Scott, J.A. (2000). Vocabulary processes. In M.L. Kamil, P.B. Mosenthal, P.D. Pearson, and R. Barr (Eds.), *Handbook of Reading Research, Vol. 3*, pp. 269–284. Mahwah, NJ: Erlbaum.

William H. Rupley
John W. Logan
William D. Nichols

Vocabulary instruction in a balanced reading program

Although somewhat overlooked in recent years, vocabulary (word meaning) development is a critical aspect of successful reading.
This article explores the role of vocabulary in reading development and suggests some classroom-tested approaches for nurturing vocabulary development and interest in students.

Children's word recognition capability, vocabulary growth, and comprehension development are essential components of a balanced reading program. Reading instruction that focuses on the growth of children's vocabulary results in enhancing their abilities to infer meanings and to better comprehend what they read. As noted by Daneman (1991), vocabulary is partially an outcome of comprehension skills, and reading comprehension is partially an outcome of vocabulary. Thus, they provide a mutual benefit in promoting reading development. As children's vocabulary grows their ability to comprehend what they read grows as well; furthermore, as their comprehension skills grow so do their abilities to learn new words from context.

Children with broad vocabulary knowledge are better able to infer the meanings of unfamiliar words in the texts that they read. Vocabulary knowledge supports the reader's text processing and interaction with the author, which in turn promote the formation and validation of concepts and learning. The author's and the reader's vocabulary and experiences are woven together to form the fabric of learning, confirming, reasoning, experiencing, enjoying, and imagining.

However, vocabulary instruction has not been a focus of recent professional writing and discussion. Although *The Reading Teacher* has published articles during the past year on word recognition and comprehension instruction, there have been no articles devoted to vocabulary instruction. Indeed, only 2% of all submissions for *The Reading Teacher* in 1997 dealt with instruction in vocabulary (Padak & Rasinski, 1998). Moreover, Cassidy and Wenrich (1998/1999) report that the consensus of literacy leaders is that vocabulary is currently *not* a hot topic.

Vocabulary instruction is an integral component of teaching children how to read both narrative and informational text. We advocate a balanced approach to teaching vocabulary— at one end of the continuum is writing word definitions and at the other end is learning vocabulary solely through contextual reading and experience. We recommend an eclectic approach in which both direct instruction and wide reading are means for fostering vocabulary development.

Children who are capable decoders often experience difficulty in reading when they encounter too many words for which they have no meaning. As students are expected to use reading to acquire new information, the role of vocabulary knowledge takes on greater importance. Not having access to the meaning of words representative of the concepts and content of what they read causes difficulty in children's comprehension of texts, limits their ability to make a connection with their existing background knowledge, and inhibits their capacity to make coherent inferences (Heilman, Blair, & Rupley, 1998). Because it further nurtures children's comprehension development, vocabulary knowledge is a critical part of a balanced reading instruction program.

Vocabulary growth

Continuous cultivation of students' language ability is the foundation for vocabulary growth. Readers and writers share meanings through their direct experiences with people, places, objects, and events and through their vicarious experiences, including interactive technology, videotapes, pictures, movies, reading, and writing. Children's vocabulary knowledge closely reflects their breadth of real-life and vicarious experiences. Without some knowledge of the concepts that written words represent, students cannot comprehend well. Vocabulary is a shared component of writing and reading—it helps the author and the reader to interact and the reader to comprehend through the shared word meanings.

Students' knowledge of words can range from simple to complex. Word knowledge can be viewed as a "continuum from no knowledge; to a general sense, such as knowing that mendacious has a negative connotation; to narrow, context-bound knowledge; to having knowledge but not being able to access it quickly; to rich decontextualized knowledge of a word meaning" (Beck & McKeown, 1991, p. 792). One form of simple level word knowledge is definitional. Definitional knowledge is word knowledge based upon a definition that may come from a dictionary, thesaurus, glossary, word bank, or other individuals. Often, however, definitions do not help a reader understand or infer the contribution of an unknown word's meanings to the text. To comprehend, a reader needs some idea of not only a word's meanings, but also the ways in which the meaning contributes to the cohesiveness of the ideas or information.

Another simple level of word knowledge is contextual. Contextual knowledge is word meaning derived from context, which can include a sentence, a passage, a discussion, or a picture (Watts, 1995). However, contextual clues have limitations in enabling children to

---

Children's vocabulary knowledge closely reflects their breadth of real-life and vicarious experiences.

---

derive the meaning of words. Use of context to derive the contribution of word meanings to the comprehension of text requires knowledge of the content and how the meanings of words combine to facilitate communication of the content through author and reader interaction. Often extracted text (sentence or short paragraphs) has inadequate context for enabling children to use their prior knowledge to know or to infer the meaning of a word. Consider the following:

Randy became very nervous as the doctor's assistant approached him with the sphygmomanometer.

The sentence context helps to some degree to understand the general setting of the event (perhaps a doctor's office), that Randy is experiencing fear or excitement, and that the sphygmomanometer is a thing. However, none of this context is helpful in inferring the meaning of the word until we read further.

She asked him to roll up his sleeve so that she could take his blood pressure. Wrapping the wide band tightly around his upper arm, she commented, "This new sphygmomanometer is so much more accurate in taking a patient's blood pressure than the old one we used to have."

Able readers integrate information as they read to construct meaning. If context is not enough to derive meaning from an unknown word, skilled readers use their language knowledge to help them infer meaning. They perform these operations so rapidly and automatically that they are not aware of them.

Vocabulary and concept development

Readers' experiential and conceptual backgrounds are extremely important in vocabulary development. Background experiences are what readers use to develop, expand, and refine concepts that words represent. Tennyson and Cocchiarella (1986) note that there are two phases in the learning of concepts. The first phase is an understanding of the function of concepts in relation to their attributes (which they refer to as prototypes) and then making connections of new concepts with existing concepts. The second phase is using procedural knowledge, which is "the classification skills of generalizing to and discriminating between newly encountered instances of associated concepts" (p. 44). In phase 1, individuals may undergeneralize and overgeneralize due to their limited experiences with concept. This is often evident in young children when, for example, they call all large animals in a pasture "cows" and all liquids for drinking "milk" or "juice." In phase 2, children can distinguish between cows and horses and various liquids for drinking. Vocabulary expands when children have numerous opportunities to encounter new words and examples that are representative of these words in rich contextual settings. Individuals do not use restricted definitions of words as they read, but construct word meaning in terms of context for the concepts that represent their background knowledge.

Active processing of vocabulary

By building connections between "old" vocabulary words and new words found in their reading, students begin to understand relationships among words they encounter. When instruction is based on building connections, students are not just asked to supply words that fit the example, but rather to describe how words fit in the stories and informational text that they read. As we visit and participate in elementary classrooms we see many children such as Matthew, who just finished reading the first chapter of *The Dinosaur Who Lived in My Backyard* (Davis & Hennessy, 1990) and used "enormous" to describe the size of the dinosaur. His teacher smiled and commented on his vocabulary, "Can you think of some other words that you might expect to find in the book?"

Matt smiled and said, "Yep, gigantic, huge, and colossal. Kinda like King Kong."

Such discussions and activities that relate and support the integration of new words and the concepts they represent to the children's past experiences help to expand their vocabularies in a meaningful manner.

Knowing a word in the fullest sense goes beyond simply being able to define it or get some gist of it from the context. Active processing that associates experiences and concepts with words contributes significantly to vocabulary growth, enhanced comprehension, and continuous learning. Vocabulary instruction that encourages children to discuss, elaborate, and demonstrate meanings of new words, and provides varied opportunities for them to use new words outside of their classroom has been shown to be effective (Beck, Perfetti, & McKeown, 1982). Such vocabulary instruction is based on and encourages active processing of word meaning.

Active process vocabulary instruction

Teaching vocabulary in a balanced reading program should be grounded in teacher-directed instruction, varied opportunities for students to practice and apply their word knowledge, and exposure to wide reading and writing activities in both narrative and informational texts. Students ought to be engaged in learning new words and expanding their understanding of words through instruction that is based on active processing. That is, students are not just memorizing definitions but are entering information and integrating word meanings with their existing knowledge to build conceptual representations of vocabulary in multiple contextual situations. The following instructional guidelines (Blachowicz & Fisher, 1996; Blachowicz & Lee, 1991) reflect the inclusion of these active processing components.

1. Select words for vocabulary instruction that come from texts that students will read in the classroom. This helps make the meanings of words relevant to the context in which they appear and helps to build connections between existing knowledge and new knowledge. Students encounter the new words in a confirmatory manner rather than as an unknown word.

2. Base instruction on language activities as a primary means of word learning. The focus of the activities should be on engaging the students in generating the learning of new words to enhance remembering and deep processing of the words. Students should be provided multiple

opportunities to use new words in their speaking, listening, reading, and writing activities.

3. Build a conceptual base for learning new words. Use analogies, language features, and other relationships to known words to activate students' background knowledge of concepts related to new words.

4. Provide a variety of instructional strategies to store word knowledge (mental pictures, visual aids, kinesthetic associations, smells, tastes, etc.).

Instructional activities that allow for a visual display of words and promote students' comparing and contrasting of new words to known words can be a beneficial means for increasing their vocabulary knowledge. Semantic mapping, semantic feature analysis, word mapping, and webbing are effective instructional strategies that incorporate many of the guidelines for active processing of vocabulary. These instructional activities enable students to expand their vocabularies, understand relationships between existing and new information, and learn. Visual displays of words can be used to preteach essential concepts and information in texts before students read. The teaching and reviewing of key concept words prior to reading help students activate their background knowledge, relate this knowledge to new concepts, and understand how new words and concepts are related.

Applications and examples of active process vocabulary instruction

It is important that vocabulary instructional practices immerse students in language-rich activities that teach words in meaningful reading experiences. Vocabulary emphases include teacher-directed instruction and appropriate practice in specific skills along with broad reading and writing opportunities. Vocabulary instruction is often criticized when it is taught in isolation of text and becomes a dictionary activity in which students copy definitions of words and then write sentences using these words. Instruction such as this, which avoids active student engagement in vocabulary and concept development, does not connect to students' previous knowledge. A richer vocabulary experience would be to have students first write sentences using the vocabulary words, then use the dictionary to confirm if the sentence context used an acceptable meaning of the word. Vocabulary instruction, whether it is focused on narrative or informational text, is most effective when it relates new words or derivations of words to existing vocabulary and background knowledge.

Vocabulary instruction that encourages children to discuss, elaborate, and demonstrate meanings of new words and that provides varied opportunities to use new words outside of their classroom has been shown to be effective.

The following classroom vignettes are illustrative of how a teacher, Ms. Marie Thomas, uses exemplary vocabulary strategies in her classroom. Ms. Thomas is an amalgamation of the countless teachers with whom we have worked. She embodies characteristics of many of the teachers we have visited, worked with, and observed over numerous years—teachers who recognize that vocabulary is the glue that holds stories, ideas, and content together and that it facilitates making comprehension accessible for children. Ms. Thomas is representative of teachers who shared with us how their learning about effective vocabulary instruction in reading, science, math, writing, and social studies gave them newfound enthusiasm for teaching. She represents the teacher in one of our staff development projects who said, "I have grown not only in my teaching but in my learning, also. I learned how to actively use vocabulary instruction in my teaching of science."

Concept wheel/circle

One instructional technique that builds on students' background knowledge, encourages brainstorming and discussion, and at the same time visually displays the connection between previous conceptual knowledge and the new word being encountered is the concept wheel/circle (see Figure 1).

Ms. Thomas teaches science to a fifth-grade class of approximately 20 students. She begins her lesson one morning incorporating the concept wheel or concept circle into her current science lesson. She explains to her class, "Today, we're going to be studying

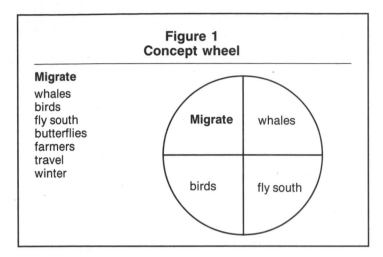

Figure 1
Concept wheel

Migrate

whales
birds
fly south
butterflies
farmers
travel
winter

| Migrate | whales |
| birds | fly south |

several terms that relate to our subject about animals and their environment." The first word she suggests is *migrate*.

She begins by asking her class, "Okay class, what are some words that come to mind when you think of migrate?"

Suzy raises her hand and calls out, "Whales! Whales in the ocean, not at Sea World!"

Ms. Thomas responds, "That's good, Suzy! Why did you think of whales?"

Suzy answers, "This weekend my mom and I watched a show on TV that said something about whales swimming from one part of the ocean to the other looking for food and stuff. My mom told me that whales that live in places like Sea World can't do that because they live in a big tank."

Ms. Thomas calls on Todd: "I think of butterflies and birds because they fly."

Greg raises his hand and responds, "Yeah, but birds don't just fly. I think they fly south or somewhere warmer."

Ms. Thomas asks the students to suggest where the birds might fly, and Amy states, "I know. Birds fly to Florida in the winter because it never snows and they can stay warm."

Ms. Thomas acknowledges that everyone has responded well and prompts the students to continue suggesting a few more words.

Scott raises his hand, and when he is called on responds, "I think that migrate means to travel or move to another city or something." When asked to explain, Scott continues, "Well, people and birds or whatever travel to places when they want to be warmer like Greg said."

"That's very good, Scott. Does anyone else have any suggestions?"

"I think migrate has something to do with winter, but I'm not sure," offers Erin.

Alicia calls out, "I think of farmers when I think of migrate because they've got animals like sheep and cows that move around from pasture to pasture."

Ms. Thomas asks the students to end the suggestions and proceeds to generate a list of words that fit appropriately with migrate. She includes all of the suggested words, and they are written on the chalkboard. Upon the completion of the list she directs the students to turn to page 342 in their science textbook, find the word *migrate*, and listen as she reads the glossary definition of the word. The students compare their generated list of words to the definition.

Ms. Thomas then tells the class, "I'd like everyone to look over these words on the board very carefully. Now based upon the definition located in the glossary, you need to decide on at least three words from this list that will help you remember the word migrate. I want you to write your selected words in your wheel and turn in your assignment at 10:30."

Suzy chooses her words and writes down *whales*, *birds*, and *fly south* in her concept wheel.

Another way to use the concept wheel is to allow students to place the correct vocabulary word with the corresponding concept wheel. Then the students identify the concept that is being completed by providing a name for the wheel. This approach has several alternative modifications to fit the various needs of teacher/student instruction.

Semantic word map

Semantic word maps allow students to conceptually explore their knowledge of a new word by mapping it with other words or phrases, which categorically share meaning with the new word. Words that function as labels for and as a means of integration of concepts do not often clearly demonstrate the meaning behind the concept when viewed alone. Word maps allow students to learn the connection among several words in order to provide a clearer definition of the concept represented. The concept becomes clearer when words are grouped together by similar criteria such as ideas, events, characteristics, examples, and so forth. Word maps work best when the teacher allows students time to brainstorm, generate a list, and participate in whole-class or small-group discussion. Once the list is generated the teacher can allow small groups to work together to create a semantic word map. It is important to remember to allow time for the groups to share their ideas on how they constructed their semantic map. Processes used by students often provide teachers with a richer, deeper understanding into students' base of understanding than will the final product.

Ms. Thomas decides to use a semantic word map while teaching her lessons on different forms of energy. She begins her class by asking, "Does everyone remember last Friday when I explained that we would be spending this week exploring different types of energy? Well, we are going to start today's lesson with solar energy as the first type of energy. I'd like everyone to brainstorm as many words as they can regarding solar energy."

For the next half hour, students give suggestions similar to Ermine's, "My dad told me that solar energy comes from the sun and is a form of power."

Ms. Thomas says, "You're right, Ermine. The sun is how the energy becomes available, and the power it gives off is an effect of solar energy."

More students respond with words related to their ideas of solar energy while Ms. Thomas affirms their examples by listing their words on the board. Once the class as a whole suggested all the words they could think of, Ms. Thomas says, "Next, I'd like you to organize the list of words that have been suggested and place the appropriate words under the categories that we discussed, such as effects, cost, education, and feasibility. You will work in small groups to complete this activity. In your groups, I want you to decide which words belong under the appropriate categories. Be sure to discuss why you placed the terms under the selected categories. I'll give you about 10 minutes to complete your word map."

Using this process the students begin to determine which words are appropriate and which words should be excluded. As each group discusses the construction of their word maps, Ms. Thomas walks around the room observing each group's progress and assisting when needed.

At the end of the 10 minutes Ms. Thomas interjects, "Okay, everyone! I saw some good work going on within your groups. I'd like to spend the rest of the period allowing each group to come up to the front of the class and present your semantic word maps."

Hector, Alicia, Donald, and Rose Marie volunteer to be first and proceed to explain their word map and how they decided to choose each word for the appropriate category. The word map in Figure 2 is an example of their work.

Webbing

A method that graphically illustrates how to associate words meaningfully and allows students to make connections between what they know about words and how words are related is semantic webbing. It allows students to see the relationship between words and concepts that they have previously experienced or read. In order to ensure that students grasp the features and purposes of webbing, the teacher can use a web with an empty center. Students can begin to understand the relationship of words in the web by choosing and considering words that might complete the center word.

Following the lesson on solar energy, Ms. Thomas introduces the next energy lesson, on electricity. "We're going to do some more brainstorming. Someone give me a word that comes to mind when you think of electricity," she asks.

As Jerome raises his hand he suggests, "I think of lightning when I think of electricity."

Ms. Thomas responds as she writes the suggestion on the board, "Good, Jerome. Can someone think of a word related to lightning or electricity?"

Tom calls out, "Yeah! Wasn't it Benjamin Franklin who flew his kite and discovered electricity?"

As the lesson progresses, one student suggests Thomas Edison while another person suggests light bulbs because Thomas Edison invented the light bulb. Along with the comments, Ms. Thomas writes the words on the board and links them together appropriately. After one student mentions Christmas lights, Rose Marie asks, "Wouldn't Santa go with Christmas lights?"

Ms. Thomas writes down her suggestion and redirects the students' comments back to electricity-related words so that the focus remains

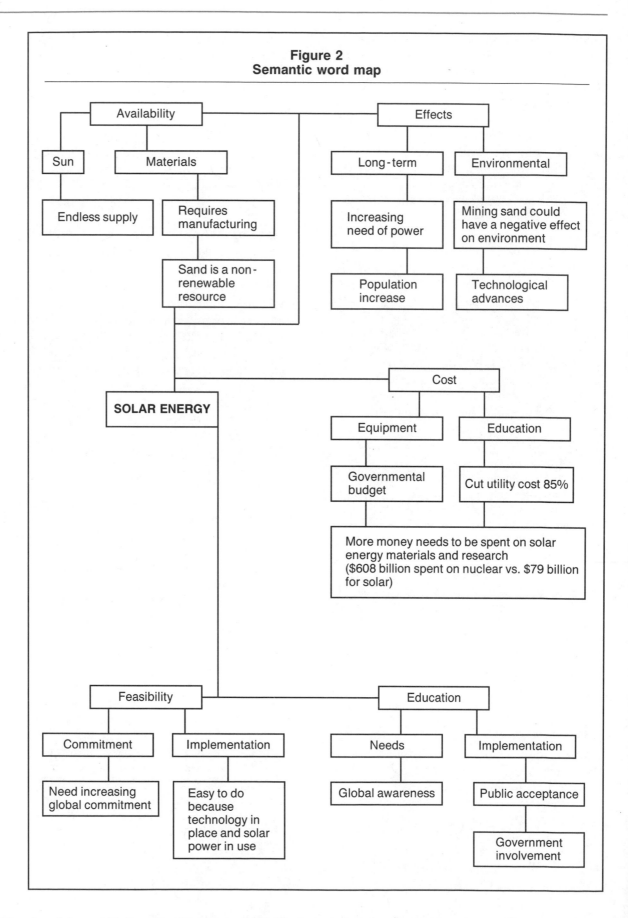

Figure 2
Semantic word map

on the key concept. The result of the class discussion can be seen in the example in Figure 3.

Concept of definition

A variation of concept mapping and webbing is a procedure that Schwartz and Raphael (1985) refer to as concept of definition, which provides a framework for organizing information in order to define new vocabulary words. Concept of definition instruction enables students to clarify the meaning of unknown terms by using a hierarchical structure to conceptualize the definition of the new term. Concept of definition makes use of categories (What is it?), properties (What is it like?), illustrations (What are some examples?), and comparisons (How are examples same or different?) in order to provide students with a clear understanding of the new term. After mapping the word, students should supply an oral or written definition for the given concept, and the teacher should pro-

vide assistance to help students realize that the amount of properties and illustrations may vary depending on the complexity of the new term.

Application of concept of definitions was evident in Ms. Thomas's class in a lesson on animals and their environment. "Let's spend some time today discussing a type of animal and related ideas. The first animal type is fish. I'd like everyone to pay attention to the following ideas: categories (What is it?), properties (What is it like?), illustrations (What are some examples?), and comparisons (How are examples same and/or different?). With each idea, brainstorm together to come up with words that you believe belong under each category."

Amy raises her hand and mentions, "I think that fish are scaly."

Ms. Thomas responds, "That's true, Amy. What do you think *scaly* means?"

"Being scaly is when you have rough skin or flakes on your body like a fish."

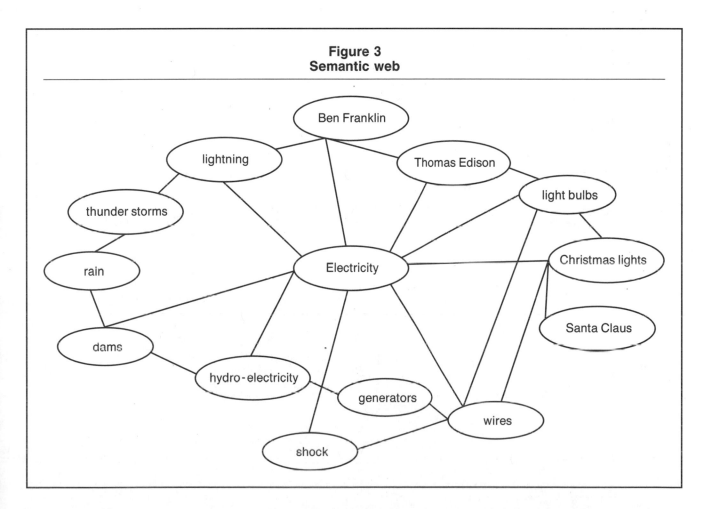

Figure 3
Semantic web

Ms. Thomas writes *scaly* on the chalkboard and asks Amy for the category of the word. Amy says, "I guess it would fall under properties because it describes what the fish is like."

As each student provides different words, Ms. Thomas asks for a definition and where the word should be placed. After the completion of the organizer Ms. Thomas asks the students to write a description of fish similar to ones located in their science text. The students then compare their written descriptions with the text. Ms. Thomas' class created the concept of definition in Figure 4.

Semantic feature analysis

Semantic feature analysis can also help students understand relationships among words and relate their background knowledge to new words. This approach is beneficial to students when words are closely related by class or common features. In order for students to analyze common vocabulary the teacher lists several familiar words that are related, such as types of fish, on a chart. Next, the teacher guides the students to discuss features or characteristics associated with the words listed. As students suggest features, these are written across the top of the chart (e.g., location, size, behavior), creating a matrix that the students can complete in terms of presence (+) or absence (–). As the students broaden and define their concepts, the teacher adds words and features to the list and analyzes them. Semantic feature analysis is a strategy that can be used

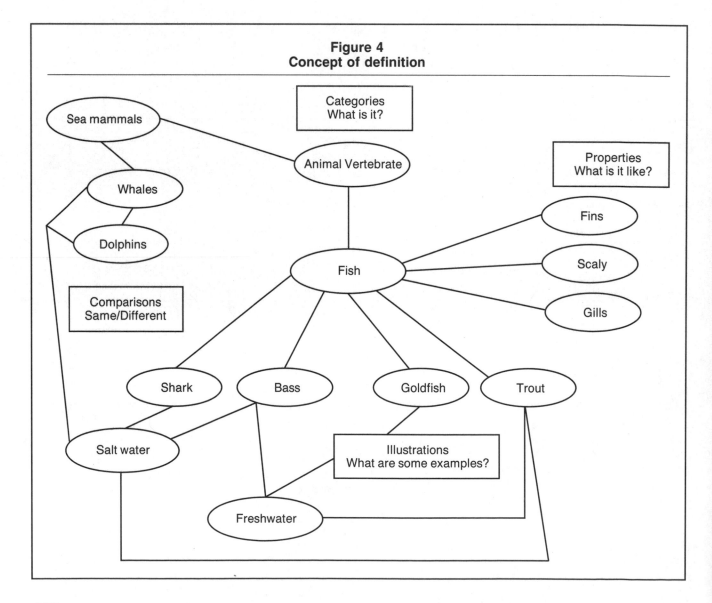

**Figure 4
Concept of definition**

for both narrative and informational texts. The arrays can be developed and expanded as students' background knowledge grows. During a subsequent lesson, Ms. Thomas brings exciting news to class, "I have thought of a good way to conclude our unit on fish. How does an aquarium set up in our classroom sound?"

The students are unanimously excited. Alicia offers an idea. "Ms. Thomas, my dad has an aquarium in his restaurant and it has goldfish in it. Could we have goldfish in ours too? They're really colorful."

Billy raises his hand and asks, "What about angelfish?"

Ms. Thomas explains, "These are all good suggestions. Let's decide which types of fish we want, where they would live in the aquarium, how big they're going to be, and how they will interact with other fish. So far we have two types, angelfish and goldfish. Let's figure out their characteristics as well as suggest some more kinds of fish."

After much discussion the students and the teacher decide on the three following characteristics: location, size, and behavior. The class reached the decision that they wanted an aquarium that was peaceful and had as many fish as possible located throughout the tank. Ms. Thomas then asked her students to complete the semantic feature analysis based on their existing knowledge about the various types of fish that they listed.

Once the students completed their organizer she said, "Now, I would like you to use the variety of texts about fish located in the science center to check your predictions and complete your semantic feature analysis."

The students enthusiastically began their scientific investigation using the selected resources provided by the teacher. Once all students had completed their organizer Ms. Thomas shared her completed organizer so that the students could compare their own research with hers (see Figure 5).

Figure 5
Semantic feature analysis

| Types of fish | Location | | | Size | | | Behavior | | |
	Bottom	Middle	Top	Small	Middle	Large	Peaceful	Aggressive	Violent
Algae Eater									
Angelfish									
Black Molly									
Dwarf Gourami									
Goldfish									
Guppy									
Neon Tetra									
Piranha									
Siamese Fighting									
Zebra-fish									

Teaching vocabulary versus incidental learning of words through wide reading should not be viewed as competing philosophies. Some students may not benefit from incidental learning but do benefit from teacher-directed instruction that initially teaches word meaning by application in meaningful narrative and expository text (McKeown, 1993). Much of the criticism leveled at vocabulary teaching concerns practices in which students are not actively involved in the personal discussion and use of words, such as defining words using a dictionary and writing sentences for those words. Any instructional practice must be called into question that neglects the teaching of words in meaningful context and fails to immerse the students in vocabulary-rich activities. Vocabulary instruction that is geared to the active process of learning and connects new information to previously learned experiences provides the means for students to make the connection between new words and their past experiences. The key to successful vocabulary instruction builds upon students' background knowledge and makes explicit the connections between new words and what they already know.

References

Beck, I., & McKeown, M. (1991). Conditions of vocabulary acquisition. In R. Barr, M. Kamil, P. Mosenthal, & P. Pearson (Eds.), *Handbook of reading research* (Vol. 2, pp. 789–814). White Plains, NY: Longman.

Beck, I., Perfetti, C.A., & McKeown, M. (1982). The effects of long-term vocabulary instruction on lexical access and reading comprehension. *Journal of Educational Psychology, 74,* 506–520.

Blachowicz, C., & Fisher, P. (1996). *Teaching vocabulary in all classrooms.* Upper Saddle River, NJ: Merrill/Prentice Hall.

Blachowicz, C., & Lee, J. (1991). Vocabulary development in the literacy classroom. *The Reading Teacher, 45,* 188–195.

Cassidy, J., & Wenrich, J.K. (1998/1999). Literacy research and practice: What's hot, what's not, and why. *The Reading Teacher, 52,* pp. 378–382.

Daneman, M. (1991). Individual differences in reading skills. In R. Barr, M. Kamil, P. Mosenthal, & P. Pearson (Eds.), *Handbook of reading research* (Vol. 2, pp. 512–538). White Plains, NY: Longman.

Davis, S., & Hennessy, B.G. (1990). *The dinosaur who lived in my backyard.* London: Puffin.

Heilman, A.W., Blair, T.R., & Rupley, W.H. (1998). *Principles and practices of teaching reading (9th ed.).* Columbus, OH: Merrill.

McKeown, M.G. (1993). Creating effective definitions for young word learners. *Reading Research Quarterly, 28,* 16–33.

Padak, N., & Rasinski, T. (1998, May). *The Reading Teacher business meeting report.* Paper presented at the annual meeting of the International Reading Association, Orlando, FL.

Schwartz, R.M., & Raphael, T.E. (1985). Concept of definition: A key to improving students' vocabulary. *The Reading Teacher, 39,* 198–205.

Tennyson, R., & Cocchiarella, M. (1986). An empirically based instructional design theory for teaching concepts. *Review of Educational Research, 56,* 40–71.

Watts, S. (1995). Vocabulary instruction during reading lessons in six classrooms. *Journal of Reading Behavior, 27,* 399–424.

Teaching Ideas

Word detectives

Dodie Ainslie

Effective, exciting vocabulary strategies are important in today's classrooms. Teachers have a lot of challenges, especially when it comes to increasing their students' abilities to read and comprehend text. The knowledge and strategies that students bring to their reading are their keys to success. As students learn more vocabulary words they are better equipped to get meaning from their reading. Students who understand how to find out the meaning of unknown vocabulary words as they read not only will become better readers, but also lifelong learners and readers. The challenge that we face as teachers is how to make this vocabulary enriching process an enjoyable one for the students.

To be effective, vocabulary instruction should provide both good definitions and illustrations of how words are used in natural contexts (Nagy, 1988). Because students "learn most of their vocabulary through the act of reading" (Weaver, 1988, p. 125), I propose a vocabulary strategy that immerses them in reading, while at the same time encourages them to find out the meaning of unknown words. How can this be done? Transform the students into "word detectives."

Student word detectives

The word detectives in my classroom take seriously the task of finding their "suspects," or new unknown words. Students have their own individual lists of unknown suspects. They add to this list every time they find an unknown word in their reading. Next to their word they write clues, such as the sentence that the word was in, the definition of that word from the dictionary, and its part of speech. They also add other word clues from the reading that might help them find out the meaning of their unknown word. These clues might take the form of another word, or an explanation of what is going on in the reading that might help them interpret their unknown word. This list of clues goes into their "detective notebook" (a small spiral notebook). This notebook is kept in the students' desks.

Every week, two students get the job of being the lead detectives for the classroom. They each pick one word from their suspect list. Then they make a graphic organizer showing their word, its definition, its part of speech, the sentence it was found in, other contextual clues that they found, and a student-created sentence example (see Figure). They make this organizer into an overhead and show it to their fellow detectives on either Monday or Tuesday. Only one suspect (word) will be shared each day. The other detectives listen to the briefing and take notes on the new word (in their detective notebooks). They may also ask questions about the word. These new words are then added to the class Word Wall and reviewed throughout the week. This review takes a questioning format, with the Lead Detective asking the other detectives questions about the word. Also, the new words will be used for bonus words in that week's spelling test (to be spelled correctly and put into a sentence).

Extensions

Extensions are limitless. As the list of unknown words grows on the Word Wall, many activities can be designed around that list to promote quick recognition and understanding of the words.

• Write the words on cards and put a ring through them so they can be used anywhere.

• When students are waiting in the hall, go down the line asking what the words are.

• If you have 5 minutes to fill, have a past detective try to stump the other detectives with an old word. The past detective might ask "Is this word being used properly in the following sentence?"

• Use the words in various cooperative learning structures, like Four Corners (Kagan, 1994). In this structure, you put four words up in the room, one in each corner. Give each student a definition, a part of speech, or a sentence that uses one of the words written on a card. At "go" the students go to their corner to share with the group, making sure they are in the right corner. Shuffle and try again.

I use this strategy successfully with my fourth-grade class, but it can easily be adapted to any level. Introduce your students to the world of word detectives. The excitement will spread throughout your class and just might make students excited about reading. Students won't shy away from unknown words, but will attack them like seasoned, professional detectives.

Graphic organizer for the suspect word *swaggered*

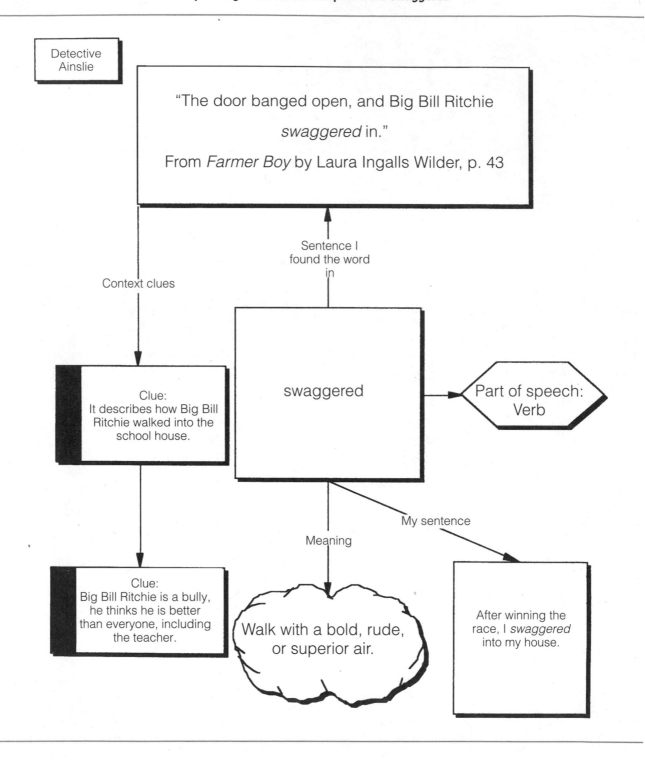

Detective Ainslie

"The door banged open, and Big Bill Ritchie *swaggered* in."

From *Farmer Boy* by Laura Ingalls Wilder, p. 43

Context clues

Sentence I found the word in

swaggered

Part of speech: Verb

Clue:
It describes how Big Bill Ritchie walked into the school house.

Clue:
Big Bill Ritchie is a bully, he thinks he is better than everyone, including the teacher.

Meaning

My sentence

Walk with a bold, rude, or superior air.

After winning the race, I *swaggered* into my house.

References

Kagan, S. (1994). *Cooperative learning*. San Clemente, CA: Kagan Cooperative Learning.

Nagy, W.E. (1988). *Teaching vocabulary to improve reading comprehension*. Urbana, IL: ERIC Clearinghouse on Reading and Communication Skills.

Weaver, C. (1988). *Reading process and practice: From socio-psycholinguistics to whole language*. Portsmouth, NH: Heinemann.

Teaching Reading

Said Webs: Remedy for tired words

Kathryn L. Laframboise

Most children enter school with oral vocabularies of a few thousand words, perhaps as many as 5,000, and reading vocabularies of only a few words. By the time these same children are in sixth grade their oral and reading vocabularies are approximately 20,000 words, and then 90,000 words by ninth grade (Anglin, 1993; White, Graves, & Slater, 1990). Clearly this explosion of word knowledge cannot occur in increments of a few words per week or by haphazard absorption through the environment. Instructional strategies such as vocabulary webs group words by meaning, so that students learn words in meaningful clusters rather than one by one. The "Said Web" is one such strategy that is most useful for examining familiar words and providing opportunities to discern their shades of meaning, to use vocabulary in discussion, and to develop increased awareness of alternatives for words that are already known.

Beck, McKeown, and Omanson (1987) distinguished three levels of vocabulary acquisition: unknown, acquainted, and established levels. For classroom purposes, I describe these three stages as the following:

1. "I haven't a clue." I don't remember ever seeing or hearing that word before, or if I did, I didn't know what you were talking about.

2. "That word seems familiar." I don't use that word in writing or speaking, but if you use it, I recognize it and usually understand what you mean.

3. "I own that word." I can use that word in writing and speaking. I understand its shades of meaning and don't confuse it with other similar words.

Classroom vocabulary instruction must be multifaceted, not only moving words out of the "I haven't a clue" category, but also moving words from familiarity to ownership. Additionally, each language user may own words in some ways, but not have complete understanding of all of the various meanings of a word. The above stages, therefore, are not discreet categories, but rather places along a continuum of vocabulary acquisition. The categories described here help children gauge their own learning of words and see it as a natural and gradual progression that occurs as a result of exposure, reflection, and practice.

The American Federation of Teachers' monograph *Teaching Reading Is Rocket Science* (Moats, 1999), concisely describes some basic premises of the knowledge base and teaching skills needed to successfully teach children to read well. Among these basic components is vocabulary instruction that includes a variety of methods that work together to explore the meanings of words through their relationships to other words. Related vocabulary instruction is taught, for example, by identifying synonyms, antonyms, associative linkages, and connotations, as well as the denotations of words. The Said Web is an instructional strategy that encourages students to examine clusters of words and their linkages to one another so that vocabulary study does not occur as lists of isolated words, but rather as meaningful groups.

These Said Webs are so-called because teachers frequently look for remedies for tired words, starting with the greatly overused word *said*. Although the stories children read or have read to them have great stores of alternatives to tired words, these words frequently do not make it into the child's speech or writing without direct instructional intervention. This webbing strategy provides mechanisms for deeper processing of the meanings of words. Some of the alternative words are unknown, and with exposure to a variety of literature become familiar. They are often skimmed over during reading because contextual cues, such as placement immediately before quotation marks, are strong indicators of the general meaning of the word. The Said Web, therefore, has three purposes: (a) to relate unknown words to known words so they will become familiar, (b) to provide deeper processing of vocabulary information in order to facilitate ownership of words, and (c) to create a reading and writing resource that encourages students to continue exploration of new words as they are encountered during further readings and discussions. The following guide describes each step of the Said Web procedure and provides a rationale for its use.

Instructional steps

1. As a class, brainstorm words the children know that are related to *said*. The brainstorming should not be

exhaustive and can be limited to a few minutes. (See sidebar for examples of word lists.) The resulting list is a "start list" to provide a core of words with which to work during the next steps in the strategy. It is interesting to note here how the children come up with words. *Shouted* may produce a synonym, *yelled*, and an antonym, *whispered*. *Explained*, on the other hand, may produce a similar sounding word, such as *exclaimed*, which is also related in meaning. Encourage the children to explore all clues.

2. Still as a class group, select and circle the words on the list that the students agree are the most common. So if the start list includes *described, answered, asked, thought, explained, whispered, yelled, shouted,* and *responded,* the children may decide that *described, shouted, asked,* and *thought* are the most familiar words and circle them.

3. Divide the class into heterogeneous groups of four or five students. Each group will need chart paper and markers in three colors. Because the result of this activity is a visual display that demonstrates the progression of ideas, for ease of differentiation provide all groups with

Said Web with words added during small group construction of web

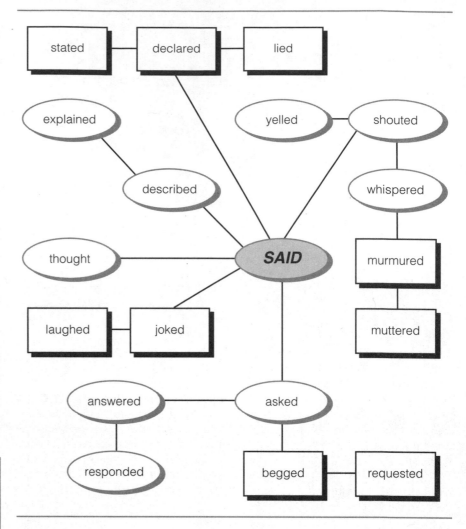

two markers in the same colors, such as red and blue, and then a third marker in a color unique to the group.

4. In the small groups, students will work with the colored markers and chart paper to create webs with the words from the start list. Begin with a single color for each group. Suggest that the words that are circled become the words for the first level of their webs, but groups may make independent decisions to use others as their first level words. They should categorize all words on the start list. Synonyms or antonyms should show their relationships to each other, such as *asked, answered,* and *responded* (see Figure). Members of the group discuss and must agree on the meanings of the words and can use resources to confirm understandings if there are disagreements

among the members. Through these discussions, students gradually refine their understandings of the connotations of words as they try to relate them to one another. As they discern the associations among the words, they may find that there are several possible meanings.

5. As the students work, individual students will remember other related words that were not part of the initial brainstorming. When they add these new words to the web, they should use the second color. (In the Figure, the start words are in the blue ovals and the added words are in the black rectangles.) As the group further refines the web during this step, they may discover that a word has different meanings depending on its related words. For example, *asked* has one connotation as the antonym of *answered* and a different connotation as

Brainstorm word lists for webs

Start words for the Said Web

added	admitted
bragged	called
claimed	cried
declared	demanded
gasped	guessed
laughed	lied
offered	ordered
pleaded	promised
reminded	retorted
sighed	suggested
wondered	

Other tired words for webs

happy	sad
mad	glad
run	walk
big	little
good	bad
laugh	cry

the synonym of *begged* and *requested*. Group members should place a word on the web only when they agree on its relationship to connected words.

6. Next, hang the chart papers around the room in areas where one of the small groups can easily cluster around them to read and make additions. This is called the "carousel." Each group brings along its third colored marker to the carousel, standing at its own web. As the carousel starts, each group moves to the next web on the carousel and has 2 to 3 minutes to read the web and add words. At the end of the designated time, each group moves to the next web on the carousel. The procedures continue until the groups are back at their original webs. They can then add to their own webs any words they learned as they moved around the carousel.

7. At this point, each web has red and blue words from the original work by the large and small groups, as well as new words in several different colors from the carousel. Students then challenge words, asking questions and making statements like, "What does that word mean? Why did you put that word in this group? We think that word should be in another group." From the unique colors of the markers, it is easy to determine which group contributed the words and direct the questions appropriately.

8. Finally, the charts are displayed, and a combined class web can be generated. The web then becomes a reading and writing resource. As additional words are discovered in future reading and writing, they are added to the web. New webs can be generated for other tired words, such as *good*, *big*, and *happy*, or for thematically related words. After the webs become part of the reading and writing center, students begin to examine new words as they encounter them in reading. Brief discussions help decide where newly discovered words belong among the various relationships on the webs.

The Said Web can be used with young children and modified for older students. It capitalizes on the shared knowledge and communication skills of students in a group to help them acquire new vocabulary and refine understandings of known words and their connotations. Through the negotiations that occur during construction of the webs and challenges made after the carousel, students talk through the meanings of words, using definitions, descriptions, and examples, and consult resources to confirm their decisions. The webs lend themselves naturally to vocabulary exploration through the graphic depiction of associations and relationships among concepts, synonyms, and antonyms. With older children who have moved past the discovery of alternatives for tired words, the webs can become a means for examining morphologically related words. The Said Webs provide a jump start for moving words from the unknown to the familiar and a focused strategy that provides reflection and practice leading to ownership of vocabulary.

References

Anglin, J.M. (1993). Vocabulary development: A morphological analysis. *Monographs of the Society for Research in Child Development*, 58, (10, Serial No. 238).

Beck, I.L., McKeown, M.G., & Omanson, R.C. (1987). The effects and uses of diverse vocabulary instructional techniques. In M.C. McKeown & M.E. Curtis (Eds.), *The nature of vocabulary acquisition* (pp. 147–163). Hillsdale, NJ: Erlbaum.

Moats, L.C. (1999). *Teaching reading is rocket science: What expert teachers should know and be able to do.* Washington, DC: American Federation of Teachers.

White, T.G., Graves, M.F., & Slater, W.H. (1990). Growth in reading vocabulary in diverse elementary schools: Decoding and word meaning. *Journal of Educational Psychology*, 82, 281–290.

Teaching Ideas

Vocabulary anchors: Building conceptual connections with young readers

Rod Winters

Recently, increasing attention has been devoted to a balance between the use of fictional texts and informational (content area) reading materials with beginning readers. While the benefits of early exposure to informational texts have been noted, it has also been widely recognized that nonfictional texts place special demands upon readers, including unique organizational patterns, sentence structures, and technical vocabulary (Feathers, 1993). Efforts to help students deal with these demands at the secondary level have resulted in the development of several instructional techniques emphasizing content area vocabulary (Readence, Bean, & Baldwin, 1995).

Given the less sophisticated resources of primary and intermediate readers, it is likely that they will need more strategies for dealing with technical vocabulary than older readers, and that they will be best served by strategies that are tailored to their developmental needs. Vocabulary anchors represent a graphic teaching strategy specifically designed to help young learners build the conceptual connections they need to understand informational text.

Early learners and concept development: What are the keys?

Three essential understandings underpin current thinking about early concept development. First, concept development is organized around schema and is primarily a problem-solving process whereby young learners make sense of a new experience by linking it to, and differentiating it from, prior knowledge (Rumelhart & Norman, 1981). By the time children enter into formal schooling, they have already engaged in extensive concept and language development through the social interaction found within the home environment. Honoring this process is likely to extend and enhance further development.

Second, the schema of young learners encompasses not just semantic information such as names, lists, and rules, but it is also thoroughly integrated with robust associations of place, context, and emotion. Cognitive scientists have repeatedly demonstrated the importance of such episodic information in easing the encoding and retrieval of information from memory (Martin, 1993).

Finally, the creation of personal meaning is not a solo operation. Concept development for young learners in particular occurs within and is greatly facilitated by informal social interaction (O'Donnell & Wood, 1992). Young children literally narrate their way through individual and group experience. The role of informal social interaction is especially critical as an opportunity for children to verbalize their developing conceptions of new knowledge (Gallas, 1994).

Existing vocabulary frames: Where have we been?

Beneficial strategies for assisting junior and senior high students with vocabulary in nonfictional texts have existed for some time. Semantic webbing has found widespread use in classrooms, with the teacher acting as scribe as students offer associations with a particular topic. The graphic that is created during such discussions provides a rich gestalt of relationships among existing pieces of background knowledge and can be used as a base for introducing new terminology (Hanf, 1971; Heimlich & Pittelman, 1986). (See Figure 1.)

Semantic Feature Analysis (Johnson & Pearson, 1984) uses a multiplication chart format to examine similarities and differences between specific exemplars of a larger category such as mammals (see Figure 2). The ability to systematically analyze what is and is not critical

Figure 1
Semantic web

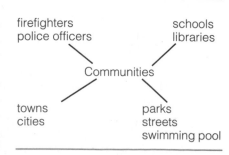

130

Figure 2
Semantic Feature Analysis

	meat eater	Africa	spots
cougar	+	–	–
leopard	+	–	+
lion	+	+	–
tiger	+	+	–

to a given concept results in increased clarity for many learners.

This interplay between example and nonexample can also be found in Verbal and Visual Word Association (VVWA) (Eeds & Cockrum, 1985). The VVWA is concerned with deep personal association for particular terms (see Figure 3). The association of personal experience provides an affective element to vocabulary learning that many students find helpful and begins to tap the narrative aspects of early language development.

Linking the new to the known, examining critical attributes of key concepts, and associating specific personal experience with new terminology have each proven to be valuable as means for assisting acquisition and retention of new vocabulary. Any attempt to create vocabulary strategies for young learners will need to use the best of these while tailoring their use to the unique nature of early language learners.

Vocabulary for young learners (Grades 2–5)

The search for a more friendly vocabulary frame began with the notion of

Figure 3
Verbal visual word association

privacy	going to bathroom in my life:
for my eyes only my definition:	public concert opposite:

developing a narrative that could serve as both a tie to immediate experience and a bridge to understanding how new words are learned. A photograph or drawing of a boat at rest in a harbor serves as a beginning point. The image of a boat floating on water is highly familiar to most young children. The frame is introduced by means of a brief narrative concerning the propensity of boats to drift. A discussion can quickly highlight the idea of an anchor being used to stop a boat from drifting aimlessly out of reach. This discussion of anchors provides a gentle platform for explaining an important aspect of comprehension—that new learning that is not connected to existing concepts in some way is likely to drift away. The use of a boat drawing can then be presented as a means of illustrating this underlying concept. Shifting to first person, a teacher can explain that "if a word or experience is to stay with us for long, we must somehow anchor it with something we already know. This is especially true when we are reading to get information about a particular topic."

A scaffold for thinking aloud

A teacher can then demonstrate the use of an anchor by beginning with a content-specific term that is fairly common. The teacher proceeds to talk through the thinking process of constructing and completing a frame for the target word. The term *hurricane* will serve to illustrate.

In this example, the teacher would draw a very simple picture of a boat on the chalkboard or overhead projector and place the target term (*hurricane*) within the boat (see Figure 4). The teacher then selects a similar word, such as *thunderstorm*, that students are likely to know and places it inside a rectangular anchor beneath the boat, connecting the two by means of a tethering line. Thinking aloud, the teacher then comments on similarities between a thunderstorm and a hurricane. Immediately below the box and to the left of the tether, the teacher notes several characteristics the two have in common using a plus sign (e.g., + rain, + wind).

The teacher then turns attention to the unique characteristics of a hurricane that set it apart from a thunderstorm and

Figure 4
Vocabulary anchor for *hurricane*

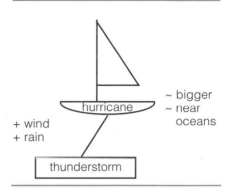

notes these critical differences to the right of the boat using a tilde sign (e.g., ~ bigger, ~ near oceans). Finally, the teacher talks briefly about a distinct memorable experience that she or he associates with the idea of a thunderstorm or hurricane.

Placing a sail on the boat, the teacher then draws a sketch or lists a few key words to serve as a trigger for recalling both the associated memory and the linked terms. It is important to emphasize to students that this last undertaking represents a unique personal memory, which would likely be different depending upon who was doing the drawing. The teacher closes the demonstration by recapping the personal significance of the drawing and reviewing why both terms would not be used interchangeably to describe an experience.

Group-negotiated applications

Once students have observed the teacher thinking aloud while working through the construction of a vocabulary anchor, the teacher can lead students through the construction of their own anchor for a targeted content term. In a recent lesson using Joanna Cole's *A Snake's Body* (1981), a vocabulary anchor was used to teach the term *molting* (see Figure 5). The teacher constructed a drawing of the boat, placing the term inside the hull. Thinking aloud, the teacher explained that molting was similar to the idea of shedding. She then engaged students in conversation about what it means when we say a dog is shedding. Through the discussion she was able to elaborate on

Figure 5
Vocabulary anchor for *molting*

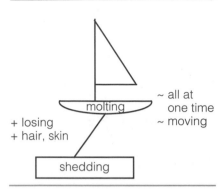

specific ways in which the two terms are similar. She then used these points as a starting gate to note key differences.

> When we see molting in this book about snakes it will mean nearly the same thing, but when snakes molt they lose their skin all at one time, and they will be climbing out of their skin, not just waiting for it to fall off.

The strategy is flexible enough to be used across multiple disciplines. *Thomas Jefferson: A Picture Book Biography* by James Giblin (1994) is a wonderful way to introduce students to the personalities behind the American Revolutionary War. With the emphasis on biography, however, concepts are often referenced without being fully developed. If students have participated in initial instruction with vocabulary anchors, a teacher can quickly introduce a term such as *colony* by noting its similarity with the familiar concept of a state. After discussing student associations for the word *state*, the teacher can call attention to the unique features of being newly settled implied by the term *colony* and the added distinction that its citizens have no power to vote on *national laws* (see Figure 6). In the final step, students would literally draw upon a strong memory of being able to vote or veto some action in their personal lives.

With younger students, it is wise initially to focus upon vocabulary anchors in a directed teaching format as a pre-reading activity. Terms that deal with animals appear to provide a strong starting point for all learners, but as a general rule, the younger the child, the more concrete the term should be. However, it is not necessary to maintain teacher control of the selection of terms to study through vocabulary anchors.

As students gain familiarity with the construction procedures, they can use partially completed Vocabulary Anchors to identify terms in their independent reading that may be confusing. Carrying out research on music composers recently, a young reader came across "Great and Glorious: Duke Ellington's Early Years" by Diana Childress (1993). Reading about Ellington's interest in and early attempts to master the "stride" style of piano playing, we are informed that he learned to play by hanging out in a pool hall next to the Howard Theater, a famous black vaudeville house. The term *vaudeville* is unfamiliar and significant enough that the student might place the word in a partially completed vocabulary anchor and keep it with a collection of other terms to be clarified back in small-group circle. Employing the strategy in this manner with older students emphasizes ongoing independent vocabulary development and echoes parts of the vocabulary self-collection strategy championed by Haggard (1992).

When, where, why?

> Students ought to be engaged in learning new words and expanding their understanding of words through instruction that is based on active processing. That is, students are not just memorizing definitions but are entering information and integrating word meanings with their existing knowledge to build conceptual representations of vocabulary in multiple contextual situations. (Rupley, Logan, & Nichols, 1999)

The frame provides a scaffold for active exploration and incorporation of newly identified content vocabulary in keeping with the spirit of active, talkative learning. As with any strategy, however, it is not a panacea.

The frame appears to work well when applied selectively. Vocabulary anchors should not be applied to every technical term students encounter. Even with the added affective element involved in the frame, young students have natural constraints on their ability to focus upon, process, and retain new terminology.

Second, vocabulary anchors are most appropriate for terms that are new to students, but have a relatively straight-

Figure 6
Vocabulary anchor for *colony*

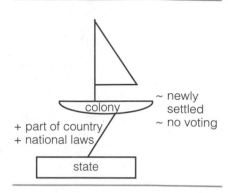

forward association with prior knowledge and experience. The frame does not lend itself well to consideration of highly complex or highly abstract concepts such as photosynthesis, nor does it highlight hierarchical relationships between terms (e.g., *state, nation*). If a teacher's purpose is to demonstrate the relationship of multiple concepts under broader classifications, other frames such as hierarchical graphic organizers (Moore & Readence, 1984) would be more appropriate.

Finally, expectations for independent use should not be hurried. In fact, it may help teachers in primary grades to think of the strategy as a way to leave footprints of a guided listening and thinking activity. The underlying process for vocabulary development is still being taught: Associate with a known word, differentiate between the known and unknown, and personalize with a meaningful memory from prior experience.

Given those clarifications, vocabulary anchors provide a needed frame for vocabulary, one tailored to young learners. Using vocabulary anchors allows a primary or intermediate-grade teacher to incorporate a user-friendly metaphor for learning while honoring the social language and unique personal experiences of his or her students. The strategy represents an innovative vehicle for building conceptual connections within informational text.

References

Eeds, M., & Cockrum, W.A. (1985). Teaching word meanings by expanding schemata vs. dictionary work vs. reading in context. *Journal of Reading, 28,* 492–497.

Feathers, K. (1993). *Infotext: Reading and learning*. Markham, ON: Pippin.

Gallas, K. (1994). *The language of learning: How children talk, write, dance, draw, and sing their understanding of the world*. New York: Teachers College Press.

Haggard, M.R. (1992). Integrated content and long-term vocabulary learning with the vocabulary self-collection strategy. In E.K. Dishner, T.W. Bean, J.E. Readence, & D.W. Moore (Eds.), *Reading in the content areas: Improving classroom instruction* (3rd ed., pp. 190–196). Dubuque, IA: Kendall/Hunt.

Hanf, M.B. (1971). Mapping: A technique for translating reading into thinking. *Journal of Reading, 14*, 225–230, 270.

Heimlich, J.E., & Pittelman, S.D. (1986). *Semantic mapping: Classroom applications*. Newark, DE: International Reading Association.

Johnson, D., & Pearson, D.W. (1984). *Teaching reading vocabulary*. Fort Worth, TX: Holt, Rinehart & Winston.

Martin, J. (1993). Episodic memory: A neglected phenomenon in the psychology of education. *Educational Psychologist, 28*, 169–183.

Moore, D.W., & Readence, J.E. (1984). A quantitative and qualitative review of graphic organizer research. *Journal of Educational Research, 78*, 11–17.

O'Donnell, M.P., & Wood, M. (1992). *Becoming a reader: A developmental approach to reading instruction*. Boston: Allyn & Bacon.

Readence, J.E., Bean, T.W., & Baldwin, R.S. (1995). *Content area literacy: An integrated approach*. Dubuque, IA: Kendall/Hunt.

Rumelhart, D., & Norman, D. (1981). Analogical processes in learning. In J.R. Anderson (Ed.), *Cognitive skills and their acquisition* (pp. 335–339). Hillsdale, NJ: Erlbaum.

Rupley, W.H., Logan, J.W., & Nichols, W.D. (1999). Vocabulary instruction in a balanced reading program. *The Reading Teacher, 52*, 338–346.

Children's books cited

Childress, D. (1993, May). Great and glorious: Duke Ellington's early years. *Cobblestone*, pp. 8–12.

Cole, J. (1981). *A snake's body*. New York: Trumpet Book Club.

Giblin, J.C. (1994). *Thomas Jefferson: A picture book biography*. New York: Scholastic.

TEACHING READING

Fun with vocabulary

Janet Towell

A word

A word is dead
When it is said,
Some say.
I say it just
Begins to live
That day.

Emily Dickinson

The following acrostic is used to introduce enjoyable and effective strategies and activities for vocabulary instruction with elementary students. (An annotated list accompanies each letter.)

V Vocabulary Self-Collection Strategy; Visual-Auditory-Kinesthetic-Tactile
O Onsets and rimes
C Color shock; clusters
A ABC books; anagrams
B Book boxes; visual configuration boxes; banks for words
U Unusual and unknown words (word attack strategies)
L List-Group-Label; Language Experience Approach
A Active involvement (music, drama and finger spelling)
R Repetition; rhymes; riddles; roots
Y Yarns

V: Vocabulary Self-Collection Strategy (VSS); Visual-Auditory-Kinesthetic-Tactile (VAKT)

Vocabulary Self-Collection Strategy (Haggard, 1986): After locating a new word in their environment, students are asked to share (a) where they found the word, (b) the context, and (c) the importance of the word and why they selected it. It is fun for the class to guess the meaning of the word from the context before the definition is read by the student who selected the word.

Visual-Auditory-Kinesthetic-Tactile: The Fernald is a popular multisensory technique (Tierney, Readence, & Dishner, 1980). Students are asked to trace the target word with a finger while pronouncing each syllable until it can be written from memory (with eyes closed at first). Ghost writing, writing in the air, or writing on a child's back can be helpful for practicing this technique. Learning disabled students benefit from using VAKT.

O: Onsets and rimes

This technique for developing phonemic awareness can help beginning readers quickly and effectively learn many sight words using word patterns. (The onset is the part of the word before the vowel; the rime includes the vowel and the rest of the letters in the word.) *Oopples and Boo-noo-noos* by Hallie Yopp and Ruth Yopp (1996) is highly recommended as a resource for learning more about phonemic awareness and word play. The book includes appropriate literature, songs, and activities.

C: Color shock; clusters

Color shock (Vitale, 1982) is a technique that was originally designed for right-brained, learning disabled students to help them remember sight words. Right-brained children seem to have a special sensitivity for bright colors. During this strategy, children write their vocabulary, spelling words, or multiplication tables in color shock (each letter or number is written in a different color, beginning with the color green for *go* to designate the beginning of the word). This technique has improved directionality, visual discrimination, and sequential memory skills in many learning disabled students.

Clusters: For vocabulary instruction to be meaningful, words should be presented in semantic frameworks through categories or clusters (Marzano & Marzano, 1988). A cluster is a set of words that relate to a single concept. Clustering is the process of relating a target word to a set of synonyms or other associated words. Clustering enables students to understand the target word better and retain it for a longer period of time.

A: ABC books; anagrams

ABC books: Alphabet books have been used successfully for teaching vocabulary, even at the secondary level (Pope & Polette, 1989). Students can be motivated to discover words through illustrations on the basis of their prior knowledge or schemata instead of memorizing the words from a required list. Through the use of complex alphabet books such as *The Ultimate Alphabet* (Wilks, 1992) and *Animalia* (Base, 1987), students are encouraged to identify synonyms, antonyms, and parts of speech for their self-selected words. Students may also enjoy creating their own ABC books based on selected themes, topics, or units of study.

Anagrams are another fun and interesting way to learn vocabulary or spelling words. In *The Eleventh Hour* by Graeme Base (1989), readers use anagrams and additional clues to solve a very complicated mystery. This book is a great way to introduce anagrams, and it appeals to all ages. (The answers are sealed in the back of the book for novice sleuths.) Students may also have fun figuring out lists of words in which the letters are scrambled. They can be "Word Detectives."

B: Book boxes; boxes for visual configuration; banks for words

Book boxes: Teachers and students collect objects or "realia" for key words or concepts in the story, placing them in a box along with the book and any other related reading materials. This technique is especially helpful for second-language learners.

Boxes for visual configuration (Thatcher, 1984): This visual discrimination technique involves drawing around words to emphasize their length and shape. It helps emergent readers distinguish between frequently confused letters and words, such as those with *b*, *p*, or *d*. They learn to recognize shapes before distinguishing individual letters or words.

Word banks: Students should have personal word banks for storing and remembering their self-selected and teacher-selected words, such as spelling words. During the year, students watch their word banks grow. These words may come from daily journals or reading materials. Index boxes, curtain rings, or blank books that are alphabetized serve as efficient organizers. Some teachers may prefer word walls that list high-frequency words or words in specific categories.

U: Unusual and unknown words

Unusual words: Sniglets, a term originally coined by Rich Hall, are fun to study in the intermediate grades and beyond (Atkinson & Longman, 1985). In one study, high school students created and defined Sniglets with common affixes and bases, including multiple meaning and parts of speech. This activity was a welcome change from the monotony of the usual vocabulary drill. An example of a Sniglet is *baldage* = hair left in the drain after showering (Hall, 1985).

Unknown words: The following word attack strategy is recommended for students in the primary grades:

1. Beep it. Say "beep" for the unknown word and read to the end of the sentence. Think of a word that would make sense in that space. Use context clues.

2. Frame it. Put index fingers around the word to separate it from the rest of the sentence.

3. Begin it. Look at the beginning sound or sounds (letter or blend).

4. Split it. Divide the word into syllables and pronounce them.

5. Find it. Look the word up in the dictionary or ask someone as a last resort.

L: List-Group-Label; Language Experience Approach

List-Group-Label (Readence & Searfoss, 1980): This is a great strategy to use with the ABC book *Animalia* by Graeme Base (1987). Working in cooperative groups, students list as many words as possible that begin with a specific letter on a piece of chart paper. (*Animalia* works well for this activity because it comes with a wall frieze that matches the book. The wall frieze comes in many different sections.) Students are give a time period to complete their lists (e.g., 15 minutes). The older the students, the more words/pictures they will be able to recognize because of their prior knowledge and schemata. After the lists of words are made and counted, students sort and label the words according to different categories. This makes the words more meaningful and easier to remember.

The *Language Experience Approach* is based on the premise that written language is actually oral language in printed form (Tierney et al., 1980). Dictated stories, word banks, and creative writing are emphasized. Language experience is an effective way to teach sight words to beginning readers or to older remedial readers who have limited sight vocabularies. Repeated reading is encouraged. There is natural motivation because the stories are usually related to the students' interests. Students are able to read successfully, perhaps for the first time. Publishing their stories in book formats for the class library can be powerful for building vocabulary as well as self-esteem.

A: Active involvement

If vocabulary instruction is to be effective, the students must be actively involved (Carr & Wixson, 1986; Nagy, 1988; Ruddell, 1986). Physical involvement such as hands-on activities to accommodate their kinesthetic-tactile learning styles can be effective. Having students do nonverbal skits, acting out the meanings of words, is another possibility (Riddell, 1988).

Music can be a motivator for learning vocabulary words or developing phonemic awareness. The vocabulary of college students improved when they used their vocabulary words in song-writing exercises (Baechtold & Algiers, 1986). For increasing phonemic awareness, Hallie Yopp (Yopp & Yopp, 1996) recommends songs based on popular tunes such as "If You're Happy and You Know It," "Someone's in the Kitchen with Dinah," "Old McDonald," and "Twinkle, Twinkle, Little Star."

Finger spelling with the manual alphabet is another strategy that actively involves students during vocabulary instruction. In the past, finger spelling has been used only for names, places, and words for which there were no signs (Sullivan & Bourke, 1980). By using 26 hand shapes, all the letters of the alphabet can be made and written in the air. Finger spelling/sign language has proven to be beneficial for improving word identification and spelling skills in both hearing and hearing-impaired children (Andrews, 1988; Isaacson, 1987; Wilson & Hafer, 1990).

R: Repetition; rhymes; riddles; roots

To facilitate comprehension of text, *repetition* of vocabulary is necessary to ensure quick and easy access of words during the reading process (Nagy, 1988). Vocabulary acquisition through repetition can be accomplished through language experience, choral reading, Readers Theatre, tape-recorded books, patterned or predictable books, basals, and rhymes in poetry.

Riddles can be used to introduce new vocabulary words for stories in basal readers or trade books. Students will enjoy writing and guessing riddles much more than writing sentences and definitions. Riddles could be a component of thematic units in an integrated curriculum. For instance, *Tyrannosaurus Wrecks* (Sterne, 1979) contains 145 riddles about dinosaurs. For example, What did the dinosaur cattle baron say to the outlaw? "Get off my terror-tory." Reading a riddle from the chalkboard each day is another exciting way for students to learn many new sight words. They may also enjoy bringing their own riddles to class.

Roots: The study of Latin, Greek, and English root words and affixes can greatly increase a student's vocabulary. Morphemic analysis and the study of etymology or word origins are especially beneficial for students in the intermediate grades and junior high. Deriving word meanings from their roots can be challenging and rewarding. For instance, the root *tele* (far) is found in the following words: *telecast, teleconference, telegram, telegraph, telephone, telescope, telethon,* and *television* (Tompkins, 1997, p. 171). Students can expand their word knowledge further through the exploration of the remaining roots in the words. For example, the root *phon* (sound) in *telephone* is found in *earphone, microphone, phonics, phonograph, saxophone,* and *symphony.* The possibilities are endless. An added benefit of this word study is to encourage students to use the dictionary.

Y: Yarns

Creating yarns or tall tales is an imaginative way for students to learn new vocabulary and/or concepts. One procedure is to divide the class into cooperative groups of four or five students. Select five meaningful vocabulary words from their next story. Challenge them to see which group can create the wildest, most exaggerated story using the same five words. Then let them read the real story and compare!

Summary

Remember to make vocabulary instruction as much fun as possible. Motivation, active involvement, repetition, and relevance lead to independent word learning, the goal of vocabulary instruction. This list of suggested strategies and activities provides a good start for teaching your students the power of words.

References

Andrews, J. (1988). Deaf children's acquisition of prereading skills using the reciprocal teaching procedure. *Exceptional Children, 54,* 349–355.

Atkinson, R., & Longman, D. (1985). Sniglets: Give a twist to teenage and adult vocabulary instruction. *Journal of Reading, 29,* 103–105.

Baechtold, S., & Algiers, A. (1986). Teaching college students vocabulary with rhyme, rhythm, and ritzy characters. *Journal of Reading, 30,* 248–253.

Carr, E., & Wixson, K. (1986). Guidelines for evaluating vocabulary instruction. *Journal of Reading, 29,* 588–595.

Haggard, M. (1986). The vocabulary self-collection strategy: Using student interest and world knowledge to enhance vocabulary growth. *Journal of Reading, 30,* 634–642.

Hall, R., & Friends. (1985). *More sniglets.* New York: Macmillan.

Isaacson, A. (1987). A fingerspelling approach to spelling. *Academic Therapy, 23,* 89–90.

Marzano, R., & Marzano, J. (1988). *A cluster approach to vocabulary instruction.* Newark, DE: International Reading Association.

Nagy, W. (1988). *Teaching vocabulary to improve reading comprehension.* Newark, DE: International Reading Association.

Pope, C.A., & Polette, K. (1989). Using ABC books for vocabulary development in the secondary school. *English Journal, 78,* 78–80.

Readence, J., & Searfoss, L. (1980). Teaching strategies for vocabulary development. *English Journal, 69,* 43–46.

Riddell, C.B. (1988). Towards a more active vocabulary. *English Journal, 77,* 50–51.

Ruddell, R. (1986). Vocabulary learning: A process model and criteria for evaluation instructional strategies. *Journal of Reading, 30,* 581–587.

Sullivan, M., & Bourke, L. (1980). *A show of hands.* New York: Harper & Row.

Thatcher, J. (1984). *Teaching reading to mentally handicapped children.* London: Croom Helm.

Tierney, R.J., Readence, J.E., & Dishner, E.K. (1980). *Reading strategies and practices: A guide for improving instruction.* Boston: Allyn & Bacon.

Tompkins, G. (1997). *Literacy for the 21st century.* Upper Saddle River, NJ: Simon & Schuster.

Vitale, B. (1982). *Unicorns are real.* Rolling Hills Estates, CA: Jalmar Press.

Wilson, R., & Hafer, J. (1990). *Come sign with us.* Washington, DC: Galludet.

Yopp, H., & Yopp, R. (1996). *Oo-pples and boo-noo-noos: Songs and activities for phonemic awareness.* New York: Harcourt Brace.

Children's literature cited

Base, G. (1987). *Animalia.* New York: Harry N. Abrams.

Base, G. (1989). *The eleventh hour.* New York: Harry N. Abrams.

Sterne, N. (1979). *Tyrannosaurus wrecks.* New York: Harper & Row.

Wilks, M. (1992). *The ultimate alphabet.* New York: Holt.

Comprehension Strategies

Reading comprehension is the construction of the meaning of a written text through a reciprocal interchange of ideas between the reader and the message in a particular text.

Findings in the National Reading Panel Report

When readers were given cognitive strategy instruction, they made significant gains on measures of reading comprehension over students trained with conventional instruction procedures.

The following specific strategies were found to be effective—comprehension monitoring, cooperative learning, graphic organizers, story structure, question answering, question generating, summarization.

Teaching a variety of reading comprehension strategies in natural settings and content areas was most effective.

Comprehension is the essence of reading. Since the 1970s, researchers have developed a substantial body of knowledge about comprehension processes and strategies. The conceptualization of comprehension in this research departed from the previous conceptualizations of comprehension as the automatic byproduct of deciphering words. Rather, comprehension was thought of as intentional thinking during which meaning is constructed through the interactions between text and reader. This conceptualization of reading comprehension as the active construction of information led to the investigation of the strategies readers use in the construction process. As specific strategies were identified, researchers moved to investigating the explicit teaching of those strategies, and the research on single strategies indicated that the strategies could be taught and that they did improve reading comprehension. Next the field investigated whether combinations of strategies could be taught, and once again the answer was affirmative. Reciprocal teaching (Palincsar, David, Winn, & Stevens, 1991), direct explanation (Duffy, 1993), and transactional strategy instruction (Pressley et al., 1992) are examples of the multiple strategy approach. Most recently, researchers have focused on the effective preparation of teachers for teaching students to use effective comprehension strategies, such as summarizing, questioning, and comprehension monitoring.

The first article, "Supporting a strategic stance in the classroom: A comprehension framework for helping teachers help students to be strategic," by Sarah L. Dowhower, provides a framework and routines for incorporating multiple comprehension strategies in classroom instruction. It organizes instruction into three phases—prereading, active reading, and postreading—and provides direction for teachers in planning and implementing multiple comprehension strategies instruction that is consistent with the NRP Report.

The last three articles in this section—"Character Perspective Charting: Helping children to develop a more complete conception of story," by Timothy and Sherrell Shanahan; "Guidelines for implementing a graphic organizer," by Donna M. Merkley and Debra Jefferies;

and "Self-monitoring in beginning reading," by Robert M. Schwartz—are all examples of single-strategy instruction for strategies deemed effective in the NRP Report—story structure, graphic organizers, and self-monitoring. All give good direction for teachers to incorporate the teaching of single strategies in their instruction. These strategies also might be incorporated in multiple strategy comprehension instruction.

References

Duffy, G. (1993). Rethinking strategy instruction: Four teachers development and their low achiever's understandings. *The Elementary School Journal, 93*(3), 231–247.

Palincsar, A.S., David, Y.M., Winn, J.A., & Stevens, D.D. (1991). Examining the context of strategy instruction. *RASE: Remedial and Special Education, 12*(3), 43–53.

Pressley, M., El-Dinary, P.B., Gaskins, I., Schuder, T., Bergman, J., Almasi, J., & Brown, R. (1992). Beyond direct explanation: Transactional instruction of reading comprehension strategies. *The Elementary School Journal, 92*(5), 513–555.

Sarah L. Dowhower

Supporting a strategic stance in the classroom: A comprehension framework for helping teachers help students to be strategic

A second grader, Colin (pseudonym), proudly announced that he has been using many of the ideas from the comprehension bulletin board to increase his understanding of books. "I've been guessing ahead, making pictures in my head, and deciding what I'm going to read for, before I start a book," he said. "These really helped me to think harder about the book and figure out what the author was trying to say when I'm reading by myself." The teacher, Mrs. E, complimented Colin for being so "strategic." The class had had strategy lessons and discussions on prediction, visual imagery, and purpose setting throughout the quarter and the children found many books that worked with these strategies. Mrs. E decided that since these three strategies were becoming independent, it was time to expand the children's repertoire. Using a flexible framework of comprehension teaching (presented in this article), she began planning how to build on what the students knew about strategies to teach two new techniques for using prior experiences and visually organizing content. These were natural extensions of the three strategies the children were already using spontaneously.

Many teachers find it challenging to take a strategic approach to comprehension. This article presents one approach that encourages strategic and student-centered processing of text.

Both the most devout whole language champion and the most adamant direct instruction advocate would concede that Colin is making good progress in learning to be strategic. Both theoretical camps would say that strategies allow readers to be autonomous and in control of the comprehension process and that good readers use them effectively. Not all, however, would agree as to how best to accomplish this strategic stance (e.g., Carnine, Silbert, & Kameenui, 1997; Clay, 1991; Weaver, 1994). Is it programmed by the teacher, naturally left to the child to do alone, or achieved by a middle ground of instruction in a natural, supportive way?

Some research suggests that there is "little teaching of cognitive strategies in contemporary classrooms" (Pressley, Symons, Snyder, & Cariglia-Bull, 1989, p. 17). Data collected over 10 years indicate that only 1 out of 10 cooperating teachers working with early field preservice elementary education students taught reading strategies (Dowhower, 1998). In a seminal study on comprehension, Durkin (1978–1979) concluded that while many teachers believe they were teaching comprehension, most often they were assessing instead of directly explaining *how* to comprehend. Although Durkin's work came under some criticism because of the criteria she used to define instruction (Heap, 1982; Hodges, 1980), there is supporting evidence that her hypothesis—teachers are more interrogators than instructors—is valid (Kurth & Greenlaw, 1980; Mason, 1983; Wendler, Samuels, & Moore, 1989).

There are valid reasons why many novice and experienced teachers find it challenging to take a strategic approach to comprehension. Preservice and inservice teachers in classes and workshops report that they "seldom saw real strategy teaching either in their K–12 schooling or college reading methods classrooms." Some confused the term *strategy teaching* with instructional techniques teachers might use rather than strategies children might learn. "Reading instruction textbooks," they said, "gave minimal assistance in learning to teach children to use strategies." Like Durkin (1981), they found little help with strategies in the basal manuals. Furthermore, research by Wendler et al. (1989) suggests that even with good teacher preparation, confusion between assessment and direct teaching of comprehension is still evident.

In an attempt to encourage teachers and their students to adopt a strategic stance like the classroom described in the scenario above, this article presents an approach to comprehension instruction that teachers and I have dubbed the comprehension strategy framework. This framework has evolved out of work

with preservice and inservice elementary teachers in our search for ways to support and encourage both strategic and student-centered processing of text. The first section gives a description of and rationale for elements of the framework, including an example of a lesson taught in Colin's second-grade class. The second section is a brief overview of how the framework fits into current literacy trends in strategy teaching. The final sections describe how to use the framework and teacher comments as to its efficacy.

Comprehension strategy framework

> Still new to the whole idea of teaching to develop strategic readers, Colin's teacher turned to the comprehension strategy framework to organize how she would present new strategies and connect them with those the children were already using. "I see the framework helping me achieve two goals," said Mrs. E, "students internalizing and self-regulating the strategies; and me, as a teacher, building a schema for good planning and strategy instruction."

The format of the framework is an adaptation of Ringler and Weber's (1984, pp. 70–72) three phases of the interactive stage of teaching (prereading, active reading, and postreading), as well as a blending of Baumann and Schmitt's (1986) "what, why, how and when" of comprehension instruction and literature teacher-student discussion techniques. The framework has three parts or phases:

The *Prereading* phase includes three activities: (a) eliciting prior knowledge, (b) building background and relating that to prior knowledge, and (c) focusing on the specific strategy to be taught—specifically *what* the strategy is and *why* it is being taught. This gives the students a simple description or definition of the strategy (declarative knowledge), how its acquisition will help them become better readers (conceptual knowledge), and a brief model of how the strategy works (procedural knowledge) (see Appendix A, Part I).

The *Active Reading* phase (see Appendix A, Part II) involves a cycle or repetition of three activities: (a) students setting a purpose for reading the specific section of text, (b) silent reading and self-monitoring, and (c) "working the story." *Working the story* means discussion that helps children become a part of what they have read as well as the process of reading. It does not include interrogation from the teacher. This conversation includes the naming and continuous personal demonstration of the strategies ("I found myself doing _____ to understand this part better"). It is where students "hear what they (the authors) have to say, but examine it, weigh it and judge for themselves" (quote by author Tyrone Edwards, source unknown). It is where the awareness of theme(s) gradually develops as the story unfolds.

The Active Reading phase is repeated with several sections of text until the end of the passage, concluding with a final discussion of the strategies learned and the text theme(s) generated. Discussion should involve *when* the strategy would be used (and not used), the kinds of text *where* the strategy works (and does not), and *how* to evaluate its use. Special care should be taken to situate the strategy in the bigger picture of the reading process and support the students' coordination of the network of strategies they are beginning to bring under control (Clay, 1991). Important to this final discussion is the constructing of themes (abstractions linking the text to other texts) that requires the students to actively process what they read at higher levels. "By providing just the right degree of scaffolding, through the use of questions and comments, the teacher can support students as they attempt to construct a theme and at the same time, shift responsibility for the task to students" (Au, 1992, p. 107)

The final *Postreading* phase (see Appendix A, Part III) entails independent activities by students either individually or in groups: (a) recall of content, (b) reader response, (c) extensions of text, (d) strategy use and transfer, and (e) informal or self-assessment. Students or teachers may choose one or more of the activities according to the text, student need, or appropriateness. For instance, to address both efferent and aesthetic responses (Rosenblatt, 1994), students might sequence the events correctly (recall of content) or write in their journals about what they got out of the text or how they would react or feel about the character or situation (reader response). The students might practice the strategies "in flight"; for example, they might talk about how they use the strategies with a partner as they reread the story (strategy use and transfer). They could retell the story into a tape recorder for the teacher to informally assess comprehension or complete a

self-assessment checksheet to indicate which strategies they used independently with new books during silent sustained reading (SSR) time (assessment). Encouraging students to recommend to peers books that fit one or more of the strategies in their repertoire is a way of weaving together strategy use and transfer and self-assessment.

To help the reader visualize the parts of the framework and how they work together to facilitate comprehension, Figure 1 gives a structural overview of the various components. The framework, as presented, is constructed as if the strategy is new for the students and this is the first time it is targeted. The components should be adapted as the students learn to use the strategy independently and integrate it with others.

Example of how the framework works

Because linking prior knowledge and constructing pictures of story content are connected with prediction and visualization (strategies that the children were already using independently), Colin's teacher decided to introduce the new strategies of Experience-Text-Relationship (ETR) and Visual Structures. ETR is a technique linking prior experiences with what is read in the text and forming some relationship between the two. Visual Structures are diagrams or pictures of the content of the text. Using the framework helped Colin's teacher plan how to present the strategies and adapt her instruction as the children became more strategic (i.e., using the strategy spontaneously during reading).

Figure 2 is the scenario of the lesson growing out of the teacher's plan represented in Appendix B. The text used, a second-grade story entitled "New Girl at School" (Delton, 1986), is about a little girl's experiences the first week in a new school. The girl's change of feelings over a week's time is not explicitly told. Because most children could relate to being in a new situation and the story lends itself well to a diagram using the 5 days of the week, Experience-Text-Relationship and Visual Structure strategies were taught together.

Rationale for framework elements

The section below discusses the rationale for elements of the framework including text division, cycles of instruction (purpose setting,

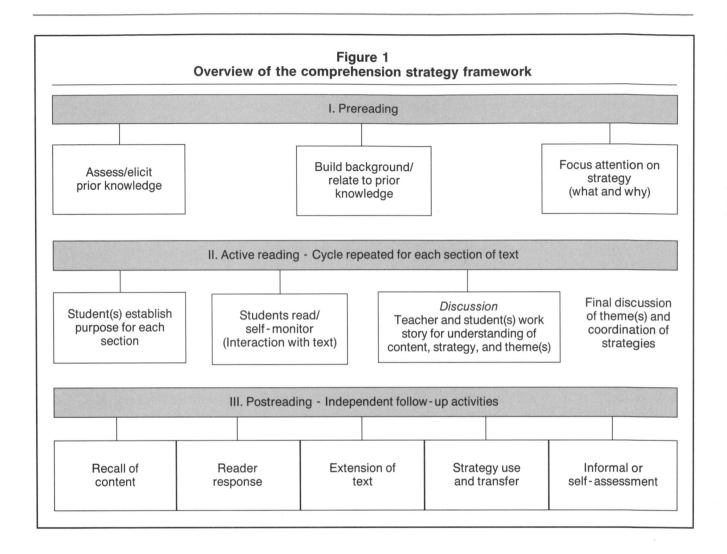

Figure 1
Overview of the comprehension strategy framework

I. Prereading		
Assess/elicit prior knowledge	Build background/ relate to prior knowledge	Focus attention on strategy (what and why)

II. Active reading - Cycle repeated for each section of text

Student(s) establish purpose for each section	Students read/ self-monitor (Interaction with text)	*Discussion* Teacher and student(s) work story for understanding of content, strategy, and theme(s)	Final discussion of theme(s) and coordination of strategies

III. Postreading - Independent follow-up activities

Recall of content	Reader response	Extension of text	Strategy use and transfer	Informal or self-assessment

silent reading, and discussion of the strategy and content), and construction of general theme(s) or central meaning of the text.

Text chunked in cycles of instruction. The framework is set up differently from the typical lesson in which teachers ask the students to read the whole text at once. Instead, the teacher divides the text into sections before the lesson. These sections can be as small as a sentence or as large as several chapters. The cycles (purpose setting, silent reading, and discussion) allow for more opportunities to stop and think publicly about what was read and the construction of understanding. Importantly, the cycles allow students to explore both the theme and the strategy throughout the story—for building big ideas (possible themes) in the story and reinforcing practice of comprehension strategies along the way.

Purpose setting emphasis. Armbruster (1991), Ogle (1986), and others (see Blanton, Wood, & Moorman, 1990, for a review of the research) suggest it is important for learners to have a clear purpose for reading because it facilitates comprehension. "Before even beginning the first sentence of a text, knowledgeable readers know how to approach and frame a reading experience with a sense of purpose, need, and direction" (*Standards for the English Language Arts*, 1996, p. 31). Thus, each cycle begins with setting a purpose for reading the specific chunk of text. Because teacher-directed purpose setting has many problems, Blanton et al. (1990) suggest that the goal be to gradually replace teacher-set purposes with jointly established ones and then ultimately to individually and independently set student purposes. By setting a reason to

Figure 2
Scenario of actual lesson plan

Lesson continued (major components of the framework in bold)

Later, in a literature circle group, Mrs. E said, "Yesterday we chose a new story to read together called 'New Girl at School.' It is a good story to learn other strategies similar to ones you have been practicing. Good readers use strategies all the time as they read. That is why we are building a list of the strategies on the bulletin board. The story is about a girl moving to a new home and school. Did that ever happen to you? How did you feel?" **(Prereading: Building background/assessing and relating to prior knowledge)**

"This story will help you to learn two new strategies to understand what you read. The first is called Experience-Text-Relationship, or ETR for short. It gets us thinking about what has happened in our lives and how that fits with the character's experiences. We are also going to draw a picture or diagram of the story's events to better see the things that happen and how they fit together (visual structures). You may have used these strategies but never realized it." **(Prereading: Focusing attention on what the strategies are and why they are good to use)**

"Look at the picture on the first page of the story. How might Marcia be feeling on her first day at the new school? Let's read pp. 13–14 silently to see if this is so." **(Active reading: Purpose setting)** After reading silently—"If we were to draw a face on our chart as to how Marcia feels, what would it be? Why? Let's list the reasons (events) below the face that caused her to feel this way. What might you be saying if you were Marcia?" **(Discussion of visual structures and ETR)** The lesson continued like this over several cycles with purpose setting and the use of the children's predictions, silent reading, discussion, and "working of the story." Students added to the chart after each section of text and also discussed how these events related to their lives and any themes they saw.

At the end of the story the teacher asked, "How is this story like an experience you had? Look at the picture we built on the chart paper and tell us what the author might be trying to say in this story. What can we learn from Marcia's experience that will help us?" **(Final discussion of theme)**

Finally, the teacher asked, "*What* did we do to understand the story better?" One student said, "We talked about how our experiences were like the girl's and drew a picture to show the parts of the story and how her feelings changed over the week at school." "Let's add ETR and visuals to our comprehension strategy bulletin board," suggested Mrs. E. "*When* could we use these strategies again?" The students suggested they could draw a picture of the parts when they were having problems remembering and making sense of a story. When the story is like something that happened to them, they could use what has happened to them to figure it out. **(Final discussion of new strategies)**

During the discussion, Colin noticed that before they were reading, the group was setting a purpose for reading by guessing (predicting) what would happen. Other students commented how they could picture various incidents with Marcia and her schoolmates as they read (visualization). These were strategies already on their strategy bulletin board and taught previously. The teacher commented that she was delighted to see the students naming as well as incorporating learned strategies with new ones as ways of building their understanding of what they read. **(Coordination of other known strategies)**

After the final culminating discussion, the children independently reread the text to find examples of events that would support the different feelings Marcia had during the story. **(Postreading: Recall using the visual)** They wrote events beside the facial expression to support Marcia's feelings (see Appendix B). They also wrote in their journals about their feelings as if they had been a new student in Marcia's classroom. **(Postreading: Reader response)**

read themselves, students have a stake in finding the answer or testing a hypothesis. They learn a behavior critical to expert reading. Other guidelines suggested by Blanton et al. (1990) include (a) setting a single purpose rather than multiple purposes, (b) sustaining the purpose throughout the selection, and (c) discussing the purpose as the first activity after the reading is completed.

Silent reading emphasis. After the purpose setting, the format requires the students to silently read a text segment. There are several reasons for asking students to read the text silently. First, much of the reading instruction in our local elementary schools occurs within the context of oral round-robin reading or some variation. There is little support for either of these oral reading practices in the literature.

Compared to independent silent reading, round-robin reading actually decreased comprehension in several studies (Lynch, 1988; Santa, Isaacson, & Manning, 1987). In addition, results of several studies suggest that silent reading is more effective for learning than oral reading (Armbruster, 1991). Oral reading draws attention to errors and increases off-task behavior. A final argument is that silent reading is more authentic to real life than oral reading. Seldom do adults read aloud, except for possibly the litany in church or a story to a young child. The bulk of our adult reading is done silently.

Strategy instruction embedded in literature discussions. As suggested by Fielding and Pearson (1994), we need to teach strategies that students can use every day within whole texts and give students time to talk about them. In other words, give "many occasions for students to talk to a teacher and one another about their responses" (p. 62). This situated cognition within good literature allows "students to internalize effective comprehension strategies through repeated situations in which they read and discuss whole text with a teacher and peers" (p. 67). These types of text discussions of content and strategies have been rare in classrooms (Durkin, 1978–1979, 1984; Mason, 1983). Furthermore, we have recent evidence that students are more highly involved and engaged in the literacy act when given opportunities to discuss by responding, challenging, questioning, and sharing opinions about the meaning of text (Almasi, McKeown, & Beck, 1996).

Theme(s) and focused discussion. A theme is the central idea of the text or the "big idea." It might be literal (e.g., girl moves to a new school); psychological, involving forces such as emotions and needs influencing the character's actions (e.g., a new girl's need for acceptance); or philosophical, encompassing universal truths (e.g., acceptance comes with time). Reading scholars suggest that themes should be at the heart of text discussions because (a) the process helps students query and develop insights beyond the literal (Lehr, 1988), and (b) "through constructing their own themes, students come to understand and appreciate literature on their own terms, not just the teacher's terms" (Au, 1992, p. 110). Teachers should scaffold the discussion with questions and comments through-

out the lesson to help students construct their own themes. While the teacher initially has several possible themes in mind that give the big picture, it is important that the final theme come from the students or be jointly constructed by the students and teacher. Likewise, different groups of students may construct multiple themes for the same text.

Using the strategy framework

As opposed to teaching just a single strategy, the framework can be a flexible, generic vehicle for teaching a repertoire of comprehension strategies. There are a number of strategic processes good readers use that can be taught. These include activating background knowledge, predicting, generating visual images, summarizing, self-questioning, analyzing text for story grammar elements, inferencing, distinguishing important information, synthesizing, monitoring, and learning to repair faulty comprehension (Goodman, Watson, & Burke, 1996; Pearson, Roehler, Dole, & Duffy, 1992; Pressley et al., 1992; Weaver, 1994).

Although there are many research-based techniques or methods in the literature that address these strategic processes, teachers new to strategy teaching find it more comfortable to concentrate on a few at first. This is consistent with what Pearson et al. (1992) suggest—initially learning a few strategies that can be applied to a wide variety of texts. Once teachers have a schema for teaching strategies, transfer to multiple strategies suggested in the literature is easier (e.g., reciprocal teaching or read aloud).

Less complex comprehension techniques include Directed Reading-Thinking Activities, Experience-Text-Relationship, Visual Structures, Story Grammars, or K-W-L (What I *K*now, What I *W*ant to Learn, What I *L*earned). These five have a classroom research base, address a range of strategic processes, can be used with varied types of text and genres, and can be adapted to various reading levels, content areas, and student needs. Importantly, there is evidence that they can transfer to independent reading. For those readers unfamiliar with these techniques the following is a brief overview with resources for further reference and exploration:

• Directed Reading-Thinking Activity (DR-TA) is a technique that encourages prediction and validation. First identified by Stauffer (1969, 1975) and applicable to both expository and narrative text, DR-TA uses a cycle in which the reader first predicts from the title or initial picture, then reads a segment of the text to validate those predictions, and predicts again from the new information. Reading, validating predictions, and then predicting again are a series of steps repeated until the end of the text. The same strategic prediction and validation cycle can be adapted to emergent readers who cannot read independently using Directed Listening-Thinking Activity (DL-TA) or Directed Seeing-Thinking Activity (DS-TA) (Dalton & Dowhower, 1985). (For other DR-TA references see Haggard, 1988; Tierney, Readence, & Dishner, 1995, pp. 213–222; Walker, 1996a, pp. 194–196.)

• Experience-Text-Relationship (ETR) is a strategy technique for linking background experiences and schemata (E) to narrative story text (T), before, during, and after reading. The result is the development of an insight or relationship (R) between the children's experiences and the text. ETR was developed from research at Kamehameha Schools with Hawaiian children (Au, 1979). (For other ETR references see Au, 1993; Mason & Au, 1990; Walker, 1996a, pp. 198–201.)

• Visual Structures is a general name given to spatial learning techniques such as graphic organizers, maps, chains, charts, continuums, webs, trees, grids, matrices, or diagrams that provide a visual representation of the content of narrative or expository text. Their purpose is to help students better understand important text ideas and how they are related. The information from a visual structure also aids summarization and allows for use of multiple modalities. (For references see Alvermann, 1991; Griffin, Malone, & Kameenui, 1995; Jones, Pierce, & Hunter, 1989; McGee & Richgels, 1985; Piccolo, 1987; Tierney et al., 1995, pp. 328–333, 346–352.)

• Story Grammar or Story Structure is perhaps the most researched comprehension technique. The terms are applicable to and include narrative story parts such as character or events, as well as the ways that content area texts (expository) are organized. Often story structure elements are written out as in frames (Cudd & Roberts, 1987; Fowler, 1982) or organized with visual structures such as maps and webs. Story structure elements are used for assessing (i.e., retelling) as well as teaching comprehension (Marshall, 1983). (For other references see Armbruster, Anderson, & Ostertag, 1989; Davis & McPherson, 1989; McGee & Richgels, 1985; Tierney et al., 1995, pp. 353–365.)

• K-W-L is a widely used self-questioning technique to help tap prior *knowledge* (K), set purposes for reading by determining what the students *want* to know (W), and identify new concepts *learned* (L). First researched by Ogle (1986), the technique is often (but not exclusively) used in the content area subjects. In its more developed form, K-W-L is called K-W-L Plus with a writing component consisting of mapping and summarization (Carr & Ogle, 1987). (For other K-W-L references see Tierney et al., 1995, pp. 379–384; Walker, 1996a, pp. 225–228.)

The changing nature of comprehension instruction

The framework described here attempts to encourage a more current perspective of strategy teaching. The last 4 decades have seen several waves of comprehension research and instruction, each very different in their emphasis. The 1960s and 1970s had a strong task-analysis flavor with both decoding and comprehension seen as sets of hierarchical skills that, taught in sequence, defined good reading instruction. The logic was that practice in completing comprehension questions and various skill activities would develop reading ability (Pearson et al., 1992). During this time there was a strong movement to teach the numerous subskills in a direct instruction mode because comprehension could best be achieved by teaching skills to some level of mastery (Rosenshine, 1980). Vestiges of this skill-based approach are still seen today in various direct instruction models (e.g., Carnine et al., 1997).

The 1980s brought a cognitive-based view of comprehension, ushering in terms such as *direct explanation* and *explicit comprehension instruction* to differentiate the approach from the *direct instruction* of the 1970s. Reading was seen by researchers as a more complex, interactive process, and teaching strategies became more credible than skills because they implied megacognitive control, higher levels of thinking, active choice, and active processing (Dole, Duffy, Roehler, & Pearson, 1991). During the 1980s and into the early 1990s, a strong cognitively focused research base suggested comprehension strategies (ways a reader monitors and makes sense of text) are important components of expert reading and can be taught (Dole et al., 1991; Fielding & Pearson, 1994; Pearson, 1985).

As productive as it was, the 1980s approach to strategy learning could be characterized as a transmission model, mostly

---

The framework described here attempts to encourage a more current perspective of strategy teaching.

---

teacher directed with large doses of direct explanation and modeling of comprehension strategies, emphasis on a few skills in isolated context, and short-term, quick-fix implementation (see Pressley et al., 1992, for a summary). Although rooted in the direct explanation tradition, there is a new look in the late 1990s to the 1980s perspective. This new look may provide potential solutions to the debate on how to facilitate strategic reading as we move into the next century. Several major shifts in thinking have occurred, in part, because of the current holistic movements in literacy.

Student's use of comprehension strategies is situated within a broader context of what a competent reader does. Researchers are seeing cognitive strategies as one facet of the overall concept of a competent reader. For example, studies in the last 5 years at the National Reading Research Center suggest that expert readers are also engaged readers who are motivated, knowledgeable, socially interactive, and strategic (Alvermann & Guthrie, 1993; Gambrell, 1996; Guthrie, 1996; Guthrie & McCann, 1997; Morrow, 1997). In addition, Almasi et al. (1996) found that use of comprehension strategies was both a sign of active engagement and a stimulus for that engagement.

Strategy development is seen in a more constructivist and collaborative light. Several theories are influencing how we currently conceptualize strategy teaching. These include

(a) Reader Response Theory/Transactional Theory (Pressley et al., 1992; Rosenblatt, 1978, 1994), (b) Motivation and Engagement Theory (Cambourne, 1988), and (c) Self-Extending/ Inner Control Theory (Clay, 1991). Literature Circles (Daniels, 1994), The Book Club (McMahon & Raphael, 1997), Questioning the Author (Beck, McKeown, Hamilton, & Kucan, 1997), and Instructional Conversations (Goldenberg, 1992–1993) are recent approaches for facilitating collaborative discussions. The general thrust of these theories and approaches is that awareness and joint social construction of strategies and meaning are best learned through teacher-student and peer-led discussions and explanatory responses during reading. When strategy use is a joint effort (by students and teacher), the teacher engages in both responsive teaching in instructional conversations (Tharp & Gallimore, 1988) and instructional scaffolding (Beck et al., 1997; Pearson & Fielding, 1991).

As opposed to strict teacher control, strategy learning is more cognitively situated in student needs and demands of the reading task. Strategies are taught in context, as part of the topic or text being explored, not in isolation. Guthrie (1996) suggests that "when students' need to know determines the type and amount of strategy instruction, strategies are likely to be adapted and used widely" (p. 438).

Because of this cognitively situated viewpoint, strategy development and use is best supported "in flight" or what Fountas and Pinnell (1996) call "on the run." This means that demonstrations of new strategies and comments that reinforce existing strategies are woven into the ebb and flow of discussion of literature, by both teachers and students (Beck et al., 1997; Clay, 1991; Fountas & Pinnell, 1996; Goodman et al., 1996; Pressley et al., 1992; Smith & Elley, 1994; Walker, 1996b; Weaver, 1994). In other words, students and teachers learn to make public or explicit their overt thinking process and ways they have found to make sense of what they read as they read.

Isolated strategy teaching is being replaced by an emphasis on learning a repertoire of strategies as well as the coordination and flexible orchestration of those strategies. Duffy (1993), in rethinking the research on strategy instruction, suggests the goal is to build a repertoire of diverse comprehension strategies—not isolated strategies learned for their own sake—an "integrated set...within an overall global plan for being strategic" (p. 243). Most recently, the International Reading Association/National Council of Teachers of English Standards for the English Language Arts support this global plan for a strategic stance. The document specifically addresses the need for students to be able to apply a wide range of strategies for comprehension, interpretation, evaluation, and appreciation to a wide range of text (*Standards for the English Language Arts*, 1996).

Also, the Standards (1996) endorse the concept that teacher explanation and modeling of reading strategies and independent practice contribute to students' proficiency in comprehension. However, direct teacher explanation, modeling, and practice are currently thought of in more fluid, informal, and less structured ways than the explicit comprehension model of the 1980s. For instance, Goodman et al. (1996) suggest more spontaneous short minilessons (individual or group) to help move readers "back in low gear" so they can focus on specific process for meaning (p. 50). Walker (1996b) suggests "phasing in to demonstrate and name strategies and phasing out to let students use new strategies independently" (p. 289). This is done with "I" statements about how one personally gains meaning—all within conversations that focus on cultivating and orchestrating a repertoire of strategies while reading.

In addition to a repertoire perspective, there is an increased emphasis on self-assessment of multiple comprehension strategies. Experts suggest the use of self-report rubrics, checklists, and portfolio entries (DeFina, 1992; Lipson & Wixson, 1991; Rhodes, 1993; Walker, 1996a, 1996b) to help students document and monitor personal strategies "in flight." The rationale is that asking students to evaluate their increasing use of strategies draws their attention to the strategies and their positive effects (Walker, 1996a) as well as empowers them to read more difficult text (Clay, 1991) and be more self-efficacious (Schunk & Zimmerman, 1997).

Developing a strategic stance

Both beginning and experienced teachers have found the comprehension strategy framework to be helpful in promoting a strategic

---

Research about strategy instruction

Descriptive and experimental strategy research findings in the 1980s and early 1990s suggest the following:

1. Expert readers use *many* strategies to process text (Pressley et al., 1992);
2. Poor and good comprehenders use the same type and number of strategies on easy text; with harder material, good comprehenders use more strategies (Kletzien, 1991; Smith, 1991; Swanson, 1988); and
3. Strategies learned transfer to independent reading situations (see Griffin et al., 1995 and Pressley et al., 1989 for a review).

In addition, studies in the 1980s to early 1990s gave practitioners several insights about explicit comprehension strategy teaching:

1. Although of questionable benefit to high readers, strategy teaching helps middle and low readers to improve their comprehension (Kern, 1989);
2. Less able readers who have been taught a strategy are often indistinguishable from good readers who had not been taught the strategy (Hansen & Pearson, 1983);
3. We can teach strategies to those students who do not use them spontaneously (Garner, 1992; Pearson & Fielding, 1991); and
4. The best teachers do more than demonstrate strategies at the beginning of a lesson; they "generate spontaneous explanations throughout the lesson, elaborating in response to student's restructured understanding of the teacher's model" (Duffy et al., 1987, p. 364).

---

stance in their classrooms. Many veterans had never viewed reading instruction this way. "I thought teaching reading was just asking comprehension questions and having some discussion on what the author meant," a first-grade teacher admitted. One fourth-grade teacher conceded that "Deep down, I didn't believe my students could be strategic and use these strategies independently—I was wrong, and I'm so proud of them." " It was not easy at first to learn to teach this way, but the terms what, why, how and when, more than anything else, gave me the actual words to explain the process of being strategic to students. The framework helped me build my own stance of teaching for strategy development," said a second-grade teacher. "This concept has changed how I teach in every subject," several others commented. Finally, teachers reported that their students approached national and the state proficiency tests more strategically and they were more confident and efficacious in reading harder material. One student teacher found that as she encouraged responsibility for strategies, the passive low achievers flourished. "I know what I can do to figure out what I'm reading!" said a remedial student.

> *Several weeks after Mrs. E's lesson*: After practicing ETR and Visuals with different stories, Mrs. E knew that the strategies had been internalized and had empowered her students when they clamored at the beginning of a new story, "Don't tell us, we know! We'll use ETR and tell all we know about this topic (referring to the title) before we start reading the story. During the story we will keep thinking about how the story is like our lives and we could also make a picture of the story parts. Right? Those are ways we can understand the story better."

Conclusion

Perhaps the fiercest theoretical debate around the issue of strategic processes today is not the concept of strategies that help readers become competent. "It is about who should control formation of that strategic system" (Clay, 1991, p. 344). Does the student do it alone, or does the teacher provide programmed help or monitoring? The various theories and models in today's literature indicate the answer lies between both positions. As opposed to the 1970s and 1980s instruction, educators view strategy use as only one facet of competency, embedding strategy learning in the ebb and flow of literature discussions, encouraging the coordination and use of a repertoire of strategies, and emphasizing student control and self-assessment "in flight" or "on the run." Fountas and Pinnell (1996) make the subtle distinction that reading instruction is teaching for strategies.

Direct instruction, in its purest sense, is often thought of as the antithesis of student-centered whole language (teacher-as-deliverer as opposed to teacher-as-facilitator). Heller (1995) suggests that a wise combination of direct instruction and student-centered activity is the goal for which classroom teachers should strive. Instructional scaffolding (challenging and assisting students to work at the edge of their competence) is one way to bridge the two contradictory models (Pearson & Fielding, 1991).

Duffy (1993) posits the most important thing is that strategic reading requires strategic teachers, which in turn requires strategic staff development (both preservice and inservice).

That is, if low achievers are to be strategic (i.e., if they are to be flexible adapters of strategies as needed to construct meanings), their teachers must themselves be strategic (i.e., flexible adapters of professional knowledge in response to students' developing concepts), and the teachers of teachers must also be strategic (i.e., adapting innovations and research findings to teachers' situations and involving them as co-constructors of knowledge rather than telling them what to do). (p. 245)

Toward these goals, I encourage both novice and experienced reading teachers, who want to establish a strategic stance, to experiment with and adapt the framework in their classrooms. However, a caveat is necessary. The framework is not a prescription or script to be followed verbatim, but a broad schema or flexible guide to be built anew, adapted, and co-constructed as the competence level of students change. By facilitating the first foray into strategy teaching, the framework can act as an instructional scaffold model for teachers and, in turn, their students.

References

Almasi, J.F., McKeown, M.G., & Beck, I.L. (1996). The nature of engaged reading in classroom discussion of literature. *Journal of Literacy Research, 28*, 107–146.

Alvermann, D.E. (1991). The discussion web: A graphic aid for learning across the curriculum. *The Reading Teacher, 45*, 92–99.

Alvermann, D.E., &. Guthrie, J.T. (1993). Themes and directions of the National Reading Research Center. *Perspectives in reading research, No. 1*. Athens, GA and College Park, MD: National Reading Research Center.

Armbruster, B.B. (1991). Silent reading, oral reading, and learning from text. *The Reading Teacher, 45*, 154–155.

Armbruster, B.B., Anderson, T.H., & Ostertag, J. (1989). Teaching text structure to improve reading and writing. *The Reading Teacher, 43*, 130–137.

Au, K.H. (1979). Using the experience-text-relationship method with minority children. *The Reading Teacher, 32*, 678–679.

Au, K.H. (1992). Constructing the theme of a story. *Language Arts, 69*, 106–111.

Au, K. H. (1993). *Literacy instruction in multicultural settings*. New York: Harcourt Brace Jovanovich.

Baumann, J.F., & Schmitt, M.C. (1986). The what, why, how, and when of comprehension instruction. *The Reading Teacher, 39*, 640–646.

Beck, I.L., McKeown, M.G., Hamilton, R.L., & Kucan, L. (1997). *Questioning the author: An approach for enhancing student engagement with text*. Newark, DE: International Reading Association.

Blanton, W.E., Wood, K.D., & Moorman, G.B. (1990). The role of purpose in reading instruction. *The Reading Teacher, 43*, 486–493.

Cambourne, B. (1988). *The whole story: Natural learning and the acquisition of literacy in the classroom*. Auckland, New Zealand: Scholastic.

Carnine, D.W., Silbert, J., & Kameenui, E.J. (1997). *Direct instruction reading* (3rd ed.). Columbus, OH: Merrill.

Carr, E., & Ogle, D. (1987). K-W-L plus: A strategy for comprehension and summarization. *Journal of Reading, 30*, 626–631.

Clay, M. (1991). *Becoming literate: Construction of inner control*. Portsmouth, NH: Heinemann.

Cudd, E., & Roberts, L.L. (1987). Using story frames to develop reading comprehension in a 1st grade classroom. *The Reading Teacher, 41*, 74–79.

Dalton, S., & Dowhower, S. (1985). *The directed seeing thinking activity and the directed listening thinking activity* (Early Education Bulletin No. 10). Honolulu, HI: Center for Development of Early Education, Kamehameha Schools—Bishop Estate.

Daniels, H. (1994). *Literature circles: Voice and choice in the student-centered classroom*. York, ME: Stenhouse.

Davis, Z.T., & McPherson, M.D. (1989). Story map instruction: A road map for reading comprehension. *The Reading Teacher, 43*, 232–240.

DeFina, A. (1992). *Portfolio assessment*. New York: Scholastic.

Delton, J. (1986). The new girl at school. In W. Durr (Ed.), *Adventures* (pp. 12–20). Boston: Houghton Mifflin.

Dole, J.A., Duffy, G.G., Roehler, L.E., & Pearson, P.D. (1991). Moving from the old to the new: Research on reading comprehension instruction. *Review of Educational Research, 61*, 239–264.

Dowhower, S. (1998). *A ten-year survey of reading strategy teaching in elementary schools*. Unpublished raw data.

Duffy, G.G. (1993). Rethinking strategy instruction: Four teachers' development and their low achievers' understanding. *The Elementary School Journal, 93*, 231–247.

Duffy, G.G., Roehler, L.R., Sivan, E., Rackliffe, G., Book, C., Meloth, M.S., Vavrus, L.G., Wesselman, R., Putnam, J., & Bassiri, D. (1987). Effects of explaining the reasoning associated with using reading strategies. *Reading Research Quarterly, 22*, 347–368.

Durkin, D. (1978–1979). What classroom observations reveal about reading comprehension instruction. *Reading Research Quarterly, 14*, 481–533.

Durkin, D. (1981). Reading comprehension instruction in five basal reading series. *Reading Research Quarterly, 16*, 515–544.

Durkin, D. (1984). Is there a match between what elementary teachers do and what basal reader manuals recommend? *The Reading Teacher, 37*, 734–744.

Fielding, L.G., & Pearson, P.D. (1994). Reading comprehension: What works. *Educational Leadership, 51*(5), 62–68.

Fountas, I.C., & Pinnell, G.S. (1996). *Guided reading*. Portsmouth, NH: Heinemann.

Fowler, G.L. (1982). Developing comprehension skills in primary students through the use of story frames. *The Reading Teacher, 37*, 176–179.

Gambrell, L.B. (1996). Creating classroom cultures that foster reading motivation. *The Reading Teacher, 50*, 14–25.

Garner, R. (1992). Metacognition and self-monitoring strategies. In S.J. Samuels & A.E. Farstrup (Eds.), *What research has to say about reading instruction* (2nd ed., pp. 236–252). Newark, DE: International Reading Association.

Goldenberg, C. (1992–1993). Instructional conversations: Promoting comprehension through discussion. *The Reading Teacher, 46*, 316–326.

Goodman, Y.M., Watson, D.J., & Burke, C.L. (1996). *Reading strategies: Focus on comprehension* (2nd ed.). Katonah, NY: Richard C. Owen.

Griffin, C.C., Malone, L.D., & Kameenui, E.J. (1995). Effects of graphic organizer instruction on fifth-grade

students. *The Journal of Educational Research, 89*(2), 98–107.

Guthrie, J.T. (1996). Educational contexts for engagement in literacy. *The Reading Teacher, 49*, 432–445.

Guthrie, J.T., & McCann, A.D. (1997). Characteristics of classrooms that promote and motivations and strategies for learning. In J.T. Guthrie & A. Wigfield (Eds.), *Reading engagement: Motivating readers through integrated instruction* (pp. 128–148). Newark, DE: International Reading Association.

Haggard, M.R. (1988). Developing critical thinking with the directed reading-thinking activity. *The Reading Teacher, 41*, 526–533.

Hansen, J., & Pearson, P.D. (1983). An instructional study: Improving the inferential comprehension of good and poor fourth-grade readers. *Journal of Educational Psychology, 75*, 821–829.

Heap, J.L. (1982). Understanding classroom events: A critique of Durkin, with an alternative. *Journal of Reading Behavior, 14*, 391–411.

Heller, M. (1995). *Reading-writing connections: From theory to practice* (2nd ed.). New York: Longman.

Hodges, C.A. (1980). Commentary: Toward a broader definition of comprehension instruction. *Reading Research Quarterly, 15*, 299–306.

Jones, B.F., Pierce, J., & Hunter, B. (1989). Teaching students to construct graphic representations. *Educational Leadership, 46*(4), 20–25.

Kern, R.G. (1989). Second language reading strategy instruction: Its effects on comprehension and word inference ability. *The Modern Language Journal, 73*, 135–149.

Kletzien, S.B. (1991). Strategy use by good and poor comprehenders reading expository text at differing levels. *Reading Research Quarterly, 24*, 67–85.

Kurth, R.J., & Greenlaw, M.J. (1980, December). *Research and practices in comprehension instruction in elementary classrooms*. Paper presented at the annual meeting of the American Reading Conference, Sarasota, FL. (ERIC Document Reproduction Service No. ED 195 931)

Lehr, S. (1988). The child's developing sense of theme as a response to literature. *Reading Research Quarterly, 23*, 337–357.

Lipson M.Y., & Wixson, K.K. (1991). *Assessment and instruction of reading disability: An interactive approach*. New York: HarperCollins.

Lynch, D. (1988). Reading comprehension under listening, silent and round robin reading conditions as a function of text difficulty. *Reading Improvement, 25*(2), 98–104.

Marshall, N. (1983). Using story grammar to assess reading comprehension. *The Reading Teacher, 36*, 616–620.

Mason, J. (1983). An examination of reading instruction in third and fourth grades. *The Reading Teacher, 36*, 906–913.

Mason, J., & Au, K.H. (1990). *Reading instruction for today* (2nd ed.). Glenview, IL: Scott Foresman.

McGee, L.M., & Richgels, D.J. (1985). Teaching expository text structure to elementary students. *The Reading Teacher, 38*, 739–748.

McMahon, S.I. & Raphael, T.E. (1997). *The book club connection*. New York: Teachers College Press.

Morrow, L.M. (1997). *Literacy development in the early years*. Boston: Allyn & Bacon.

Ogle, D.M. (1986). K-W-L: A teaching model that develops active reading of expository text. *The Reading Teacher, 39*, 564–570.

Pearson, P.D. (1985). Changing the face of reading comprehension instruction. *The Reading Teacher, 38*, 724–737.

Pearson, P.D., & Fielding, L. (1991). Comprehension instruction. In R. Barr, M. Kamil, P. Mosenthal, & P.D. Pearson (Eds.), *Handbook of reading research, Vol. II* (pp. 815–860). New York: Longman.

Pearson, P.D., Roehler, L.R., Dole, J.A., & Duffy, G.G. (1992). Developing expertise in reading comprehension. In S.J. Samuels & A.E. Farstrup (Eds.), *What research has to say about reading instruction* (2nd ed., pp. 145–199). Newark, DE: International Reading Association.

Piccolo, J. (1987). Expository text structure: Teaching and learning strategies. *The Reading Teacher, 40,* 838–847.

Pressley, M., El-Dinary, P.B., Gaskins, I., Bergman, J.L., Almasi, J., & Brown, R. (1992). Beyond direct explanation: Transactional instruction of reading comprehension strategies. *The Elementary School Journal, 92,* 513–555.

Pressley, M., Symons, S., Snyder, B., & Cariglia-Bull, T. (1989). Strategy instruction research comes of age. *Learning Disability Quarterly, 12*(1), 16–31.

Rhodes, L.K. (1993). *Literacy assessments.* Portsmouth, NH: Heinemann.

Ringler, L.H., & Weber, C. (1984). *A language-thinking approach to reading.* New York: Harcourt Brace Jovanovich.

Rosenblatt, L.M. (1978). *The reader, the text, the poem: The transactional theory of literacy work.* Carbondale, IL: Southern Illinois University Press.

Rosenblatt, L.M. (1994). The transactional theory of reading and writing. In R.B. Ruddell, M.R. Ruddell, & H. Singer (Eds.), *Theoretical models and processes of reading* (4th ed., pp. 1057–1092). Newark, DE: International Reading Association.

Rosenshine, B. (1980). Skill hierarchies in reading comprehension. In R.J. Spiro, B.C. Bruce, & W.F. Brewer (Eds.), *Theoretical issues in reading comprehension* (pp. 535–554). Hillsdale, NJ: Erlbaum.

Santa, C.M., Isaacson, L., & Manning, G. (1987). Changing content instruction through action research. *The Reading Teacher, 40,* 434–438.

Schunk, D.H., & Zimmerman, B.J. (1997). Developing self-efficacious readers and writers: The role of social and self-regulatory processes. In J.T. Guthrie & A. Wigfield (Eds.), *Reading engagement: Motivating readers through integrated instruction* (pp. 34–50). Newark, DE: International Reading Association.

Smith, M.W. (1991). Constructing meaning from text: An analysis of ninth-grade reader responses. *Journal of Educational Research, 84,* 263–271.

Smith, J.W.A., & Elley, W.B. (1994). *Learning to read in New Zealand.* Katonah, NY: Richard C. Owen.

Standards for the English Language Arts. (1996). Newark, DE: International Reading Association and Urbana, IL: National Council of Teachers of English.

Stauffer, R.G. (1969). *Directing reading maturity as a cognitive process.* New York: Harper & Row.

Stauffer, R.G. (1975). *Directing the direct reading-thinking process.* New York: Harper & Row.

Swanson, B.B. (1988). Strategic preferences of good and poor beginning readers. *Reading Horizons, 28,* 255–261.

Tharp, R., & Gallimore, R. (1988). *Rousing minds to life: Teaching, learning and schooling in a social context.* Cambridge, England: Cambridge University Press.

Tierney, R.J., Readence, J.E., & Dishner, E.K. (1995). *Reading strategies and practices: A compendium* (4th ed.). Boston: Allyn & Bacon.

Walker, B.J. (1996a). *Diagnostic teaching of reading* (3rd ed.). Englewood Cliffs, NJ: Merrill.

Walker, B.J. (1996b). Discussions that focus on strategies and self-assessment. In L.B. Gambrell & J.F. Almasi (Eds.), *Lively discussions!* (pp. 256–296). Newark, DE: International Reading Association.

Weaver, C. (1994). *Reading process and practice: From socio-psycholinguistics to whole language* (2nd ed.). Portsmouth, NH: Heinemann.

Wendler, D., Samuels, S.J., & Moore, V.K. (1989). Comprehension instruction of award-winning teachers, teachers with master's degrees, and other teachers. *Reading Research Quarterly, 24,* 382–400.

APPENDIX A
Comprehension strategy framework

Text:_____

Central theme/relationship: _____
(Possible Big Idea(s) to be worked by teacher and students)

I. **Prereading:** Enabling Activities
  A. Assess/elicit prior knowledge
  Teacher determines with students what they already know about the topic, ideas, structure, or contents of the text to be read. Also, the teacher checks students' knowledge of what a "strategy" is and if they have ever used the particular strategy targeted or others to increase their understanding of what they have read.

  B. Build background/relate to prior knowledge
  Teacher and students build bridges from known to unknown through use of questions, statements, and activities. What do the students know that will help them understand the text and the new strategies introduced here?

  C. Focus attention on strategy
  Teacher establishes *what* comprehension strategy students are going to learn and *why* it will help the students. The teacher gives a model or brief description of *how* the strategy works.

II. **Active reading:** Interaction between Students, Teacher, and Text
  A. *Cycle 1:*

  Establish purpose for reading Reasons for reading the section are set by either the students or teacher, or jointly.

  Read silently pages xx Students should be encouraged to self-monitor, think about and react to what they are reading, and to use the strategy, as well as other strategies they know, to understand what they are reading.

  Discuss/work the story Together students and teacher negotiate the meaning of the section. The teacher includes 1–2 open-ended questions for discussion, starting first with the purpose(s) set for reading. Utmost in the teacher's mind is working toward meaningful themes. The teacher also supports strategy construction by naming the strategy and showing how she or he uses it personally.

  B. *Cycle 2* and beyond:

  Establish purpose

  Read silently pages xx

  Discuss/work the story

  Repeat Cycle as needed.

  C. *Final Discussion*: Theme and comprehension strategy
  Teacher includes 1–2 open-ended questions that get at the heart of the story (*theme*) and tie the discussion of the sections together. It is important for the students to explicitly discuss *what* strategy they learned, *why* it helped comprehension, and *when* they could use the strategy again in other texts, particularly in their independent reading. Encourage students to identify other comprehension and decoding strategies that they used as they read.

III. **Postreading:** Independent Activities
  These activities are done after reading and working the text. They are done alone or in small groups without the teacher.

(continued)

A. *Recall of content*

This may include the traditional activities of answering comprehension questions, sequencing the text parts, drawing a picture of an important episode, etc.

B. *Reader response*

Students respond in some fashion to the text. This may include both efferent and aesthetic responses.

C. *Extension of text*

Students go beyond text doing other reading, writing, listening, or speaking activities that are related, such as repeated reading, partner reading, taping the story, Readers Theatre, or writing a new ending.

D. *Strategy use and transfer*

Students practice the strategy with the specific text or a new text.

E. *Informal or self-assessment*

Students may retell the story or demonstrate comprehension of the text and strategy use in some way. Also, students might explain and evaluate how effectively they were using certain strategies "in flight" by recording and rating them as they read.

IV. **Evaluation of teaching:** Reflection

How clear were your explanations of the strategy? How well did you use "what, why, how and when" and continue to reinforce the strategy throughout the lesson? How well do you think the students understand the strategy and how to apply it to help their comprehension? In what ways did you support the coordination and use of other strategies? How well did the students appreciate and develop understanding of the text on their own terms? Why was the theme(s) constructed appropriate?

APPENDIX B
Example of a plan using the comprehension strategy framework:
Mrs. E's introduction of ETR and visual structure strategies

Text: "The New Girl at School," *Adventures*, Houghton-Mifflin, pp. 12–20.

Central theme(s): Things get better over time. Bad situations can become good. Change is hard. We all need acceptance.

I. **Prereading:**
  A. Assess prior knowledge:
    1. Content: This story is about a girl moving to a new home. Has anyone done this? How did you feel? What problems were there?
    2. Strategies: What are reading strategies? What strategies do you use to figure out meaning?
  B. Build background:
    1. Content: Imagine how it would feel if you went some place new and didn't know anyone. The people there already had friends. This is what happens in our story. How might you feel? What might you do?
    2. Strategies: We have learned to make pictures in our head and to guess what was coming next in order to help understand the story. There are other similar strategies that good readers use.
  C. Focus attention on strategy: Today we are going to read a story and learn to understand it better by talking about our own experiences and how they are like the character's. Also, instead of visualizing in our heads, we are going to draw a picture of the events of the story so we can better know what happened to the little girl. (Strategy—what, why, and how)

II. **Active Reading:**
  Cycle 1
  Establish purpose: The first page of our story gives us a general purpose for reading the story (p. 12). What do you think we will find out as we read? (Discuss predictions of how Marcia might feel going to a new school.)

  Read silently pages 13–14 to find out how Marcia feels the first day.

  Discuss/work story: If we were to draw a face on our chart as to how Marcia feels, what would it be (Visual Structure)? Why? Let's list the reasons she is unhappy (see attached visual). What is so funny about the words in parentheses? Relate her comments to what you would be saying to yourself (ETR).

  Cycle 2
  Establish purpose: How would you react the next day? What do you think will happen to Marcia the next day?

  Read silently pages 15–16 to see if you made a close guess.

  Discuss/work story: Were you close? What happened the next two days? (Add to chart.) Did something ever happen to you like this (ETR)?

  Cycle 3
  Establish purpose: What gives us a clue that things are changing for the better? How would you feel if you were Marcia?

  Read silently pages 17–18 to see if your feelings were the same.

  Discuss/work story: How would you be feeling if you were in this situation (ETR)? How did Marcia's feelings change by the end of the week? Why? Would you have stayed at that school (ETR)? Why? (Add to chart.)

(continued)

APPENDIX B (continued)
Example of a plan using the comprehension strategy framework:
Mrs. E's introduction of ETR and visual structure strategies

Final discussion: (Theme) How is this story like an experience you had? Look at the picture we built on the chart and tell us what the author might be trying to tell us in this story. What can we learn from Marcia's experience that will help us? (Strategy) What did we do to understand the story better? (talked about how our experiences were like the girl's and drew a picture to show the parts of the story and how her feelings changed over the week at school). When could we use ETR and visuals again? What other times could we use these to understand a story better? (When you are having problems re-membering and making sense of a story, you could draw a picture of the parts. Also when the story is like something that happened to you, you could use what you know to figure it out.) What other strategies did you use as you read the story?

III. **Postreading:**
   A. Recall: Reread the story again with a partner and find one example to support the feelings in each of the five faces on the worksheet (see attached).
   B. Reader Response: In your journal, write about the feelings you would have if you were a new student in that classroom. Tell the theme or important idea you got out of the story and why you think it is important.

IV. **Evaluation**
   Example of visual structure

Monday	Tuesday	Wednesday
Everyone stared	No one to sit with on bus	Didn't get picture up
Everyone had friends	By self at lunch	Got to second base
Couldn't do subtraction		

Thursday	Friday
Put airplane up	New girl doesn't get subtraction
Skirt noticed	Asked to sleep over

(continued)

APPENDIX B (continued)
Example of a plan using the comprehension strategy framework:
Mrs. E's introduction of ETR and visual structure strategies

"The New Girl at School"

1. Name the day beside the face.

2. Write one sentence from the story that supports (proves) each feeling.

Timothy Shanahan
Sherrell Shanahan

Character Perspective Charting: Helping children to develop a more complete conception of story

Character Perspective Charting is an instructional technique that fosters story understanding.

The scene is a fourth-grade suburban U.S. classroom. Students have finished reading a short story, and now their desks are pushed together into five small groups. The students in each group are engaged in a sometimes spirited conversation about the story. One boy says, "No, no…I don't think those characters have the same intentions."

"Yes, they do. They both want the same thing," answers another group member.

"If we can't agree, how do I fill it in?" a third child, waving a Character Perspective Chart, appeals to the teacher. The students, as if one, open their books and begin to reexamine the story without any direction from the teacher. It is evident that these children are thinking deeply about the story and particularly about the relationships between characters' intentions and goals. As one youngster told us, "You never know the complete story without this activity."

We developed Character Perspective Charts (CPCs) to help children gain access to a more complete and appropriate understanding of stories. The purpose of this article is to describe the use of Character Perspective Charts in elementary reading classes.

Story mapping and what we used to believe about story comprehension

CPC is a technique that has its roots in the story summary charts or story maps that have been a popular activity in elementary classrooms for several years (McConaughy, 1980). Tim, one of the authors of this article, teaches undergraduate and graduate teacher education courses, and over the years he has often recommended the use of these story mapping techniques. Sherry, the other author, is a reading specialist in an elementary school district, and she has used mapping with students and has recommended it to the teachers in her school.

Most reading textbooks now recommend such charts or maps, and many articles for teachers have appeared showing how they can best be used (e.g., Beck & McKeown, 1981; Marshall, 1983; Reutzel, 1985; Sadow, 1982; Whaley, 1981). It has become commonplace to have elementary school children fill in charts with information about main characters, their problems, attempts to solve them, outcomes, and other plot elements.

The source of such activities can be traced directly to the story grammar research conducted by cognitive psychologists during the 1970s (Mandler & Johnson, 1977; Stein & Glenn, 1979). Story grammar was an attempt to describe the rules that people use to create and remember stories. Like sentence grammars, a story grammar is a set of structural rules. For example, all well-formed sentences must have a subject and predicate, and the predicate describes the action of the subject. Similarly, according to story grammar rules, stories are expected to have a main character who is confronted with some type of problem.

Story grammars were remarkable in that they seemed to describe the powerful mental tools that people use for remembering stories, drawing inferences about them, and creating new stories. Stein's work (Stein & Glenn, 1979) was particularly persuasive, possibly because of the simple labels that she used for her categories and the elegance of her experiments (Shanahan & Neuman, in press). In one study, for instance, she told children stories that omitted some key structural information. Students tended to fill in the gap with structurally appropriate information when they remembered the story. Or if the structural information was told out of sequence, children would remember the story in story grammar order instead of as it was actually told. Thus, story grammars seemed to offer a sound description of the abstract categorical structures used to remember stories; as a result, teachers and curriculum designers developed a variety of instructional techniques based on them. That was why we, and others, thought story maps were such a good idea.

But what if story grammars—and the instructional story maps and charts based upon them—could not provide a full summary of most stories? What if these activities mislead teachers and students into thinking about stories in ways that are not especially accurate?

Quite by accident, we became aware of these troubling possibilities a few years ago. Since then we have been field testing a technique for helping children to develop fuller and more appropriate conceptualizations of stories. Given the dramatic increase in the availability of high-quality literature for teaching reading, this is a particularly opportune time for the development of instructional methods that reflect the actual complexity of stories. In the rest of this article we will describe CPC, a practical instructional alternative to story mapping, that appears to help children to better understand, interpret, and appreciate stories. We will describe how we developed CPC and some of the ways that we have used it with children in Grades 2–6 at Sherry's school.

A different way of looking at stories

A few years ago, Tim was preparing a presentation on story mapping for an undergraduate reading course that he was teaching. He used *The Big Orange Splot* by Daniel Pinkwater (1977) as his example and filled in each of the categories in the chart with information about that story. (See left side of the Figure.) It worked beautifully. All essential information from the story was used, all of the blanks in the chart were filled, and a somewhat conventional theme emerged. But, what if...? Tim began to anticipate questions that students might ask.

But what if...story maps and charts... mislead teachers and students into thinking about stories in ways that are not especially accurate?

"What if a child erred? What if a child charted it incorrectly?" If a child made a mistake, the chart wouldn't come out right, he assumed. Surprisingly, given the popularity of these techniques, there are no examples in the literature of their diagnostic use. He proceeded to develop an example with a mistake in it so that these beginning teachers would recognize the implications of errors that might occur.

To fill in the chart Tim had to think about who the main character was. It is a simple story, and the only choices for main character are Mr. Plumbean or the neighbors. We usually tell children to choose the main character based upon who has the important problem, and in this case he thought it was Plumbean; after all, it was his house that was messed up. So, to get it wrong, he chose the neighbors as the main character for this second chart. (See right side of the Figure.) Despite this fundamental error in choice, he found that he could, again, summarize all important information from the story. He was able to fill in all of the spaces on the chart and, surprisingly, could still arrive at a reasonable theme. Even more surprising was the fact that the themes for the two charts were in conflict.

As he examined the charts, he began to appreciate the depth of *The Big Orange Splot* in new ways. This simple children's story emerged as a cleverly designed tale that captured the fundamental tensions between two very different world views. Any summary of the story without a description of its conflict of perspectives would miss the point. Clearly the story mapping chart alone was insufficient. It allowed a reasonable summary of the story, but it also focused the reader's attention on only a single perspective. By charting the story from both characters' points of view, however, he arrived at a greater

Character Perspective Chart	
Main character: Who is the main character? MR. PLUMBEAN	Main character: Who is the main character? MR. PLUMBEAN'S NEIGHBORS.
Setting: Where and when does the story take place? PLUMBEAN'S NEIGHBORHOOD	Setting: Where and when does the story take place? PLUMBEAN'S NEIGHBORHOOD
Problem: What is the main character's problem? PLUMBEAN'S NEIGHBORS PESTER HIM.	Problem: What is the main character's problem? BIRD DROPS PAINT ON PLUMBEAN'S HOUSE.
Goal: What is the main character's goal? What does the character want? TO DECORATE HIS HOUSE AND GET NEIGHBORS TO LEAVE HIM ALONE	Goal: What is the main character's goal? What does the character want? TO MAKE NEIGHBORHOOD ALL THE SAME AGAIN.
Attempt: What does the main character do to solve the problem or get the goal? DECORATES HOUSE AND TALKS TO EACH NEIGHBOR	Attempt: What does the main character do to solve the problem or get the goal? TRY TO CONVINCE HIM TO CHANGE THEN EACH CHANGES TO BE LIKE HIM
Outcome: What happened as a result of the attempt? PLUMBEAN'S HOUSE LOOKS LIKE HIS DREAMS AND NEIGHBORS ACCEPT IT.	Outcome: What happened as a result of the attempt? ALL HOUSES IN NEIGHBORHOOD ARE DECORATED IN SAME WAY.
Reaction: How does the main character feel about the outcome? HAPPY.	Reaction: How does the main character feel about the outcome? HAPPY.
Theme: What point did the author want to make? FOLLOW YOUR DREAMS.	Theme: What point did the author want to make? IT IS IMPORTANT TO BE THE SAME.

understanding and appreciation. Instead of structural elements being a kind of static property of story—a stable set of building blocks that, when properly assembled, add up to a story—this procedure encouraged an awareness of the dynamic interconnections between theme and structure. The original story grammar research never considered multiple character perspectives, conflict, or even the dynamic relationship of theme and structure. (Theme in most maps is just one more structural property of story, one more box to fill in.) By thinking about the story from a second perspective, Tim had deepened his understanding and appreciation of this story and of stories in general.

As a result of this peculiar discovery, we began to wonder about the prevalence of social conflict within stories and to investigate how useful this kind of dual charting might be for helping children to think more effectively about what they read. In this process, we went back to read the original research on story grammars again and found that as persuasive as the story grammar work had been, there were other conflicting theories and studies that challenged the story grammar findings. Unfortunately, these theories had not been translated into instructional activities or procedures, so they exerted little or no influence on comprehension instruction. These alternative views were more in accord with the kind of dual charting that Tim had used with *The Big Orange Splot*.

For example, Bertram Bruce and his colleagues described stories on the basis of character plans and goals. They illustrated how stories gained depth when characters' plans interacted and claimed that "much of the complexity of stories in which characters interact arises because the story is about a *conflict* between the goals of two characters" (Bruce & Newman, 1978, p. 196). Elsewhere (Steinberg & Bruce, 1980), they quoted the novelist John Le Carré as pithily saying, "The cat sat on the mat is not a story. The cat sat on the dog's mat is a story" (p. 1). Unfortunately, this economy of description was not preserved in their analysis, and these ideas did not find their way into the instructional literature. Bruce and his colleagues found that character conflicts of this type were common in children's books. They examined a sample of 32 stories (half primary, half intermediate) and found that 29 of them

contained such conflicts, and all but one of these was an example of interpersonal conflict.

More recently, Trabasso (1989) pointed out that "when we understand a series of events in a text, we do not experience them as isolated, individual occurrences," but as "a *coherent* sequence of happenings" (p. 68). He concluded that to achieve this coherence, a reader must draw inferences about the protagonist's plan or goal-directed sequences. Trabasso criticized the static quality of story grammar categories but, like us, did not simply reject them. Instead, he provided a reconceptualization of the categories. These categories, in Trabasso's view, "activate information we have stored about intentional action and use to infer relations from this knowledge about plans" (p. 75). His work demonstrated that children, ages 3–9, recognize the need for a goal plan for their main characters (Trabasso, Stein, Rodkin, Munger, & Baughn, 1992). This study found that story memory can be described better when we consider causal connections based upon readers' theories of characters' intentions.

Even more relevant to our concerns is the work of Golden and Guthrie (1986). They examined student responses to a story and wondered about the sources of the interpretive differences that occurred. After careful analysis, they concluded that both text and reader factors were implicated. Interpretations depended on whether readers felt empathy for particular characters, and empathy depended both on readers' personal experiences and on how "the text presents the points of view of two characters...and thus evokes different kinds of emotional involvement" (p. 417). They noted that "A favorable disposition toward one character may lead the reader to construct meaning in which that character is central" (p. 419). Thus, readers who focus on the perspective of a single character, something that they may be predisposed to do by their own experiences or the art of the author, can end up with an incomplete understanding of a story. Golden and Guthrie found that readers often disagreed about who was actually in conflict within a story, and, therefore, multiple plausible plot summaries were possible. They argued that conflict, because of its close connection to theme and character intentions, transcends plot details. Traditional story mapping or summarizing procedures could mask this inherent complexity, as they focus attention only on the main character's point of view. Emery and Mihalevich (1992) have demonstrated that children can have trouble understanding a literary work when they focus too narrowly on the main character's perspective.

Given these findings, it is surprising that story mapping has been so widely recommended. Story mapping focuses attention so heavily on the problems of a single character that it can only reinforce the notion of a single correct interpretation. Authors and children's book publishers have recognized the importance of character perspective or goal conflict; witness *The True Story of the Three Little Pigs* (Scieszka, 1989) in which the author tells the

---

Literary interpretation and, indeed, reading are constructive acts. To be good at them, the reader must learn to do this interpretive work on his or her own.

---

story and explains the conflict from the wolf's point of view. But as enjoyable and useful as a book like this can be, it should be remembered that it is the author and not the children who is doing the hard interpretive work.

Literary interpretation and, indeed, reading are constructive acts. To be good at them, the reader must learn to do this interpretive work on his or her own. Story maps emphasize static structural properties of text over these more dynamic and interactive qualities. The dual CPC charting that Tim happened upon seemed promising as an instructional technique because of the possibility that it would provoke children to interpret character perspective in ways more in accord with these richer views.

Character Perspective Charts and how we use them

This is where Sherry got involved. She was looking for some new techniques for teaching comprehension and thought Tim's CPC idea might be just the thing. This led her—and some of the teachers at her school— to try it out with children in Grades 2–6, with very promising results.

Stories or novels used with CPC should have two or more characters with separate goals. The technique can be applied to any story with more than one character, but it is most revealing when the characters' goals are in conflict. Fairy tales often have this structure. Think of the conflicting goals of Cinderella and her grasping stepsisters, Rumplestiltskin and the clever peasant's daughter, or the three bears and Goldilocks.

Sherry's school has both a K–8 basal anthology and the early levels of a 6–12 litera-

---

Table 1
Some recent Caldecott winners for Character Perspective Charting

Caldecott winners	Characters in conflict
Rathman, Peggy. (1995). *Officer Buckle and Gloria*. New York: Putnam.	Buckle/Gloria
Say, Allen. (1993). *Grandfather's journey*. Boston: Houghton Mifflin.	Grandfather/Grandchild
McCully, Emily Arnold. (1992). *Mirette on the high wire*. New York: Putnam.	Mirette/Bellini
Wiesner, David. (1991). *Tuesday*. New York: Trumpet Club.	Frog/Policeman
Macaulay, David. (1990). *Black and white*. Boston: Houghton Mifflin.	Boy at home/Parents
Young, Ed. (1990). *Lon Po Po: A red-riding hood story from China*. New York: Scholastic.	Children/Wolf
Ackerman, Karen. (1988). *Song and dance man*. New York: Knopf.	Grandpa/Children
Yolen, Jane. (1987) *Owl moon*. New York: Philomel.	Father/Daughter
Yorinks, Arthur. (1986). *Hey, Al*. New York: Farrar Straus & Giroux	Al/Bird
Van Allsburg, Chris. (1985). *The Polar Express*. Boston: Houghton Mifflin.	Boy/Santa

ture series. She examined the stories in these and found that such conflict was evident in more than 60% of the selections; this is attenuated a bit because of the existence of nonstory materials from science and social studies and stories with only single characters. In other words, it is very easy to find appropriate selections. (See Tables 1 and 2 for lists of some popular books and stories that can be used with CPC.) Although the technique was developed for use with short stories, such as those in a typical picture book format, Sherry found that it worked even better with longer and more complex novels such as *The Black Cauldron* by Lloyd Alexander (1990) or *Ramona Forever* by Beverly Cleary (1979). The idea of CPC is to help children to think about stories at a deeper

level, and most novels recommended for classroom use have the kind of depth that makes such an analysis worthwhile. In these stories each chapter poses new problems and character actions. Each chapter can be charted separately for a detailed understanding of the whole novel.

CPC works well with historical fiction, also. When fifth graders charted *The Fighting Ground* by Avi (1987), a story about 24 hours during the American Revolution, they developed a fuller understanding of how perspectives of war differed between common soldiers and officers. The many events, problems, and conflicts support two opposing themes, which made for a lively class discussion about the glory and realities of war. We have a hunch

---

Table 2
Other popular stories for Character Perspective Charting

Stories for various grade levels	Characters in conflict
Grade 2	
Henry and Mudge by Cynthia Rylant	Henry/Mudge
The Wednesday Surprise by Eve Bunting	Grandma/Anna
The Mysterious Tadpole by Steven Kellogg	Louis/Miss Seevers/Alphonse
The Best Friends' Club by Elizabeth Winthrop	Lizzie/Harold
Grade 3	
Dr. DeSoto by William Steig	Dr. DeSoto/Fox
Grandfather Tang's Story by Ann Tampert	Chou/Wu Ling
The Patchwork Quilt by Valerie Flournoy	Grandma/Tanya/Mama
Ramona Forever by Beverly Cleary	Ramona/Mr. Quimby
Dream Wolf by Paul Goble	Tiblo/Wolf
Grade 4	
The Lost Lake by Allen Say	Dad/Luke
Sarah, Plain and Tall by Patricia MacLachlan	Sarah/Anna
Yeh-Shen by Ai-Ling Louie	Yeh-Shen/Stepmother
The Three Little Pigs and the Fox by William Hooks	Hamlet/Fox
Mufaro's Beautiful Daughters by John Steptoe	Nyasha/Manyara
Grade 5	
The Talking Eggs by Robert San Souçi	Rose/Blanche/Old Woman
The Voyage of the Dawn Trader by C.S. Lewis	Eustace/Lucy
Willie Bea and the Time Martians Landed by Virginia Hamilton	Willie Bea/Toughy Clay
The Best Bad Thing by Yoshiko Uchida	Rinko/Aunt Hattie
The Shimmershine Queens by Camille Yarbrough	Angie/Ms. Collier
Grade 6	
Zlateh the Goat by Isaac Bashevis Singer	Aaron/Reuven
Dragon, Dragon by John Gardner	Dragon/Youngest Son
Greyling by Jane Yolen	Fisherman/Wife
The American Slurp by Lensey Namioka	Maibon/Dwarf
The Wise Old Woman by Yoshiko Uchida	Emperor/Old Woman/Farmer

that CPC would also work with factual historical narratives in a similar fashion, although we have not yet had the opportunity to try it out with them.

CPC is likely to be especially helpful with those stories and novels that reveal variations in life experiences that we hope children will learn to bridge. For example, using CPC with a story such as *Princess Poo* by Kathleen Muldoon (1989) helped a classroom of second graders become more aware of and sensitive to physical handicaps by charting the story from the points of view of two sisters, one confined to a wheelchair and the other jealous of the attention that her sister received.

Moreover, CPC is likely to become more useful as teachers increasingly try to use literature that reflects the experiences of various racial, ethnic, and linguistic groups. Books such as *Baseball in April and Other Stories* by Gary Soto (1990), Virginia Hamilton's (1993) *Anthony Burns: The Defeat and Triumph of a Fugitive Slave*, or Lois Lowry's (1989) *Number the Stars* do more than just describe characters of particular cultural heritages; they illuminate the difficulty of maintaining positive relationships among those from different backgrounds. CPC, because of its emphasis on the conflicting intentions and goals of various characters, seems like a natural companion to explorations of this type of literature.

When Sherry first introduces CPC to children, she provides a demonstration of how it works. This usually takes 30–40 minutes depending on the length and complexity of the story used. All the children read the same story, and the teacher does the initial charting—with assistance from the children. It is easier, of course, if the children have already had experience charting stories, but in any event, it is a good idea to review the story elements included in the form. This is especially true of characters' goals/decisions/plans, characters' reactions, and themes. Research shows that children become aware of more subtle aspects of stories, such as characters' goals and reactions, relatively late (Stein & Glenn, 1979); moreover, such items are often omitted from the maps or charts used in schools. For the initial discussion, it is enough to define each and give an example from a story that the children already know.

Next, Sherry presents two blank charts and tells students that they are going to fill them

in together. Each chart is labeled with a main character, whom the children thoroughly describe and discuss. Sherry explains that, "Each of these characters has his or her own point of view. Each character has different goals. If we want to fully understand the story, we need to know how these goals differ and see what problems arise because of them." She then asks questions that will help the children fill in the charts.

Setting is usually a shared element, that is, it is the same for the two characters, so that is an easy place to start. Problems, on the other hand, are inextricably bound up in the characters' plans, goals, or intentions, and these reflect the conflicting perspectives of the characters. Initially, we didn't have a separate box in the chart for characters' goals or intentions; we had assumed that stating the problem was sufficient. However, without a careful consideration of intentions, it is easy to misunderstand the entire sequence of events that follows. Some stories pose more than a single problem for the character, and it is essential that we recognize how he, she, or they interpret the situation.

It is worth discussing these intentions thoroughly, and the problems need to be stated in terms consistent with the characters' actions and feelings. In *The Big Orange Splot*, for instance, when a bird drops a can of orange paint on Mr. Plumbean's house, this apparently is not a problem for him (although without a separate consideration of intentions, both children and adults see this initiating event as his problem). He neither does anything about it nor seems particularly concerned. In fact, his later actions suggest that he kind of likes the splot and wishes that he could decorate his house even more. Mr. Plumbean's real problem, the one that moves him to action, is that his neighbors are upset about how his house looks and are pestering him. For the neighbors, the orange paint—and the later decorations—are the problem; Mr. Plumbean fails to conform to community tastes. These differences are then summarized in the two charts.

With different problems and goals, not surprisingly, the two characters take different actions. Mr. Plumbean decides that if the neighbors are going to bug him anyway, he might as well decorate his house as he chooses. When the pestering neighbors try to get him to make his house like theirs, he convinces them, instead, to go on their own decorating binges. The neighbors want conformity and try to induce Plumbean to change his style. When they fail to persuade him to live as they do, they decide to make their homes more like his. Again, this information is filled into the two charts.

In the end, the charts reflect that both characters had positive reactions to the events; they have accomplished their goals. Plumbean wanted to follow his individual vision without interference, and, in fact, his house "reflects his dreams" and has support of his community. The neighbors wanted conformity, and when they couldn't get Plumbean to be like them, they conformed to his standards. Given the striking differences in the two points of view for this story, we arrive at two different themes. For one the idea is that we should follow our dreams, and the other is more of a "if you can't beat them, join them" kind of tale. One story champions personal freedom of expression and individuality and the other the importance of group cohesion and social agreement. The striking differences between these two themes are unusual. In our experience, themes differ depending on which character is the focus of study, but they tend to be either variations on the same theme—such as good is rewarded, evil is punished—or very separate issues altogether. In a case such as this one, part of the richness of the story comes from the tension between the opposing themes.

After a demonstration, and the spirited conversation that it entails, it is worthwhile to encourage students to reflect on the types of thinking strategies that they used, including remembering details, developing vocabulary, drawing inferences or conclusions, and comparing the goals and actions of characters. It can be a good time to raise issues of critical reading or author's craft, as well. How did the author advantage one point of view over another? Or what did the author include to build sympathy for either of the perspectives?

Most students have been able to use CPC independently or in small groups after only a single demonstration, although second graders may need some additional assistance with the ideas of point of view and theme. With these younger children, it might be wise to do several CPCs together over time; some of the

teachers that Tim works with even prefer to use it as a type of guided reading lesson for a class or group under teacher direction. We have tried many variations on the technique, and all seem to work pretty well. It would be wise to experiment to see what works best with your students.

Some other ways to use CPC

In the demonstration described above, both charts were completed simultaneously. With this simultaneous charting, students do not seem to get as locked into the idea of a single point of view, whichever one they started with, as being correct. However, it can be easier with relatively difficult material, or for younger or disabled readers, to chart a story one way and then to chart it again from a second perspective afterwards. The size of the boxes in the chart are an important issue with younger children, too. The boxes need to be reasonably large to accommodate their larger printing and script styles, but multiple-paged charts have proven cumbersome.

Another variation that we have tried has been to divide a class into two groups, with each group assigned responsibility for developing one of the charts. This is an excellent cooperative learning activity that engenders a lot of productive discussion. In this case, it is probably best for students to know which character they are to focus on before reading, or the activity may require additional time for rereading. Once the two charts are developed, the groups come together to compare and discuss their separate findings.

Although most of our experiences with CPC have been in small-group or whole-class situations, it has worked well with individuals also. One third grader went so far as to use the charts independently to help write a book report. Nevertheless, most students tell us that they prefer to work with CPCs in cooperative pairs or groups; they value the discussion and support that their classmates provide.

CPC can also be used in combination with other popular instructional techniques. Many teachers, for instance, have used Venn diagram charts to compare story characters (Routman, 1996). This can still be done. We think that children might be better able to delve into character similarities and differences, however, once they have explored their contrasting points of view using CPC. Children who have difficulty getting beyond the superficial in book club discussion groups (Goatley, Brock, & Raphael, 1995) might use CPC as a kind of warm-up activity that could better prepare them for productive book conversation. Also, Emery (1996) has suggested that teacher-led discussions can encourage children to think about character perspectives more thoroughly, and we think combining such discussion procedures with CPC might be helpful to some children.

In some cases, such as with *The Big Orange Splot*, children may have difficulty, even with CPC, sorting out subtle themes or those that do not match well with their life's experiences. With this story, younger children sometimes have trouble seeing that a new kind of conformity descends on the neighborhood, because each house is wildly decorated in its own way. In such cases, it can help to introduce another story with a related issue or theme. With *Splot*, we have found *The Araboolies of Liberty Street* (Swope, 1989) to be a useful companion book. In this story, again, all the houses are the same initially, until the arrival of a new family. A general who lives on the street is so concerned that he calls in the army to destroy the house "that's different." To save the newcomers, the other neighbors quickly make their houses different, too, so that only the general's stands out when the tanks arrive.

Finally, we have tried out CPC as a postreading assessment tool. Teachers have seen it as a way of appraising students' understanding of a story. As one explained, "If a student is able to think about a story from two characters' perspectives, then that student probably has a pretty complete understanding of the story."

What children learn from CPC

Sherry has field tested CPC with several classes of students and observed its use by other teachers; she has interviewed children about their experiences with it; and we have examined hundreds of charts that they have developed. Some children, mainly younger ones, such as second and third graders, have indicated that they liked the activity because it helped them to think more about the different characters' actions and personalities. Not surprisingly, children at this stage focus heavily on the separate elements of the story. Their responses seemed to show deep understanding

of particular characters or events, but this information does not appear to be any better coordinated as a result of CPC.

However, for children a bit older, we saw many examples of better understanding of the relationships between characters and their actions. A fourth-grade student, for instance, remarked that now he could understand "two sides of the same story," as in the story of the Three Little Pigs. He could make sense of "how both the pigs and the wolf felt" in their dealings with each other. Fifth graders said that they could better appreciate "what a character was going through and why they made the decisions that they did." They often related the characters' decisions to their own lives, too. Most fifth graders realized, for instance, that they have conformed to peer pressure just like the neighbors in *The Big Orange Splot*.

Often students indicated that they appreciated the story more as a result of the insights developed from CPC, and some showed how they had used this new awareness. A fourth grader volunteered that he had used this activity when watching the movie *Grumpy Old Men* and that he liked the story only if he thought about it from one of the character's points of view, but not from the other's. Similarly, several sixth graders noted that they found that they liked or disliked characters depending on how their own points of view matched with those of the characters. These comments reflect appropriate literary understandings and the availability of useful cognitive tools for critical reading and interpretation.

Most students, no matter what the grade level, claimed that the technique led them to think about a story more thoroughly. According to these students, before the use of CPC they usually considered only a single interpretation of a story. They like CPC in part because it encourages them to read the story more completely.

In conclusion

We were not attempting to conduct a formal research study here, nor should readers think of our descriptions as being based on statistically significant evidence proving CPC to be better than anything else at improving reading comprehension. Nevertheless, CPC is a practice that is more consistent with the basic research findings from cognitive psychology and theories of literary interpretation than is the popular story mapping technique. Our investigations show that it is a practical technique that can be used in a variety of ways with children as early as second grade, and that they generally seem to enjoy its use and appreciate the insights they gain. Finally, the technique encourages the development of multiple perspectives on a story, something that is not usually evident in other instructional techniques. We can only speculate on the implications of this for reading achievement or even for student use of these insights in other reading situations. With regard to the latter, the various student attempts to use this on their own that we have described make it seem rather promising.

Although simple story structure charts support children's comprehension by helping them to recognize and remember structural elements of stories, they can mislead as well. Approaching stories from only a single perspective can foster the misconception that there is only a single meaning. Thus, such charts emphasize comprehension (understanding what is there), rather than interpretation (wondering about meaning). Character Perspective Charting is valuable because it encourages children to use structural information as a base for interpretation. By requiring the reader to enter the minds of the various characters and to consider events from their alternative perspectives, children come to a fuller understanding of story and theme. Character conflict is a central property of a large proportion of stories, novels, and factual narratives, and Character Perspective Charting can help children as early as second grade to develop more mature and complete conceptions of such texts.

References

Beck, I.L., & McKeown, M.G. (1981). Developing questions that promote comprehension: The story map. *Language Arts, 58,* 913–918.

Bruce, B., & Newman, D. (1978). Interacting plans. *Cognitive Science, 2,* 195–233.

Emery, D.W. (1996). Helping readers comprehend stories from the characters' perspectives. *The Reading Teacher, 49,* 534–541.

Emery, D.W., & Mihalevich, C. (1992). Directed discussion of character perspectives. *Reading Research and Instruction, 31,* 51–59.

Goatley, V., Brock, C.H., & Raphael, T.E. (1995). Diverse learners participating in regular education "Book Clubs." *Reading Research Quarterly, 30,* 352–380.

Golden, J.M., & Guthrie, J.T. (1986). Convergence and divergence in reader response to literature. *Reading Research Quarterly, 21,* 408–421.

Mandler, J.M., & Johnson, N.S. (1977). Remembrance of things parsed: Story structure and recall. *Cognitive Psychology, 9,* 111–151.

Marshall, N. (1983). Using story grammar to assess reading comprehension. *The Reading Teacher, 36,* 616–620.

McConaughy, S.H. (1980). Using story structure in the classroom. *Language Arts, 57,* 157–165.

Reutzel, D.R. (1985). Story maps improve comprehension. *The Reading Teacher, 38,* 400–405.

Routman, R. (1996). *Invitations.* Portsmouth, NH: Helnemann.

Sadow, M.W. (1982). The use of story grammar in the design of questions. *The Reading Teacher, 35,* 518–522.

Shanahan, T., & Neuman, S.B. (in press). Literacy research that makes a difference. *Reading Research Quarterly.*

Stein, N.L., & Glenn, C.G. (1979). An analysis of story comprehension in elementary school children. In R.O. Freedle (Ed.), *New directions in discourse processing* (Vol. 2, pp. 53–120). Norwood, NJ: Ablex.

Steinberg, C., & Bruce, B. (1980). *Higher-level features in children's stories: Rhetorical structure and conflict* (Reading Education Rep. No. 18). Urbana, IL: Center for the Study of Reading, University of Illinois.

Trabasso, T. (1989). Causal representation of narratives. *Reading Psychology, 10,* 67–83.

Trabasso, T., Stein, N.L., Rodkin, P.C., Munger, M.P., & Baughn, C.R. (1992). Knowledge of goals and plans in the on-line narration of events. *Cognitive Development, 7,* 133–170.

Whaley, J.F. (1981). Story grammars and reading instruction. *The Reading Teacher, 34,* 762–771.

Children's books cited

Alexander, L. (1990) *The black cauldron.* New York: Dell.

Avi. (1987). *The fighting ground.* New York: Harper & Row.

Cleary, B. (1979). *Ramona forever.* New York: Dell.

Hamilton, V. (1993). *Anthony Burns: The defeat and triumph of a fugitive slave.* New York: Borzoi Spinder/A.A. Knopf.

Lowry, L. (1989). *Number the stars.* New York: Dell.

Muldoon, K. (1989). *Princess Poo.* Niles, IL: A. Whitman.

Pinkwater, D. (1977). *The big orange splot.* New York: Scholastic.

Scieszka, J. (1989). *The true story of the three little pigs.* New York: Scholastic.

Soto, G. (1990). *Baseball in April and other stories.* San Diego, CA: Harcourt Brace.

Swope, S. (1989). *The Araboolies of Liberty Street.* New York: Clarkson N. Potter.

Donna M. Merkley
Debra Jefferies

Guidelines for implementing a graphic organizer

This article suggests attributes for effective graphic organizer implementation accompanied by a sample classroom prereading dialogue.

In 1985, the National Academy of Education's Commission on Education and Public Policy, along with the National Institute of Education, published *Becoming a Nation of Readers* (Anderson, Hiebert, Scott, & Wilkinson, 1985). The intent was to bring together panels of experts on reading instruction and leaders in the field of education to promote the policies and practices deemed necessary for academic achievement and school success. A special section within the research report was dedicated to extending the elementary literacy focus from "learning to read" to "reading to learn." That is, the experts acknowledged the importance of teaching students how to read narrative materials, but further emphasized the need to develop proficiency in content area reading as well. The National Council of Teachers of English and the International Reading Association (1996) have recommended within their standards that students develop an understanding of a wide variety of literature genres including expository material and, more important, that teachers equip students with a flexible set of skills and strategies to comprehend expository text.

Reading expository material

Although students are often avid readers of narrative materials and can comprehend and recall information from narrative texts, many students have difficulty effectively comprehending and recalling expository material (Griffin &

Tulbert, 1995; Taylor, 1985; Winograd, 1984). Expository text, written with the primary intent of communicating information, facts, and ideas, presents a challenge for elementary students because it includes text structures that are often different from those students have encountered in narrative material (May, 1990; McCormick, 1995). Text structure in expository material contains a complex organization of concepts arranged in a certain order so that relationships such as cause and effect, compare and contrast, problem and solution, and sequence classification, are conveyed (McCormick, 1995). Expository materials often contain specialized vocabulary that is necessary in order to impart the intended meaning. The high density of concepts often makes expository passages difficult for readers to digest.

In addition, since expository text is written specifically to communicate information, facts, and ideas, students need to systematically activate background knowledge in order to make the necessary connections for learning to occur (Farnham-Diggory, 1992; Fry, 1989; Recht & Leslie, 1988; Rumelhart, 1980). Ausubel's premise (1968) that "the most important single factor influencing learning is what the learner already knows" (p. iv) is echoed by Novak (1991), who maintained that "new meanings must be constructed on the basis of knowledge students already possess" (p. 45). In response to the challenges posed by expository text, teachers plan prereading instructional techniques designed to activate students' schema, guide students' comprehension, and enhance students' retention of new information (Carr & Thompson, 1996; Pearson, Hansen, & Gordon, 1979).

Research on graphic organizers

A number of authorities have addressed the impact of graphic organizers on students' reading comprehension and recall. Graphic organizers developed as a result of Ausubel's research (1960) into the benefits of using an *advance organizer* in the form of an introductory prose passage to enhance the reader's acquisition of new knowledge. Ausubel concluded that when used as a prereading tool, an advance organizer has the potential to link prereading information with a reader's existing schema.

Researchers such as Barron (1969), Earle (1969), and Baker (1977) continued investigating the use of advance organizers, but modified the prereading introduction to an outline format, called a *structured overview*, in place of Ausubel's prose passage. As practitioners and researchers expanded the application of structured overviews to include a hierarchically organized visual display of information, they adapted structured overview use for prereading, during-reading, and postreading tasks, and the term *structured overview* was replaced with the term *graphic organizer* (GO) (Dunston, 1992; Griffin, Simmons, & Kameenui, 1991). Novak and Gowin (1984) adapted the GO to develop concept mapping as a metacognitive tool for science learning, emphasizing the importance of labeled links between concepts in order to specify relationships.

Hawk's research (1986) favored the GO strategy because it provided (a) an overview of the material to be learned, (b) a reference point for putting new vocabulary and main ideas into orderly patterns, (c) a cue for important information, (d) a visual stimulus for written and verbal information, and (e) a concise review tool.

Research on GOs by Alvermann and Boothby (1986) suggested that the effects upon comprehension are increased when GOs are partially constructed by students as a during-reading or postreading activity. Novak (1991) indicated that learner-constructed concept maps (GOs with labeled links) reflected learners' understanding of science concepts better than traditional forms of testing. Bean, Singer, Sorter, and Frasee (1986) reported enhanced results when

GOs were combined with other metacognitive training such as summarizing and retelling. However, in a review of research relating to graphic organizers, Rice (1994) wrote that

> The findings suggest that currently there is no systematic approach to analyzing graphic organizer research resulting in a lack of explanations for why graphic organizers work or do not work.... Further, instructional implications are tenuous at best due to the lack of explanations of how graphic organizers work or do not work. (p. 39)

Constructing graphic organizers

Although instructional implications from the research are debatable, reading methodology textbooks typically include the GO strategy and provide directions for construction accompanied by examples from various content areas (Cooper & Flynt, 1996; Richardson & Morgan, 1997; Roe, Stoodt, & Burns, 1998; Ruddell, 1997). The suggestions for creating GOs usually include the following steps:

1. Analyze the learning task for words and concepts important for the student to understand.
2. Arrange them to illustrate the interrelationships and pattern(s) of organization.
3. Evaluate the clarity of relationships as well as the simplicity and effectiveness of the visual.
4. Substitute empty slots for certain words in order to promote students' active reading.

Implementing graphic organizers

There appears to be no source, however, that provides implementation guidelines for the teacher who is a novice GO user. We have observed that teachers inexperienced with GOs have a tendency to use the GO visual as a "worksheet" distributed to students, and to lecture from the GO visual with scant provision for student participation. The findings of Moore and Readence (1980, 1984) support the argument that the GO suffers from a lack of systematic operational procedures. Methodology textbooks typically offer fairly vague suggestions for GO implementation such as "Introduce students to the learning task by displaying the graphic and informing them why the terms are arranged in the given manner. Encourage students to

Figure 1
Deep Freeze Bees

Rain or shine, wind or snow, an Arctic bee must eat! Luckily, it's got neat ways to beat the bitter cold.

By Jack Kelley

It's early summer in the Arctic. But patches of snow still cover the ground and a cold wind is blowing. The temperature is only 44° F. Yet a black and yellow bee about the size of a peanut battles the cold and goes about its business.

To the Arctic bumble bee, the snow, cold and wind are no problem. Some flowers are in bloom and the bee does what it must—gather pollen and nectar for itself and the many other bees in its nest.

Of the 400 different kinds of bumble bees, only a few can survive in the Arctic. It is very hard to stay alive in their harsh environment, so Arctic bumble bees don't always behave just like ordinary bumble bees. And if you look at them very, very carefully, you can see that they don't look exactly the same either.

While many of their southern cousins nest in the underground burrows of other animals, Arctic bumble bees do not. Instead, they build nests on top of the ground. That's because underground nests in the Arctic are colder and wetter than nests above the ground. The floor, walls, and roof of an Arctic bumble bee nest are made of dried mosses, leaves, and grasses. The door of the nest faces the warm sun much of the day.

To get from their nests to their feeding grounds, Arctic bumble bees have to fly through the cold air. So to cut down on "commuting" time, they build nests close to clumps of flowers. They also choose the warmest, least windy route possible. That means they fly closer to the ground than ordinary bees.

Arctic bumble bees are also better "dressed" for cold weather than ordinary bumble bees. They have longer, thicker hair. These heavier "fur coats" are better at keeping their body heat from escaping. Their coats are darker too. And dark colors take in the sun's heat better than light colors do. So while the bees sip nectar, their dark coats soak up lots of warm sunshine. Neither cold nor wind can stop the amazing Arctic bumble bee. It survives in a harsh climate because it has its own special ways of keeping warm.

The End

contribute as much as possible." The next sections of this article suggest guidelines for GO implementation, provide a sample implementation, and identify and discuss attributes of effective GO implementation.

In formulating GO implementation guidelines, we turned to the literature on schema (Beers, 1987; Clark, 1991; Gordon & Rennie, 1987; Rumelhart, 1980; Sadoski, Pavio, & Goetz, 1991), classroom discussions (Clark, 1991; Darch, Carnine, & Kameenui, 1986; Nelson-Herber, 1986; Pearson et al., 1979; Stahl & Vancil, 1986), and concept development (Hawk, 1986; Kinnison & Pickens, 1984; Robinson & Schraw, 1994). After analyzing the research and the thinking in these three areas, we offer five attributes for effective GO implementation. When presenting the GO to students, the teacher should do the following:

- verbalize relationships (links) among concepts expressed by the visual,

- provide opportunity for student input,

- connect new information to past learning,

- make reference to the upcoming text, and

- seize opportunities to reinforce decoding and structural analysis.

The teacher should take care that the GO visual is detailed enough to present an overview of the material, yet not so detailed that reading the text is not required.

Sample graphic organizer implementation

The example in the Table is designed to illustrate GO implementation, highlighting the occurrence of the five guidelines in the left margin. A brief discussion of each guideline follows the example. Note that in this example the GO is presented to students on an overhead transparency sheet, removing sticky notes to uncover the GO elements as the prereading discussion proceeds. This enables the teacher to direct students' attention to the GO element under consideration. Figure 1 contains the text students used. Figure 2 is the actual graphic organizer.

Script for graphic organizer for "Deep Freeze Bees"

GO attribute(s)	Script
Student input and connecting old to new	Boys and girls, for the past 2 weeks, we have been studying various insects. Let's name these insects, listing their characteristics and their feeding habits. (Pause for student input.)
Verbalize relationships Student input: reference to upcoming text	One of the insects mentioned in our review was the bee. Today, you will be reading an article about bees, but before you read the selection let's look at the big ideas and how they fit together. The article is titled "Deep Freeze Bees." (Remove note to show the title.) What do you suppose this article will be about? (Pause for student input.)
Connecting old to new	The article will describe the Arctic bumble bee. (Remove note to show "Arctic.") Now think about our geography study this year. Who can come to the map to show us where the Arctic region is located? (Pause for student input.) What words can we use to describe the Arctic region? (Pause for student input.)
Reinforcing decoding	Compared with other regions, the Arctic could be described as ... (remove note to show "harsh"). Look carefully at this word. What do we know about pronouncing a vowel that precedes an *r*? (Pause for student input.) Who can pronounce this word?
Reinforce structural analysis	What does *harsh* mean? So, the Arctic region can be said to have a harsh environment. (Remove note to show "environment.") What do we know about the Arctic climate? (Pause for student input.) The article will report an early summer temperature of 44° F. (Remove note to show 44°.) This is about 7° C. So the temperature reflects a harsh environment. The root of this word, *environ*, comes from French, meaning vicinity or surroundings. How could we define *environment*? (Pause for student input.) The dictionary defines *environment* as the conditions surrounding the development of an organism. What other words with this same root can you think of? (Pause and discuss *environmental, environmentalist.*)
Verbalize relationships Reinforce decoding	So, the harsh environment of the Arctic influences how the bumblebee can...(remove note to show "survive"). Who can pronounce this? How can we guess the sound *i* will have? (Student input to generate the generalization.)
Reference to upcoming text Student input	How the Arctic bumblebee survives in the harsh environment will be described in your reading. What conditions of the bumblebee's existence in the Arctic do you think will be different from bumblebees in Iowa or Florida? (Pause—students may anticipate how the bee looks, what it eats, or where it lives.)
Verbalize relationships: pattern of organization Vocabulary Student input Reference to upcoming text Student input	Because of the harsh environment the nests of the Arctic bumblebee are important. (Remove note to show "nest.") The article states that Arctic bees do not nest in burrows. (Remove note to show "burrows" and put an X through "burrows.") They build a nest above ground. (Remove note to show "top of ground.") Why do you suppose? (Remove note to show "?" and pause for student input.) The article will explain why. Look for that explanation as you read. The article will also describe other features of Arctic bees' nests. As you read, look for these features (remove note to show the two blank boxes) and we will discuss the difference these make. Who can guess what any of these might be? (Pause for student input.)

(continued)

Script for graphic organizer for "Deep Freeze Bees" (continued)

GO attribute(s)	Script
Connect old/new Relationships: 1. vocabulary 2. pattern of organization Reference to upcoming text	What else do you think that we will learn about Arctic bees? (Pause for student input.) In addition to their nests, the harsh Arctic environment influences the bees' feeding habits. (Remove note to show "feeding habits.") Think back to what we said about the feeding habits of bees. Arctic bees do gather pollen and nectar. (Remove note to show "pollen & nectar.") How might bees feed because of the very cold climate, the harsh environment of the Arctic? (Pause for student input.) As you read look for two additional details about the bees' feeding habits. We will come back to this after you read.
Student input Relationship: Vocabulary	So, we will discover in our reading how the nests and the feeding habits distinguish, or set apart, the Arctic bumble bee from other bees. What else do you suppose is different? (Pause for student input.) Yes. How they look is called their...(remove note to show "appearance") appearance. The article states that they are peanut size. (Remove note to show "peanut size.") How else do you suppose their appearance has been affected by the harsh Arctic environment? (Pause for student input.) As you read (remove note to show the two blank places), the article will explain how their appearance helps the bees in the harsh Arctic environment. (Remove note to show the two boxes with "?".) Look for these as you read.
Reference to upcoming text	Class, you will each receive a sheet just like the one I am showing on the overhead. Read the article, take your copy, and fill in information from the selection in these boxes. After you have filled in the boxes, write a two- or three-sentence summary of "Deep Freeze Bees" in the space provided. Remember this summarizing will be like the summaries we have been practicing. We will compare information and summaries in about 20 minutes. If you finish early, use the back of your sheet to sketch and label something you have learned about Arctic bees. What questions do you have?

Discussion of the implementation guidelines in the example

Verbalize relationships (links) among concepts expressed by the visual. The teacher's verbal presentation of the GO elements attempted to reinforce the relationships and links between and among concepts, reminding students that the GO is an overview of material they will encounter during reading. ("Before you read the selection, let's look at the big ideas and how they fit together.") Main ideas were emphasized, and new vocabulary had a reference point. The teacher's verbal presentation, likewise, reinforced the cause and effect pattern of organization within the material. ("Because of the harsh environment....") This was especially important because a pattern of organization signal words was not present in the selection.

Provide opportunity for student input. With frequent pauses for student input, the teacher used the GO elements for brief, focused prereading discussion. The teacher encouraged student comments about GO elements to see what students already knew about the GO elements ("What do we know about the Arctic climate?") and to assess relationships that students understood. Note that the teacher's questions were open ended, avoiding yes or no responses and inviting hypotheses. ("What do you suppose the article will be about?" "How else do you suppose their appearance has been affected by the harsh Arctic environment?")

Connect new information to past learning. The teacher's presentation of the GO elements was designed to guide students in activating stored experiences, in recalling previously

Figure 2
Graphic organizer for "Deep Freeze Bees"

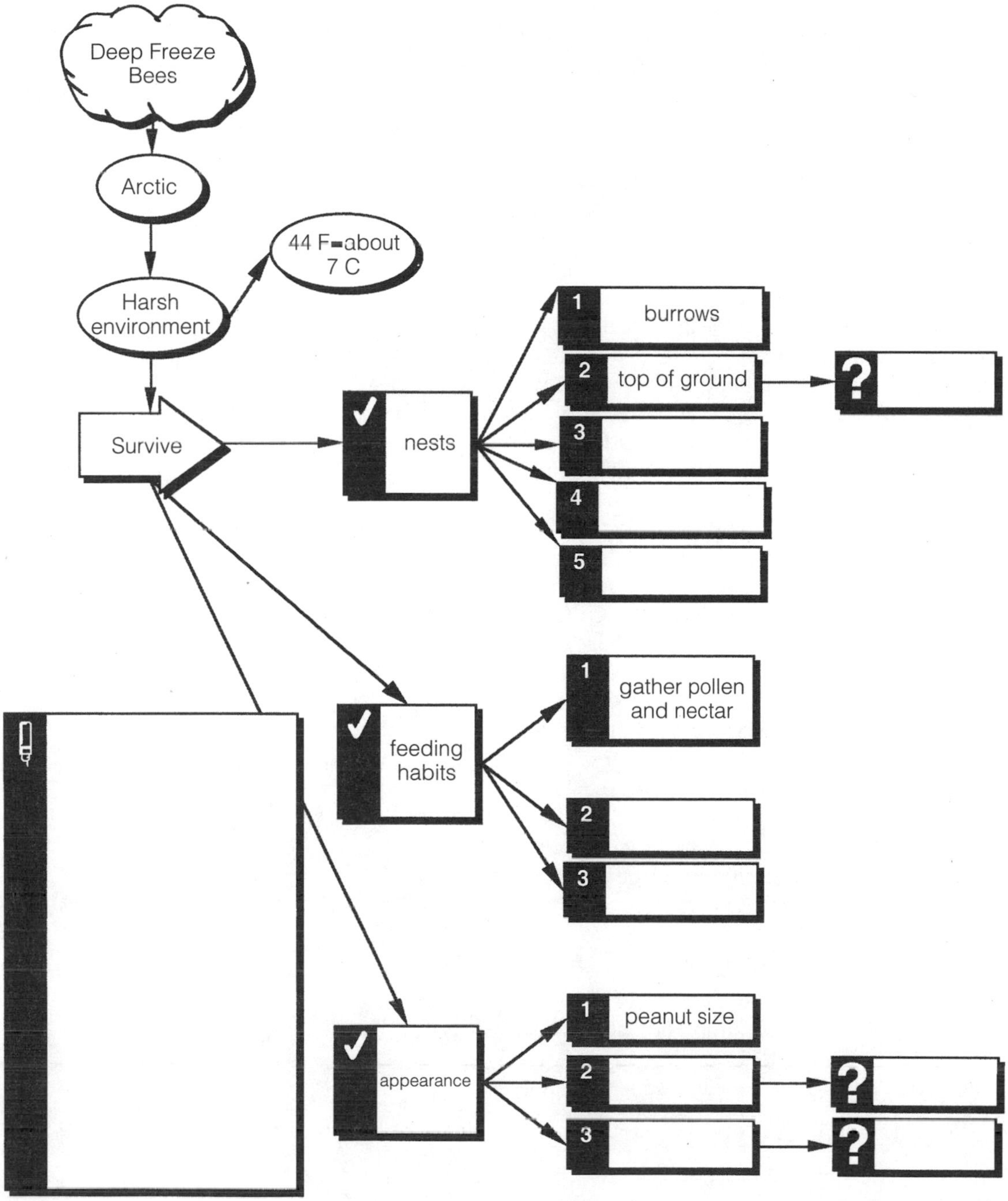

encountered information ("For the past 2 weeks we have been studying insects. Let's name these insects, listing...."), and in making connections with previously encountered information. ("Now think about our geography study this year.") Depending on student responses, the teacher could correct errors in understanding or challenge students to read the upcoming information carefully to justify or to revise their thinking.

Make reference to the upcoming text. As suggested earlier, the teacher should be careful that the GO visual and discussion are detailed enough to present an overview of the material, yet not so detailed that reading the text is not required. In this example the teacher used the GO elements to raise students' expectations about meaning and provided students with frequent reminders that the upcoming reading would explain certain concepts or provide additional details. ("The article will explain why." "Look for these as you read.") Tasks for students to complete after reading were clearly and carefully explained.

Seize opportunities to reinforce decoding and structural analysis. Because the GO elements contained technical vocabulary, the teacher capitalized on this context-relevant opportunity and used GO elements to remind students about relevant phonics generalizations ("What do we know about pronouncing a vowel that precedes an *r*?" "How can we guess the sound the *i* will take on?") and structural analysis applications ("environment"). It is important, however, that this conversation not detract from the comprehension emphasis of the GO strategy.

A step beyond worksheets

The GO strategy offers considerable potential to enhance students' comprehension of expository text. Thoughtful construction of the visual reflects how the teacher chooses to emphasize the important concepts in a selection, underscores the relationships between and among those concepts, and highlights the selection's explicit or inferred pattern of organization. In the sample lesson the GO visual had a top-to-bottom, left-to-right format. It is important to note that although this is a frequently occurring format, it is not a "standard" format. In our experience a reading selection with a tight, obvious pattern of organization often results in a top-to-

bottom, left-to-right, fairly symmetrical GO visual. For other reading selections, the GO visual may seem less "organized." In fact, one that is *not* well organized may be the reading for which students need the most guidance. Drawing from his work with GO-based concept mapping, Novak (1991) concluded, "My experience has been that whenever teachers (including university professors) constructed a concept map for a lecture, demonstration, book chapter, or laboratory experiment they wish to teach, they gain new insight into the meaning of that subject matter" (p. 48).

It is important, however, that GO planning extend beyond construction of the visual to the deliberate consideration of the teacher's strategies to elicit prereading dialogue to accompany the visual. It is this guided dialogue, stimulated by the visual, that elevates the GO strategy above the "worksheet" or the "lecture" level. The teacher-directed, prereading dialogue serves to stimulate students' prior knowledge, assist students' anticipation of upcoming text, and encourage students' active reading. These potential benefits depend on the teacher's carefully executed implementation of a skillfully crafted GO.

References

Alvermann, D.E., & Boothby, P.R. (1986). Children's transfer of graphic organizer instruction. *Reading Psychology: An International Quarterly, 7*, 87–100.

Anderson, R.C., Hiebert, E.H., Scott, J., & Wilkinson, I.A.G. (1985). *Becoming a nation of readers: The report of the commission on reading*. Washington, DC: National Institute of Education.

Ausubel, D.P. (1960). The use of advanced organizers in the learning and retention of meaningful behavior. *Journal of Educational Psychology, 51*, 267–272.

Ausubel, D.P. (1968). *Educational psychology: A cognitive view*. New York: Holt, Rinehart & Winston.

Baker, R.L. (1977). Meaningful reception learning. In H.L. Herber & R.T. Vacca (Eds.), *Research in reading in the content areas: The third report* (pp. 32–50). Syracuse, NY: Syracuse University, Reading and Language Arts Center.

Barron, R.F. (1969). The use of vocabulary as an advance organizer. In H.L. Herber & P.L. Sanders (Eds.), *Research in reading in the content areas: First year report* (pp. 29–39). Syracuse, NY: Syracuse University, Reading and Language Arts Center.

Bean, T.W., Singer, H., Sorter, J., & Frasee, C. (1986). The effect of metacognitive instruction in outlining and graphic organizer construction on students' comprehension in a tenth-grade world history class. *Journal of Reading Behavior, 18*, 153–169. (ERIC Document Reproduction Service No. 393 484)

Beers, T. (1987). Schema-theoretic models of reading: Humanizing the machine. *Reading Research Quarterly, 22*,

369–377. (ERIC Document Reproduction Service No. 355 395)

Carr, S.C., & Thompson, B. (1996). The effects of prior knowledge and schema activation strategies on the inferential reading comprehension of children with and without learning disabilities. *Learning Disability Quarterly*, *19*(1), 48–61. (ERIC Document Reproduction Service No. 519 854)

Clark, S.R. (1990). *Schema theory and reading comprehension.* (ERIC Document Reproduction Service No. 325 802)

Cooper, R.B., & Flynt, E.S. (1996). *Teaching reading in the content areas.* Englewood Cliffs, NJ: Merrill.

Darch, C.B., Carnine, D.W., & Kameenui, E.J. (1986). The role of graphic organizers and social structure in content area instruction. *Journal of Reading Behavior, 18*, 275–295. (ERIC Document Reproduction Service No. 393 401)

Dunston, P.J. (1992). A critique of graphic organizer research. *Reading Research and Instruction, 31*(2), 57–65. (ERIC Document Reproduction Service No. 441 050)

Earle, R.A. (1969). Use of the structured overview in mathematics classes. In H.L. Herber & P.L. Sanders (Eds.), *Research in reading in the content areas: First year report* (pp. 49–58). Syracuse, NY: Syracuse University, Reading and Language Arts Center.

Farnham-Diggory, S. (1992). *Cognitive processes in education* (2nd ed.). New York: HarperCollins.

Fry, E.B. (1989). Reading formulas—maligned but valid. *Journal of Reading, 32*, 292–297.

Gordon, C.J., & Rennie, B.J. (1987). Restructuring content schemata: An intervention study. *Reading Research and Instruction, 26*, 126–188. (ERIC Document Reproduction Service No. 353 735)

Griffin, C.C., Simmons, D.C., & Kameenui, E.J. (1991). Investigating the effectiveness of graphic organizer instruction on the comprehension and recall of science content by students with learning disabilities. *Reading, Writing, and Learning Disabilities, 7*, 355–376. (ERIC Document Reproduction Service No. 441 315)

Griffin, C.C., & Tulbert, B.L. (1995). The effect of graphic organizers on students' comprehension and recall of expository text: A review of the research and implications for practice. *Reading and Writing Quarterly, 11*, 73–89. (ERIC Document Reproduction Service No. 496 028)

Hawk, P.P. (1986). Using graphic organizers to increase achievement in middle school life science. *Science Education, 70*, 81–87. (ERIC Document Reproduction Service No. 332 059)

Kinnison, R.L., & Pickens, I.R. (1984). *Teaching vocabulary to the L.D. student from an interactive view of reading comprehension.* Canyon, TX: West Texas State University. (ERIC Document Reproduction Service No. 276 222)

May, F.B. (1990). *Reading as communication: An interactive approach* (3rd ed., pp. 396–426). Columbus, OH: Merrill.

McCormick, S. (1995). *Instructing students who have literacy problems.* Englewood Cliffs, NJ: Prentice Hall.

Moore, D.W., & Readence, J.E. (1980). A meta-analysis of the effect of graphic organizers on learning from text. In M.L. Kamil & A.J. Moe (Eds.), *Perspectives in reading research and instruction.* 29th yearbook of the National Reading Conference (pp. 213–217). Chicago: National Reading Conference.

Moore, D.W., & Readence, J.E. (1984). A quantitative and qualitative review of graphic organizer research. *Journal of Educational Research, 78*, 11–17.

National Council of Teachers of English & International Reading Association. (1996). *Standards for the English language arts.* Urbana, IL: National Council of Teachers of English.

Nelson-Herber, J. (1986). Expanding and refining vocabulary in content areas. *Journal of Reading, 29*, 626–633.

Novak, J.D. (1991). Clarifying with concept maps. *The Science Teacher, 58*(7), 45–49.

Novak, J.D., & Gowin, D.B. (1984). *Learning how to learn.* Ithaca, NY: Cornell University Press.

Pearson, P.D., Hansen, J., & Gordon, C.J. (1979). The effect of background knowledge on young children's comprehension of explicit and implicit information. *Journal of Reading Behavior, 11*, 201–209.

Recht, D.R. & Leslie, L. (1988). Effect of prior knowledge on good and poor readers' memory of text. *Journal of Educational Psychology, 80*(1), 16–20. (ERIC Document Reproduction Service No. 384 774)

Rice, G.E. (1994). Need for explanations in graphic organizer research. *Reading Psychology, 15*, 39–67.

Richardson, J.S., & Morgan, R.F. (1997). *Reading to learn in the content areas.* Belmont, CA: Wadsworth.

Robinson, D.H., & Schraw, G. (1994). Computational efficiency through visual argument: Do graphic organizers communicate relations in text too effectively? *Contemporary Educational Psychology, 19*, 399–415. (ERIC Document Reproduction Service No. 498 458)

Roe, B.D., Stoodt, B.D., & Burns, P.C. (1998). *The content areas.* Boston: Houghton Mifflin.

Ruddell, M.R. (1997). *Teaching content reading and writing.* Boston: Allyn & Bacon.

Rumelhart, D.E. (1980). Schemata: The building blocks of cognition. In R.J. Spiro, B.C. Bruce, & W.F. Brewer (Eds.), *Theoretical issues in reading comprehension* (pp. 33–58). Hillsdale, NJ: Erlbaum.

Sadoski, M., Pavio, A., & Goetz, E.T. (1991). A critique of schema theory in reading and a dual coding alternative. *Reading Research Quarterly, 26*, 463–484. (ERIC Document Reproduction Service No. 435 546)

Stahl, S.A., & Vancil, S.J. (1986). Discussion is what makes semantic maps work in vocabulary instruction. *The Reading Teacher, 40*, 62–69.

Taylor, B.M. (1985). Toward an understanding of factors contributing to children's difficulty summarizing textbook material. In J.A. Niles & R.V. Lalik (Eds.), *Issues in literacy: A research perspective* (pp. 125–131). Rochester, NY: National Reading Conference.

Winograd, P.N. (1984). Strategic difficulties in summarizing texts. *Reading Research Quarterly, 19*, 404–425.

Robert M. Schwartz

Self-monitoring in beginning reading

This article discusses the development of self-monitoring and searching behaviors in beginning readers.

Have you ever played the game of 20 Questions with a 5- or 6-year-old? They have their own style. When my son, Michael, was that age he would point to different objects asking, "Is it this?" After 7 or 8 guesses, I was tempted to say "Yes! You got it!" To be helpful, I could explain how more general questions reduce the options and lead to a quick solution. Unfortunately, in my experience this never works! So I take a turn trying to guess what he is thinking. Is it on this side of the room? Is it on the floor? Is it bigger than a bread box (as if any 6-year-old knows what that is)? If this demonstration succeeds at all, Michael might begin his next turn asking, "Is it on this side of the room?" before switching back to his original strategy, "Is it this?"

Clay (1993b) finds a useful analogy between the processing involved in this simple game and reading. "The smarter readers ask themselves the most effective questions for reducing uncertainty; the poorer readers try lots of trivial questions and waste their opportunities to reduce their uncertainty" (p. 9). As primary teachers, we see this processing game played out every day. Our high-progress students are driven by questions like, What is this

story about? Did my attempts make sense in this story? Does it look right and make sense? What can I do to solve this problem?

Struggling readers are still trying to figure out the game. Over the last 5 years, I've used Reading Recovery® procedures to help some of the lowest performing first-grade students become literacy players. I've also observed hundreds of other similar students as they work with Reading Recovery teachers to build effective strategies. You can see and hear them working on the game. Marty, a first grader I worked with, said things like, "No, that's not right!" "Don't tell me. I can get it!" or "Uh oh!" as he worked to solve the problems he encountered.

Teaching for strategies is a key part of literacy instruction in the primary grades and for older students struggling with reading. The difficulty is that telling students what to do is even less effective in a complex task like reading than in the simpler context of the 20 Questions game (Cazden, 1992). The purpose of this article is to describe how we can foster this type of processing. First, I set the stage by describing reading strategies and cues we use rather automatically. Then I distinguish between two types of processing strategies that play a central role in learning to read: monitoring and searching. Next, I present oral reading samples to show how children extend the set of cues they use to monitor their reading. Finally, I provide some classroom implications for assisting young readers to develop effective processing strategies.

Cues we use

The following passage engages readers in processing a variety of cues (based on Goodman, 1993, p. 94). Try to read it out loud with good phrasing.

> The Boat
>
> A man was building a boat in his
> cellar. As soon as he had finished
> the boot he tried to take it through the
> the cellar door. It would not go though
> the door. So he had to take it a part.
> He should of planed better.

This brief passage is filled with opportunities for checking cues, many that you probably noticed as you read aloud. In normal reading, we coordinate a variety of cues from the text. Visual and phonological information within words (print cues), the grammatical structure of the text (sentence structure cues), and the meaning derived from prior sections of the text (meaning cues) provide information sources that interact with the reader's knowledge to support ongoing word recognition and comprehension strategies (Adams, 1990; Clay, 1991; Goodman, 1985, 1993; Rumelhart, 1994). The problems inserted in this passage create conflicts among these cues. Readers may notice these conflicts, just as you might notice an error made while reading normal text. Most readers get to the word *boot* and notice the conflict between print cues from the letters and meaning cues from the context of the story. At this point, they often shift from a meaning orientation to a proofreading task giving greater emphasis to gathering print cues. Proofreaders sometimes work backwards through a document to avoid meaning cues that might cause them to overlook typographical errors. In this passage, since many of the print cues in altered words combine with meaning to confirm incorrect responses, the reader might say *through* for *though* or *planned* for *planed*. Many readers will not notice these slight visual conflicts caused by a single letter difference.

Should of raises additional problems in place of *should've*. The print cues are easily processed and recognized, both *should* and *of* are known words. The substitution even sounds right (phonological and sentence structure cues) within the overall context. With this degree of agreement among cues the rather vague meaning conflict between *of* and *have* is often not noticed. *A part* for *apart* raises similar problems.

By far, the most difficult problem to notice is the *the the* repetition between the third and fourth lines. Early in first grade, Marty would have had no difficulty reading both *the's* in this type of situation because he was very carefully looking at (and often pointing to) each word he said. Let's hope he would have complained that this didn't sound right. As good readers, we read with expression and phrasing by letting our eyes work ahead of our voice. As we gather information on the fly, our processing systems coordinate or ignore partial information from two glances (fixations). Our normal use of meaning, sentence structure, and print cues almost ensures that we will not see the second *the*.

The processing you did in reading this passage demonstrates the complex set of mental strategies that readers need in order to coordinate cues from different information sources, evaluate their progress, and shift between comprehension and word recognition processes when difficulties arise. This set of in-the-head strategies is much more complex than any set of rules or suggestions that we can tell children. Much of what we do is difficult to describe even in the most detailed text on the psychology of reading. Even if we could somehow describe what we do (like our suggestions for the 20 Questions game), it is unlikely that describing rules or processes would be helpful.

So how can we help? By carefully observing reading behaviors, we can infer the types of cues and strategies children use. Given these tentative theories of processing, we can then support their efforts to extend the set of cues they attend to and strategies they use as they read. The degree and type of support needed will vary among children until their network of strategies is sufficiently developed that they can extend their own strategies to meet the demands of increasingly complex texts. This is what Clay (1991) calls a self-extending system.

Two types of processing strategies

The conflicts among cues in *The Boat* passage require readers to coordinate two major types of processing strategies, searching and monitoring. Searching strategies enable us to gather cues for an initial attempt to read a text, make multiple tries at difficult words, and self-correct some errors. Self-monitoring strategies enable us to evaluate our attempts and decide if further searching is needed. Most discussions of methods for beginning reading instruction focus on searching strategies and largely ignore the role of monitoring. Teaching procedures like phonics instruction, use of context cues for word recognition, and solving words by analogy to known words are designed to foster searching strategies.

When self-monitoring has been considered in beginning reading instruction, the focus has usually been to encourage children to check whether their attempts make sense. This is important, but ignoring other types of monitoring strategies and cues can be self-defeating. It is a little like having a teenager who can do a variety of household tasks. Now that my son is almost a teen, he can do many chores and usually doesn't even mind doing them. But somehow he never notices that a chore needs to be done. I can nag him to do each task, but unless he notices the cues in the environment himself, like cans and dishes by the TV or soccer clothes on the bathroom floor, real independence never develops. Attending to the situation and noticing when things aren't quite right is monitoring. Extending the set of cues a child searches for when reading depends on the child noticing that his/her current attempt requires further work.

Monitoring strategies involve checking one's attempts to coordinate the variety of cues found in texts. These monitoring strategies develop gradually, often over a period of years, and play a critical role in learning to read (Clay, 1991). Self-correction is an observable behavior from which we can infer that the reader has engaged in monitoring and searching strategies. Self-correction means that the reader has used some cues from the text to generate an attempt, then either immediately, or after reading on in the text, s/he monitors a conflict among the cues. This is illustrated in *The Boat* passage when the reader reaches *boot*. If the print cues generate an accurate response, a skilled reader usually notices that this does not fit the meaning. In a normal text, monitoring an error would lead the reader to search for additional cues to resolve the conflict. If this effort is completely successful an error would be replaced with an accurate response, self-correction. It is more important to foster the development of monitoring strategies in beginning readers than to stress highly accurate responding.

Observing cues used for self-monitoring

Clay (1991) has developed a theory of literacy learning that assigns a central role to monitoring strategies. An important question for beginning instruction is, "How can we support the development of a highly efficient and coordinated set of monitoring and searching strategies?" A necessary first step is to carefully observe the types of behaviors that signal strategic processing. Our best window into the child's processing comes from analyzing errors or miscues (Goodman & Goodman, 1994). A correct response neatly fits all the available cues. But this does not imply that a child accurately reading a simple pattern book is using or monitoring all cues. By analyzing the child's errors, we can infer the types of cues used and those neglected. Behaviors at the point of error, or shortly after an error, suggest the types of cues the child is monitoring. Monitoring is indicated when an error is followed by rereading all or part of the sentence, by making several attempts at a word (including self-correction), by showing signs of dissatisfaction, or by appealing for help (Clay, 1991).

The Figure is a modified version of Clay's (1993a) representation of the primary cue systems used in reading. Any given error can be analyzed in terms of the cues or information sources that are used and those that are neglected. These include meaning cues from the illustrations or the context of the story; sentence structure cues from the word sequence within the sentence and the child's developing knowledge of oral language and the more formal language of books; print cues from words and letters and the reader's knowledge of how these visual cues relate to sounds (phonological cues); and cues from the relationship of sound-to-letter expectations. A child's pattern of responses and whether s/he checks or notices conflicts between attempts and other possible cues indicate his/her level of monitoring. An important question for instruction is not Does the child monitor? but rather, What types of cues does the child use to monitor his/her attempts?

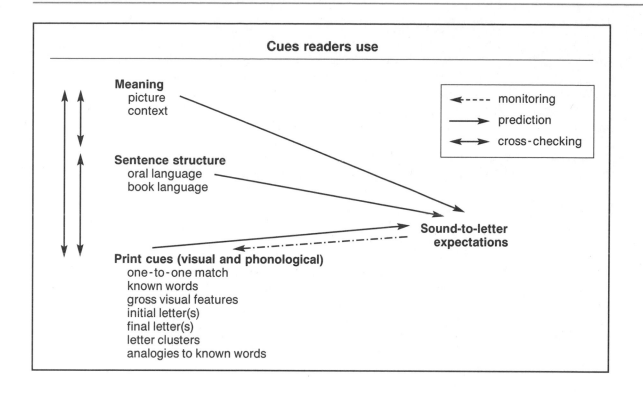

Cues readers use

Meaning
picture
context

Sentence structure
oral language
book language

Print cues (visual and phonological)
one-to-one match
known words
gross visual features
initial letter(s)
final letter(s)
letter clusters
analogies to known words

Sound-to-letter expectations

←----- monitoring
→ prediction
↔ cross-checking

One-to-one matching. Consider some possible readings of the text in Example 1. In a one-line pattern book with illustrations of different things a baby can do, the first reading (R1: "The baby is smiling and playing a trick") would clearly fit the meaning and an acceptable language structure. The match to print cues is more problematic. Marty read simple books in this manner at the beginning of first grade. He accepted this reading without hesitation. He monitored for meaning and sentence structure but had not yet come to terms with reading for a precise message or monitoring for a match between his developing concept of a word in oral language and words in print. For many young children, this is an appropriate response on which future learning can build. The child uses knowledge of the world and language to "problem solve" the task at hand and reaches an acceptable solution. Within a few lessons, Marty began to extend his monitoring strategies on new books, commenting, "I know it doesn't say all that" after this type of response.

Example 1

Text: Baby can laugh.
R1   The baby is smiling and playing a trick.
R2   Baby laughing.
R3   The baby laughed.
R4   Baby is laughing.

The second reading (R2) represents another child's solution to the challenge of this text. Again meaning is maintained, but the one-to-one correspondence of words in oral and written language doesn't match. This could represent progress over the previous response. The child pointed to each word in the text and monitored the correspondence between oral and written language. So why doesn't he notice he is one word short? In a long word like *laughing*, beginning readers often operate on a theory of matching one word in print to each beat in oral language. Saying and hearing the syllables in *hippopotamus* can cover quite a few written words for a reader operating on this theory. The concepts of a word in oral language and a word in written language are complex. Children like Marty, who enter school with little knowledge about print, require many literacy experiences and demonstrations before they monitor their own reading consistently by cues of one-to-one matching (Clay, 1991; Morris, 1992).

The third reading (R3) fits meaning, structure, and matches one-to-one. The fact that this attempt doesn't fit all the print cues is irrelevant if matching oral words to word spacing is the level of processing the child is ready to notice. The fourth reading (R4) again fits the previously used cue types with much more visual similarity on the first and third words. If, however, the child knows the word *can* or *is*, perhaps as part of his/her writing vocabulary, we might expect some signs of monitoring discrepancies related to print cues from known words.

As you can see, reading even a simple text requires complex problem solving and the coordination of a variety of cues. With enough repetitions, a child can learn to read much more complex texts accurately, but this serves little purpose if s/he does not develop strategies that will support problem solving in other texts. We support independent problem solving by praising children's uses of cues in their initial miscues and prompting them to extend the types of cues they use to monitor these attempts. This is particularly important for young children who are just beginning to use print cues. It can also be important for older readers who are having difficulty because of an imbalance in the cues they use for problem solving.

Known words. The remaining examples focus on extending the kinds of print cues used for self-monitoring. Example 2 relates to monitoring by "known words." This text comes from a slightly more complex pattern book with a supportive illustration in which a child waves to different friends who drive by as he waits for the school bus. The first reading (R1) again fits meaning, structure, and print cues, and the printed words match one-to-one with words in the child's oral reading. Since Marty has demonstrated knowledge of *my*, *to*, and *the* in writing stories and is matching one-to-one, he could use this knowledge to monitor his attempts. Words controlled in writing are a better indication of knowledge of words than accurate reading of the words in stories. The fact that a child has correctly responded to a word may not mean that he knows it. Accurate book reading could be achieved solely based on the use of meaning and structure cues.

Example 2

Text: I wave to my friend the car driver.
R1 I wave at the man driving the car.
R2 I will to my friend the car man.

But even detailed knowledge of a word does not ensure that this information will be used to monitor reading in context. For Marty and many other beginning readers it is quite a complex task to coordinate meaning, sentence structure, and print cues from known words. A supportive teacher might promote this type of processing by allowing the child to complete the sentence and then reading back the sentence to him or her as s/he said it, encouraging monitoring in this shared context: "Was that right?"

The second reading (R2) in this example achieves a better visual fit across the sentence with all known words read accurately. But meaning and structure cues have been ignored to achieve this visual fit. We would hope the child would monitor this discrepancy and attempt to reprocess the sentence. This early, tentative strategic processing where one type of cue is searched to produce an initial guess and is then checked against another cue type is called cross-checking (see double arrows on the left side of the Figure). Our goal is to help the child extend the set of cues s/he monitors, not to shift attention from meaning to visual cues.

Sound-to-letter expectations. Example 3 focuses on monitoring cues from sound-to-letter expectations where there are gross differences between the child's prediction and the visual features of a word in text. The text again comes from a slightly more complex pattern book with a supportive illustration. Different animals make suggestions to a boy about what he might like on his sandwich. A cat suggests a mouse; a lizard suggests a spider; and then on this page, a bird makes a suggestion. The picture shows a fat purple worm on bread.

The difficulty comes because of the insertion of the adjective into the established language pattern. Marty initially tried to read this as "would you like a worm," but monitoring of one-to-one matching triggered another attempt. Marty's first reading (R1) is a reasonable solution to this problem using meaning cues from the picture. But since he is beginning to generate sound-to-letter expectations, this prediction was rejected because of the lack of agreement between the dominant sounds in *purple* and the visual features of *fat*. Another attempt results in the second reading (R2). Since *funny* shares some visual features with *fat*, Marty accepts this as a reasonable solution to the problem.

Example 3

Text: Would you like a fat worm?
R1 Would you like a purple worm?
R2 Would you like a funny worm?

How do children learn to monitor gross visual features within words? Early writing experiences help children learn to hear and record sounds in words, as do procedures that promote invented spelling during group or individual writing (Lyons, Pinnell, & DeFord, 1993) or various forms of phonics instruction (Cunningham & Allington, 1994). The ability to go from a word in oral language to using letters to represent sounds in the word is a major accomplishment. This sound-to-letter emphasis is different from the letter-to-sound emphasis often associated with early phonics instruction.

The process Marty used to monitor gross visual features is illustrated in the Figure. Marty's initial search of meaning, structure, and/or visual cues produced a word prediction, which allowed him to access his knowledge of sound-to-letter expectations. If he said the predicted word slowly and thought about the letters he expected to see, as Marty does to write unfamiliar words, he could check these letter expectations against the print, e.g., "I think it will say *purple*. I hear two *p*s, but I don't see them, so it can't be *purple*." Eventually this process becomes integrated with other strategies to provide a rapid form of visual monitoring of words identified based on a limited set of cues. Monitoring by sound-to-letter expectations is gradually refined to detect more detailed discrepancies between predictions based on multiple cue sources and print cues from initial letters, final letters, familiar letter clusters, or analogies to known words.

Some children will need prompting to apply this knowledge to monitoring their reading. The miscue is my opportunity to foster self-monitoring and searching strategies. I could validate the good processing reflected in Marty's first reading by confirming that it made sense. Then prompting Marty to check if it looks right and makes sense will encourage him to engage in the reading work that will extend his set of strategies (Clay, 1993a).

If I just focused on searching strategies, I might point to the word *fat* after the substitution of *purple* and prompt Marty to "get his mouth ready" for the initial sound. But pointing to the error eliminates Marty's opportunity to self-monitor. Now if he rereads and integrates the initial visual cue with meaning and sentence structure cues to generate *funny*, I might ignore this successful processing and continue to nag him to sound out the word. However, these would be serious mistakes in my efforts to assist Marty's development of independent processing strategies. "It is more important that the child comes to check on his own behavior than that he be required to use all sources of cues at this stage" (Clay, 1993a, p. 41).

Clay (1991) notes that children making good progress learning to read

> were using "predict and check" in many cases as a substitute for letter-sound decoding, in situations where their print knowledge was inadequate. These intermediate skills enable a reader to use prediction to narrow the field of possibilities and to reduce the decoding load. (p. 254)

Checking or monitoring is critical. Instruction that encourages prediction without fostering increasingly complex forms of monitoring runs the risk of producing readers who are limited by inefficient orthographic and phonological processing (Schwartz & Stanovich, 1981; Stanovich, 1980).

Phonics-based instruction, on the other hand, fosters attention to visual and phonological cues, but at a cost. The mental effort of processing and blending even one or two letters is considerable for young readers. This requires children to shift attention away from meaning and sentence structure cues. Many children need our support to extend the cues they find effective, rather than changing to a purely visual approach. We risk creating poor readers who take a word-by-word approach to reading when we prompt primarily for searching visual cues in order to "sound it out" (Clay, 1993a; Lyons, 1994).

Letter-sound knowledge and strategies can be effectively developed in the context of reading books and writing stories. Using meaning, structure, and a gradually increasing set of print cues for initial searching helps to reduce the processing required for successful reading. Monitoring many accurate predictions and some errors increases knowledge of the relationship among meaning, structure, and print cues. Teachers can help children extend the set of cues used to monitor their reading and then gradually integrate these newly noticed cues with others used in searching. This is a critical mechanism that supports development of reading strategies.

Fostering self-monitoring in primary classrooms

High-progress readers monitor their reading and extend the set of cues they use within the context of literate classroom and home environments. Low-progress readers, like Marty, tend not to construct this system of strategies without instructional support. This support can also benefit primary-level readers.

In many classrooms, self-monitoring during oral reading seems almost impossible. Children may monitor for the reader, informing him or her immediately and loudly when an error occurs. However, group contexts can be established to foster self-monitoring. A poster like the following might help establish this context.

> Readers know that:
> 1. Good readers think about meaning.
> 2. All readers make mistakes.
> 3. Good readers notice and fix some mistakes.

These simple tenets can lead to negotiating procedures: (a) to allow each reader time to discover and fix his/her own mistakes; (b) to provide help when requested; and (c) to enable members of the group to note, analyze, and suggest errors (only one or two) for discussion after a student has finished reading and the meaning of the section has been established. With initial teacher modeling, these discussions can shift the focus of reading from accuracy to interpretation and strategy development (Brown & Palincsar, 1989; Pressley et al., 1992; Taylor & Nosbush, 1983).

Low-progress readers, like Marty, tend not to construct this system of strategies without instructional support.

Goodman (1996) describes several settings in which readers engage with their teacher or peers to analyze and discuss miscues and strategies. The following transcript is an excerpt from a guided reading lesson (Fountas & Pinnell, 1996) for a group of Title 1 second-grade students. Early in the year the group generated questions to help them when they encounter difficulties in reading. The teacher recorded these questions on a chart and modeled how they might be used to assist a student at points of difficulty. One rule was that no person should tell another student a word without first prompting that student to "problem solve" the word. After the teacher introduced the story, each child read the story as the teacher circulated, observing reading behaviors and providing assistance at points of difficulty. Early in the year, children read these stories quietly, aloud to themselves; later they read silently. When the group finished this initial reading and had a short discussion of the story, the children were invited to find a part in the story that was tricky for them. This led to the following collaborative problem-solving discussion:

John:	(reading) Before, when I was wild, I slept in the … (stops at the word *stable*).
Teacher:	Who can help him? What can he try?
Arianna:	Where would a horse sleep? What would make sense?
John:	In a barn…but, that doesn't look right.
Arianna:	Think of something that would make sense and begin with those letters.
John:	(reading) Before, when I was wild, I slept in the st–st–sta–ble? Stable?
Teacher:	Yes, a stable is like a barn. In this story, the horse slept in the stable.

John identified a part of the text that caused him difficulty. After Arianna prompted him to consider meaning cues, John made a meaning-based attempt, *barn*, but monitored the conflict between this attempt and the print cues in *stable*. Arianna then prompted him to search both meaning and print cues. John reread to gather meaning and structure and then used print cues from letter clusters. Even with all this successful processing, John was still a bit unsure about his solution, so the teacher stepped in to confirm his strategy use by clarifying the meaning of *stable*.

Admittedly, this is an example of a highly effective interaction, but it does illustrate what is possible. This type of interaction allows the teacher to develop tentative theories about cues children use for monitoring and searching, which can then be used to provide "critical moment teaching" (Goodman, 1996). In this type of activity setting, both teachers and students take an active role in teaching and learning.

Why is this important? Lev Vygotsky suggests that social interactions drive cognitive development.

> Any function in the child's cultural development appears twice, or on two planes. First it appears on the social plane, and then on the psychological plane. First it appears between people as an interpsychological category, and then within the child as an intrapsychological category. (Wertsch, 1990, p. 113)

This is a gradual process. The issues and procedures discussed by the group or with the teacher are interpreted, organized, altered by experience, and internalized as the basis for mental strategies. I suspect this is why telling a child how to play the game of 20 Questions is so ineffective. If we really want him/her to improve, we'd play as a team, hinting, prompting, modeling, and puzzling out the solution together as the child's strategies and independence increased.

Shared problem solving centered around self-monitoring, searching, and self-correction is the mechanism that Clay (1993a) has detailed in the Reading Recovery program to support the hardest-to-teach children. High-progress students often appear to develop this system of strategies with only minimal support from literate classroom or home environments. These high-progress readers learn from what we decide to teach, but they also fill in the gaps to construct a balanced set of monitoring and searching strategies.

Yet, for far too many children in our primary classrooms, learning to read has remained confusing, frustrating, and fraught with feelings of failure. Careful observation and attention to fostering self-monitoring strategies can help us ease this transition into literacy for many students (Lyons et al., 1993). As Clay (1991) concludes, "literacy activities can become self-managed, self-monitored, self-corrected and self-extending for most children, even those who initially find the transition into literacy hard and confusing" (p. 345).

Author notes

Marty is a pseudonym for one particular Reading Recovery student. Although I had him in mind as I wrote this article, the examples are a composite of his behaviors and my experience in working with and observing other children in the program. I would like to thank Mary Fried, Reading Recovery clinical trainer at The Ohio State University, Columbus, Joan Bohn,

Reading Recovery teacher, Birmingham Public Schools, Michigan, and Linda Dorn from the University of Arkansas at Little Rock for providing some of the examples used in this article.

References

Adams, M.J. (1990). *Beginning to read*. Cambridge, MA: MIT Press.

Brown, A.L., & Palincsar, A.S. (1989). Guided, cooperative learning and individual knowledge acquisition. In L.B. Resnick (Ed.), *Knowing, learning, and instruction: Essays in honor of Robert Glaser* (pp. 392–451). Hillsdale, NJ: Erlbaum.

Cazden, C.B. (1992). Revealing and telling: The socialisation of attention in learning to read and write. *Educational Psychology*, *12*(3 –4), 305–313.

Clay, M.M. (1991). *Becoming literate: The construction of inner control*. Portsmouth, NH: Heinemann.

Clay, M.M. (1993a). *Reading Recovery: A guidebook for teachers in training*. Portsmouth, NH: Heinemann.

Clay, M.M. (1993b). *An observation survey*. Portsmouth, NH: Heinemann.

Cunningham, P.M., & Allington, R.L. (1994). *Classrooms that work: They can all read and write*. New York: HarperCollins.

Fountas, I.C., & Pinnell, G.S. (1996). *Guided reading: Good first teaching for all children*. Portsmouth, NH. Heinemann.

Goodman, K.S. (1985). A linguistic study of cues and miscues in reading. In H. Singer & R. Ruddell (Eds.), *Theoretical models and processes of reading* (pp. 129–134). Newark, DE: International Reading Association.

Goodman, K.S. (1993). *Phonics phacts*. Portsmouth, NH: Heinemann.

Goodman, Y.M. (1996). Revaluing readers while readers revalue themselves: Retrospective miscue analysis. *The Reading Teacher*, *49*, 600–609.

Goodman, Y.M., & Goodman, K.S. (1994). To err is human: Learning about language processes by analyzing miscues. In R.B. Ruddell, M.R. Ruddell, & H. Singer (Eds.), *Theoretical models and processes of reading* (pp. 104–123). Newark, DE: International Reading Association.

Lyons, C.A. (1994). Reading Recovery and learning disability: Issues, challenges, and implications. *Literacy, Teaching and Learning*, *1*(1), 109–119.

Lyons, C.A., Pinnell, G.S., & DeFord, D.E. (1993). *Partners in learning: Teachers and children in Reading Recovery*. New York: Teachers College Press.

Morris, D. (1992). Concept of word: A pivotal understanding in the learning-to-read process. In S. Templeton & D. Bear (Eds.), *Development of orthographic knowledge and the foundations of literacy* (pp. 53–77). Hillsdale, NJ: Erlbaum.

Pressley, M., El-Dinary, P.B., Gaskins, I., Schuder, T., Bergman, J.L., Almasi, J., & Brown, R. (1992). Beyond direct explanation: Transactional instruction of reading comprehension strategies. *Elementary School Journal*, *92*, 513–555.

Rumelhart, D.E. (1994). Toward an interactive model of reading. In R.B. Ruddell, M.R. Ruddell, & H. Singer (Eds.), *Theoretical models and processes of reading* (pp. 864–894). Newark, DE: International Reading Association.

Schwartz, R.M., & Stanovich, K.E. (1981). Flexibility in the use of graphic and contextual information in good and poor readers. *Journal of Reading Behavior, 13,* 264–269.

Stanovich, K.E. (1980). Toward an interactive compensatory model of individual differences in the development of reading fluency. *Reading Research Quarterly, 16,* 32–71.

Taylor, B.M., & Nosbush, L. (1983). Oral reading for meaning: A technique for improving word identification skills. *The Reading Teacher, 37,* 234–237.

Wertsch, J.V. (1990). The voice of rationality in a sociocultural approach to mind. In L.C. Moll (Ed.), *Vygotsky and education: Instructional implications and applications of sociohistorical psychology* (pp. 111–126). Cambridge, England: Cambridge University Press.

Putting It All Together

The five essential components in the Reading First portion of the No Child Left Behind Act are based on the findings of the *Report of the National Reading Panel*. Each of the previous sections began with a brief summary of the findings related to one of the five essential components—phonemic awareness, phonics, reading fluency, vocabulary development, and comprehension strategies. Indeed, the findings of the panel document the positive effects of instruction in each of these areas on reading development.

The NRP Report provides a list of five specific types of instruction that "work." However, there is much that the report does not and cannot provide. This list is not an exhaustive list and the panel did not intend it to be exhaustive; they had limited time and resources and included in their topics those they believed to be most important. The panel members would be the first to acknowledge that although the report is important and worthy of serious consideration by all reading educators, it is not a prescription for providing good reading instruction.

An analogy may help: The five essential components are the equivalent of a list of ingredients. For some of the ingredients (phonemic awareness and phonics) there is information about the amounts (5–18 total hours for phonemic awareness and 2–3 years for phonics) and timing (pre-K–K for phonemic awareness and K–2 for phonics), but this information is lacking for the other components. The Report, because of its approach and organization, cannot provide the mixing and cooking instructions that will turn the list of ingredients into a successful reading program. A reading program that taught a rotation of lessons on the five essential components would be unsuccessful because instruction in these components must be combined in a coherent instructional design.

The articles included in this section emphasize the ways that skilled professionals incorporate the five essential components in coherent instructional designs. None of the articles refer to all five of the components and all the articles focus on more than one component. The first article, "Effective schools/accomplished teachers," by Barbara M. Taylor, P. David Pearson, Kathleen F. Clark, and Sharon Walpole, summarizes the results of a study designed to uncover the practices of effective teachers. The article highlights several findings. In relation to time, the findings show that in the most effective schools, teachers spent more time working with small groups. The NRP findings addressed small-group issues in some of the areas and found that small groups were effective—in some cases more effective than one-to-one instruction. Taylor et al. also report that the most effective and moderately effective schools spent more time in independent reading, adding to the correlational evidence that supports independent silent reading. The authors also found that in the area of phonics, explicit direct instruction of phonics was present in all the schools and that what distinguished the most effective schools was coaching in how to use phonics knowledge during reading. The observations of comprehension instruction indicated that the effective schools were distinguished by higher level comprehension questions.

"Singing and songwriting support early literacy instruction," by John A. Smith, describes activities organized around songs that teach letter names and sounds, phonemic awareness, print conventions, background knowledge and vocabulary, and word identification. The author describes familiar routines with whimsical songs that can provide opportunities for both direct instruction and practice.

In "Sharing informational text with young children," Ruth Helen Yopp and Hallie Kay Yopp share ways to incorporate informational text into the primary grade literacy program. They note that alphabet books can be used to help children learn letter names and sounds, support development of phonemic awareness, build vocabulary, and are an excellent environment for using comprehension strategies such as graphic organizers. They also provide an annotated bibliography of alphabet books.

In "'Doing' literature: Using drama to build literacy," Jennifer Catney McMaster suggests a number of drama activities that can be used to provide both direct instruction and practice related to the five essential components. For example, she explains how drama can be used for direct vocabulary instruction in ways that help students acquire definitions that go beyond surface verbalizations. She also writes about developing comprehension monitoring and mental imaging through the use of drama.

Linda D. Labbo, in "12 things young children can do with a talking book in a classroom computer center," lists activities that focus on several of the essential components. She explains how repeated reading can be integrated with computer technology; how word searches for similar letter-sound elements such as beginning sounds, vowel patterns, and syllable structures can be used to reinforce phonics; and how telling how one screen fits with other screens can encourage inferencing and the development of higher order thinking skills.

The final article, "Promoting reading comprehension, content learning, and English acquisition through Collaborative Strategic Reading (CSR)," by Janette K. Klingner and Sharon Vaughn, demonstrates another way to combine the essential components in teaching routines.

CSR specifically combines several of the strategies found effective by the panel, including cooperative learning with previewing, click and clunk, getting the gist, and wrapup.

In each of these articles, the authors have used some of the essential components and combined them in a coherent instructional design. The articles describe teaching routines or practices that allow for direct instruction and practice. Each of the articles provide examples of accomplished teachers' abilities to coordinate complex instructional needs and to facilitate systematic and explicit instruction in phonemic awareness, phonics, vocabulary development, reading fluency, and comprehension strategies. The provision of excellent reading instruction extends far beyond the teaching of five discrete components of reading. Teacher expertise is the most important component in excellent reading instruction (Jordan, Mendro, & Weerasinghe, 1997; Sanders & Rivers, 1996; Whitehurst, 2002). Skilled teachers go beyond the bounds of these articles to orchestrate activities and routines that are effective, efficient, and include the five essential components and more, with the goal of meeting the needs of all the children they teach.

References

Jordan, H.R., Mendro, R., & Weerasinghe, D. (1997, July). Teacher effects on longitudinal student achievement: A preliminary report on research on teacher effectiveness. Paper presented at the National Evaluation Institute, Indianapolis, IN.

Sanders, W., & Rivers, J. (1996). Cumulative and residual effects of teachers on future student academic achievement. Knoxville, TN: University of Tennessee Value-Added Research and Assessment Center.

Whitehurst, G.J. (2002, March). Research on Teacher Preparation and professional development. Paper presented at the White House Conference on Preparing Tomorrow's Teachers.

Center for the Improvement of Early Reading Achievement

Barbara M. Taylor, P. David Pearson, Kathleen F. Clark, Sharon Walpole

Effective schools/accomplished teachers

To assist United States schools in reaching the national goal of all children reading by Grade 3, scholars have been combing research archives in search of relevant findings and good advice for teachers and administrators. Researchers and professional organizations have synthesized research on learning to read (Snow, Burns, & Griffin, 1998), effective school reform programs (Herman, 1999), early reading interventions (Hiebert & Taylor, in press), and effective classroom practices for the primary grades (Learning First Alliance, 1998; Morrow, Tracey, Woo, & Pressley, 1999). Others have examined the characteristics of effective schools (Puma et al., 1997; Stringfield, Millsap, & Herman, 1997) and effective primary-grade teachers (Wharton-MacDonald, Pressley, & Hampston, 1998).

What is missing from this wealth of valuable information is research that weds effective classroom teaching and effective school programs. To fill this need, a group of us at the Center for the Improvement of Early Reading Achievement (CIERA) conducted a national study of effective schools and accomplished teachers. These patterns of effective schools and accomplished teachers will become the foundation for CIERA's projects with aspiring schools—schools that are committed to increasing the reading achievement of their students.

Our goal was to uncover the practices of accomplished teachers within schools that were promoting high achievement among students for whom failure is a common experience. To accomplish this goal, we investigated school and classroom practices in effective (unexpectedly high-achieving) schools and compared them with what was happening in moderately effective and less effective schools.

Method

Seventy Grade 1–3 teachers from 14 schools in Virginia, Minnesota, Colorado, and California participated. To get a picture of their instructional practices, we observed each teacher for an hour of reading instruction each month from December through April. Additionally, we asked them to keep a weekly time log of instructional activities in reading/language arts for a week in February and a week in May, and to complete a questionnaire on school and classroom practices related to reading. We also interviewed a subset of teachers and all building principals.

In each classroom, we gathered performance data for two low and two average readers in the fall and in the spring. In the fall, Grade 1 children were tested on letter names, phonemic segmentation and blending, and a word list (comprising common sight words and some words with predictable spellings). In the fall (for Grades 2–3)

and spring (Grades 1–3) students were assessed on words correct per minute on a grade-level passage, retelling on an instructional-level passage, and a word list (again comprising common sight words and some words with predictable spellings).

To secure an index of overall school effectiveness, we created a composite score based upon the overall school mean for students' gains on the individually administered reading measures (words correct per minute, reading words in isolation, and retelling of a passage) and the school's average on whatever standardized test was used for Grade 3 students. The resulting distribution of composite scores suggested three clusters of schools. Four schools were judged to be most effective, six were classified as moderately effective, and four were judged to be least effective. Relevant data on these groups of schools are presented in Table 1.

On the basis of the observations, logs, questionnaires, interviews, and case studies, we constructed several teacher (classroom-level) variables as potential candidates to explain differences between more and less effective schools.

- Level of home communication
- Student engagement
- Time spent in small- or whole-group reading instruction
- Time spent in independent reading

- Approaches to word recognition instruction (Grades 1 and 2 only)
- Approaches to comprehension instruction

Home communication and student engagement were ratings based upon a set of criteria we developed for scaling comments from our observations. The two time indices were taken from the weekly logs. The last two indices are not quite as transparent. In Grades 1 and 2 frequently observed approaches to word recognition instruction included phonics in isolation, coaching in word attack as children were reading, and sight word practice. Additionally, in Grades 1–3, frequently observed approaches to comprehension instruction included asking literal-level oral questions after reading, asking higher level oral questions after reading, and having students write in response to what they had read.

Results

Time spent in small-group instruction for reading distinguished the most effective schools from the other schools in the study and was offered by teachers in these schools as a reason for their success. Reading instruction included teacher-directed reading of narrative and expository text, literature circles, and instruction in phonics, vocabulary, and comprehension. Across these activities, students in the more effective schools spent more time in small-group instruction than students in the moderately and least effective schools (see Table 2).

This time for small-group instruction was not achieved by each teacher working in isolation. To the contrary, all four of the most effective schools used a collaborative model for reading instruction in which Title I, reading resource, special education, and regular teachers (as well as ELL [English Language Learners] teachers in one school) worked together to provide small-group instruction. In three schools, resource teachers came into the classroom for 60 minutes a day. In one school, children went to resource teachers to work in groups of two or three for 45 minutes a day. The staff in three of the four schools pointed to early reading interventions in Grades K–3 for those students most at risk as one reason for their success.

The small groups in these four schools tended to be based on ability. The rationale given by teachers and administrators for this decision was a desire to maximize individual participation and ensure that all students were working on skills and materials that were within their reach. While this practice may seem reminiscent of an earlier age when we tracked students in Grade 1 into groups in which they would remain for the rest of their school lives, it was different in these schools. Movement across groups was common because of their commitment to regular, systematic assessment and to early interventions. The assessments gave them the evidence they needed to take stock of progress on a regular basis (at least three times per year); the interventions provided the means to accelerate the growth of those most at risk. Thus group boundaries were quite permeable; children were not doomed to lifetime, or even yearlong, membership in particular reading groups.

Children in most and moderately effective schools spent more time in independent reading (28 and 27 minutes per day) than children in least effective schools (19 minutes per day). Teachers in the most effective schools mentioned

Table 1
School effectiveness level by poverty level and reading performance

	Percentage Free/reduced-price lunch	Mean Grade 3 standardized reading test percentile
3. Most effective schools	59	51
2. Moderately effective schools	69	40
1. Least effective schools	45	43

Table 2
Time spent in reading instruction by school effectiveness level

	Minutes spent in small group	Minutes spent in whole group	Minutes spent in independent reading	Total minutes in reading
3. Most effective schools	60	25	28	134
2. Moderately effective schools	26	37	27	113
1. Least effective schools	38	30	19	113
	3>2=1		3=2>1	

time for students to read authentic texts as a factor contributing to their success.

Phonics instruction provided an interesting contrast across levels of effectiveness. As documented in Table 3, explicit phonics was common in all the schools. However, what really set the teachers in the most effective schools apart from their counterparts was their use of coaching children in how to apply the word identification skills they were learning in phonics while they were reading everyday texts.

These differences struck us as important enough to illustrate more vividly. A majority of Grade 1 and 2 teachers across levels of school effectiveness were frequently observed teaching phonics in isolation, including working with words on an erasable board, chart, or worksheet; working with word cards dealing with word study or word families; making words; writing words; and reading words with a particular phonic element. However, in addition to teaching phonics in isolation, a majority of teachers in the most effective schools, unlike those in the other schools in the study, also taught word recognition by coaching children in the use of strategies to figure out unknown words while they were reading. Instead of the teacher or another child calling out a word when a child was stuck, the teacher used prompts such as,

• Why don't you sound it out and think of what would make sense?

• Does that make sense? (*pick* for *quick*)

• Do you see a chunk you know? (*ell* in *fell*)

In other words, children weren't simply practicing reading by reading aloud. Through their coaching, teachers were helping students learn how to apply word recognition strategies to real reading. While more research is needed, the results from this study suggest that conversations about systematic phonics instruction and opportunity to practice need to be broadened to include on-the-spot coaching as children are actually reading.

Table 4 portrays our findings on comprehension instruction practices. Differences emerged in the use of higher level questions, with the clear nod going to the teachers in the most effective schools. There were no reliable differences in the observed use of text-based questions or writing in response to reading. Two other trends are worth noting. First, the teachers in the most effective schools were more balanced in their use of instructional tools compared with their counterparts. Second, when all is said and done, there was not much comprehension activity in these classrooms in general.

Compared with the teachers in the moderately and least effective schools, teachers in the most effective schools communicated more with parents. They were more likely to

• call home at least once a month,

• send notes or newsletters home weekly, and

• send home traveling folders weekly.

In two of the four most effective schools, teachers specifically mentioned good home–school connections as a reason for their success.

In all four of the most effective schools, teachers mentioned that reading was a priority in their building and that this was a factor contributing to their success. The teachers in the most effective schools spent 134 minutes a day on reading (including small- and whole-group reading instruction, independent seatwork, independent reading, and writing in response to reading) compared with teachers in the moderately and least effective schools who averaged 113 minutes a day (in both levels of school effectiveness) on reading.

Summary

We hope that teachers and administrators find this brief overview of some of our results useful and provocative. In our view, nothing could be more important than documenting practices that help teachers in high-poverty schools scaffold their students' learning and achievement. While some of the news in these findings supports earlier research (small-group instruction, overall commitment to reading, time for reading independently, and the importance of higher level questions), we hope it is welcome news, especially at a time when the policy pressures to focus our curriculum in particular ways are stronger than ever.

Some of the news points us in new directions. We think the role that scaffolded word identification during reading of stories played in these effective schools is an important finding. Equally important, we think, is the strong relationship found between school effectiveness and teacher communication with parents (which, by the way, is even stronger when examined as a building-level phenomenon). Finally, the interaction between strong building communication and the capacity to offer high levels of small-group instruction is reassuring; undoubtedly, the one begets the other.

It is clear from this study that a combination of sound building decisions, such as the collaborative model for reading instruction, and effective classroom practices contributed to success in our most effective schools. What is needed now, we believe, is research on

Table 3
Percentage of teachers frequently observed using various approaches to word recognition instruction in Grades 1 and 2 by school effectiveness level

	Coaching during reading	Phonics in isolation	Drill on sight words
3. Most effective schools	54	60	27
2. Moderately effective schools	17	61	0
1. Least effective schools	13	60	40
	3>2=1		3>2,1>2

ways to help aspiring schools and teachers learn from effective schools and accomplished teachers so they too may beat the odds in teaching all children to read. This is the area some of us within CIERA are turning to next.

This research was conducted as part of CIERA and supported under the Educational Research Development Centers Program, PR/Award Number R305R70004, as administered by the Office of Educational Research and Improvement, U.S. Department of Education. The contents of the described report do not necessarily represent the positions or policies of the National Institute on Student Achievement, Curriculum, and Assessment, or the National Institute on Early Childhood Development, or the U.S. Department of Education, and you should not assume endorsement by the federal government of the United States. Please check the CIERA Web site at www.ciera.org for a more complete report of this research study.

References

Herman, R. (1999). *An educator's guide to schoolwide reform*. Arlington, VA: Educational Research Service.

Hiebert, E.H., & Taylor, B.M. (in press). Beginning reading instruction: Research on early interventions. In R. Barr, M. Kamil, P. Mosenthal, & P.D. Pearson (Eds.), *Handbook of reading research* (Vol. 3). New York: Longman.

Learning First Alliance. (1998). Every child reading: An action plan of the Learning First Alliance. *American Educator, 22*(1–2), 52–63.

Morrow, L., Tracey, D., Woo, D., & Pressley, M. (1999). Characteristics of exemplary first-grade literacy instruction. *The Reading Teacher, 52*, 462–479.

Puma, M.J., Karweit, N., Price, C., Ricciuitti, A., Thompson, W., & Vaden-Kiernan, M. (1997). *Prospects: Final report on student outcomes*. Washington, DC: Planning and Evaluation Service, U.S. Department of Education.

Snow, C.E., Burns, S., & Griffin, P. (1998). *Preventing reading difficulties in young children: Report of the Committee on the Prevention of Reading Difficulties in Young Children*. Washington, DC: National Academy Press.

Stringfield, S., Millsap, M.A., & Herman, R. (1997). *Urban and suburban/rural special strategies for educating disadvantaged children: Findings and policy implications of a longitudinal study*. Washington, DC: U.S. Department of Education.

Wharton-MacDonald, R., Pressley, M., & Hampston, J.M. (1998). Literacy instruction in nine first-grade classrooms: Teacher characteristics and student achievement. *The Elementary School Journal, 99*, 101–128.

Table 4
Percentage of teachers frequently observed using various approaches to comprehension instruction in Grades 1–3 by school effectiveness level

	Text-based questions	Higher level questions	Writing in response to reading
3. Most effective schools	37	37	47
2. Moderately effective schools	34	7	24
1. Least effective schools	45	0	27
		3>2=1	

Teaching Reading

Singing and songwriting support early literacy instruction

John A. Smith

Daddy's taking us to the zoo tomorrow,
Zoo tomorrow, zoo tomorrow,
Daddy's taking us to the zoo tomorrow,
And we can stay all day.

Twenty-three emerging readers enthusiastically singing Tom Paxton's song *Going to the Zoo* (1997, Rounder Records) don't realize that they are reinforcing important reading skills as they follow along with a class-mate who points to the lyrics printed on chartpaper.

Advocates of the arts in education have linked art, music, dance, and dra-ma activities to a variety of academic, social, and personal benefits for stu-dents (Dean & Gross, 1992; Eisner, 1992; Hanna, 1992). Meta-analyses of arts education research studies suggest that music activities in particular are strongly associated with nonmusical curricular outcomes. Music activities can enhance students' academic perfor-mance (Miller & Coen, 1994), social skills (Surace, 1992), and content learn-ing (Kassell, 1997).

Music activities can also complement a wide range of literacy learning activi-ties. Educators have suggested ways to use music to help students learn alpha-bet sounds and letters (Page, 1995), de-velop phonemic awareness (Ericson &

Juliebo, 1998; Yopp & Yopp, 1997), and build vocabulary (Jalongo & Ribblett, 1997). McCracken and McCracken (1998) describe activities for using nursery rhymes and songs to teach print conventions and basic spelling patterns. Fountas and Pinnell (1999) recommend having students "sing songs of such delight that the lyrics remain in the memory forever" (p. 92).

The purpose of this article is to pro-vide examples of singing and songwrit-ing activities that can support early literacy instruction in the areas of letter names and sounds, phonemic aware-ness, print conventions, background knowledge, vocabulary, decoding, and writing. Readers should adapt and ex-pand upon these ideas to create their own singing and songwriting literacy activities.

Letter names and sounds

Millions of English-speaking chil-dren have learned the names of the al-phabet letters more easily because someone set them to the tune of *Twinkle Twinkle Little Star*. Once students have learned to sing the ABC song confi-dently, they can learn to recognize the printed alphabet letters using an ABC song chart with the alphabet letters printed (vowels in blue) in a configura-tion that matches the song (see Figure).

Pointing to the letters on the ABC song chart while singing the song helps my students establish a visual represen-tation for each letter. This also helps them learn that *lmnop* is not a single let-ter. Follow-up activities to further rein-

ABC song

a	b	c	d		
e	f	g			
h	i	j	k		
l	m	n	o	p	
q	r	s			
t	u	v			
w	x				
y	z				

Now I know my ABCs
Next time won't you sing with me?

force learning of the letter names in-clude having students chant the letter names as the teacher points to them in random order, and matching activities with alphabet letter cards or plastic magnetic letters. As students become familiar with the letter names, they can use letter cards to reconstruct the ABC song chart on the floor or a tabletop.

Ericson and Juliebo (1998) provided many suggestions for adapting familiar songs and nursery rhymes to teach letter names and sounds. For example, my students and I have enjoyed singing the following adaptation to the tune of *Old MacDonald Had a Farm*:

Old MacDonald had some (chickens, cheese, chocolate)
ee-i-ee-i-oh
With a *ch*, *ch* here
And a *ch*, *ch* there
Here a *ch*, there a *ch*,
Everywhere a *ch*, *ch*
Old MacDonald had some (chickens, cheese, chocolate)
ee-i-ee-i-oh.

I've also used *Twinkle Twinkle Little Star* to help my first-grade beginning readers understand that vowel letters make both long and short sounds. I printed the following words on chart paper, sang them with my students, then distributed copies of the song in the form of individual booklets that children illustrated, read to one another, and took home.

Short and Long Vowel Song

Short *A* sounds like *bat bat bat,*
Long *A* sounds like *bait bait bait.*
Short *E* sounds like *set set set,*
Long *E* sounds like *seat seat seat.*
Short *I* sounds like *bit bit bit,*
Long *I* sounds like *bite bite bite.*
Short *O* sounds like *knot knot knot,*
Long *O* sounds like *note note note.*
Short *U* sounds like *cut cut cut,*
Long *U* sounds like *cute cute cute.*

In between each verse we sang the chorus:

Vowels are short and vowels are long,
Oh we love to sing this song.

Phonemic awareness

Singing is a fun way for students to learn that letter sounds can be manipulated and recombined to create many spoken words (Ericson & Juliebo, 1998; Yopp & Yopp, 1997). The popular traditional song *Oopples and Boo-noo-noos* (Yopp & Yopp, 1997) gets students to create silly new words as they substitute the five long vowel sounds into the words, "I like to eat eat eat, apples and bananas."

I like to ate ate ate, ay-pples and bay-nay-nays
I like to eat eat eat, ee-pples and bee-nee-nees.

A similar lively song, *B-A-Bay,* by the 1960s folk trio The Limelighters requires students to substitute consonant sounds to make the verses. Each time we sing this song I let the class choose eight favorite consonant letters that I write on the board. We alternate singing two verses and then a chorus. My students often find it hilarious to see what the last two words of each verse will be (*boo boo, moo moo, zoo zoo,* etc.).

B	A	bay
B	E	be
B	I	biddybye
B	O	bo
Biddy	bi	bo
B	U	boo
Biddy	bi	bo
Boo	boo	

Print conventions

A wonderful way to teach left-to-right, top-to-bottom, and punctuation skills is a musical version of the language experience approach (Nelson & Linek, 1999). I select a popular song in which the first line is repeated several times such as *The Farmer in the Dell* or *She'll Be Coming Round the Mountain* (see the list of repetitive songs in the Sidebar). We then choose a favorite line, and the students will suggest words to substitute for a rewritten version. For example, in the song *Skip To M'Lou,* the structure of the line "chicken in the breadpan pickin' out dough" lends itself well to original rewriting, focusing on the verse's elements of animal (chicken), place (in the breadpan), and action (pickin' out dough). My students have come up with a variety of original lines such as "Cow in the bedroom sleeping on the bed." We sing each line three times followed by the words "Skip to M'Lou my darling" to constitute a verse. We also sing the chorus between verses. As in the language experience approach, I write the students' dictated words on chartpaper, commenting on directionality, letters and words, sentences, and punctuation. Our follow-up print activities such as matching word cards and sentence strips and making individual illustrated song booklets provide further opportunities for helping teach and reinforce print conventions.

Background knowledge and vocabulary

As emergent readers hear, sing, discuss, play with, and write songs they are building important background knowledge that they will draw upon during later reading and writing experiences. With each new song, students learn concepts and word meanings that they will encounter in print (Foye & Lacroix, 1998; Gilles, Andre, Dye, & Pfannenstiel, 1998). For example, while learning the popular song *Grandma's Featherbed* my students learned words, concepts, and idioms including *tick, ballad, bolt of cloth, soft as a downy chick,* and *cobwebs filled my head.* Similarly, while laughing and singing *Clementine,* they learned words and concepts including *cavern, canyon, excavating, mine,* and *forty-niner.*

I also teach my students background knowledge and vocabulary through writing and singing simple songs that contain content concepts. I write several informational phrases (transportation is moving things around) about a topic and set them to the melody of one of the repetitive songs in the Sidebar. For example, using the tune of the chorus of *Glory, Glory, Hallelujah:*

Transportation is moving things around,
Transportation is moving things around,
Transportation is moving things around,
Things and people move from town to town.
Ships carry goods across the ocean,
Ships carry goods across the ocean,
Ships carry goods across the ocean,
And bring them to our country.
Trucks carry goods on the highway,
Trucks carry goods on the highway,
Trucks carry goods on the highway,
And bring them to our town.

Word identification

My favorite way to teach word identification concepts through music is an adaptation of shared reading (Fountas & Pinnell, 1996). Shared singing is singing together as a class while following along with the lyrics printed on chartpaper or an overhead transparency ("big lyrics" instead of Big Books). Mooney's (1990) model of *to, with,* and *by* lends itself very well to shared singing. I begin by singing the song to the students or playing it on a tape or CD player. Much like the initial read-aloud in a shared reading lesson, this first singing familiarizes students with the song.

I then display the lyrics printed on chartpaper or an overhead and read them to the students, pointing to the words and explaining vocabulary and concepts as needed. I read the lyrics with the students, choral fashion, while pointing to the words. The students then read the lyrics back to me. The best follow-up activity is singing and enjoying the song together. Other activities can focus on print features such as spelling patterns and word parts.

Nursery rhymes printed on chartpaper also lend themselves very well to shared singing activities. Many nursery rhymes can be put to one or more of the

Familiar tunes for songwriting activities

Familiar tunes
Achy Breaky Heart
Act Naturally
Amazing Grace
Army Life
Ballad of Jed Clampett
Camptown Races
Davy Crockett
Down in the Valley
Ghost Riders in the Sky
Gilligan's Island Theme
Glory, Glory, Hallelujah
Greensleeves
Home on the Range
Let My People Go
Oh Where Has My Little Dog Gone
Polly-Wolly Doodle
Pop Goes the Weasel
Red River Valley
Rock Around the Clock
Row, Row, Row Your Boat
Sweet Betsy From Pike
The Hokey Pokey
The Rose
This Old Man
Three Blind Mice
Twinkle, Twinkle Little Star
Yankee Doodle
Yellow Rose of Texas
Yellow Submarine
You Are My Sunshine
Your Cheatin' Heart

Repetitive songs
Are You Sleeping

A-Hunting We Will Go
Buffalo Gals
Crawdad Song
Did You Ever See a Lassie
Frère Jacques
Go Tell Aunt Rhody
Head, Shoulders, Knees, and Toes
Here We Go Round the Mulberry
    Bush
If You're Happy and You Know It
It Ain't Gonna Rain No More
Jimmy Crack Corn
Lazy Mary Will You Get Up
London Bridge
Mama Don't Allow
Mary Wore Her Red Dress
99 Bottles of Beer on the Wall
She'll Be Comin' Round the Mountain
Shortnin' Bread
Skip to My Lou
The Ants Go Marching
The Bear Went Over the Mountain
The Other Day, I Met a Bear
The Wheels on the Bus
This Little Light of Mine
This Old Man
Three Blind Mice

Cumulative songs
Green Grass Grew All Around
Hush, Little Baby
Old MacDonald
There Was an Old Lady Who
    Swallowed a Fly

then sorted the words into columns. My students then went on a 2-day word hunt to find additional /oi/ words and add them to the list. Some of these included the following:

joy	oink
Troy	point
oyster	join
ahoy	asteroid
boysenberry	oil
noisy	boil

An important consideration when using songs and other forms of literature is to balance the teaching of print concepts against maintaining the literary integrity of the piece. Rosenblatt (1980) cautioned against analyzing the print and grammatical features of literary works because this may diminish the quality of students' esthetic experiences with these works. My personal experience with teaching literacy through singing is that using printed song lyrics to highlight common spelling patterns and word parts does not diminish students' enthusiasm for learning and singing the songs. Instead, focusing on some print features increases students' attention to the words and their ability to participate more fully in the enjoyment of the songs.

Throughout the school years, as our classroom collection of favorite songs has grown, I have typed and bound these songs in classroom song anthologies. I make multiple copies so that each student can keep one in his or her desk. These booklets are very handy for sing-alongs and are popular during sustained silent reading.

tunes listed in the Sidebar. For example, the nursery rhyme *Three Little Kittens* can be sung very easily to the tunes of *Ghost Riders in the Sky*, *Home on the Range*, or *Your Cheatin' Heart*. *Mary Had a Little Lamb* can be sung to the tunes of *Greensleeves*, *The Rose*, or *Yankee Doodle*.

One of my favorite follow-up activities for shared reading and shared singing is to guide students to underline common spelling patterns and word parts on the chart paper or an overhead transparency (Pinnell & Fountas, 1998). For example, after singing *Grandma's Featherbed*, my students examined the chartpaper lyrics and underlined words

containing consonant blends (*floor, bread, bolt, spit*), digraphs (*shed, choice, featherbed*), and *-ing* (*sing, morning, fishing*).

Wagstaff (1994, 1998) describes an instructional procedure that uses rhyming words from poems to build word families using onsets and rimes (Adams, 1990). This procedure works well as a follow-up activity to shared singing. For example, after singing Tom Paxton's song *The Marvelous Toy* recently, my students pointed out that the first two rhyming words in the song are *boy* and *toy*. We then brainstormed words that contained the /oi/ sound, discovered the two spelling patterns, and

Songwriting

Just as writing activities are a necessary companion to reading instruction, songwriting complements the joys and learning opportunities associated with singing. Helping students rewrite original lyrics to an existing song makes use of the song's text and melodic patterns to support students' songwriting efforts. Repetitive and cumulative songs (see song list in the Sidebar) provide extra support for initial songwriting in the same way that pattern and predictable books provide extra support for initial reading. For example, after singing *Put Your Finger in the Air*, my students and I brainstormed other places to put their fingers, generated rhyming words, and wrote verses about it. Here are some favorites:

Put your finger on your shoe, and then walk to the zoo.
Put your finger on your food, and you'll be very rude.
Put your finger on your teacher, and see if you can reach her.

While learning the Appalachian folksong *Mama Don't Allow No Guitar Playing 'Round Here*, our class rewrote verses to create our own song *Teacher Don't Allow*. The first verse goes as follows:

Teacher don't allow no book readin' 'round here,
Teacher don't allow no book readin' 'round here,
Well we don't care what the teacher don't allow
We'll read books anyhow,
Teacher don't allow no book readin' 'round here.

Subsequent verses dealt similarly with other curriculum areas: story writin', number countin', and science learnin'. This song, like many others, was written on chartpaper and became part of our daily shared singing. Here is the last tongue-in-cheek verse:

Teacher don't allow no happy students 'round here,
Teacher don't allow no happy students 'round here,
Well we don't care what the teacher don't allow
We'll be happy anyhow,
Teacher don't allow no happy students 'round here.

Active participation

In 1998 the International Reading Association and the National Associa-tion for the Education of Young Children released a joint position statement outlining principles and practices of appropriate education for young children, which pointed out that "high-quality book reading occurs when children feel emotionally secure and are active participants in reading" (pp. 198–199). Anyone who has appreciated the shining faces of children in song can testify that music provides emotional security and active participation. Singing and songwriting activities can bring many additional opportunities for students to respond and participate during classroom literacy instruction. Former U.S. Supreme Court justice Oliver Wendell Holmes understood the importance of singing when he wrote the following:

Alas for those who never sing,
but die with all their music in them.

References

Adams, M. (1990). *Beginning to read: Thinking and learning about print*. Cambridge, MA: MIT Press.

Dean, J., & Gross, I.L. (1992). Teaching basic skills through art and music. *Phi Delta Kappan, 73*, 613–618.

Eisner, E. (1992). The misunderstood role of the arts in human development. *Phi Delta Kappan, 73*, 591–595.

Ericson, L., & Juliebo, M.F. (1998). *The phonological awareness handbook for kindergarten and primary teachers*. Newark, DE: International Reading Association.

Fountas, I.C., & Pinnell, G.S. (1996). *Guided reading: Good first teaching for all children*. Portsmouth, NH: Heinemann.

Fountas, I.C., & Pinnell, G.S. (1999). *Voices on word matters: Learning about phonics and spelling in the literacy classroom*. Portsmouth, NH: Heinemann.

Foye, M.M., & Lacriox, S.E. (1998). Making connections through integrated curriculum. *National Association of Laboratory Schools Journal, 22, 3*, 1–4.

Gilles, C., Andre, M., Dye, C., & Pfannenstiel, V. (1998). Constant connections through literature: Using art, music, and drama. *Language Arts, 76*, 67–75.

Hanna, J.L. (1992). Connections: Arts, academics, and productive citizens. *Phi Delta Kappan, 73*, 601–607.

International Reading Association and National Association for the Education of Young Children. (1998). Learning to read and write: Developmentally appropriate practices for young children. *The Reading Teacher, 52*, 193–215.

Jalongo, M.R., & Ribblett, D.M. (1997). Using picture books to support emergent literacy. *Childhood Education, 74*, 15–22.

Kassell, C.P. (1997). Music in the classroom. *Primary Voices K–6, 2*, 26–31.

McCracken, R., & McCracken, M. (1998). *Stories, songs, and poetry to teach reading and writing*. Winnipeg, MB: Peguis.

Miller, A., & Coen, D. (1994). The case for music in the schools. *Phi Delta Kappan, 75*, 459–461.

Mooney, M.E. (1990). *Reading to, with, and by children*. New York: Richard C. Owen.

Nelson, O., & Linek, W.M. (1999). *Practical classroom applications of language experience*. Boston: Allyn & Bacon.

Page, N. (1995). *Music as a way of knowing*. New York: Stenhouse.

Pinnell, G.S., & Fountas, I.C. (1998). *Word matters: Teaching phonics and spelling in the reading/writing classroom*. Portsmouth, NH: Heinemann.

Rosenblatt, L. (1980). What facts does this poem teach you? *Language Arts, 57*, 386–394.

Surace, E. (1992). Everyone wants to join the chorus. *Phi Delta Kappan, 73*, 608–612.

Wagstaff, J. (1994). *Phonics that work: New strategies for the reading/writing classroom*. New York: Scholastic.

Wagstaff, J. (1998). Building practical knowledge of letter-sound correspondences: A beginner's word wall and beyond. *The Reading Teacher, 51*, 298–304.

Yopp, H.K., & Yopp, R.H. (1997). *Oopples and boo-noo-noos: Songs and activities for phonemic awareness*. New York: Harcourt Brace.

Ruth Helen Yopp
Hallie Kay Yopp

Sharing informational text with young children

Focusing on informational alphabet books, the authors describe several strategies for before, during, and after reading to support content and literacy development.

Recently, numerous educators have challenged the predominance of narrative in primary-grade classrooms, arguing that young students should have many more experiences with informational books than they currently have. Moss, Leone, and Dipillo, (1997), for example, while applauding teachers' increased use of trade books for literacy instruction, lamented that the literature of choice is most often story. Moss et al. argued that students need greater familiarity with nonfiction if they are to survive in the Information Age, and commented that teachers cannot assume that children will transfer their ability to read narrative into competent reading of informational text as they advance through school. Pappas (1991) also challenged the "narrative as primary" notion, stating that an exclusive emphasis on story in early grades means that young children have limited experiences with other text forms, possibly resulting in a "barrier to full access to literacy" (p. 461).

Others agree that if we do not offer young students many experiences with informational texts we are contributing to future difficulties with these materials (Duthie, 1994). The so-called "fourth-grade slump" (Chall, 1983; Chall, Jacobs, & Baldwin, 1990), wherein students often show a decline in the rate of progress in reading or there is a decrease in the number of students reading at "good levels" (Snow, Burns, & Griffin, 1998, p. 78), has been blamed on the shift in materials that students are expected to read at this grade level. Traditionally, fourth-grade students are required to read informational materials to a much greater extent than in previous grades. Without significant previous exposure to informational texts, students have difficulties reading to learn with these materials. This is because informational text differs from narrative.

Narrative, or story, typically consists of a setting, characters, and a plot. The text is usually temporally ordered and goal based. Informational text, by contrast, makes use of compare/contrast, problem/solution, or other text structures. In addition, unlike narrative, informational text often makes use of many of the following features (Duke & Kays, 1998): (a) timeless verb constructions (e.g., "The lifecycle of every butterfly begins with an egg" in *The Butterfly Alphabet Book* by Brian Cassie and Jerry Pallotta, 1995); (b) generic noun constructions (e.g., "Batik designers create a picture in wax on a piece of cloth" in *A Is for Asia* by Cynthia Chin-Lee, 1997); (c) relational/existential verbs, that is, forms of to have and to be (e.g., "Indigo is a blue powder made from the indigo plant" in *K Is for Kwanzaa* by Juwanda G. Ford, 1997); (d) general statements at the opening and closing; (e) use of technical vocabulary; and (f) repetition of the topical theme. These different text structures and features place different demands on the reader.

In addition to placing different demands on the reader, different text structures and features influence classroom literacy interactions in different ways. In the report of the Committee on the Prevention of Reading Difficulties in Young Children, Snow et al. (1998) reviewed the educational impact of sharing nonfiction with young children. Research by Mason, Peterman, Powell, and Kerr (1989) revealed that the nature and focus of discussions and activities accompanying different text genres shift consistently and dramatically depending on the type of text used. Snow et al. concluded that "the potential value of reading different genres with children *extends well beyond any properties of the texts themselves*" and that "the kinds of activities and discussion associated with each genre make distinctive contributions toward developing children's appreciation of the nature, purposes, and processes of reading" (p. 181, italics added).

In addition to gaining exposure to a variety of text structures and features, children learn about their world from these texts. Much research in the past few decades has demonstrated that what we learn from a text is influenced by what we already know. Fielding and Pearson summarized the research by saying that comprehension "depends heavily on knowledge" (1994, p. 62). Early classroom experiences with informational texts help children build the background knowledge they will need in order to experience success with future reading materials.

Doiron (1994) called for an increase in the use of nonfiction for affective reasons. He argued that teachers must include informational books in read-aloud programs, or reading for enjoyment will be perceived only as reading fiction. Reading nonfiction text can be enjoyable, he asserted, as children are not bored by facts; rather, they are curious about and interested in learning about their worlds.

Indeed, nonfiction may be a catalyst for literacy development—a way into literacy for some children (Caswell & Duke, 1998). Informational texts can capitalize on children's interests and lead them to be more purposeful and active readers. A colleague of ours often discusses his own reading difficulties as a young boy (Bishop & Bishop, 1996). The turning point in his self-described cycle of failure was when a teacher noticed him hurdling benches at lunchtime and later presented him with an informational book about a track star with perfect hurdling form. Our colleague's desire to read that book was so intense that he struggled through it until he could read it. The book, followed by numerous additional informational sports books, served as a catalyst for his literacy development. Too often, unfortunately, teachers fail to capitalize on the fascination that facts hold for children (Moss, Leone, & Dipillo, 1997). In fact, an informal survey we recently conducted of 126 primary-grade teachers suggests that nonfiction may make up only a small portion of read-alouds in primary-grade classrooms. In our sample, only 14% of the materials teachers reported reading aloud on a given day were informational in nature.

Contributing to teachers' disinclination to use nonfiction may be a belief that children cannot or do not like to read nonfiction materials. Pappas (1991) expressed concern about an "unacknowledged ideology" about the primacy of story. Many educators and some reading experts, she said, send explicit and implicit messages that young children are unable to make sense of anything unless it is a story and that children's abilities to understand narrative precede their ability to understand nonfiction. Narrative text is thought to be easier than informational text, particularly for young children. Although there continues to be debate on this issue, Pappas's work suggests that young children are as capable of understanding informational text as narrative text. However, she warned that this initial competence will fade if teachers provide students with only stories. Similarly, the work of Duke and Kays (1998) and Kamil and Lane (1997) provided evidence that young children are capable of interacting with informational text, and that they grow in their ability to interact with informational text with opportunities to do so.

Our experiences with our own children support the notion that young children are interested in and capable of thinking about information. Figure 1 shares a list of questions asked spontaneously by our children. Over the course of several days, we surreptitiously recorded questions asked by 5-year-old Erica and 6-year old Danny and found that a preponderance of their inquiries were about their social and natural world. Their questions reveal that they are curious about many things and that no effort is required by adults to initiate conversations about nonfiction topics. Further, many of their questions required extended responses—and sometimes research, in

Figure 1
Questions spontaneously asked by two young children

Questions asked by 5-year-old Erica	Questions asked by 6-year-old Danny
What does an owl look like?	Every minute is God making babies?
Can owls have any color of eyes?	How do they make hammerhead sharks?
What do bats sound like?	Is this rope strong enough to hold this?
Who was the first person? How did babies get started?	What does it look like inside a grape?
What does outside of our world look like?	Why does the air hold up a napkin?
When we go in rockets, how do we leave the earth?	Why don't you see black when you blink really fast?
How do plants grow when you give them water?	Are people only brown and white? Or do they come in other colors too, like blue and purple?
How did the first people get born in the world?	How many different languages are in different places?
If there's a first baby in the world, how does he grow up and get his own food?	Why does black smoke come up from the candle when you blow on it?
How do you get pictures out of cameras?	Can this world end?
Where do people get needles from?	Can a duck fly above the clouds?
Why do people have to go to the bathroom all the time?	When you go up higher, is there lesser air, lesser air, lesser air?
Are there people on other planets?	What does a snake bite feel like?
Why do things so far away seem so small?	What if there were no poison in a snake bite?
Where do shooting stars land?	How big are meteors?
Is day longer than nighttime or is nighttime longer than day?	Can a rocket blast into the sun?
How do you get chicken pox? How did the first person get it?	If a tiny meteor crashed into the ground, would it cause shaking like an earthquake?
When there are twins in a mom, which baby comes out first?	If you landed on Mars, what would it look like?
How do snowflakes come from the clouds?	How fast can snakes go?
If all the insects in the world tried to take you up in the sky, who would win—them or gravity?	Why do lizards take off their tails?
What are bricks made out of?	How fast can lizards run?
What do drugs look like?	How does soap work?

which they eagerly participated. Children's questions such as these provide adults with evidence of their interest in information and their ability to think about it. They also provide adults with opportunities to engage in rich and elaborated oral language interactions and to look into the pages of informational texts with their children—opportunities that should not be ignored.

In summary, informational books serve numerous purposes in primary-grade classrooms (see Figure 2). They provide children with exposure to a variety of text structures and features, helping to mitigate the fourth-grade slump when reading materials and requirements shift. Informational books expose children to concepts and specialized vocabulary, building background knowledge and language that students can draw upon when reading more complex books later. Informational texts cause a shift in the focus of discussion and nature of activities accompanying the reading experience, thus contributing to children's understanding of the purposes and processes of reading. Also, informational texts capitalize on children's interests, whet their appetites for more information, and motivate them to read.

In the remainder of this article, we share ways to incorporate informational texts into the primary-grade literacy program. Then we focus on a particular type of informational book—the informational alphabet book—that can be used by teachers to expose children to new concepts, new vocabulary, and nonfiction text structures, and we offer suggestions for before, during, and after reading activities for extending interactions with these books. Finally, we provide an annotated bibliography of 3 dozen informational alphabet books.

Using informational materials in primary-grade classrooms

Informational materials—including trade books, textbooks, magazines and newspapers, and multimedia materials—can be incorporated into primary-grade literacy programs in a variety of ways (summarized in Figure 3). As noted previously, informational materials can be used as read-alouds. What teachers choose to read aloud to their students can have a significant impact on their students' independent book selections, and therefore their experiences with some types of texts. Indeed, the work of Robinson, Larsen, Haupt, & Mohlman (1997) revealed that when given opportunities to choose books, preschool and kindergarten children select familiar books more frequently than unfamiliar books. Therefore, sharing informational books aloud may pique children's interest in these books and prompt children to select them when given the opportunity.

A second way to use informational material is to pair it with a narrative read by or to the class. As students read or listen to stories, questions often arise (Moss et al., 1997). After listening to *The Very Quiet Cricket* by Eric Carle, for example, students may want to know more about crickets. Nonfiction works, such as *Chirping Crickets* by Melvin Berger, may address many of their questions. Conversely, before reading the story *Owl Moon* by Jane Yolen, the students might listen to *Tiger With Wings: The Great Horned Owl* by Barbara J. Esbensen and *Owl* by Mary Ling. The information shared in these nonfiction books will enrich the students' understanding of and appreciation for the story. In other words, not only can fiction spark the questions that lead children to nonfiction, but nonfiction can build the background knowledge that allows children to more deeply appreciate fiction.

Third, informational trade books and other materials can be paired with content area textbooks. For example, before or after reading a selection about simple machines in a science textbook, one small group of children might read copies of a trade book or other materials about wheels and axles, another group might read informational text about levers, and a third group might read about pulleys. Before or after reading a chapter about weather, small groups of chil-

dren might study rain, wind, and snow through informational texts. Expert groups then can share their findings with classmates.

Fourth, informational texts can be used as the literature of reading instruction. Because nonfiction is a small proportion of basal reader selections at the first-grade level (Hoffman et al., 1994), teachers must incorporate informational trade books and other nonfiction materials as they teach children how to read.

Fifth, informational books should constitute a significant portion of the classroom library so they are readily available to students during free reading or book choice periods.

Informational alphabet books

Like other informational books, informational alphabet books expose children to expository text structures, expand their vocabulary, and build their knowledge of the world. The use of informational alphabet books with intermediate and middle-grade students has been advocated

Figure 2
Some purposes for sharing informational books in primary-grade classrooms

- Expose children to a variety of text features and structures.
- Expose children to specialized vocabulary.
- Expose children to new concepts, building background knowledge.
- Shift nature of accompanying discussions and activities, contributing to understanding of purposes and processes of reading.
- Serve as a catalyst to literacy.

Figure 3
Some ways to incorporate informational materials into literacy programs

- Use as read-alouds.
- Pair with narrative selections.
- Pair with content-area textbooks.
- Use as the literature of reading instruction.
- Include in the classroom library.

because these books allow students to examine language patterns, vocabulary, topics, and illustrations (Chaney, 1993; Thompson, 1992). Informational alphabet books, of course, also have a critical place in classrooms of beginning readers because they support many early literacy understandings as well as provide experiences with informational text (Bishop, Yopp, & Yopp, 2000).

For example, alphabet books have long been used to help children learn letter names and sounds, and knowledge of letters and sounds is considered one of a number of key learnings in early literacy programs. Alphabet books are particularly useful for helping children learn letters because the print is made salient. Indeed, research has shown that conversations about print are more likely to take place with alphabet books than with other genres of children's literature (Bus & van Ijzendorn in Murray, Stahl, & Ivey, 1996; Yaden, Smolkin, & MacGillivray, 1993). Conversations about print are powerful vehicles for literacy development (Snow et al., 1998).

Alphabet books also can support development of phonemic awareness, the insight that the speech stream consists of small units of sound—phonemes—and that these units can be manipulated. Phonemic awareness has a significant relationship with literacy development; children's emerging insights about the phonemic structure of spoken language support their efforts to interact with an alphabetic orthography (Yopp & Yopp, 1996a). Alphabet books present connections between letters and the phonemes they represent ("*a* is for apple," "*b* is for banana"), and as children work to make sense of those connections by attending to spoken words, they begin to understand the phonemic structure of their language (Murray et al., 1996).

Sharing informational alphabet books

As with other types of informational texts, teachers can use informational alphabet books in multiple contexts and support young readers' interactions with them by engaging in before, during, and after reading activities (Yopp & Yopp, 1996b). *Before reading activities* help children access and build relevant background knowledge, guide them to set purposes for reading, and arouse their curiosity and motivate them to read. Prior to sharing *Things That Go: A Traveling Alphabet* by Seymour Reit, for example, the teacher might encourage the students to build a semantic map by brainstorming vehicles in three categories: air, land, and water (see Figure 4). The teacher records their thoughts on an erasable board or butcher paper that can be kept and added to later. The teacher also might have the students participate in home or school activities in which they look for vehicles and share what they have seen. Before listening to Jerry Pallotta's *The Icky Bug Alphabet Book*, students might explore the schoolyard for insects, discussing their findings with one another.

Students might participate in developing a K–W–L chart (Ogle, 1986) before listening to *The Yucky Reptile Alphabet Book* by Jerry Pallotta. Background knowledge is activated and extended as students discuss and record what they already know about reptiles. In the KWLA chart, Mandeville (1994) added a column for students to indicate how they feel about the topic (*A* is for affect). Though Mandeville suggested this column be completed after reading, asking students what they feel before reading may evoke aesthetic responses to the topic and the text and increase the desire to read. Feelings based on past experiences or misconceptions may be challenged or supported by the text.

Before reading *Farm Alphabet Book* by Jane Miller the students might do a quickdraw to depict what they think of when they hear the word *farm*. Like the other prereading activities, these drawings can spark conversations and reveal what children know about a topic (Guillaume, 1998). Completing each of these activities again after the students have read informational materials will reveal students' growth in understanding of the concept or topic.

During reading activities may be used to build comprehension, focus children's attention on particular content or language, and encourage efferent or aesthetic responses to the text. One reading activity that we tried with kindergartners during a reading of *Amazon Alphabet* by Martin and Tanis Jordan is the contrast chart (Yopp & Yopp, 1996b). Figure 5 shows one that was developed during the reading of this book. As each page was shared, children indicated whether or not they were familiar with the animal. The animal was listed in a column on the left side of a large sheet of butcher paper if most of the students indicated that they had heard of it before. Those animals that the majority of students said

Figure 4
Semantic map developed before reading *Things That Go: A Traveling Alphabet*

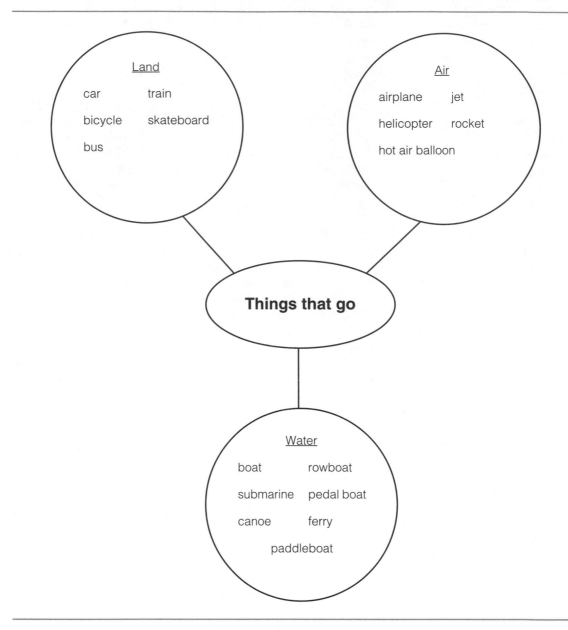

they had never heard of were listed in a column on the right side. This activity stimulated considerable conversation as students told where they had heard about a particular animal or noted that very few of them had heard of it. Furthermore, this activity led the students to the discovery that our world is rich with a diversity of life. Contrast charts can be displayed in the classroom and revisited as children engage in further study. For example, later when they listen to *A Walk in the Rain Forest* by Kristin Joy Pratt, children might record, letter by letter, the plants and animals shared in this book and note similarities and differences in the two authors' selections of life forms from this region of the world, as in Figure 6. At some future point, when students are listening to *V for Vanishing: An Alphabet of Endangered Animals* by Patricia Mullins, they

Figure 5
Contrast chart for *Amazon Alphabet* developed by kindergartners

Animals we have heard about	Animals that are new to us
Butterfly	Agouti
Dolphin	Caiman
Eagle	Giant Armadillo
Frog	Jaguar
Hummingbird	Kinkajou
Iguana	Leaf-Nosed Bat
Toucan	Macaw
	Night Monkey
	Ocelot
	Piranha
	Quetzal
	Red Ouakari
	Sloth
	Umbrella Bird
	Vine Snake
	White-Collared Peccary
	X-ray Fish
	Yapok
	Zorro

may be interested to revisit either chart and note which of the animals listed previously is identified as an endangered species.

After reading activities for an informational alphabet book might include the teacher having young students construct their own alphabet books on the topic. The pages shown in Figure 7 were developed by a first grader who authored an alphabet book about his favorite foods after reading *Eating the Alphabet: Fruits and Vegetables from A to Z* by Lois Ehlert.

Students might follow up a reading of *Jambo Means Hello: Swahili Alphabet Book* by Muriel Feelings by sharing ways of saying hello in other languages. The teacher can record the greetings and identify the languages shared by the students on separate pieces of paper. For instance, one child might share that "hola" is *hello* in Spanish. The teacher records this on a piece of paper and affixes it to a large world map in a region of the world where Spanish is spoken. Children might be encouraged to interview family members and examine books and other resources to research additional ways of saying hello.

After reading *K Is for Kwanzaa* by Juwanda G. Ford, students might work in small groups to develop Venn diagrams comparing this celebration with another of their choosing. Children identify ways the two celebrations are similar and the ways they are different.

Postreading activities such as those described provide children with opportunities to organize and reflect on what they learned from the text, extend what they learned, and make connections with their own experiences.

Informational alphabet books provide opportunities for young readers to interact with informational texts, exposing them to text features and structures (other than narrative) as well as to specialized knowledge and vocabulary. In addition, they provide information on topics that may arouse curiosity, spark questions, and serve as catalysts to language and literacy. Further, informational alphabet books may facilitate young readers' emerging literacy understandings, such

Figure 6
Comparison of life form used for each letter of the alphabet for *Amazon Alphabet* and *A Walk in the Rain Forest*

Letter	Amazon Alphabet	A Walk in the Rain Forest
A	Agouti	Anteater
B	Butterfly	Bromeliad
C	Caiman	Cock-of-the-Rock
D	Dolphin	Dragonfly
E	Eagle	Emerald Tree Boa
F	Frog	Fern
G	Giant Armadillo	Gorilla
H	Hummingbird	Hummingbird
I	Iguana	Iguana
J	Jaguar*	Jaguar*
K	Kinkajou	Kapok
L	Leaf-nosed Bat	Leaf-Cutter Ants
M	Macaw*	Military Macaws
N	Night Monkey	Native
O	Ocelot	Ocelot
P	Piranha	Poison-Arrow Frogs
Q	Quetzal	Quetzal
R	Red Ouakari*	Red-Eyed Tree Frog
S	Sloth*	Sloth*
T	Toucan	Toucan
U	Umbrella Bird	Urania Butterfly
V	Vine Snake	Vanilla Orchid
W	White-Collared Peccary	Water
X	X-ray Fish	-
Y	Yapok	-
Z	Zorro	-

* identified in *V for Vanishing* as an endangered species

as alphabet knowledge, sound-symbol correspondences, concepts about print, and phonemic awareness.

Annotated bibliography of informational alphabet books

We offer here an annotated bibliography of 36 informational alphabet books that are appropriate for primary-grade children. The bibliography is organized alphabetically by title within topics.

Teachers should remember that some authors take liberty when pairing letters with words to represent the letter sounds. Although pairing between consonant letters and their sounds is typically consistent with what we teach young children, vowel letters are more problematic. Some authors select words that begin with the long-vowel sounds (e.g., *A* is for ape); others use words that begin with the short-vowel sounds (e.g., *A* is for apple). Some authors switch between long- and short-vowel sounds. In some cases, neither the long nor short vowel is heard in the paired word. For example, in one book the author wrote "*a* is for artist." In another book, we found "*a* is for anemone." *A* is for artist when it is part of the *ar* team. *A* is for anemone when the vowel occurs in the unaccented syllable in the word (that is, it is a schwa). We recommend that teachers preview each book before reading it to the children and note unfamiliar sound-symbol correspondences. Then, they may choose to either avoid the book with some groups of children or to highlight and explain these usages with their young students. If uncommon or irregular usages are not discussed, confusion, frustration, or misunderstanding may result.

Figure 7
Pages from a first grader's alphabet book on foods

A i S f OR apple

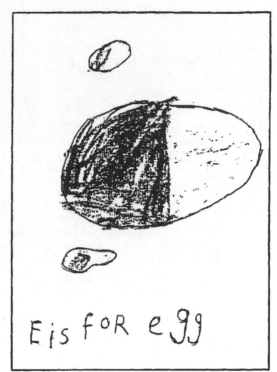

E i s f OR e gg

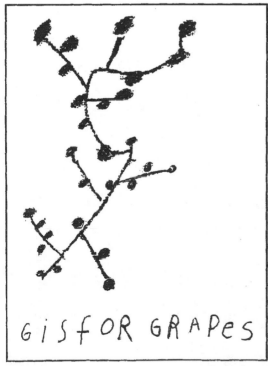

G i S f OR GRA P e s

S i s F OR spa g hetti

Animals

Amazon Alphabet by Martin and Tanis Jordan. New York: Kingfisher, 1996.

This large book with spectacular, colorful illustrations introduces 26 animals that inhabit the area around the Amazon. One sentence for each animal makes up the basic text (e.g., "Jj is for Jaguar preparing to prowl"), and a paragraph about each animal is included at the end of the book for additional information. A pronunciation guide is provided for less familiar animals. This book is a wonderful companion to *A Walk in the Rainforest*.

Animal Alphabet by Sybil Rebman. La Jolla, CA: Green Tiger Press, 1985.

This clever alphabet book was originally published in 1917. One animal for each letter of the alphabet is presented in a rhyme that provides some information about the animal. For *A*: "A for Alligator—His jaws open wide. He has a long tail and a leathery hide." Illustrations of each animal are made with the letters in the spelling of the animal. For example, the letters in the word *alligator* are printed in such a way as to form the shape of an alligator.

Animals A to Z by David McPhail. New York: Scholastic, 1989.

There is more to this simple book than meets the eye at first glance. For each letter of the alphabet from one to three animals are identified. For instance, on the page for *C* is written, "Cricket, Crocodile, Crow" with all three in the illustration. Looking closer at the illustration, however, we find at least three additional items that begin with *C* pictured: a castle, clouds, and a crown.

The Butterfly Alphabet Book by Brian Cassie and Jerry Pallotta. Watertown, MA: Charlesbridge, 1995.

The spectacular diversity of butterflies is displayed in this book, beginning with the Apollo butterfly and ending with the Zephyr Metalmark. Children will be surprised by the variety of butterflies and learn many scientific concepts such as camouflage, the life cycle of the butterfly, species endangerment, transparency, the features of a butterfly, and more.

The Icky Bug Alphabet Book by Jerry Pallotta. Watertown, MA: Charlesbridge, 1986.

From *A* for ant to *Z* for zillions of zebra butterflies, we are introduced to the diversity of nature and learn some fascinating information. The water spider (for *W*), for example, weaves a special web that allows it to bring air underwater where it makes its home.

Roger Tory Peterson's ABC of Birds: A Book for Little Birdwatchers with text by Linda Westervelt. New York: Universe, 1995.

Through photographs, drawings, and informative text, readers and listeners learn about birds and avian features. Developed by internationally acclaimed birdwatcher Roger Tory Peterson, this book shares his enthusiasm for nature. The text makes use of the traditional "A is for..." form and rhyme to introduce and share information about birds from around the globe.

V for Vanishing: An Alphabet of Endangered Animals by Patricia Mullins. New York: HarperCollins, 1993.

Colorful torn tissue paper collages illustrate the pages of this book that introduces the reader or listener to endangered animals. The text is simple, providing the common and scientific name of each animal as well as its country of habitat. We also learn about several extinct animals on the pages that present *X* (*X* is for extinct). On these pages, animals that no longer exist are shown in far less vibrant tones than those in the colorful pages in the rest of the book. The author provides the approximate year of extinction for each animal depicted.

The Wildlife ABC: A Nature Alphabet Book by Jan Thornhill. New York: Simon & Schuster, 1988.

Detailed illustrations of North American wildlife fill the pages of this book, one for each letter of the alphabet. In this rhyming book, children learn about a variety of animals: "Ee is for Eagle Seeking salmon to eat, Ff is for Frog With webbed hind feet." "Ss is for Salmon Swimming up a creek, Tt is for Turtle Her mouth is a beak." Each animal is elaborated upon in a section of Nature Notes at the end of the book. Also, children have the opportunity to identify additional animals on the *Z* page (*Z* is for zoo), which is followed by a key so their identifications can be checked.

The arts

A Is for Artist: A Getty Museum Alphabet. Los Angeles: The J. Paul Getty Museum, 1997.

Details from paintings housed in the Getty Museum are the subject of this alphabet book. "J is for jar," for example, shows a close up of a jar from the Paul Cézanne painting entitled "Still Life with Apples." "U is for umbrella" shows the umbrella from the Edgar Degas painting entitled "Waiting." This book exposes young children to famous pieces of art as they learn the alphabet. On the last pages of the book is a gallery of the complete paintings.

Musical Instruments From A to Z by Bobbie Kalman. New York: Crabtree, 1998.

This book provides interesting information about a variety of musical instruments. Children learn about history (long ago, people used instruments made of shells, wood, and horns to call to one another) and science (long pipes make low sounds and short pipes make high sounds) as well as music in this richly detailed book.

Careers

a b c I can be by Verna Wilkins. Singapore: Tamarind Books, 1993.

Children are exposed to realistic role models from a variety of cultural and ethnic backgrounds for a wide range of careers. Males and females are not depicted in stereotypical roles: For *A*, Anna is an astronomer; for *N*, Nick is a nurse.

Celebrations

K Is for Kwanzaa by Juwanda G. Ford and Ken Wilson-Max. New York: Scholastic, 1997.

From "A is for Africa" to "Z is for Zawadi" listeners learn about the African American holiday, Kwanzaa, letter by letter. This simple informative book is illustrated with brilliant colors. The origin of the holiday, the seven Kwanzaa principles, celebration traditions, and aspects of African heritage are introduced.

Cultures/regions

A Is for Africa by Ifeoma Onyefulu. New York: Cobblehill, 1993.

Photographs of objects from A to Z share much about Africa's diversity. "B is for the Beads a girl may wear on her head, ears, or neck..." "I is for Indigo, a blue powder from the indigo plant that is used to dye clothes."

A Is for Asia by Cynthia Chin-Lee. New York: Orchard, 1997.

The author introduces this book with "A is for Asia, one-third of the earth" and from there proceeds to share information about this culturally diverse region of the world. She describes the Indonesian craft of batik, the camel races in Saudi Arabia, the Korean national pastime of kite-flying, the art of paper folding in Japan, the celebration of the Chinese New Year, and the Muslim holy book, the Qur'an.

Alaska ABC Book by Charlene Kreeger and Shannon Cartwright. Homer, AK: Paws IV Publishing, 1991.

Alliteration is used in this alphabet book about Alaska. For *G* the authors write, "Goats gliding down a glacier." For *T* they write, "Two tall totem poles." Although some of the material in this book is silly (e.g., "Whale watering a walrus" for *W* shows a cartoonish whale with water coming out of its spout and landing on a walrus), young listeners are exposed to many animals that inhabit the region, the climate and geography of the region, and the lifestyle of some Alaskans.

C Is for China by Sungwan So. Parsippany, NJ: Silver Press, 1998.

This beautiful book of photographs and text offers considerable information about the daily life, history, and beliefs of the peoples of China. From "A is for Abacus" to "Z is for Zen," children get a flavor of some of the ancient and modern customs shared by many in this region of the world.

Jambo Means Hello: Swahili Alphabet Book by Muriel Feelings. New York: Dial, 1974.

Readers are introduced to Swahili words for each letter of the alphabet. Information about African culture, traditions, and geography is included. For instance, we learn that a pundah (for *P*) is a donkey and that this is an important animal to farmers of some areas as it transports harvested crops from the fields to the homes. The illustrations, too, offer much information.

A Walk in the Rainforest by Kristin Joy Pratt. Nevada City, CA: Dawn, 1992.

An ant goes for a walk in the rainforest and sees an amazing anteater, a beautiful bromeliad, a comely cock-of-the-rock, and so on, letter by letter, through the alphabet. Use of alliteration for each letter draws the listeners' attention to the sounds of language. In addition to the main text, there is subtext on each page that provides information about the rainforest.

Desert life

Agave Blooms Just Once by Gisela Jernigan. Tucson, AZ: Harbinger House, 1989.

The author uses rhyme to introduce the reader or listener to 26 dwellers (one for each letter of the alphabet) of the Sonora desert in Arizona, including the agave plant, bobcat, and coyote, and provides a small amount of information about each.

Dinosaurs

The Dinosaur Alphabet Book by Jerry Pallotta. New York: The Trumpet Club, 1991.

"A is for Ankylosaurus"—a dinosaur that, we discover, was armored with spikes that stuck out of its back and that had a club on the end of its tail that it could swing and use as a weapon. "B is for Baryonyx," a fish-eating dinosaur with two large claws and a head the shape of a crocodile's head. The topic of dinosaurs is appealing to many young children, and this book provides considerable information about dinosaurs, including a brief discussion of different hypotheses about their extinction.

Farm

Farm Alphabet Book by Jane Miller. Englewood Cliffs, NJ: Prentice-Hall, 1983.

On each page of this book is a photograph of a farm animal or activity. The author briefly describes each item, teaching us about incubators, orchards, and tractors, for example. Additionally, we learn the names of female, male, and baby animals. For instance, for the letter *P*, we learn about pigs. A mother pig is a sow, a father pig is a boar, and a young pig is a piglet.

Food

Alpha-Bakery by Gold Medal Flour. Minneapolis: General Mills, 1997.

This book presents recipes for children to enjoy preparing with an adult. From apple crisp to lemon squares to zebra cookies, there is a recipe for each letter of the alphabet!

Eating the Alphabet: Fruits and Vegetables From A to Z by Lois Ehlert. New York: Trumpet Club, 1989.

A number of fruits and vegetables are pictured for each letter of the alphabet, including more and less familiar ones. Large colorful drawings help listeners identify these foods. Although throughout the book only the names are included (for *B*, the following are pictured and labeled: blueberry, Brussels sprout, bean, beet, broccoli, banana), at the end the author provides a brief description of each fruit and vegetable mentioned. Here we learn, for instance, that the blueberry was a wild North American berry. Native Americans taught settlers how to dry the berries for use all winter long.

Geography

Geography From A to Z: A Picture Glossary by Jack Knowlton. New York: HarperCollins, 1988.

The text and colorful illustrations provide information about 63 geographic features of our earth from A to Z. Paragraph definitions and descriptions are offered for features such as badlands and beaches; glaciers, gulches, and gulfs; two types of waterfall; and five climatic and geographic zones. This book is an excellent resource for learning about our world. An index concludes the book.

The ocean

ABSea by Bobbie Kalman. New York: Crabtree, 1995.

Colorful photographs and informative text are provided about sea animals and their environment for each letter of the alphabet. For example, the reader learns that coral reefs are made up of millions of coral animals, some living and some dead. These reefs serve as home to thousands of animals.

The Ocean Alphabet Book by Jerry Pallotta. Watertown, MA: Charlesbridge, 1986.

> Another informational alphabet book by Jerry Pallotta, *The Ocean Alphabet Book* describes fish and other sealife in the North Atlantic Ocean letter by letter.

The Sailor's Alphabet by Michael McCurdy. Boston: Houghton Mifflin, 1998.

> "Oh, A is for anchor and that you all know, B is the bowsprit that's over the bow." This singsong book identifies objects relevant to sailing vessels in a rhyme format. Subtext is included on each page to offer more information for the interested listener.

A Swim Through the Sea by Kristin Joy Pratt. Nevada City, CA: Dawn, 1994.

> A seahorse explores the ocean and encounters sea life for each letter of the alphabet. Alliteration is used on each page. For *F*, the author states that the seahorse would "find phosphorescent Flashlight fish"; for *G*, "he'd greet a gargantuan Grouper gladly getting groomed." In smaller type, the author provides considerable information about each of the animals depicted. Beautiful colorful drawings are included.

Plants

Alison's Zinnia by Anita Lobel. New York: Mulberry, 1996.

> Children learn about the tremendous variety of flowers that exist as Alison acquires an amaryllis for Beryl who then buys a begonia for Crystal who cuts a chrysanthemum for Dawn, and so on. This book makes use of alliteration as it moves its way through the alphabet. Illustrations beautifully display the flowers identified in this book.

The Victory Garden Alphabet Book by Jerry Pallotta and Bob Thomson. Watertown, MA: Charlesbridge, 1992.

> Learn about a variety of vegetables that can be grown in a garden, from asparagus to zucchetta. A brief description of each vegetable is given, and we learn much about the growth of different plants. Peanuts, for instance, grow underground from shoots that have turned downward and buried themselves. Leeks are naturally pest free; insects and animals do not like to eat them.

Transportation

The Airplane Alphabet Book by Jerry Pallotta and Fred Stillwell. Watertown, MA: Charlesbridge, 1997.

> The authors provide information about airplanes from the AT6 to the Zero. For children who are fascinated with flying machines, this book is an interesting resource. Children learn a bit about the history of flight as well as about the variety of airplane designs and purposes.

Things That Go: A Traveling Alphabet by Seymour Reit. New York: Bantam, 1990.

> A different means of transportation for every letter of the alphabet is introduced in this book, beginning with an ambulance and ending with the zeppelin. A brief description of each is included. For *S* we learn that spaceships carry people and equipment beyond the earth's atmosphere and that the spaceship *Columbia* circled the earth in 110 minutes on its first voyage.

United States history

Cowboy Alphabet by James Rice. Gretna, LA: Pelican, 1990.

> Aspects of western life, including rodeo lore, desert wildlife, and cowboy dress, are revealed through the letters of the alphabet in this humorous and delightfully illustrated book.

The Folks in the Valley: A Pennsylvania Dutch ABC by Jim Aylesworth. New York: Harper Trophy, 1992.

> Through simple rhyming text and colorful illustrations, we get a glimpse of the daily life of the Amish, Mennonites, Moravians, and others whose ancestors came to rural Pennsylvania in the 17th century seeking political and religious freedom. *C* shows cows getting milked in the milking shed; *Q* shows a group of women stitching a quilt at a quilting bee.

Many Nations: An Alphabet of Native America by Joseph Bruchac. Mahwah, NJ: BridgeWater Books, 1997.

> The diversity of Native American cultures is depicted in this book as we read about "Blackfeet riders following buffalo herds," and "Dakota children listening to the storyteller's words" as well as numerous other

Native American tribes. Colorful paintings delight readers and listeners.

Other

Apples, Bubbles, and Crystals: Your Science ABCs by Andrea T. Bennett and James H. Kessler. New York: McGraw-Hill, 1996.

From *A* is for apple to *Z* is for zoom, the authors provide a poem and step-by-step instructions for a scientific activity for each letter of the alphabet. Children, with the supervision of an adult, make their own glue, construct a kazoo, move objects with magnets, and write secret messages with wax. Explanations of the scientific principles for each of the activities are included.

References

Bishop, A., & Bishop, S. (1996). *Teaching phonics, phonemic awareness, and word recognition*. Westminster, CA: Teacher Created Materials.

Bishop, A., Yopp, R.H., & Yopp, H.K. (2000). *Ready for reading: A handbook for parents of preschoolers*. Boston: Allyn & Bacon.

Caswell, L., & Duke, N. (1998). Non-narrative as catalyst for literacy development. *Language Arts, 75*, 108–117.

Chall, J. (1983). *Stages of reading development*. New York: McGraw-Hill.

Chall, J., Jacobs, V., & Baldwin, L. (1990). *The reading crisis: Why poor children fall behind*. Cambridge, MA: Harvard University Press.

Chaney, J. (1993). Alphabet books: Resources for learning. *The Reading Teacher, 47*, 96–104.

Doiron, R. (1994). Using nonfiction in a read-aloud program: Letting the facts speak for themselves. *The Reading Teacher, 47*, 616–624.

Duke, N., & Kays, J. (1998). "Can I say 'Once upon a time'?": Kindergarten children developing knowledge of information book language. *Early Childhood Research Quarterly, 13*, 295–318.

Duthie, C. (1994). Nonfiction: A genre study for the primary classroom. *Language Arts, 71*, 588–595.

Fielding, L.G., & Pearson, P. D. (1994). Reading comprehension: What works. *Educational Leadership, 51*(5), 62–68.

Guillaume, A. (1998). Learning with text in the primary grades. *The Reading Teacher, 51*, 476–486.

Hoffman, J., McCarthey, S., Abbott, J., Christian, C., Corman, L., Curry, C., Dressman, M., Elliott, B., Matherne, D., & Stahle, D. (1994). So what's new in the new basals? A focus on first grade. *Journal of Reading Behavior, 26*, 47–73.

Kamil, M., & Lane, D. (1997). *A classroom study of the efficacy of using information text for first grade reading instruction*. Paper presented at the American Educational Research Association meeting, San Diego, CA.

Mandeville, T.F. (1994). KWLA: Linking the affective and cognitive domains. *The Reading Teacher, 47*, 679–680.

Mason, J., Peterman, C.L., Powell, B.M., & Kerr, M.K. (1989). Reading and writing attempts by kindergarteners after book reading by teachers. In J. Mason (Ed.), *Reading and writing connections* (pp. 105–120). Old Tappan, NJ: Allyn & Bacon.

Moss, B. (1995). Using children's nonfiction tradebooks as read-alouds. *Language Arts, 72*, 122–126.

Moss, B., Leone, S., & Dipillo, M. (1997). Exploring the literature of fact: Linking reading and writing through information trade books. *Language Arts, 74*, 418–429.

Murray, B., Stahl, S., & Ivey, M.G. (1996). Developing phoneme awareness through alphabet books. *Reading and Writing: An Interdisciplinary Journal, 8*, 307–322.

Ogle, D. (1986). K–W–L: A teaching model that develops active reading of expository text. *The Reading Teacher, 39*, 564–570.

Pappas, C. (1991). Fostering full access to literacy by including information books. *Language Arts, 68*, 449–462.

Robinson, C., Larsen, J., Haupt, J., & Mohlman, J. (1997). Picture book selection behaviors of emergent readers: Influence of genre, familiarity, and book attributes. *Reading Research and Instruction, 36*, 287–304.

Snow, C., Burns, M.S., & Griffin, P. (Eds.). (1998). *Preventing reading difficulties in young children*. Washington, DC: National Academy Press.

Thompson, D. (1992). The alphabet book as a content area resource. *The Reading Teacher, 46*, 266–267.

Yaden, D.B., Smolkin, L.B., & MacGillivray, I. (1993). A psychogenetic perspective on children's understanding about letter associations during alphabet book readings. *Journal of Reading Behavior, 25*, 43–68.

Yopp, H.K., & Yopp, R.H. (1996a). *Oo-pples and boo-noo-noos: Songs and activities for phonemic awareness*. Orlando, FL: Harcourt Brace.

Yopp, H.K., & Yopp, R.H. (1996b). *Literature-based reading activities* (2nd ed.). Boston: Allyn & Bacon.

Children's books cited

Berger, Melvin. (1998). *Chirping crickets*. New York: HarperTrophy.

Carle, Eric. (1997). *The very quiet cricket*. New York: Putnam.

Esbensen, Barbara J. (1991). *Tiger with wings: The great horned owl*. New York: Orchard.

Ling, Mary. (1992). *Owl*. New York: DK.

Yolen, Jane. (1987). *Owl moon*. New York: Philomel.

Jennifer Catney McMaster

"Doing" literature: Using drama to build literacy

This article explores the use of drama as a teaching tool to promote students' interest in literacy.

The students in Adele Toney's third-grade class at Roberts Elementary School in Syracuse, New York, USA, are learning about Frederick Douglass. Ms. Toney reads aloud from a biography about this famous American, which discusses his childhood as a slave in Baltimore and mentions that Frederick was not permitted to learn to read or write. "Why do you think slaves were not allowed to learn to read and write?" Ms. Toney asks the class. The students aren't sure.

Ms. Toney asks a student for a scrap of paper. She scribbles something on the paper, folds it, and surreptitiously hands it to a student, Patrina, whispering, "Read this and pass it on." The entire class pays rapt attention as Patrina reads the note and hands it to another student who also reads it and passes it on. Then Patrina and several others quietly get up from their desks and sneak out the door following Ms. Toney, while the rest of the class watches in wondering silence. Seconds later the group reappears and Ms. Toney asks Patrina to read aloud from the piece of paper. Patrina unfolds the note and reads, "Let's escape tonight!"

Then Ms. Toney repeats her earlier question, "Why do you think slaves were not allowed to learn to read and write?" This time the students are full of answers: "So the slaves couldn't plan an escape!" "So they couldn't communicate!" "Because if they could read they could learn how to get away!" This drama activity, observed during a clinical practicum experience, lasted for less than 5 minutes, but created a vivid mental representation that the teacher and students were able to draw upon for future classroom discussion.

The use of drama as a teaching tool is based on the simple premise that an involved child is an interested child, an interested child will learn, and drama directly involves the child (Smith, 1972). However, a study by Bolton (1985) showed that in North American schools, students and teachers overwhelmingly thought classroom drama was the equivalent of "doing a play," a project usually associated with an elaborate production. Thus, teachers may avoid using drama in the classroom because they fear it will involve tedious, time-consuming preparations. Unfortunately, this view can cause educators to overlook what is an important tool for teaching in general, and for the teaching of reading and language arts in particular.

Drama is an invaluable tool for educators because it is one of the few vehicles of instruction that can support every aspect of literacy development. Drama encompasses all four of the language arts modalities and is an effective medium for building decoding, vocabulary, syntactic, discourse, and metacognitive knowledge. Drama activities encourage the affective aspects of reading and emergent literacy, accomplishing this within a valuable social context. Drama begins with the concept of meaningful communication and provides multiple opportunities for social interaction and feedback. These interactions offer the kind of support Vygotsky (1978) deems necessary for internalizing new knowledge. Above all, drama activities are extremely effective in fostering a community of learners who choose to participate in independent reading activities.

One of the important features of drama is the variety of communication experiences it offers to children. Drama is thinking out loud; it develops oral language skills as the child defines, articulates, expresses, and verbalizes thoughts in the context of improvised activities. By participating in drama activities, children develop listening skills on two levels: (a) the basic listening skills that are required in order for the sessions to continue, such as listening for cues; and (b) the evaluative listening skills that develop as children act as audience members, considering how the activities are progressing and what they would do differently if they were performing (Stewig, 1974).

Drama is an invaluable tool for educators because it is one of the few vehicles of instruction that can support every aspect of literacy development.

Children experience the chance to improve their speaking skills as they take on different roles, selecting the language most appropriate to the situation. Oral language development has a crucial impact on learning to read, as "a solid oral language foundation allows [children] to generalize from what they already do well" (Leu & Kinzer, 1995, p. 241). Children engaged in dramatic play use literate language. This language use, which includes defining references to pronouns, clarifying ambiguous terms, choosing objects to symbolize other objects, and clearly introducing topics, will later transfer into their learning of written language (Pellegrini, 1980, 1982, 1984).

Drama activities can be used to develop writing skills by expanding on students' oral language development. Yaffe (1989) used dramatic improvisation to capture the interest of

his students and allow them to experience success in creating scenes orally before attempting to do so in writing. The students were then led to the realization that improvising was really just "writing on their feet" and that they were good at it; they were subsequently able to transfer their words to paper.

Finally, drama activities can focus students directly on print and can expand their receptive written language skills. This article will focus on how drama activities can specifically develop central components of literacy acquisition: affective aspects; emergent literacy and automaticity; and syntactic, decoding, vocabulary, discourse, and metacognitive knowledge.

Developing affect through drama

One of the most agreed-upon uses for drama in the reading program is as a means of developing affect in learners. Drama creates interest and motivation, which are crucial factors in facilitating students' understanding and response. "Drama has a positive effect on personal attitudes often associated with language growth: self-confidence, self-concept, self-actualization, empathy, helping behavior and cooperation" (Wagner, 1988, p. 48). The students involved in Yaffe's (1989) writing activity

> learned a valuable lesson—that they had something to say, that they could say it well, that other people were interested in hearing it. For the at-risk student with a history of failure, this was a startling revelation. Self-esteem and self-confidence grew. These pupils became learners because they came to think of themselves as capable of learning. (p. 30)

Heinig (1987) pointed out the value of drama as a way to let children experience a role that is new to them, such as "a powerful king, a hero, or a brave person. They see themselves in a new light, with a strength they never knew they had within them. Sometimes they discover talents they never had a chance to express before" (p. 4). A student involved in a drama program in Toronto eloquently stated the impact drama had on her affect:

> When I started drama three years ago, I was very shy and didn't say much in a group. I didn't think anybody would listen or care. In drama you realize nobody will criticize. I can now talk in a group even if others disagree with me and I've learned how to listen to others. (Yau, 1992, p. 5)

Drama can be a major force in boosting a child's self-concept and desire to be an active part of the learning community. However, drama is also a direct motivator for reading. When dramatizing books is a regular activity in the classroom, children naturally desire to act out more stories, which encourages them to seek out more reading experiences. They are inspired to find the "perfect" story to dramatize and may read several selections to find the best one (Ross & Roe, 1977).

Miccinati and Phelps (1980), reading instructors and dramatists, found drama to be a strong motivator on many levels. First, the students must read to find the story they wish to dramatize. They then read further to pick the best parts to act out. Additional reading is required to understand the characters and actions more completely. Even more reading is motivated if the students are engaged in script writing or in dramatizing nonfiction, as they do further research about their characters, setting, and props. When the students subsequently act out the stories they've read, they see for themselves that the words on the page have meaning, both for them and for others.

The excitement of performing scenes for an audience, whether their class, school, or parents, adds another level of motivation for drama participants. Bidwell (1990), a reading teacher who regularly employs drama in her classroom, elaborated:

> Students know that eventually they will be performing, so they want to do it right as soon as possible. Repeated readings and modelings help them know they can do it right. The more they perform successfully, the greater their self-concept—and the downward spiral starts moving up. (p. 40)

Teachers DeRita and Weaver (1991) used drama to increase motivation when they paired their fourth-grade reading class with kindergarten drama partners. This pairing resulted in extremely positive attitudes in the fourth graders, who "looked forward to doing their work because they had a real purpose for doing it and a real audience to appreciate it" (p. 247). Students' excitement about performing leads to increased motivation to read their parts well, which in turn creates successful drama experiences. Successful experiences allow students to perceive themselves as good readers, thus continuing the cycle.

Drama builds on something children do naturally—pretending. By building on a natural ability, all students can experience success from the start. These initial successes may not involve any actual reading; in fact, they may

be chiefly pantomime. However, with each success, the child is more willing to take risks, allowing script work to be introduced. Bordan's work (1970) using drama to motivate poor readers led her to comment,

> I know of no faster way of getting a class…to read, than to present each child with his own personal mimeographed copy of a play he feels he has had a hand in creating…. Children, who for three years have never realized the purpose of reading and have considered it dreary, frustrating drudgery suddenly acquire an inner motivation. (p. 22)

Successful participation in a drama after learning one or two lines of dialogue by reading and repeating them over and over can change a child's entire view toward reading. Reading is suddenly something the child can succeed in and is self-fulfilling as well. The knowledge that reading can be its own reward comes to many as a complete surprise and becomes a source of increased motivation for reading (Bordan, 1970).

Above all else, the reason drama is cited again and again as an effective method for building interest and motivation in reading is that children enjoy it. Drama is just plain fun. It allows learners to use their feelings, their thoughts, and their imaginations to express themselves to and with others, all the time growing in language ability (Flennoy, 1992).

Developing emergent literacy through drama

Drama can be an important source of scaffolding for the emergent reader, especially by providing children with rich background experiences to draw upon in future reading. Story enactments in the kindergarten and pre-K classrooms can create curiosity about literature before independent reading begins. These experiences allow children to take on the role of storyteller long before they can read or write. Teacher Adele Toney, whose classroom was described at the beginning of the article, chooses action-filled stories such as *Anansi and the Moss-Covered Rock* (Kimmel, 1988) for her class to dramatize while she slowly reads aloud. The students pay close attention to her reading as they know they will be acting out the story. They listen intently as they pantomime or wait for their opportunity to act. In places where dialogue occurs, the students repeat it after their teacher. In subsequent group discussions, students reveal a deep understanding of the events and sequence of the story. This type of activity is easy to carry out and provides emergent readers with a valuable model of story form and book language. It allows nonreaders to participate fully in a literary event with their reading peers and encourages further exploration of books as students look for more stories to dramatize.

Dramatizations can also provide students with vicarious experiences that they can draw upon when learning to read. Although direct experiences such as field trips are the strongest source of background knowledge, drama experiences can be a viable alternative (May, 1990). When students participate in dramatization, they "become" whatever it is they are enacting. Nonfiction dramatizations in particular become event representations for the children, transforming facts, vocabulary, and concepts into scenarios that the children experience and thus retain (Putnam, 1991).

Students can experience an event, such as a trip to the zoo, through a drama framework that begins with the class members sharing their own personal knowledge of what a zoo is like, with the teacher acting as facilitator. This is followed by a dramatization during which students assume the roles present at the event, such as animals, zookeepers, and visitors. The enactment is followed by a discussion of their experience (Schickedanz, 1978). Finally, the class may read a story about the zoo. In this way, students can experience what they read, rather than simply experience the act of reading (DuPont, 1992). Use of dramatizations in the early grades can successfully build students' background knowledge:

> Key incidents in the lives of famous people, important historical events, customs practiced in other cultures, animal behavior, natural phenomenon like the growth of plants, biological processes like the movement of blood through the body—all these can be made accessible through the descriptions and explanations of nonfiction. Those descriptions and explanations can, in turn, be made more accessible to young children through dramatization. (Putnam, 1991, pp. 468–469)

As we know from watching children at play, they are natural dramatists who use make-believe as a way of understanding life around them. The goal of drama in emergent literacy is to capitalize on something children already do naturally, by using dramatization to build a reservoir of experiences that can be connected to new information encountered in later learning.

Developing decoding knowledge through drama

Vygotsky (1978) indicated the significance of dramatic play as a foundation for literacy. Dramatization leads to the development of skill in symbolic representation and the use of decontextualized language. In order to act out a scene, children must be able to indicate who they are portraying and where they are in space (and/or time), as well as what they are doing in the fictitious world they have established. Meaning is attached to symbols or signs, used to represent objects that are not present (Wagner, 1988). The awareness of symbolic representation and the ability to manipulate symbols in dramatic play is the same basic understanding children require in order to grasp the alphabetic principle. This concept that symbols (letters) represent sounds, which have meaning, must be internalized before children can make sense of printed material. The child's development of representational skills in drama can thus serve as a basis for development of the representational skills required for literacy (Schickedanz, 1978).

Later in the reading process, the teacher can use drama activities to address specific decoding challenges directly. For example, to work on consonant blends, the teacher might play "What's my word?" In this activity, a blend is written on the blackboard (e.g., *gr*). The teacher has a grab bag filled with word endings, such as *in*, *ab*, *oan*, and *ow*. The student picks an ending, holds it up to the blend written on the board, and the entire group reads the resulting word aloud. The group then acts out the word, thus providing a visual, aural, and kinesthetic memory cue for the word.

Bordan (1970) experienced positive results using drama to teach her second-grade nonreaders sight words. She began with simple verbs such as *jump* and the students' names, which were often the only words they could read. At different points during the day she would write a student's name on the board, followed by an action verb (e.g., "Jack, jump!"). The student would then read the phrase and perform the action. The students looked forward to learning each new verb and became actively engaged in remembering words in the hopes that they would get to perform them.

Developing fluency through drama

In order for children to extract meaning from print, they must move beyond plodding word-by-word decoding and achieve fluency in reading. Research shows that in order to develop fluency, students need opportunities for repeated reading of the same material (Bidwell, 1990). Repetition and practice are inherent in many drama activities, with the added incentive that the repetition is meaningful for students. Students read and reread with the purpose of selecting a piece of literature for performance, choosing the parts to dramatize, practicing and switching roles, trying different line readings, underlining words for emphasis, and discussing different interpretations in a small-group setting (Wolf, 1993). According to Bidwell (1990):

> Reading something over and over may sound good to the researchers, but youngsters hate to do it unless we can "trick" them into wanting to reread. In Grades 1 through 8, I haven't found anyone who has minded rehearsing a part many times for the purpose of performing in front of a real audience. (p. 40)

In Flennoy's (1992) study with low-achieving first graders, drama activities led to the students reading with more expression, enthusiasm, and fluency. Hoyt (1992) found that participating in choral readings of Readers Theatre resulted in improved fluency among third-grade students in a Chapter 1 program. Much like repeated practice of a piece of music allows a young violinist to develop playing proficiency, repetitious work with a script in drama activities allows a new reader to develop fluency in reading.

Developing vocabulary knowledge through drama

New vocabulary presented in the drama context has the benefit of being acted out, thus providing students with a strong mental image of the word, one that has been experienced visually, aurally, and kinesthetically. When new words are defined and then reinforced through a drama activity, students have concrete examples in multiple modalities to complete their understanding of the word.

A good example of using drama to develop vocabulary can be seen in the following excerpt from a kindergarten class. The teacher, Pat Thompson, reads aloud to her class from a book about rodeo star Bill Pickett. She uses dramati- zation to teach her class the new word *bulldogging*, which she has just read from the text:

> Let's act this part out. All right, stand up. All right, you're Bill Pickett on your horse, Spradley. Look at the way you're on your horses. Okay, now, what do you have to do? Leap, leap out of your saddle. Oh, that's right. That's the way you leap. Good, good.... Here's your pretend steer. Grab him by those what? Horns. Now, take those hands and twist his head sideways. Now roll him on the ground. Excellent. You're great Bill Picketts. And what you did is called bulldogging. (Putnam, 1991, p. 466)

By pausing for this brief activity during the reading of a nonfiction text, the teacher provides the students with a strong association for their new vocabulary word. Vocabulary words can also be reinforced during an extended improvisation. Adele Toney uses this technique while teaching her class about the water cycle. As the class acts out "a day in the life of a drop of water," she integrates the new terms they have encountered in their reading, giving directions such as: "All right, now you are meeting up with some other *molecules* of water up in the sky.... Now join together with them...okay, you are getting too heavy to stay in the sky, so start to *precipitate*..." As the class acts out her descriptions, she can easily monitor if any students are having difficulty with the vocabulary and, if so, can immediately expand upon the problematic word (e.g., "Remember, *evaporation* happens when the liquid water gets so much energy it turns into a gas...show me your energy!").

By tying word meanings to experience, drama activities help students acquire definitions for new words that go beyond surface verbalizations (Duffelmeyer & Duffelmeyer, 1979). A sample activity might include introducing a new word list to the class, then assigning one or two words from the list to small groups. Each group must create a skit that uses the word and then perform it for the class. For example, after the "mule" refuses to plow for the "farmer," the child playing the farmer might say, "My mule, Sam, sure is acting *obstinate* today," while Sam holds up his group's word, *obstinate*, on a card (Reuse, 1977). The entire class benefits from the representation of the word.

Children can be led to differentiate between similar vocabulary words by acting out the distinctions, such as portraying the actions of the various animals in the poem "The Sandhill Crane" as they *scuttle*, *hide*, *stalk*, and *whisper* (Stewig, 1974). Vocabulary gains are also made as students act out favorite stories and must represent the distinction between various character traits (e.g., a greedy giant vs. a dejected giant vs. an angry giant) (Ross & Roe, 1977). Another vocabulary-oriented drama activity involves writing vocabulary words on cards that students then select and act out for their team to guess—a variation on charades.

Finally, drama activities can be successfully used to help define new concepts, such as "civil rights." Justine Winslow introduced this term to her kindergarten class by leading them through a reenactment of the story of Rosa Parks, providing them with a deeper understanding of the concept than a verbal definition alone could give (Putnam, 1991).

Developing syntactic knowledge through drama

Drama can help students become more aware of syntactic structure, or the knowledge that word order, phrasing, and punctuation all contribute to the meaning of a written selection. Pellegrini (1980) found a significant correlation between dramatic play used with kindergartners and their understanding of syntactic structures. This relationship may be due to the fact that children involved in drama activities are constantly experimenting with different ways of talking, which leads to a higher awareness of the variations in language they encounter during reading experiences.

Teachers can use drama activities to direct students' attention to syntactic patterns and punctuation. One has to attend to details of punctuation and phrasing in order to give a good acting performance, which makes paying attention to these details purposeful for students. Group discussion of how a certain character should sound when speaking can lead to valuable insights into syntactic clues about meaning. Ross and Roe (1977) found students' oral reading skills improved as a result of "thinking the dialogue" as they read. Once the students are guided to the character insights they can find in punctuation cues, they attend more strongly to them while reading. Teachers can start with very basic ideas, such as pointing out that the actors' words are found inside quotation marks. A simple line reading activity can be developed by placing a sentence on the chalkboard, changing the ending punctuation from a period to a question mark to an excla-

mation point, and having different students demonstrate how this would change the way a character would say the line.

Another effective beginning strategy is to photocopy story pages and let the students highlight the dialogue with colored markers, locating these sections by paying attention to quotation marks (Bidwell, 1992). This lesson can be further elaborated by marking different punctuation with different symbols, for example, underlining exclamatory sentences and circling questions. The students then read the selections aloud, exaggerating the clues they have discovered. In this way students can become "drama detectives" who attempt to find as many "clues" about their characters as possible within the text.

Students dramatizing text often work as a group, writing down the main events their scene should include and in what order, thus reinforcing event-sequencing skills. If students attempt to act out a scene that is not correctly sequenced, their error will quickly come to their attention, and they can self-correct by inserting the missing event or rearranging the sequence.

In the DeRita and Weaver (1991) cross-age literacy program, teachers used playwriting to reinforce syntactic knowledge. After several experiences working with scripts written by adults, groups of older children selected a simple story to rewrite in script form for the younger children to perform. Each group wrote one part of the script, which they edited for sentence structure and spelling. Then the groups assembled all of the parts into one script, an activity that reinforced their sequential knowledge. This activity also provides a meaningful opportunity to reinforce punctuation skills with questions such as "How do you want the children to say that line?" and "How can you let them know that by how you write it?" The playwriting aspect of drama can thus reinforce syntactic knowledge on several levels simultaneously.

Developing discourse knowledge through drama

Drama activities can be used to help students learn what to expect when reading different forms of discourse. It is especially useful as a way to familiarize children with nonfiction works early in their reading careers. The teachers in Putnam's (1991) review used dramatizations to introduce kindergarten students to such diverse nonfiction topics as thunderstorms, dinosaurs, volcanoes, photosynthesis, and the earth's rotation. In order to help the students process the new organizational structures in expository text, the teachers stopped their nonfiction read-alouds frequently to dramatize important information. For example, in a lesson about the Pilgrims' journey to North America, one teacher paused in her reading to let the class experience what it felt like to be crowded onto the *Mayflower*; the children briefly became Pilgrims, squashed together into a small section of the classroom as their teacher described the experience. The use of such dramatizations gives nonfiction texts more of the excitement inherent in fiction. Students have a meaningful frame for the concepts and vocabulary of nonfiction, thus increasing retention of new information (Dewey, 1994).

Drama activities are also useful in helping children acquire knowledge about narrative structure. By reading and rereading a story to prepare to act it out, students "sharpen their sense of how a story 'works,' how the elements of character, plot, action and setting work together" (Miccinati & Phelps, 1980, p. 270). For example, a useful way to reinforce the idea that narratives include problems that need to be solved is to read aloud from a narrative, stopping at a high point and having students work in small groups to create their own ending, which must resolve the conflict. The groups perform for the class, and the class discusses which ending they think the author might choose. The teacher then reads the author's ending. On a more basic level, Cooper (1993) found that pantomiming stories as they are read aloud provides kindergarten students with a clear model of story form that they can draw upon for understanding in later reading.

Teachers can also direct their students to compare and contrast plays and stories. After reading a story, the class can discuss the main ideas that should be present in a dramatization—the "play version" of the story. They can generate a list of the characters, the setting, and the major actions. The class can also discuss what will be left out of the play version and why this is necessary, thus exploring the differences in the two discourse types.

Stewig (1974) advocates teaching the features inherent in "good stories for drama." His students' written stories are used as the basis for class improvisations, but only those stories containing his four requirements of a good drama can be selected. Students are careful to include active characters, an arresting beginning and logical form, a clear storyline, and a climax and satisfying conclusion so that their work can be considered for performance. Stewig uses this activity not only to make his students aware of the elements that make up a good drama, but also to create in them a desire to produce these elements in their own writing.

Developing metacognitive knowledge through drama

Drama can be a strong vehicle for developing metacognitive knowledge, both in the area of comprehension monitoring and in developing strategies for more effective reading. The very act of portraying a character leads to analyzing one's part—asking "Am I convincing?" and "If not, why, and how can I change?" Teachers can further this tendency by providing students with self-questioning worksheets to complete as they work on drama activities that extend over longer periods of time. These sheets ask students to respond to questions such as "Am I pleased with how I am doing in the play so far? Why or why not?" "What can I do during this class time to make the play better?" "What needs to happen before next week to make the play better?" (Bidwell, 1990, p. 40).

Drama can also teach specific strategic knowledge. Jacob (1976) found a strong link between good readers and mental imaging, the process of creating clear pictures in one's mind of what has been read. Mental imaging is a comprehension strategy that aids readers in storing information for retrieval. Students gain valuable practice in this strategy when they are called upon to act out material they have read. Studies by Gambrell and Bales (1986, as cited in DuPont, 1992) found that students taught to use mental imaging were "more successful at monitoring their own comprehension" (p. 51) than those readers unfamiliar with this skill. DuPont's (1992) study of 11-year-olds involved a control group, which read and discussed children's literature, and a treatment group, which read the same literature but participated in drama activities following the readings rather than in group discussion. The students in the treatment group scored significantly higher than the control group on a standardized comprehension test at the completion of the 6-week program, which DuPont attributes to the valuable practice the students gained in creating mental images of written materials as they were called upon to act it out. The most important aspect of this study is that the reading material tested was not related to the content of instruction, so students were able to transfer their newly acquired strategy, mental imaging, to the comprehension of unrelated reading materials that they did not have the opportunity to dramatize.

Ross and Roe (1977) similarly found mental imaging (in their words "visualization") to enhance comprehension. Their study used a drama game called "Stretching the Imagination" to specifically build students' mental imaging ability. The students were later able to apply the strategy to entire story selections. During the game, students were given a list of items that they had to imagine and then react to appropriately. The list included items such as a lemon, a skunk, and a seashore, and the students were encouraged to make use of all their senses in their visualization. A more story-specific mental imaging activity, "Who am I?", requires students to take turns portraying a character from their current reading—demonstrating the character's walk, talk, and any other important details. The rest of the group then attempts to identify the character.

In order to develop understanding of character for drama activities, students must read strategically.

In order to develop understanding of character for drama activities, students must read strategically. This is especially true in dramatizations of content area reading, in which students research a historical period, gathering appropriate information for dramatization. Students learn to use a variety of sources, skim for references that are appropriate to their scene, and make use of headings and subheadings for guidance (Bidwell, 1992).

Cullinan (1993) demonstrated this use of dramatization in her social studies class. Before beginning a unit on the Gold Rush in the U.S., students enacted a scene in a mining town. Each student introduced the character he or she would be portraying to the class, then the brief enactment began. The students discovered that they needed to know more about the historical period in order to make the scene real. Cullinan used this experience to segue into "reading to discover" strategies, and the class discussed the specific information they wanted to look for in order to elaborate on their scene. At the end of the Gold Rush unit the students were given an opportunity to dramatize the same scene again, this time incorporating their newfound knowledge of the time period.

One reason that drama is such an effective tool for the development of metacognition is that students preparing a scene are actually recreating an entire story, rather than simply recalling bits of what has been read. If children can't find the detail they need for the scene (whether it's what happens next, a town's name, or the attitude of a character), they must reread, confer with peers, or look in other sources to supply the missing pieces (Hoyt, 1992). Otherwise the scene cannot continue. Children have to self-evaluate and participate in group evaluation consistently during the various stages of a dramatization.

Flynn and Carr (1994) used drama to help their students make predictions and raise questions during the reading of *Lon Po Po* by Ed Young (1989). During this story of three sisters who open their door to a wolf pretending to be their grandmother, Flynn alternated narration and role play, letting the students predict what they thought would happen next and then act on it. After dramatizing their predicted ending to the tale, the students listened to the author's ending and saw how well their forecasts fit with the story.

This dramatization can also be a transition into higher level questioning about the story. Having the students maintain their roles as the children who had outsmarted the wolf, the teacher assumed the role of their returning "absent mother" and asked them questions in character, such as "Why did you let a wolf in?"

(Flynn & Carr, 1994, p. 42). Although drama activities can be used to target the individual components of literacy, such as metacognitive knowledge, many activities naturally support the development of higher level thinking skills and the overall comprehension of extended text.

Using drama to develop comprehension of extended texts

Drama activities lend themselves to the development of comprehension on literal, inferential, and evaluative levels. According to the curriculum guidelines published by the Ontario Ministry of Education: "A student involved in a drama activity will be called upon to practice several thinking skills, such as: inventing, generating, speculating, assimilating, clarifying, inducing, deducing, analyzing, accommodating, selecting, refining, sequencing, and judging" (Yau, 1992, p. 4).

Ross and Roe (1977) maintain that drama requires the same skills that are fundamental for reading comprehension, namely an understanding and ability to express the details of the plot, characters, sequence of events, cause-and-effect relationships, word meanings, motivations and main events of the story, and the ability to sense the mood of the selection. Students who participated in a 3-month drama in the language arts program showed improvement in the areas of finding the main idea, sequencing, identifying the theme, interpreting the author's purpose, and identifying characteristics of setting and characters (Siks, 1983). Bordan (1970) found that children who could not understand the morals of fables after hearing them read aloud were able to do so after dramatizing them. Similarly, Galda's research (1982) with 108 kindergarten, first, and second grade students found those children participating in creative drama activities following read-alouds showed significantly greater comprehension than those children who followed reading with either drawing or discussion activities. The drama group outscored their peers in the areas of remembering, understanding, and solving and analyzing questions, as well as in sequential recall.

Why do drama activities have such strong effects on comprehension? The effect may be due to the constant use of reflective and imaginative powers during improvisational activities, which leads to greater ability in perspective tak-ing, mental imaging, and creative thinking (Yau, 1992). Acting requires reading between the lines, making judgments, and going beyond the text to analyze why a character behaves in a specific way (DuPont, 1992). The students in the enactment of *Lon Po Po* actually experienced making the decision to let the wolf into the house. From their position "in the shoes" of the character it is much easier to answer evaluative questions like "Why did you let the wolf in?" in an insightful way (Flynn & Carr, 1994).

Teachers can enhance students' inferential and evaluative skills by having them write extensive descriptions of their characters, detailing how they look, how they act, and why they do the things they do. Stewig (1974) suggested expanding on minor characters, such as the stepsisters in Cinderella, asking questions such as "Were they always that way?" and "If not, what happened to make them change?" He also encouraged students to delve into the details of character, inferring what they can about the characters' physical appearance, feelings, thoughts, and even social and home life. This type of activity fosters creativity as well as inferential and evaluative insights.

Swartz (1992) described an effective method for encouraging deep evaluation of character motivation called "Conscience Alley." His 11-year-old students were listening to the novel *Weasel* (DeFelice, 1990), the story of two young children, Nathan and Molly, haunted by a murderous man named Weasel. Swartz stopped his read-aloud at the point when Nathan is faced with the opportunity to kill his enemy. In "Conscience Alley" each student had the chance to say one sentence to Nathan (played by the teacher) to convince him to kill Weasel. Then each student approached him with a reason against killing. Finally, the class formed an "alley" down which Nathan slowly walked. As he passed each student, they chose to give either pro or con advice. The experience let students see the complexity of Nathan's decision and gave them the opportunity to voice their own thoughts about his choice.

Direct Point of View (POV) activities are another useful way to explore higher level thinking about reading selections. In these activities students take on the role of a character and respond to an interviewer's questions. POV avoids the abstract quality of questions such as "How did you think James felt when he saw the giant peach?" by allowing the student to answer directly as the character. This technique helps prevent the vague answers that are the result of "standing outside the story looking in." If a student still has trouble being specific, the questions can be changed to "show me" requests, such as "Be Mary Lennox. Open the door and walk into the secret garden for the first time" (Cullinan, 1993).

POV can be extended into prediction and problem solving. In one variation, the story is stopped at a high point of the conflict, and the character is asked what he or she plans to do next. After the teacher collects several POV answers from different students, groups of students briefly enact these various predictions. The class evaluates whether the prediction makes sense in the story and if they think the characters made wise choices. They then read on to see how the author dealt with the problem (Cullinan, 1993). Drama activities that take place before and at intermittent pauses in extended text, or as accompanying projects for thematic units, seem to be most beneficial for developing comprehension.

Drama as a means of assessment

An added bonus to using drama in the classroom is that it provides useful and immediate feedback about students' understanding of new materials. Students can summarize what they have learned by acting it out (Dewey, 1994). If the class has just finished reading a selection about the life cycle of a butterfly, a brief dramatization of this occurrence can be useful to evaluate the extent of their understanding of what they read. By attending to the students' actions and words, the teacher can assess what areas of the text may need additional reinforcement. Drama is also a way for teachers to assess whether there is a discrepancy between what children comprehend and their ability to express that comprehension. Drama activities provide "an outlet, both physical and verbal, for students who might otherwise have no way to express their understanding or feeling about what they have read or heard. These kids can show what they mean" (Miccinati & Phelps, 1980, p. 270).

Using drama to support all learners

Mem Fox (1987) voiced one of the chief benefits of drama as method when she said, "One of the loveliest advantages of drama is that it gives all children the chance to be successful" (p. 4). Dramatist Ruth Heinig (1987) agreed that:

> Often children who have difficulty with other classroom tasks find success and a place for themselves in drama, a discovery that gives them a renewed interest in learning. Enjoyment and success together lead to self-confidence, a prime requisite for becoming a thinking, feeling, and creative person able to face life's challenges. (p. 9)

Drama activities also help to create a cooperative community of learners, especially as dramatizations allow students to experience life vicariously. Acting gives children the opportunity to see life from a different perspective, which leads to respect for others' ways of thinking.

Drama is an artistic response to reading; there is no absolute right or wrong in drama activities. One of the primary lessons of drama is that each individual's contribution is important. Children who experience anxiety about their own worth cannot focus outward on learning. Drama can provide a forum for children to participate and have their opinions reinforced as valuable. Providing such reinforcement is one of the teacher's most crucial roles in classroom drama (Bordan, 1970). Clift's study (1985) on the use of drama showed that not only do dramatizations result in more expressions of interest in students than the traditional lecture/seatwork approach, they also evoke fewer expressions of fear of being singled out or having attention drawn to the fact that one doesn't know the right answer. A review of studies on the social effects of drama shows an increase in collaboration skills, cooperation, negotiation, compassion, empathy, and social tolerance among student participants.

Along with teaching the specific skills needed for success in reading, drama activities nurture students' self-concepts and help to foster cooperative learning communities. Students of all ages like "doing," and drama provides all students with the opportunity to "do" literature. Finally and foremost, drama activities motivate students to read and keep on reading and thus assist teachers in reaching their ultimate goal: creating and nurturing lifelong learners.

References

Bidwell, S.M. (1990). Using drama to increase motivation, comprehension, and fluency. *Journal of Reading*, *34*, 38–41.

Bidwell, S.M. (1992). Ideas for using drama to enhance reading instruction. *The Reading Teacher*, *45*, 653–654.

Bolton, G. (1985). Changes in thinking about drama in education. *Theory Into Practice*, *24*, 151–157.

Bordan, S.D. (1970). *Plays as teaching tools in the elementary schools*. New York: Parker.

Clift, R. (1985). High school students' responses to dramatic enactment. *Journal of Classroom Interaction*, *21*(1), 38–44.

Cooper, P. (1993). *When stories come to school: Telling, writing, and performing stories in the early childhood classroom*. New York: Teachers and Writers Collaborative.

Cullinan, B.E. (1993). *Children's voices: Talk in the classroom*. Newark, DE: International Reading Association.

DeFelice, C. (1990). *Weasel*. New York: Avon.

DeRita, C., & Weaver, S. (1991). Cross-age literacy program. *Reading Improvement*, *28*, 244–248.

Dewey, M.L. (1994). *Combining literature with drama*. (ERIC Document Reproduction Service No. 376 508)

Duffelmeyer, F.A., & Duffelmeyer, B.B. (1979). Developing vocabulary through dramatization. In N.H. Brizendine & J.L. Thomas (Eds.), *Learning through dramatics: Ideas for teachers and librarians* (pp. 58–61). Phoenix, AZ: Oryx.

DuPont, S. (1992). The effectiveness of creative drama as an instructional strategy to enhance the reading comprehension skills of fifth-grade remedial readers. *Reading Research and Instruction*, *31*(3), 41–52.

Flennoy, A.J. (1992). *Improving communication skills of first grade low achievers through whole language, creative drama, and different styles of writing*. (ERIC Document Reproduction Service No. 352 599)

Flynn, R.M., & Carr, G.A. (1994). Exploring classroom literature through drama: A specialist and a teacher collaborate. *Language Arts*, *71*, 38–43.

Fox, M. (1987). *Teaching drama to young children*. Portsmouth, NH: Heinemann.

Galda, L. (1982). Playing about a story: Its impact on comprehension. *The Reading Teacher*, *36*, 52–55.

Heinig, R.B. (1987). *Creative drama resource book*. Englewood Cliffs, NJ: Prentice-Hall.

Hoyt, L. (1992). Many ways of knowing: Using drama, oral interactions, and the visual arts to enhance reading comprehension. *The Reading Teacher*, *45*, 580–584.

Jacob, S.H. (1976). Contexts and images in reading. *Reading World*, *15*, 167–175.

Kimmel, E. (1988). *Anansi and the moss-covered rock*. New York: Holiday House.

Leu, D.J., & Kinzer, C.K. (1995). *Effective reading instruction* (3rd ed.). Englewood Cliffs, NJ: Prentice-Hall.

May, F.B. (1990). *Reading as communication: An interactive approach* (2nd ed.). Columbus, OH: Merrill.

Miccinati, J.L., & Phelps, S. (1980). Classroom drama from children's reading: From the page to the stage. *The Reading Teacher*, *34*, 269–272.

Pellegrini, A.D. (1980). The relationship between kindergartners' play and achievement in prereading, language, and writing. *Psychology in the Schools*, *17*, 530–535.

Pellegrini, A.D. (1982). The effects of thematic-fantasy play training on the development of children's story comprehension. *American Educational Research Journal*, *19*, 443–452.

Pellegrini, A.D. (1984). Symbolic functioning and children's early writing: The relationship between kindergartners' play and isolated word-writing fluency. In R. Beach & L. Bridwell (Eds.), *New directions in composition research* (pp. 274–284). New York: Guilford.

Putnam, L. (1991). Dramatizing nonfiction with emerging readers. *Language Arts*, *68*, 463–469.

Reuse, R.B. (1977). All it takes is a little incentive. In N.H. Brizendine & J.L. Thomas (Eds.), *Learning through dramatics: Ideas for teachers and librarians* (pp. 42–43). Phoenix, AZ: Oryx.

Ross, E.P., & Roe, B.D. (1977). Creative drama builds proficiency in reading. In N.H. Brizendine & J.L. Thomas (Eds.), *Learning through dramatics: Ideas for teachers and librarians* (pp. 52–57). Phoenix, AZ: Oryx.

Schickedanz, J. (1978). "You be the doctor and I'll be sick": Preschoolers learn the language arts through play. In N.H. Brizendine & J.L. Thomas (Eds.), *Learning through dramatics: Ideas for teachers and librarians* (pp. 44–51). Phoenix, AZ: Oryx.

Siks, G.B. (1983). *Drama with children* (2nd ed.). New York: Harper & Row.

Smith, E.C. (1972). Drama and schools: A symposium. In N.H. Brizendine & J.L. Thomas (Eds.), *Learning through dramatics: Ideas for teachers and librarians* (pp. 4–14). Phoenix, AZ: Oryx.

Stewig, J.W. (1974). Drama: Integral part of the language arts. In N.H. Brizendine & J.L. Thomas (Eds.), *Learning through dramatics: Ideas for teachers and librarians* (pp. 33–41). Phoenix, AZ: Oryx.

Swartz, L. (1992). How far can you see with your eyes? Some thoughts about a drama curriculum. *The Drama Theatre Teacher*, *4*(2), 6–11.

Vygotsky, L.S. (1978). *Mind in society*. Cambridge, MA: Harvard University Press.

Wagner, B.J. (1988). Research currents: Does classroom drama affect the arts of language? *Language Arts*, *65*, 46–55.

Wolf, S.A. (1993). What's in a name? Labels and literacy in Readers Theatre. *The Reading Teacher*, *46*, 540–545.

Yaffe, S.H. (1989). Drama as a teaching tool. *Educational Leadership*, *46*, 29–32.

Yau, M. (1992). Drama: Its potential as a teaching and learning tool. *Scope Research Services*, *7*(1), 3–6.

Young, E. (1989). *Lon Po Po*. New York: Philomel.

Teaching Reading

12 things young children can do with a talking book in a classroom computer center

Linda D. Labbo

The following scene is a familiar one to most early childhood educators. A teacher, sitting in a comfortable chair with an open storybook on her lap, asks her students if they have ever felt like the main story character. The energy level in the classroom moves up a notch as the young children, sitting on a large rug with their legs folded in front of them, breathlessly and earnestly share personal experiences that relate to the story. This is an immediately familiar scene because reading books aloud to young children is a cherished activity that is a beneficial part of the daily routine.

Teachers know that when they read and discuss quality children's literature with their young students, the children will have many opportunities to develop rich vocabularies (Dickinson & Tabors, 1991), gain insights into literary conventions (Purcell-Gates, 1988), and develop an appreciation for reading. Indeed, when I ask teachers in graduate-level classes, workshops, or inservice sessions to brainstorm suggestions for how to share children's literature and list literacy benefits for children, the resulting ideas fill a large chalkboard. However, when I follow up that activity by asking them to shift the focus to CD-ROM talking books, the chalkboard lists only one

or two ideas, and the teachers admit that they have few strategies to suggest.

With the growing presence of computers in elementary school classrooms (Becker, 1993), many teachers find themselves with a fairly new technology and a growing collection of CD talking books but little guidance on developmentally appropriate practice. It is important that educators of young children begin to grapple with issues of ascertaining the quality and appropriateness of using CD-ROM talking books with youngsters. This article offers a dozen suggestions for ways that young children can interact with CD-ROM talking books to support their traditional print-based literacy development in a classroom computer center. I first describe talking books, provide a brief commentary on teachers' questions about developmentally appropriate use, and provide a rationale. Next, I offer a dozen suggestions for using talking books in computer centers. I close with a few concluding comments.

What are CD-ROM talking books and how might they foster young children's literacy development?

CD-ROM talking books are interactive, digital versions of stories that employ multimedia features such as animation, music, sound effects, highlighted text, and modeled fluent reading. As such, they offer a new venue for engaging students with stories. For example, much-loved children's stories such as *Stellaluna* (1996) and *Dr. Seuss's ABC* (1995) literally come to life as the stories are told in a multimedia presentation through fluent, ex-

pressive text narration and the animated performance of story characters who talk, sing, move, and dance across the computer screen. Many talking book screens are interactive because the software allows children to use the mouse to access words that are pronounced, passages that are reread, illustrations that become animated, and special effects that produce visual or auditory responses. It is the interactive nature of CD-ROM talking books that creates the potential to support young children's developing literacy.

Although there has been a slow increase in the numbers of these books due to copyright issues and a tendency for many of them to be traditional works of literature that do not fall under copyright laws, there are a growing number of CD-ROM talking books available on the market. Research on the effectiveness of various types of talking books to support young children's literacy development has produced mixed results at best. However, the suggestions provided in this article are drawn from guidelines provided by National Association for the Education of Young Children (1992), selected research, and well-established traditional, text-based approaches to literacy development.

What are teachers' questions and concerns about CD-ROM talking books and why should teachers consider using them?

Many teachers I work with indicate that they have some concerns about using digital versions of stories in class. For example, they wonder if children's interactions in play mode, a software feature that presents 20 to 40 responsive screen operations, are actually detrimental for literacy and literary development. Might children be distracted by too many bells and whistles on the screen (Burrell & Trushell, 1997)? Teachers wonder if watching a talking story unfold on the screen might foster passivity in children that is similar to a TV-watching mode. Additionally, they wonder about how to best manage children's time in a classroom computer center when some research suggests that children are willing to spend up to 45 minutes or an hour interacting with CD-ROM talking books (Labbo & Kuhn, 1999).

However, in spite of these concerns and potential difficulties, I believe that there are developmentally appropriate ways to foster children's interactions with CD-ROM talking books. Teachers I talk to in various educational settings are also intrigued by the interactivity of the technology and are excited about the potential of CD-ROM talking books to provide unique opportunities for young children's engagement with stories and computer-related literacy development in a classroom center.

What are 12 things young children can do with a talking book?

It is important to note that teachers need to do more than simply post the list of 12 suggestions in the classroom and assume that children will benefit. Teachers need to be prepared to first model the strategies, then mentor children's use of the strategies, and finally oversee or manage strategy use in various ways.

Model: Teachers need to model the purposes, outcomes, and strategies for software use involved in each of the suggestions. This can be accomplished in brief whole- or small-group demonstrations and discussions. For example, demonstrating how children can use the mouse to click on particular features of the software for particular strategic purposes will enable them to access words that they know.

Mentor: After introducing and modeling a strategy, teachers need to find ways to support young children's initial and ongoing computer encounters with digital stories. We can't assume that the software alone will serve as an adequate first or ongoing scaffold. Mentors, those who will sit beside the child in the computer center and offer assistance or direction for implementing a suggested activity, may consist of the teacher, a paraprofessional, parent volunteers, student teachers, cross-age computer buddies from intermediate grades, or more capable peers in class.

Manage: It is important to find easy ways to manage children's use of the computer in the center. Just as they do in other classroom situations and centers, teachers will need to state expected behaviors and outcomes for each of the suggestions as it is introduced. Set reasonable limits for the amount of time children can spend at the computer center. A reasonable amount of time will allow the child to accomplish the tasks involved in a selected activity. Set a timer to ring about 5 minutes before the child needs to bring closure to the activity.

Teachers can also guide what children do in the center by making an assignment from the list of suggestions or by offering children a free choice. After becoming familiar with the different suggestions, teachers will be better equipped to match children to specific activities that are likely to support targeted literacy needs. Posting the dozen suggestions on a wall in the center will serve as a good reminder to children who have a free choice.

Peer pairs may also work at a computer center simultaneously; however, to avoid "mouse wars" it is important to establish and enforce procedures for sharing the decision making involved in each suggested activity. Once the center is well established, expectations are clear, and guidelines are posted, the center should become self-sustaining and require little assistance from the teacher.

Following are descriptions of the 12 suggestions along with a brief rationale for each. See also the list of the activities that may be discussed and then posted in the classroom. The list of activities relies on children having access to the CD-ROM books for multiple readings and rereadings over time. It is organized with a focus on (a) initial interaction level; (b) story-, fluency-, and comprehension-level interactions; (c) word-level interactions; and (d) metacognitive-level interactions.

Initial interaction level

1. Listen to the story first. Watch, listen to, interact with, think about, and talk about the story. Children should have the opportunity to enjoy the digital, multimedia features of the story and to take the stance of an appreciative audience member. In listening students have occasions to enjoy the multimedia and cinematic effects of a digital storytelling experience. After introducing children to this activity, or perhaps later when mentoring them, it may be helpful to draw their attention to concepts about print that are being presented on screen. For example, mentors will want to note the directional aspects of reading print as the text is highlighted from left to right. This is important because some

---

12 things to do with a talking book in computer center

1. Listen to the story first.
2. Read along with the story.
3. Echo read the story.
4. Read it first, then listen.
5. Partner read in digital Readers Theatre.
6. Look for letters or words you know.
7. Select words with same sounds.
8. Select rhyming words.
9. Read along with a book copy.
10. Tell how one screen fits with other screens.
11. Tell how special effects fit the story.
12. Tell about similar stories.

CD-ROM talking books present simultaneous animation that continues to draw attention away from the print even upon subsequent viewings.

Fluency and comprehension level

The four suggestions in this section focus on ways children can engage in various levels of supported, contextualized repeated readings. When children are invited to interact in different ways with CD-ROM talking books on multiple occasions it is possible that they will have unique opportunities to develop comprehension and fluency that are similar to those benefits reported for repeated readings of traditional text (Samuels, 1997). Teachers will want to carefully model each of the strategies in this section, drawing attention to the rhythms or tempo of each type of repeated reading. Additionally, students may need to be reminded that the focus of oral reading is to understand and express the meaning of the stories.

2. Read along with the story. This form of digital choral reading is helpful for less confident students who can read and who have some automatic sight word recognition, but lack fluency and need support. Children should not attempt to read along with the text throughout an entire story, but may select a few passages at a time. Reading along with the story allows students to read words or phrases that they know and to be supported in figuring out words or phrases that they don't know.

3. Echo read the story. This form of reading is especially helpful for children who need support with sight words and decoding (Heckelman, 1969). Children may repeat words or phrases as they are read aloud to them on screen. Reading along after phrases are read allows some children to focus on recognizing sight words in context.

4. Read it first, then listen. Students who need practice and a safe environment for taking risks in attempts to read aloud may benefit from attempting to read phrases first, then listening to the text read aloud on screen. Connected text, phrases, sentences, passages, or pages may be read. In addition, students may benefit from having immediate feedback on their attempts to recognize or decode words in the context of connected text. Many interactive CD-ROM stories offer different options for a read-it-first, then listen-to-it mode. For example, in some CDs a child can read an entire passage and then access the digitally provided story reader's oral reading (e.g., the CD-ROM series Living Books published by Broderbund). In other CD-ROMs a child can attempt a word-by-word reading, checking the accuracy of each attempt by clicking on each word and hearing it pronounced (e.g., the Living Books series). Other CD-ROMs give a child the option of recording his or her own voice and then replaying (e.g., *Tronic Phonics* published by Macmillan/McGraw-Hill).

5. Partner read in digital Readers Theatre. Invite a small group of children to gather at the computer center. Each child is involved in casting the experience by either being assigned or given a choice of a story character. As the text is presented on screen, students read the dialogue for their characters, serve as narrator, or read one line at a time. This activity can foster supported expressive reading, capitalize on peer collaboration, invite reluctant readers to practice, and result in more fluent reading for hesitant oral readers.

Word level

The three activities in this section are not intended to represent an exhaustive list of suggestions for CD-ROM talking book word-level interactions. The activities should be viewed as a core of basic activities children can engage in when considering word recognition, vocabulary knowledge, and phonic analysis. That is, the activities are not meant to be a complete or an adequate word study program. Rather, they are intended to be supplemental to an ongoing program of systematic word-level study in the literacy curriculum. Because the words available to children on the screen have been encountered in the meaningful context of a previous initial viewing and subsequent repeated readings, the shift to a more narrow word-level focus is appropriate.

In all of the instances, children can be invited to keep a dated list of words they recognize so they can chart their growing sight word vocabulary. Directions for keeping a chart of words involve students in some simple record keeping: (a) Put the title of the CD and the date on top of a blank sheet of paper, (b) list each word recognized, (c) write down the total, and (d) see if the number of words recognized increases over multiple readings. When combined with a math lesson, the data may be used in a bar-graphing activity.

6. Look for letters or words you know. Young children who are just gaining the concept of letters may benefit from sitting down with a mentor and pointing out letters that they recognize. Children who have a stable concept of words and an emerging sight word vocabulary may select words they recognize. This activity involves students in selecting words they automatically recognize and understand. Immediate feedback is available to students when they locate a word, read it aloud, then check their accuracy by accessing the talking book pronunciation.

7. Select words with same sounds. Almost any CD-ROM story may be used as a springboard for a same-sound word search. Indeed, children who have a developing sense of the concept of words and of the phonic elements in words may benefit from a search to select and ultimately sort out words that have some common sound. By focusing on the same beginning sounds, vowel patterns, or syllable structures, young children may have opportunities to confirm their working hypotheses about orthographic patterns and phonic elements. For example, children may enjoy and benefit from searching for all of the words on a page screen that begin with the /st/ beginning sound. In doing so, they may learn how to scan the screen for the unique *st* configuration of letters in words they see. As they pronounce the /st/ sound when noticing words such as *store, stay,* and *stop,* their hypothesis may be tested by simply clicking on the word and hearing it pronounced by the narrator.

8. Select rhyming words. When word patterns are studied in class during ongoing literacy instruction, children will wish to seek out similar rhyming patterns in words they encounter in CD-ROM talking books that use rhyme patterns. Additionally, when rhyming pattern stories are presented on the computer screen, children will enjoy highlighting words that rhyme within a text. For example, after learning about the -am word family, children will enjoy noticing words with the -am pattern in the CD-ROM version of *Green Eggs and Ham by Dr. Seuss* (1995). After clicking on the word, children will hear the narrator's voice expressively read the words aloud. Additionally, if a child selects a word with a similar pattern (e.g., *them*), the narrator's pronunciation provides relevant feedback.

Metacognitive and story response level

9. Read along with a book copy. Children may be invited to pay closer attention to the unique features of CD-ROM talking books when they are asked to compare the digital version with a book version of the story. As they do a "screen and book read along" (Labbo & Ash, 1998, p. 189), children are likely to note that the formatting, illustrations, and arrangement of the text on the screen are qualitatively different from the story as told on the printed page. Children should have many opportunities to discuss their insights. These activities may help children build a more complex schema for conventions of CD-ROM talking books and digital story structures.

10. Tell how one screen fits with other screens. A higher order thinking skill that is helpful for students' comprehension of print-based books involves the use of intratextual connections; that is, connections that children make across and within a story. Children are more likely to make inferences, draw conclusions, understand sequence of events, or figure out cause and effect when they engage in meaning making across different segments of the story. Asking children to explain how events from one screen relate to previous screens may help them learn to make digital intratextual connections that support a metacognitive, strategic approach to making meaning. For example, asking children to explain what they learned about the eating habits of fruit bats by comparing a screen of Stellaluna, a little bat, savoring a mango to an earlier screen of her choking down a bug helps them learn more about drawing conclusions from various parts of a digital story.

11. Tell how special effects fit the story. One of the unique features of CD-ROM talking books is the use of multimedia special effects such as music, dynamic color tones (as when a sunny sky turns to a pastel sunset on a screen), sound effects, and cinematic animation. Children who are invited to note how multimedia effects are used by software animators may come to appreciate unique aesthetic qualities of digital storytelling related to tone, texture, and mood. These activities may also help children learn how to interpret story content. For example, the feelings of warmth and contentment experienced by Stellaluna, a young bat separated from her mother, are enhanced and reinforced when her surrogate mother, a bird, croons a lullaby to the musical accompaniment of soft stringed instruments. Discussions of how special effects fit the story may be similar to discussions teachers have with children about how illustrations enhance storytelling in printed books.

12. Tell about similar stories. Intertextual connections, recalling how events in one story are similar to other stories or to personal experiences, are a central part of the type of comprehending in which good readers engage (Block, 1999). When children are invited to reflect on how the CD-ROM talking book connects to their own stories and their own experiences, they have occasions to make personally relevant meaning. When they are invited to reflect on how the CD-ROM talking book connects to other stories they have read, they are likely to begin to reflect on story themes, events, and genre structures.

Another way to support children

Teachers have excellent reasons for sharing literature as a significant part of the literacy curriculum. Teachers read books aloud in order to model language structures, motivate children to read, and bridge students' prior experiences with lessons. CD-ROM talking books have the potential to serve as another vehicle for children's engagement with stories in ways that support their literacy development; however, we have much more to learn about developmentally appropriate practices. Many of the suggestions offered in this article consist of

best guesses that are based on established practices and an emerging body of computer-related research. More research is needed to continue to define best computer-related literacy instruction in the early childhood classroom.

References

Becker, H.J. (1993). Decision making about computer acquisition and use in American schools. *Computers and Education, 20,* 341–352.

Block, C.C. (1999). Comprehension: Crafting understanding. In L.B. Gambrell, L.M. Morrow, S.B. Neuman, & M. Pressley (Eds.), *Best practices in literacy instruction* (pp. 98–118). New York: Guilford Press.

Burrell, C., & Trushell, J. (1997). "Eye-candy" in "interactive books"—A wholesome diet? *Reading, 31*(2), 3–6.

Dickinson, D., & Tabors, P. (1991). Early literacy: Linkages between home, school and literacy achievement at age five. *Journal of Research in Childhood Education, 6,* 30–46.

Heckelman, R.G. (1969). A neurological-impress method of remedial-reading instruction. *Academic Therapy, 4,* 277–282.

Labbo, L.D., & Ash, G.E. (1998). Supporting young children's computer-related literacy development in classroom centers. In S. Neuman & K. Roskos (Eds.), *Children achieving: Instructional practices in early literacy* (pp. 180–197). Newark, DE: International Reading Association.

Labbo, L.D., & Kuhn, M. (1999, July). *Kindergarten children make sense of CD stories as a new genre.* Paper presented at the Annual United Kingdom Reading Association Conference, London.

National Association for the Education of Young Children. (1992). Guidelines of appropriate curriculum content and assessment in programs serving children ages 3 through 8. In S. Bredenkamp & T. Rosengrant (Eds.), *Reading potentials: Appropriate curriculum and assessment for young children, Vol. I* (pp. 9–27). Washington, DC: Author.

Purcell-Gates, V. (1988). Lexical and syntactic knowledge of written narrative held by well-read-to-kindergartners and second graders. *Research in the Teaching of English, 22,* 128–160.

Samuels, S.J. (1997). The method of repeated readings. *The Reading Teacher, 50,* 376–381.

Talking books cited

Dr. Seuss's ABC. (1995). Living Books series. Novato, CA: Random House—Broderbund Software.

Green Eggs and Ham by Dr. Seuss. (1995). Living Books series. Novato, CA: Random House—Broderbund Software.

Stellaluna by Cannon. (1996). Living Books series. Novato, CA: Random House—Broderbund Software.

Tronic phonics. (1997). New York: Macmillan/McGraw-Hill Software.

Janette K. Klingner
Sharon Vaughn

Promoting reading comprehension, content learning, and English acquisition through Collaborative Strategic Reading (CSR)

CSR combines two instructional approaches that teachers may implement: reading comprehension strategy instruction and cooperative learning. Procedures are described for teaching CSR to students.

Albert and Pablo are classmates in a diverse, heterogeneous class that includes 10- and 11-year-old students at a range of achievement levels. Albert is a high-achieving student and Pablo is a student identified as learning disabled who uses English as a second language (ESL). Their teacher, Lucille Sullivan, taught the class to use an instructional approach called Collaborative Strategic Reading (CSR) (Klingner, Vaughn, & Schumm, 1998). One aspect of CSR is learning to help members of your group "de-clunk" (better understand) vocabulary words in social studies and science. Listen in on a conversation between Albert and Pablo:

Albert: Does anyone have a clunk (a word they don't understand)?

Pablo: Calcium.

Albert: Try to read sentences in the back and in the front to try to get a clue...did you get anything?

Pablo: No.

Albert: OK, now I do, I get something. It [calcium] is a tiny crystal-like mineral. Do you know what a mineral is?

Pablo: Yeah.

Albert: What is it?
Pablo: It's like a kind of vitamin.
Albert: OK, calcium is a type of element that there is in the bones. And, the bones need that. Calcium helps the bones in order to make them strong. Do you now understand what calcium is?
Pablo: Yes.
Albert: What is it again, one more time?
Pablo: It is a type of element that helps the bones grow.
Albert: OK, good.

Pablo and Albert, as well as the rest of their classmates, discuss the benefits of CSR enthusiastically, "It helps us learn new information from books and articles better than other ways," "Also, it helps me learn new words," and "It helps me be a better reader." When asked what they liked best about CSR, students' top response was "helping each other learn." They noticed improvement in their reading comprehension, vocabularies, and test scores. In this article, we describe procedures for teaching CSR. The examples we provide are from real teachers' classrooms.

Overview of CSR

CSR combines two instructional approaches that many teachers already implement: reading comprehension strategy instruction (e.g., Palincsar & Brown, 1984) and cooperative learning (e.g., Cohen, 1986; Johnson & Johnson, 1989). In CSR, students of mixed reading and achievement levels work in small, cooperative groups to assist one another in applying four reading strategies to facilitate their comprehension of content area text. These reading strategies are (a) preview (prior to reading a passage, to recall what they already know about the topic and to predict what the passage might be about); (b) click and clunk (to monitor comprehension during reading by identifying difficult words and concepts in the passage and using fix-up strategies when the text does not make sense); (c) get the gist (during reading, to restate the most important idea in a paragraph or section); and (d) wrap-up (after reading, to summarize what has been learned and to generate questions "that a teacher might ask on a test"). Initially, the classroom teacher presents the strategies to the whole class using modeling, role playing, and teacher think-alouds. After students have developed proficiency applying the strategies through teacher-facilitated activities, they are divided into heterogeneous groups where each student performs a defined role as students collaboratively implement the strategies (see Figure).

Research support for CSR's effectiveness

Research validates the effectiveness of the instructional approaches that were combined to form CSR, as well as CSR itself. Comprehension strategy instruction has improved learning opportunities for students with learning disabilities (LD) (for reviews see Pressley, Brown, El-Dinary, & Afflerbach, 1995; Weisberg, 1988) and limited English proficient (LEP) students (Anderson & Roit, 1996; Chamot & O'Malley, 1996; Hernandez, 1991; Klingner & Vaughn, 1996). Cooperative learning has also produced favorable results for students with LD (e.g., Madden & Slavin, 1983; Stevens & Slavin, 1995) and LEP students (e.g., Durán & Szymanski, 1995; Jacob, Rottenberg, Patrick, & Wheeler, 1996; Long & Porter, 1985). This type of peer interaction increases opportunities for meaningful communication about academic content (Cazden, 1988; Richard-Amato, 1992) and allows LEP students to draw on native language support from bilingual peers (Cohen, 1986). The use of native discussions to clarify meaning when reading English-language texts has been found to increase comprehension, with the conceptual knowledge transferring to English when the appropriate English vocabulary is learned (Cummins, 1984; Díaz, Moll, & Mehan, 1986; Hakuta, 1990).

CSR has consistently yielded positive findings in investigations of its effectiveness. In one study, the reading comprehension, content learning, and vocabulary acquisition of 10- and 11-year-old bilingual (Spanish-speaking) English language learners improved when students used CSR with their science textbook (Klingner, 1997; Klingner & Vaughn, 1998). In another study, 9- and 10-year-old students in three culturally and linguistically diverse classrooms that included struggling readers, English language learners, and average and high-achieving students implemented CSR with a unit from their social studies text. Students' reading comprehension scores on a standardized reading test improved at significantly higher levels than their peers who did

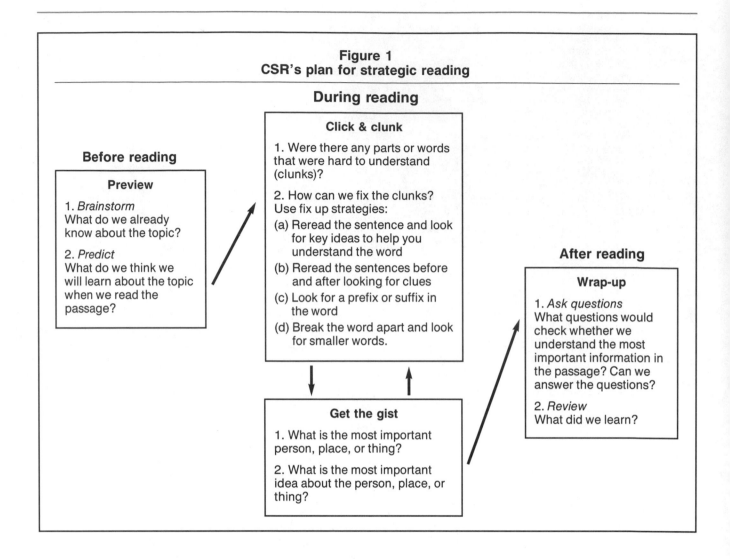

Figure 1
CSR's plan for strategic reading

During reading

Before reading

Preview

1. *Brainstorm*
What do we already know about the topic?

2. *Predict*
What do we think we will learn about the topic when we read the passage?

Click & clunk

1. Were there any parts or words that were hard to understand (clunks)?

2. How can we fix the clunks? Use fix up strategies:
(a) Reread the sentence and look for key ideas to help you understand the word
(b) Reread the sentences before and after looking for clues
(c) Look for a prefix or suffix in the word
(d) Break the word apart and look for smaller words.

After reading

Wrap-up

1. *Ask questions*
What questions would check whether we understand the most important information in the passage? Can we answer the questions?

2. *Review*
What did we learn?

Get the gist

1. What is the most important person, place, or thing?

2. What is the most important idea about the person, place, or thing?

not use CSR (Klingner, Vaughn, & Schumm, 1998). Chinese-speaking English language learners with learning disabilities who implemented CSR improved in content learning, English acquisition, and reading comprehension (Chang & Shimizu, 1997). In addition, teachers noted that students' participation in group discussions increased. Thus, CSR provides an environment in which students, with the assistance of the teacher and their peers, increasingly become more proficient at applying comprehension strategies and constructing knowledge while reading from the content area texts.

Teaching CSR strategies through whole-class instruction

The teacher initially teaches the CSR comprehension strategies to the whole class, grad-

ually increasing students' involvement as they become more proficient at applying the strategies. On the first day of instruction, the teacher models the entire CSR plan for strategic reading so that students get the big picture. On subsequent days, the teacher provides explicit instruction in how to implement each of the CSR strategies.

We introduce CSR by explaining to students that they will learn some strategies that will help them understand and remember what they read. These strategies are what many good readers already do when they read, often automatically and "in their heads." On the first day, we model the strategies using a think-aloud procedure, verbalizing our thinking as we apply each of the strategies while reading a sample passage. Here is an example of one teacher's think-aloud while "declunking" a word after reading a paragraph about Vietnam:

Uh oh, here is a word I don't understand, *paddies*. Let me see if there are any clues that can help me figure it out. I'll try reading the sentence without the word, "U.S. troops fought in the jungles and rice_____." Well, it has to be a place, because it is where they fought, and maybe it is sort of like a jungle. Also, it must have to do with rice. I'll bet it's a place where they grow rice. That makes sense. I'll write that in my Learning Log.

Preview. Students learn that before reading a passage, they should quickly scan the material searching for clues as to what the text will be about. The primary goals of previewing are for children to (a) generate interest and questions about the text they will read; (b) stimulate their background knowledge and associations with the text; and (c) facilitate their ability to make predictions about what they will learn. We allow approximately 8 minutes for students to survey the text, to think about what they already know about the topic and what they predict they'll learn, and to share their ideas with others.

We teach children to preview by asking if they have ever been to the movies and seen a preview. We prompt them to think about what they learn from a movie preview. After students generate responses, the teacher highlights some of the key information as it relates to reading by saying, "When you use the preview strategy, you develop your own preview for the text you are about to read. You look for the following types of information:

- *what* the passage is mainly about,
- *who* is described in the text,
- *when* the passage takes place, and
- *where* the text is describing information you already know about the topic.

Also, the teacher asks students what information in the text can help them in previewing. Using students' responses, the teacher prompts students to look at (a) headings and subheadings; (b) words that are italicized, bolded, or underlined; (c) pictures, tables, and graphs; and (d) questions or key information highlighted in the columns.

Connie Solis (pseudonym) teaches a fourth-grade class with 34 students. When she implements previewing she allows her students 2 minutes to survey the material and put the preview together in their heads. She then allows about 5 minutes for students to share their best ideas. Mary Brown, a fifth-grade teacher, first introduces the topic for the day and then asks students to brainstorm and record in their CSR learning logs everything they already know about the topic. Students share what they know with one another. Then they "take a peek" at the text they will be reading, write down what they think they will learn, and share their favorite predictions.

Click and clunk. Clicking and clunking refer to the self-monitoring strategy that students are taught to apply while reading. When students "click" it means that they recognize information that they know well and understand, clicking along smoothly while proceeding through the text. When students "clunk" it means that they identify words, concepts, or ideas they don't understand or need to know more about. The image is of the student running into a brick wall—a big clunk. We teach students to monitor their reading comprehension, to identify when they have breakdowns in understanding, and to use fix-up strategies to declunk words.

During reading students record clunks that later will be discussed with their peers and perhaps the teacher. The class learns to declunk words by using fix-up strategies. These fix-up strategies are written on clunk cards that assist students in declunking words. Figure 2 provides a pattern for making clunk cards.

Lucille Sullivan encourages her students to click and clunk throughout the school day. She told us, "Another reason I like this technique is that there is a transfer. The students will be reading in the cafeteria, and they'll say, 'hey, look at this clunk word, what does it mean?' and that just thrills me" (Klingner & Vaughn, 1998b). Her bilingual students become quite proficient at translating for each other.

Get the gist. When the students get the gist, they identify the main idea or the most critical information in a section of text (one or two paragraphs). Students are taught to identify the most important point in the text and to rephrase the key idea in their own words. The intent is to assist students in providing the gist in as few words as possible while conveying the most meaning and excluding unnecessary details.

Lourdes Garcia (pseudonym) gets the gist this way. She asks her students to read a two-paragraph section and while reading think about who or what the paragraph was about. She then encourages students to put in their own words the most important idea about the who or what—limiting their responses to 10 words or less (Fuchs, Fuchs, Mathes, & Simmons, 1997). She calls on several students, continually referring back to the class to get their feedback about what aspects of their gist should be kept or dropped. She ends by asking each student to write the gist in their own words, thus refining the skills of all of the students.

Wrap-up. When students wrap up, they formulate questions and answers about what they have read and review key ideas. The purpose of wrap-up is to teach students to identify the most important ideas of the entire section they have read to improve their knowledge, understanding, and memory of what was learned. While students learn to get the gist for every paragraph or two, they wrap up only at the end of the material they have covered during that session, usually about 12–14 paragraphs.

Figure 2
Pattern for making clunk cards

Clunk card 1

Reread the sentence with the clunk and look for key ideas to help you figure out the unknown word. Think about what makes sense.

Clunk card 2

Reread the sentences before and after the clunk looking for clues.

Clunk card 3

Look for a prefix or suffix in the word that might help.

Clunk card 4

Break the word apart and look for smaller words that you know.

Directions: Cut out the clunk cards and glue them onto different colors of posterboard or tagboard cut in squares.

When Tiffany Royal teaches her 10- and 11-year-olds to wrap up, she tells them to think about questions a good teacher would ask about the passage. She asks them to think about question starters that include "the 5 W's and one H" (who, what, when, where, why, and how). Often she gives students index cards and asks them to write one or two questions on one side of the card and the answers on the other side. She then gives students an opportunity to ask one another questions about what they have read. Students are taught to ask questions that involve higher level thinking skills as well as literal recall. She teaches students to use the following question stems (adapted from Rosenshine & Meister, 1992):

- How were _____ and _____ the same? Different?
- What do you think would happen if _____?
- What do you think caused _____ to happen?
- What might have prevented the problem of _____ from happening?
- What are the strengths and weaknesses of _____ ?

To review, students write about the most important ideas they learned from the day's reading assignment in their learning logs. They then take turns sharing what they learned with their group. Lucille Sullivan also conducts a whole-class review. Many students can share their best idea in a short period of time, providing the teacher with valuable information about each student's level of understanding.

Implementing CSR in cooperative groups

Students who are accustomed to working together cooperatively quickly learn to implement CSR in small groups (i.e., 4–5 students) once they have developed proficiency applying the comprehension strategies with their teacher's guidance. Within cooperative learning groups students are given two responsibilities: to complete the assigned task and to make sure that all other members of their group do likewise (Johnson & Johnson, 1989). Students discuss the material to be learned with one another, help one another to understand it, and encourage one another to do their best. The essential components of cooperative learning described by Johnson and Johnson are built into CSR: (a) positive interdependence, (b) considerable face-to-face interaction, (c) individual accountability, (d) learning social skills, and (e) posttask evaluation.

Students who do not have experience working in cooperative learning groups will need to learn the social skills essential for working collaboratively prior to implementing CSR. Learning groups are not productive unless members are skilled in cooperating with one another. We teach social skills through a three-step process whereby we first define the target behavior, next model the behavior, and finally provide opportunities for students to practice the behavior, using simulation and role-playing. We teach one social skill at a time, posing each behavior on a chart for reference as it is learned. Students learn how to listen attentively, ask clarifying questions, take turns speaking, provide positive feedback, and resolve conflicts.

Within cooperative groups, each student performs a designated role. Roles are an important aspect of CSR because cooperative learning seems to work best when all group members have meaningful tasks. Roles rotate so that students can experience a variety of roles and so that everyone takes a turn being the leader. We have found that all students can successfully lead their groups when provided with a cue sheet and encouragement. Students can perform more than one role at a time if necessary. CSR roles include the following:

Leader: Leads the group in the implementation of CSR by saying what to read next and what strategy to apply next. Asks the teacher for assistance if necessary.

Clunk expert: Uses clunk cards to remind the group of the steps to follow when trying to figure out a difficult word or concept.

Gist expert: Guides the group toward the development of a gist and determines that the gist contains the most important idea(s) but no unnecessary details.

Announcer: Calls on different group members to read or share an idea. Makes sure everyone participates and only one person talks at a time.

Encourager: Watches the group and gives feedback. Looks for behaviors to praise. Encourages all group members to participate in the discussion and assist one another. Evaluates how well the group has worked together and gives suggestions for improvement.

Leyda Caride relies on modeling to teach her students the roles they will perform while using CSR in peer-led learning groups. She invites a group of expert 11- and 12-year-old students to demonstrate the CSR roles to her 8- and 9-year-olds. Then, while her students implement CSR in cooperative groups for the first time, the expert students each sit in with a different group to provide assistance.

CSR materials

Cue cards. Cue cards outline the procedures to be followed in cooperative learning groups and provide structure and support for students while they are learning CSR. Each role comes with a corresponding cue card (or set of cards) that explains the steps to be followed to fulfill that role (see Figure 3 for a sample set of the cue cards). Cue cards help students stay focused and on task and increase their confidence. The cards can also be used as bookmarks or placeholders while reading.

CSR learning logs. CSR learning logs enable students to keep track of learning in English or another language and provide a springboard for follow-up activities. We encourage students to record their ideas, initially in either language and later translating ideas into English. Logs promote active group participation. Students can record ideas while applying some of the strategies (e.g., clunks and key ideas). A different learning log can be created for each social studies or science unit. These logs provide written documentation of learning, thus assuring the individual accountability that facilitates cooperative learning. Logs also become excellent study guides. See Figure 4 for an example.

Figure 3
CSR student leaders cue cards

Before reading	During reading	After reading
Preview S: We know that today's topic is _____. S. Let's brainstorm and write everything we already know about the topic in our learning logs. S: Who would like to share their best ideas? S: Now let's predict. Look at the title, pictures, and headings and think about what we might learn today. Write your ideas in your learning logs. S: Who would like to share their best ideas?	**Read** S: Who would like to read the next section **Click and clunk** S: Did everyone understand what we read? If you did not, write your clunks in your learning log. S: (if someone has a clunk): Clunk Expert, please help us out. **Get the gist** S: Gist Expert, please help us out. S: Now we will go around the group and each say the gist in our own words. *Go back and do all of the steps in this column over for each section that is read.*	**Wrap-up** S: Now let's think of some questions to check if we really understood what we read. Remember to start your questions with who, when, what, where, why, or how. Everyone write your questions in your learning log. S: Who would like to share their best question? S: In our learning logs, let's write down as much as we can about what we learned. **Compliments and suggestions** S: The Encourager has been watching carefully and will now tell us two things we did really well as a group today. S: Is there anything that would help us do even better next time?

Adapted from Klingner & Vaughn (1998b)

Figure 4
CSR learning log

Today's topic _____ Date _____

Before reading
Preview

What I already know about the topic	Questions about the important ideas in the passage
What I predict I will learn	What I learned

After reading
Wrap-up

During reading
Clunks

Reading materials. CSR was designed to be used with expository text found in content area textbooks. Teachers have successfully used CSR with their social studies and science textbooks and also with newspapers, children's news magazines, and other nonfiction publications. Although CSR will "work" with any expository text, initially students should use well-formed, interesting passages that are conducive to strategy application. Such text is characterized by (a) clues that help students predict what they will be learning, (b) definitions for key vocabulary built into the text, (c) one main idea per paragraph, and (d) context that helps students connect information. As students gain more experience with the strategy, they can work with less supportive materials.

The teacher's role: Monitoring groups

Once students have learned the strategies and their roles and have begun working in cooperative learning groups, the teacher's role is to circulate among groups and provide ongoing assistance. If necessary, teachers can clarify difficult words, model strategy usage, encourage students to participate, and model a helpful attitude. Joyce Duryea, an inclusion specialist, values the opportunity CSR affords her to engage in kidwatching. She continually monitors individual and group progress. Sometimes when the students are struggling to understand a difficult clunk, she listens without interrupting but makes a note to bring up the clunk later with the whole class. At other times she models how to figure out the word (or get the gist, as the case may be). There are also occasions when she merely drops a hint or gives a clue, enabling students who were stuck to continue on their own. She compliments students who are doing a good job and encourages reticent students to participate.

Follow-up activities

A variety of activities can be used to reinforce key vocabulary and important concepts and also help the teacher to monitor learning. English language learners can create bilingual dictionaries with their clunks. Or each group might complete a different follow-up activity and then share their products with the rest of the class (see Figure 5). Products generated through follow-up activities can be written on overhead transparencies to facilitate sharing with the entire class. Students can also prepare games and activities as homework.

Conclusion

We and our colleagues have taught CSR to numerous teachers in Florida, Texas, and California (see Vaughn, Hughes, Schumm, & Klingner, 1998). Teachers have told us that they really like the fact that once students learn the strategies (preview, click and clunk, get the gist, and wrap-up), they can apply them independently in cooperative groups. This enables the teachers to circulate around the classroom, monitor individual and group progress, and provide assistance where needed. Teachers value the benefits for their students from using CSR. Tiffany Royal, an expert CSR implementer, told us, "What I like best is that my students learn how to understand what they read while they improve their vocabulary. Also

---

Figure 5
CSR follow-up activities

Bilingual dictionaries: English language learners write their clunks with definitions in English and their native language and add illustrations.

Bulletin board: Each student writes a clunk and a sentence that demonstrates the meaning of the clunk on a large index card, with a picture. These can be arranged on a bulletin board entitled "From Clunks to Clicks."

Clunk books: Students create flip books that include clunks and illustrations that represent their meanings.

Clunk concentration: Students use small index cards. On one card they write a clunk and on another the definition. These can be used to play concentration games with a partner or a small group.

Crossword puzzles: Students develop a crossword puzzle using the clunks or other key words related to the topic. The puzzle can then be shared with other group members or passed along to another group.

Mnemonic devices: Students apply memory strategies to help them remember what they have learned. Students might create a rhyme (e.g., "In 1492, Columbus sailed the ocean blue"), an acronym (e.g., HOMES to represent each of the U.S. Great Lakes), or a spatial layout (e.g., given a list of items to be remembered, students mentally place an item in a different room of their house; to recall the items they retrace their steps and retrieve each item from where it was placed).

Numbered heads together: Students in each group number off from 1 – 4 or 1 – 5 (depending upon how many students are in each group). The teacher asks a review question. Students in each group then "put their heads together" to discuss the question and make sure that everyone in the group knows the answer. The teacher then rolls two dice. The number on one die indicates which group is selected; the number on the second die indicates which student within the group answers the question.

Quizzes: Each group writes its best question on the board and the class then answers all of the questions as a homework or in-class assignment.

Send a problem: Each group selects the best question it has generated and passes that question to a different group to answer.

Theme pictures: Students draw pictures about the topic that was just read. Throughout the picture they write key words about the topic that correspond with their illustrations.

Venn diagrams: Each group draws two large intersecting circles on paper or an overhead transparency. First students compare two different ideas by generating a list of similarities and writing these in the overlapping portion of the circles. Then they contrast the two ideas and write differences in the two portions of the circles that are not connected.

Web: Students categorize words or ideas and place these in a semantic map that visually represents the relationships among ideas. Students write the topic in a circle in the middle of the paper and then write related words in categories arranged around the topic.

it helps on our end of the year Stanford Achievement Tests" (Klingner & Vaughn, 1998b). Referring to her LEP students, Lucille Sullivan noted, "I can't believe how well they did, how much they learned. I've seen so much improvement in their English. And they are participating more in other subjects, too. They seem more confident."

References

Anderson, V., & Roit, M. (1996). Linking reading comprehension instruction to language development for language-minority students. *Elementary School Journal, 96*, 295–309.

Cazden, C.B. (1988). *Classroom discourse: The language of teaching and learning.* Portsmouth, NH: Heinemann.

Chamot, A.U., & O'Malley, J.M. (1996). The Cognitive Academic Language Learning Approach: A model for linguistically diverse classrooms. *Elementary School Journal, 96*, 259–273.

Chang, J., & Shimizu, W. (1997, January). *Collaborative strategic reading: Cross-age and cross-cultural applications.* Paper presented at the Council for Exceptional Children Symposium on Culturally and Linguistically Diverse Exceptional Learners, New Orleans, LA.

Cohen, E.G. (1986). *Designing groupwork: Strategies for the heterogeneous classroom.* New York: Teachers College Press.

Cummins, J. (1984). *Bilingualism and special education: Issues in assessment and pedagogy.* San Diego, CA: College Hill.

Díaz, S., Moll, L., & Mehan, H. (1986). Sociocultural resources in instruction: A context-specific approach. In California State Department of Education, *Beyond language: Social and cultural factors in schooling language minority students* (pp. 187–230). Los Angeles: California State University Evaluation, Dissemination, and Assessment Center.

Durán, R.P., & Szymanski, M.H. (1995). Cooperative learning interaction and construction of activity. *Discourse Processes, 19*, 149–169.

Fuchs, D., Fuchs, L.S., Mathes, P., & Simmons, D. (1997). Peer-assisted learning strategies: Making classrooms more responsive to student diversity. *American Educational Research Journal, 34*, 174–206.

Hakuta, K., (1990). *Bilingualism and bilingual education: A research perspective.* Washington, DC: George Washington University, Center for Applied Linguistics.

Hernandez, J.S. (1991). Assisted performance in reading comprehension strategies with non-English proficient students. *Journal of Educational Issues of Language Minority Students, 8*, 91–112.

Jacob, E., Rottenberg, L., Patrick, S., & Wheeler, E. (1996). Cooperative learning: Context and opportunities for acquiring academic English. *TESOL Quarterly, 30*, 253–280.

Johnson, D.W., & Johnson, R.T. (1989). Cooperative learning: What special educators need to know. *The Pointer, 33*, 5–10.

Klingner, J. (1997, March). *Promoting English acquisition and content learning through collaborative strategic reading.* Paper presented at the annual meeting of the American Educational Research Association, Chicago.

Klingner, J.K., & Vaughn, S. (1996). Reciprocal teaching of reading comprehension strategies for students with learning disabilities who use English as a second language. *Elementary School Journal, 96*, 275–293.

Klingner, J.K., & Vaughn, S. (1998a). *The helping behaviors of bilingual fifth-graders during collaborative strategic reading (CSR) cooperative learning.* Unpublished manuscript.

Klingner, J.K., & Vaughn, S. (1998b). Using collaborative strategic reading. *Teaching Exceptional Children, 30*, 32–37.

Klingner, J.K., Vaughn, S., & Schumm, J.S. (1998). Collaborative strategic reading during social studies in heterogeneous fourth-grade classrooms. *Elementary School Journal, 99*, 3–21.

Long, M., & Porter, P. (1985). Group work, interlanguage talk, and second language acquisition. *TESOL Quarterly, 19*, 207–228.

Madden, N.A., & Slavin, R.E. (1983). Mainstreaming students with mild handicaps: Academic and social outcomes. *Review of Educational Research, 53*, 519–569.

Palincsar, A.S., & Brown, A.L. (1984). The reciprocal teaching of comprehension-fostering and comprehension-monitoring activities. *Cognition and Instruction, 1*, 117–175.

Pressley, M., Brown, R., El-Dinary, P.B., & Afflerbach, P. (1995). The comprehension instruction that students need: Instruction fostering constructively responsive reading. *Learning Disabilities Research and Practice, 10*, 215–224.

Richard-Amato, P.A. (1992). Peer teachers: The neglected resource. In P.A. Richard-Amato & M.A. Snow (Eds.), *The multicultural classroom: Readings for content-area teachers* (pp. 271–284). White Plains, NY: Longman.

Rosenshine, B., & Meister, C. (1992). The use of scaffolds for teaching higher-level cognitive strategies. *Educational Leadership, 49*, 26–33.

Stevens, R.J., & Slavin, R.E. (1995). Effects of a cooperative learning approach in reading and writing on academically handicapped and nonhandicapped students. *Elementary School Journal, 95*, 241–262.

Vaughn, S., Hughes, M.T., Schumm, J.S., & Klingner, J. (1998). A collaborative effort to enhance reading and writing. *Learning Disability Quarterly, 21*, 57–74.

Weisberg, R. (1988). 1980's: A change in focus of reading comprehension research: A review of reading/learning disabilities research based on an interactive model of reading. *Learning Disability Quarterly, 11*, 149–159.

What Is Evidence-Based Reading Instruction? A Position Statement of the International Reading Association

There are few instructional tasks more important than teaching children to read. The consequences of low achievement in reading are costly both to individuals and society. Low achievement in literacy correlates with high rates of school drop-out, poverty, and underemployment (Snow, Burns, & Griffin, 1998; Wagner, 2000). The far-reaching effects of literacy achievement have heightened the interest of educators and noneducators alike in the teaching of reading. Policymakers, parents, administrators, and teachers seek the same end—to provide literacy instruction that is most likely to lead to high rates of achievement for all children.

As we pursue this goal, we must be mindful of the critical lesson provided by investigations of the past and of the present: There is no single instructional program or method that is effective in teaching all children to read. Rather, successful efforts to improve reading achievement emphasize identification and implementation of evidence-based practices that promote high rates of achievement when used in classrooms by teachers with diverse instructional styles with children who have diverse instructional needs and interests (Bond & Dykstra, 1967/1997; National Clearinghouse for Comprehensive School Reform, 2001)

Also, as we seek effective programs and practices, we must remain mindful of the powerful influence teachers have. Time and again,

research has confirmed that regardless of the quality of a program, resource, or strategy, it is the teacher and learning situation that make the difference (Bond & Dykstra, 1967/1997). This evidence underscores the need to join practices grounded in sound and rigorous research with well-prepared and skillful teachers.

What does the term *evidence-based reading instruction* mean?

In its simplest form, *evidence-based reading instruction* means that a particular program or collection of instructional practices has a record of success. That is, there is reliable, trustworthy, and valid evidence to suggest that when the program is used with a particular group of children, the children can be expected to make adequate gains in reading achievement. Other terms that are sometimes used to convey the same idea are *research-based instruction* and *scientifically based research*.

This relatively simple concept becomes more complicated when we attempt to define the types of evidence that are reliable and trustworthy indicators of effectiveness. The central question is, What counts as evidence of success? In general, educators agree that such evidence should be as follows:

- objective—data that any evaluator would identify and interpret similarly

- valid—data that adequately represent the tasks that children need to accomplish to be successful readers
- reliable—data will remain essentially unchanged if collected on a different day or by a different person
- systematic—data that were collected according to a rigorous design of either experimentation or observation
- refereed—data that have been approved for publication by a panel of independent reviewers

In addition to evaluating the quality of the data by which programs or practices are judged, teachers also must examine the generalizability, or fit, of the evidence. In other words, teachers might ask if the children in their classrooms closely resemble the children from whom the evidence was collected: Are they the same age? Do they have similar language and cultural backgrounds? Do they have similar learning profiles? Teachers might also ask if the learning contexts are the same: Are class sizes and teacher-student ratios similar? Is the allocation of instructional time and resources similar? Do teachers have similar funds of knowledge? Has more than one study produced particular findings? If the answer to all of these questions is *yes*, then teachers might conclude that there is a good fit and that their students might be expected to make similar achievement gains with the same program or practice. If, however, the answers to some or all of these questions is *no*, then it is difficult to predict whether similar results might be achieved.

Research studies used to collect evidence about programs and practices may have a variety of designs. In general, studies that demonstrate effectiveness using experimental designs (studies that compare results from the program or practices of interest to results from a control group with random assignment to the groups), and quasi-experimental designs (studies that do not use random assignment to the program or comparison group, but use adequate statistical procedures to control preexisting differences) give the strongest evidence of effects of a program or practice on the "average" student—particularly when the studies are carried out in naturalistic environments. Quantitative studies such as these generally investigate program ef-

fects on relatively large numbers of students. In addition, they can be aggregated by using meta-analysis. In contrast, qualitative studies typically focus on small samples or on individuals and are especially valuable in helping teachers understand how particular programs or approaches affect individuals who may not represent the mainstream or average student.

However, no single study ever establishes a program or practice as effective; moreover, it is the convergence of evidence from a variety of study designs that is ultimately scientifically convincing. When evaluating studies and claims of evidence, educators must not determine whether the study is quantitative or qualitative in nature, but rather if the study meets the standards of scientific research. That is, does it involve "rigorous and systematic empirical inquiry that is data-based" (Bogdan & Biklen, 1992, p. 43).

What is the difference between evidence-based programs and evidence-based practices?

The quest to find the "best programs" for teaching reading has a long and quite unsuccessful history. Most notable among such efforts is a group of studies conducted in the mid-1960s that became known as the First-Grade Studies (Bond & Dykstra, 1967/1997). This series of U.S. federally funded investigations examined popular approaches to teaching beginning reading. Included were examinations of basal reading, phonics, language experience, and linguistics approaches to reading instruction. The collection of 27 studies comparing different methods and materials found as many differences between and among teachers using the same program or approach as there were between and among teachers using different programs or approaches, leaving the authors unable to identify a "best" program. Instead, the results led the authors to conclude,

> Children learn to read by a variety of materials and methods.... No one approach is so distinctly better in all situations and respects than the others that it should be considered the one best method and the one to be used exclusively. (Bond & Dykstra, 1967/1997, p. 416)

Indeed, many large studies have come to similar conclusions. For example, consider the recent findings related to the evaluations of Comprehensive School Reform. Once again the focus was on reading programs and methods, and the findings echo those of the First-Grade Studies, that "no models had uniformly positive effects, and no models had uniformly negative or neutral effects. In other words, no model worked in every case and every situation" (National Clearinghouse for Comprehensive School Reform, 2001, p. 2).

Despite many attempts at program studies in the years since the First-Grade Studies, and many claims of program excellence, literacy scholars (e.g., Allington, 2001; Stahl, Duffy-Hester, & Stahl, 1998) argue that careful examination of such studies reveals the use of either flawed designs or selective reporting of the available data. Furthermore, attempts to find the "right program" for large-scale implementation is complicated by the diversity of student needs, teaching styles, and classroom conditions that exist in any school or group of schools.

Whereas efforts to find "best programs" have centered largely on the materials teachers use, attempts to identify best practices have focused on the actions teachers take and the practices in which they routinely engage students. In contrast to the discrepant findings of studies designed to identify best programs, examinations of best practices have led to highly consistent results when such studies have been rigorously designed and systematically analyzed and compared. The results of the First-Grade Studies again provide a relevant starting place. Although findings failed to show superiority of any particular approach or program, evidence did indicate strong relationships between particular practices and high achievement. Most recently, the National Reading Panel (National Institute of Child Health and Human Development, 2000) took a similar approach to its study of effective instruction of reading, examining evidence related to practices in phonemic awareness, phonics, fluency, vocabulary, and comprehension instruction. They found 22 phonics programs that varied along several dimensions that were effective. The results support a conclusion that it is particular practices and not the specific programs that are effective.

Current critical and comprehensive research reviews (e.g., Gambrell, Morrow, Neuman, & Pressley, 1999; Guthrie & Alvermann, 1999; Kamil, Mosenthal, Pearson, & Barr, 2000; National Institute of Child Health and Human Development, 2000; Pressley, Wharton-McDonald, Hampson, & Echevarria 1998; Taylor, Pressley, & Pearson, 2002) indicate widespread agreement among literacy experts concerning the particular literacy practices and experiences in which effective teachers routinely engage children. The following list of 10 research-based best practices posed by Gambrell et al. (1999) is representative of the current state of literacy knowledge and provides an effective template for understanding best literacy practices:

1. Teach reading for authentic meaning-making literacy experiences for pleasure, to be informed, and to perform a task.
2. Use high-quality literature.
3. Integrate a comprehensive word study/phonics program into reading/writing instruction.
4. Use multiple texts that link and expand concepts.
5. Balance teacher- and student-led discussions.
6. Build a whole-class community that emphasizes important concepts and builds background knowledge.
7. Work with students in small groups while other students read and write about what they have read.
8. Give students plenty of time to read in class.
9. Give students direct instruction in decoding and comprehension strategies that promote independent reading. Balance direct instruction, guided instruction, and independent learning.
10. Use a variety of assessment techniques to inform instruction. (p. 14)

What resources might be useful when examining evidence to support particular programs or practices?

A list such as the one presented above provides an important starting point in the development of evidence-based reading instruction. But how might we learn more about each of these practices and the steps toward effective implementation? Rigorous, peer-reviewed, comprehensive research syntheses provide an excellent starting place for teachers, administrators, and policymakers who wish to learn more about effective teaching of reading. Such syntheses are important and useful because they are based on comprehensive and systematic reviews of many studies, and allow us to predict outcomes when the practices are used under similar conditions with children similar to those who participated in the reported investigations.

There are at least three types of research syntheses: large-scale reviews conducted by a team of researchers appointed by a funding agency; edited handbooks, generally compiled by a team of researchers who invite professional colleagues to provide comprehensive reviews of particular topics within a series of chapters; and individual analyses of a particular topic. Individual analyses may be published as book-length monographs, as articles in refereed research journals, or as chapters in edited volumes. The following list gives examples of these types of works, as well as names of refereed research journals.

Large-scale, U.S. federally funded research reviews

Anderson, R.C., Hiebert, E.H., Scott, J.A., & Wilkinson, I.A.G. (1985). *Becoming a nation of readers: The report of the Commission on Reading*. Washington, DC: National Institute of Education.

Bond, G.L., & Dykstra, R. (1997). The cooperative research program in first-grade reading instruction. *Reading Research Quarterly, 32*, 348–427. (Original work published 1967)

National Institute of Child Health and Human Development. (2000). Report of the National Reading Panel. *Teaching children to read— An evidence-based assessment of the scientific research literature on reading and its implications for reading instruction* (NIH Publication No. 00-4769). Washington, DC: U.S. Government Printing Office. (Available at http://www.nichd.nih.gov/publications/nrp/smallbook.htm)

Snow, C.E., Burns, M.S., & Griffin, P. (Eds.). (1998). *Preventing reading difficulties in young children*. Washington, DC: National Academy Press.

Edited handbooks

Barr, R., Kamil, M.L., Mosenthal, P.B., & Pearson, P.D. (Eds.). (1991). *Handbook of reading research* (Vol. 2). White Plains, NY: Longman.

Flood, J., Lapp, D., Squire, J.R., & Jensen, J.M. (Eds.). (2002). *Handbook of research on teaching the English language arts* (2nd ed.). Mahwah, NJ: Erlbaum.

Kamil, M.L., Mosenthal, P.B., Barr, R., & Pearson, P.D. (Eds.). (2000). *Handbook of reading research* (Vol. 3). Mahwah, NJ: Erlbaum.

Neuman, S.B., & Dickinson, D.K. (Eds.). (2001). *Handbook of early literacy research*. New York: Guilford.

Pearson, P.D., Barr, R., Kamil, M.L., & Mosenthal, P.B. (Eds.). (1984). *Handbook of reading research*. New York: Longman.

Research journals

American Educational Research Journal
Journal of Educational Research
Journal of Learning Disabilities
Journal of Literacy Research
Reading Psychology
Reading Research and Instruction
Reading Research Quarterly
Remedial and Special Education

Recommendations

The challenge that confronts teachers and administrators is the need to view the evidence that they read through the lens of their particular school and classroom settings. They must determine if the instructional strategies and routines that are central to the materials under review are a good match for the particular children they teach. That is, are the instructional practices likely to provide their students with the types of experiences that research predicts will result in successful reading? The list of best practices in literacy presented previously may be used to frame questions that will be useful when considering whether there is a good fit between the program or approach under examination and a particular school or classroom setting. The International Reading Association recommends teachers and administrators ask the following questions when reviewing materials:

- Does this program or instructional approach provide systematic and explicit instruction in the particular strategies that have been proven to relate to high rates of achievement in reading for the children I teach?

- Does the program or instructional approach provide flexibility for use with the range of learners in the various classrooms where it will be used? Are there assessment tools that assist teachers in identifying individual learning needs? Are there a variety of strategies and activities that are consistent with diverse learning needs?

- Does the program or instructional approach provide a collection of high-quality literary materials that are diverse in level of difficulty, genre, topic, and cultural representation to meet the individual needs and interests of the children with whom it will be used?

In addition to examining the match between the instructional approach or program and the children they teach, administrators and teachers also must consider the match between the instructional approach or program and the resources available for implementation (e.g., Hayes, 1997; Richardson, 1994). Questions such as the following may help teachers and administrators assess appropriateness of resources and professional development opportunities:

- What instructional personnel will be required to effectively implement the program or instructional approach? That is, can the program be implemented by a classroom teacher alone, or will it require additional instructional personnel within or outside the classroom?

- What types of professional development will be necessary for effective implementation of the program or instructional approach?

- What adjustments to existing academic programs and practices will be necessary for effective implementation of the program or instructional approach?

References

Allington, R.L. (2001). *What really matters for struggling readers: Designing research-based programs.* New York: Longman.

Bogdan, R.C., & Biklen, S.K. (1992). *Qualitative research for education: An introduction to theory and methods* (2nd ed.). Boston: Allyn & Bacon.

Bond, G.L., & Dykstra, R. (1997). The cooperative research program in first-grade reading instruction. *Reading Research Quarterly, 32,* 348–427. (Original work published 1967)

Gambrell, L.B., Morrow, L.M. , Neuman, S.B., & Pressley, M. (1999). *Best practices in literacy instruction.* New York: Guilford.

Guthrie, J.T., & Alvermann, D.E. (Eds.). (1999). *Engaged reading: Processes, practices, and policy implications.* New York: Teachers College Press.

Hayes, D.A. (1997). Models of professional practice in teacher thinking. In S.A. Stahl & D.A. Hayes (Eds)., *Instructional models in reading* (pp. 31–58). Mahwah, NJ: Erlbaum.

Kamil, M.L., Mosenthal, P.B., Pearson, P.D., & Barr, R. (2000). *Handbook of reading research* (Vol. 3). Mahwah, NJ: Erlbaum.

National Clearinghouse for Comprehensive School Reform. (2001). *Taking stock: Lessons on comprehensive school reform from policy, practice, and research.* Benchmarks, 2, 1–11.

National Institute of Child Health and Human Development. (2000). Report of the National Reading Panel. *Teaching children to read—An evidence-based assessment of the scientific research literature on reading and its implications for reading instruction* (NIH Publication No. 00-4769). Washington, DC: U.S. Government Printing Office. (Available http://www.nichd.nih.gov/publications/nrp/smallbook.htm)

Pressley, M., Wharton-McDonald, R., Hampson, J.M., Echevarria, M. (1998). The nature of literacy instruction in ten grade 4–5 classrooms in upstate New York. *Scientific Studies of Reading, 2,* 159–194.

Richardson, V. (1994). *Teacher change and the staff development process: A case study in reading instruction.* New York: Teachers College Press.

Snow, C.E., Burns, M.S., & Griffin, P. (1998). *Preventing reading difficulties in young children.* Washington, DC: National Academy Press.

Stahl, S.A., Duffy-Hester, A.M., & Stahl, K.A.D. (1998). Everything you wanted to know about phonics (but were afraid to ask). *Reading Research Quarterly, 33,* 338–355.

Taylor, B.M., Pressley, M.P., & Pearson, P.D. (2002). Research-supported characteristics of teachers and schools that promote reading achievement. In B.M. Taylor & P.D. Pearson (Eds.), *Teaching reading: Effective Schools, accomplished teachers* (pp. 361–373). Mahwah, NJ: Erlbaum.

Wagner, D.A. (2000). EFA 2000 thematic study on literacy and adult education: For presentation at the World Education Forum, Dakar (April, 2000). Philadelphia: International Literacy Institute.

Note: This brochure may be purchased from the International Reading Association in bulk quantities, prepaid only. (Please contact the Association for pricing information.) Single copies are free upon request by sending a self-addressed, stamped envelope. Requests from outside the U.S. should include an envelope, but postage is not required. Single copies also can be downloaded free for personal use through the Association's website: www.reading.org/positions.html (requires Adobe's Acrobat Reader).

Related Resources From the International Reading Association

International Reading Association Journals

The Reading Teacher (RT)

This top-rated journal contains useful information and practical insights for educators of children ages 5 to 12. A peer-reviewed, professional journal published eight times yearly, *RT* gives thoughtful consideration to practices, research, and trends in literacy education and related fields. It takes an active stance on issues affecting education today: appraising and extending the profession, promoting literacy worldwide, embracing pluralism, transforming teaching, owning technology, and connecting with the community.

Journal of Adolescent & Adult Literacy (JAAL)

JAAL is a peer-reviewed journal published eight times a year and intended as an open forum for the field of literacy education. Its goals are to encourage innovative ways of teaching and studying literacy. *JAAL* publishes material directed to professionals who work with learners from about age 12 through adulthood. These individuals include students in middle school; junior high school; secondary school; colleges or universities; and adults in literacy programs set in communities, institutions, or the workplace.

Reading Research Quarterly (RRQ)

RRQ is the leading peer-reviewed professional research journal for those committed to scholarship on questions of literacy among learners of all ages. *RRQ* supports the spirit of inquiry that is essential to the ongoing development of literacy research, and provides a forum for multidisciplinary research, alternative modes of investigation, and variant viewpoints about the nature of literacy practices and policies of diverse groups of persons around the world. *RRQ* is now also available in an online version; see http://www.reading.org/rrqonline/ for more information on *RRQ Online*.

Lectura y Vida

Lectura y Vida is the Association's Spanish-language quarterly. Published in Argentina, it is of particular interest to those working in Latin America and elsewhere in the Spanish-speaking world. Each issue offers insightful articles on research, theory, and practice applicable to all teaching levels. For more information on this journal, please visit the *Lectura y Vida* website, http://www.lecturayvida.org.ar/.

Reading Online (ROL)

ROL is a peer-reviewed electronic journal of classroom literacy practice and research for K–12 educators. A special mission of *ROL* is to support professionals as they begin to integrate digital and networked technologies within their classrooms. *ROL* was created as an interactive journal, not an electronic version of a traditional print publication. It provides opportunities for dialogue between and among contributors and readers while delivering information in new formats that expand our understanding as readers, teachers, and learners.

Thinking Classroom/Peremena

Thinking Classroom (also published in Russian as *Peremena*, which means "change") provides perspectives and descriptions of teaching experiences from around the world. This quarterly journal explores how schools can contribute to improving society by helping students create, question, and apply knowledge responsibly. Peer-reviewed articles discuss active inquiry, student-centered and cooperative learning, problem solving, critical thinking, alternative assessment, and ways that educators can bridge cultural divides.

Articles can be accessed through the Association's website http://www.reading.org. Click on the Article Archive link and then the ProQuest Archiver icon.

Reading Research Quarterly Articles Cited in the National Reading Panel Report

Adams, A., Carnine, D., & Gersten, R. (1982). Instructional strategies for studying content area texts in the intermediate grades. *Reading Research Quarterly, 18,* 27–55.

Anderson, R.C., Wilkinson, I.A.G., & Mason, J.M. (1991). A microanalysis of the small-group, guided reading lesson: Effects of an emphasis on global story meaning. *Reading Research Quarterly, 26,* 417–441.

Armbruster, B.B., Anderson, T.H., & Meyer, J.L. (1991). Improving content-area reading using instructional graphics. *Reading Research Quarterly, 26,* 393–416.

Armbruster, B.B., Anderson, T.H., & Meyer, J.L. (1991). "Improving content-area reading using instructional graphics": Erratum. *Reading Research Quarterly, 27,* 282.

Armbruster, B.B., Anderson, T.H., & Ostertag, J. (1987). Does text structure/summarization instruction facilitate learning from expository text? *Reading Research Quarterly, 22,* 331–346.

Atkinson, R. (1968–1969). A reply to reaction to computer-assisted instruction in initial reading: The Stanford Project. *Reading Research Quarterly, 3,* 418–420.

Atkinson, R., & Hansen, D. (1966–1967). Computer-assisted instruction in initial reading: The Stanford Project. *Reading Research Quarterly, 2,* 5–26.

Ball, E., & Blachman, B. (1991). Does phoneme awareness training in kindergarten make a difference in early word recognition and developmental spelling? *Reading Research Quarterly, 26,* 49–66.

Baumann, J.F. (1984). The effectiveness of an instruction paradigm for teaching main idea comprehension. *Reading Research Quarterly, 20,* 93–115.

Baumann, J.F. (1986). Teaching third-grade students to comprehend anaphoric relationships: The application of a direct instruction model. *Reading Research Quarterly, 21,* 70–90.

Berkowitz, S.J. (1986). Effects of instruction in text organization on sixth-grade students' memory for expository reading. *Reading Research Quarterly, 21,* 161–178.

Biemiller, A. (1977–1978). Relationships between oral reading rates for letters, words, and simple text in the development of reading achievement. *Reading Research Quarterly, 13,* 223–253.

Bond, G., & Dykstra, R. (1967/1998). The cooperative research program in first grade reading. *Reading Research Quarterly, 2,* 5–142.

Calfee, R.C., & Piaotkowski, D.C. (1981). The reading diary: Acquisition of decoding. *Reading Research Quarterly, 16,* 346–373.

Dahl, K.L., Sharer, P.L., Lawson, L.L., & Grogran, P.R. (1999). Phonics instruction and student achievement in whole language first-grade classrooms. *Reading Research Quarterly, 34,* 312–341.

Dickinson, D.K., & Smith, M.W. (1994). Long-term effects of preschool teachers' book readings on low-income children's vocabulary and story comprehension. *Reading Research Quarterly, 29,* 104–122.

Dole, J.A., Valencia, S.W., Greer, E.A., & Wardrop, J.L. (1991). Effects of two types of prereading instruction on the comprehension of narrative and expository text. *Reading Research Quarterly, 26,* 142–159.

Dowhower, S.L. (1987). Effects of repeated reading on second-grade transitional readers' fluency and comprehension. *Reading Research Quarterly, 22,* 389–406.

Dressman, M. (1999). On the use and misuse of research evidence: Decoding two states' reading initiatives. *Reading Research Quarterly, 34,* 258–285.

Duffy, G.G., Roehler, L.R., Meloth, M.S., Vavrus, L.G., Book, C., Putnam, J., & Wesselman, R. (1986). The relationship between explicit verbal explanations during reading skill instruction and student awareness and achievement: A study of reading teacher effects. *Reading Research Quarterly, 21,* 237–252.

Duffy, G.G., Roehler, L.R., Sivan, E., Rackliff, G., Book, C., Meloth, M., Vavrus, L., Wesselman, R., Rutnma, J., & Bassiri, D. (1987). Effects of explaining the reasoning associated with using reading strategies. *Reading Research Quarterly, 22,* 347–368.

Durkin, D. (1979). What classroom observations reveal about reading comprehension. *Reading Research Quarterly, 14,* 518–544.

Durkin, D. (1981). Reading comprehension instruction in five basal reading series. *Reading Research Quarterly, 14,* 481–533.

Ehri, L., & Wilce, L. (1987b). Does learning to spell help beginners learn to read words? *Reading Research Quarterly, 22,* 48–65.

Fleischer, L.S., Jenkins, J., & Pany, D. (1979). Effects on poor readers' comprehension of training in rapid decoding. *Reading Research Quarterly, 14,* 30–48.

Gambrell, L.B., & Bales, R.J. (1986). Mental imagery and the comprehension-monitoring performance of fourth and fifth-grade poor readers. *Reading Research Quarterly, 21,* 454–464.

Guthrie, J.T., et al. (1996). Growth of literacy engagement: Changes in motivations and strategies during concept-oriented reading instruction. *Reading Research Quarterly, 31,* 306–332.

Herman, P.A. (1985). The effect of repeated readings on reading rate, speech pauses, and word recognition accuracy. *Reading Research Quarterly, 20,* 553–565.

Jenkins, J.R., Matlock, B., & Slocum, T.A. (1989). Two approaches to vocabulary instruction: The teaching of individual word meanings and practice in deriving word meaning from context. *Reading Research Quarterly, 24,* 215–235.

Judy, J.E., Alexander, P.A., Kulikowich, J.M., & Wilson, V.L. (1988). Effects of two instructional approaches and peer tutoring on gifted and non gifted sixth-grade students' analogy performance. *Reading Research Quarterly, 23,* 236–256.

Kameenui, E., Carnine, D., & Freschi, R. (1982). Effects of text construction and instructional procedures for teaching word meanings on comprehension and recall. *Reading Research Quarterly, 17,* 367–388.

Lie, A. (1991). Effects of a training program for stimulating skills in word analysis in first-grade children. *Reading Research Quarterly, 26,* 234–250.

Linden, M., & Wittrock, M.C. (1981). The teaching of reading comprehension according to the model of generative learning. *Reading Research Quarterly, 17,* 44–57.

Lundberg, I., Frost, J., & Peterson, O. (1988). Effects of an extensive program for stimulating phonological awareness in preschool children. *Reading Research Quarterly, 23,* 263–284.

Lysynchuk, L.M., Pressley, M., d'Ailly, H., Smith, M., & Cake, H. (1989). A methodological analysis of experimental studies of comprehension strategy instruction. *Reading Research Quarterly, 24,* 458–470.

McGuiness, D., McGuiness, C., & Donohue, J. (1995). Phonological training and the alphabet principle: Evidence for reciprocal causality. *Reading Research Quarterly, 30,* 830–852.

McKeown, M.G., Beck, I.L., Omanson, R.C., & Pople, M.T. (1985). Some effects of the nature and frequency of vocabulary instruction on the knowledge and use of words. *Reading Research Quarterly, 20,* 522–535.

Miller, G.E. (1985). The effects of general and specific self-instruction training on children's comprehension monitoring performances during reading. *Reading Research Quarterly, 20,* 616–628.

Morrison, C., Harris, A.J., & Auerbach, I.T. (1969). Staff aftereffects of participation in a reading research project: A follow-up study of the craft project. *Reading Research Quarterly, 4,* 366–395.

Nagy, W., & Anderson, R.C. (1984). How many words are there in printed school English? *Reading Research Quarterly, 19,* 304–330.

Peters, E.E., & Levin, J.R. (1986). Effects of a mnemonic imagery strategy on good and poor readers' prose recall. *Reading Research Quarterly, 21,* 179–192.

Pinnel, G., Lyons, C., DeFord, D., Bryk, A., & Seltzer, M. (1994). Comparing instructional models for the literacy education of high-risk 1st graders. *Reading Research Quarterly, 29,* 9–39.

Pfaum, S.W., & Pascarella, E.T. (1980). Interactive effects of prior reading achievement and training in context on the reading of learning-disabled children. *Reading Research Quarterly, 16,* 138–158.

Rack, J., Snowling, M., & Olson, R. (1992). The nonword reading deficit in developmental dyslexia: A review. *Reading Research Quarterly, 27,* 29–53.

Raphael, T.E., & Wonnacott, C.A. (1985). Heightening fourth-grade students' sensitivity to sources of information for answering comprehension questions. *Reading Research Quarterly, 20,* 282–296.

Reinking, D. (1988). Computer-mediated text and comprehension differences: The role of reading time, reader preference, and estimation of learning. *Reading Research Quarterly, 23,* 484–498.

Reitsma, P. (1988). Reading practice for beginners: Effects of guided reading, reading-while-listening, and independent reading with computer-based speech feedback. *Reading Research Quarterly, 23,* 219–235.

Reutzel, D.R., & Hollingsworth, P.M. (1988). Highlighting key vocabulary: A generative-reciprocal procedure for teaching selected inference types. *Reading Research Quarterly, 23,* 358–378.

Rinehart, S.D., Stahl, S.A., & Erickson, L.G. (1986). Some effects of summarization on reading and studying. *Reading Research Quarterly, 21*(4), 479–530.

Roth, S., & Beck, I. (1987). Theoretical and instructional implications of the assessment of two microcomputer word recognition programs. *Reading Research Quarterly, 22,* 197–218.

Santa, C., & Hoien, T. (1999). An assessment of early steps: A program for early intervention of reading problems. *Reading Research Quarterly, 34,* 54–79.

Scott, J., & Nagy, W. (1997). Understanding the definitions of unfamiliar verbs. *Reading Research Quarterly, 32,* 184–200.

Senechal, M., & Cornell, E.H. (1993). Vocabulary acquisition through shared reading experiences. *Reading Research Quarterly, 28,* 360–374.

Shany, M.T., & Biemiller, A. (1995). Assisted reading practice: Effects of performance for poor readers in grades 3 and 4. *Reading Research Quarterly, 30,* 382–395.

Shaywitz, B., Holford, T.R., Holahan, J.M., Fletcher, J.M., Steubing, K.K., Francis, D.J., & Shaywitz, S.E. (1995). A Matthew effect for IQ but not for reading: Results from a longitudinal study of reading. *Reading Research Quarterly, 30,* 894–906.

Singer, H., & Donlan, D. (1982). Active comprehension: Problem-solving schema with question generation for comprehension of complex short stories. *Reading Research Quarterly, 17*(2), 166–186.

Spache, G. (1968–1969). A reaction to computer-assisted instruction in initial reading: The Stanford Project. *Reading Research Quarterly, 3,* 101–109.

Stanovich, K.E. (1986). Matthew effects in reading: Some consequences of individual differences in the acquisition of literacy. *Reading Research Quarterly, 21,* 360–406.

Stevens, R.J., Madden, N.A., Slavin, R.E., & Farnish, A.M. (1987). Cooperative integrated reading and composition: Two field experiments. *Reading Research Quarterly, 22,* 433–454.

Taylor, B.M., & Beach, R.W. (1984). The effects of text structure instruction on middle-grade students' comprehension and production of expository prose. *Reading Research Quarterly, 19,* 134–136.

Tharp, R.G. (1982). The effective instruction of comprehension: Results and description of the Kamehameha early reading education program. *Reading Research Quarterly, 17*, 503–527.

Troia, G. (1999). Phonological awareness intervention research: A critical review of the experimental methodology. *Reading Research Quarterly, 34*, 28–52.

Uhry, J., & Shepherd, M. (1993). Segmentation/spelling instruction as part of a first-grade reading program: Effects on several measures of reading. *Reading Research Quarterly, 28*, 218–233.

Underwood, N.R., & McConkie, G.W. (1985). Perceptual span for letter distinctions during reading. *Reading Research Quarterly, 20*, 153–162.

Wasik, B., & Slavin, R. (1993). Preventing early reading failure with one-to-one tutoring: A review of five programs. *Reading Research Quarterly, 28*, 179–200.

Wixson, K.K. (1986). Vocabulary instruction and children's comprehension of basal stories. *Reading Research Quarterly, 21*, 317–329.

The Reading Teacher Articles Cited in the National Reading Panel Report

Allington, R.L. (1983). Fluency: The neglected reading goal in reading instruction. *The Reading Teacher, 36*, 556–561.

Au, K.H., & Scheu, J.A. (1989). Guiding students to interpret a novel. *The Reading Teacher, 43*, 104–110.

Babbs, P.J. (1984). Monitoring cards help improve comprehension. *The Reading Teacher, 38*, 200–204.

Baumann, J., Hoffman, J., Moon, J., & Duffy-Hester, A. (1998). Where are teachers' voices in the phonics/whole language debate? Results from a survey of U.S. elementary classroom teachers. *The Reading Teacher, 51*, 636–650.

Boodt, G.M. (1984). Critical listeners become critical readers in remedial reading class. *The Reading Teacher, 37*, 390–394.

Brown, R., El-Dinary, P.B., Pressley, M., & Coy-Ogan, L. (1995). A transactional strategies approach to reading instruction (National Reading Research Center). *The Reading Teacher, 49*, 256–258.

Chall, J., & Feldmann, S. (1966). First grade reading: An analysis of the interactions of professed methods, teacher implications, and child background. *The Reading Teacher, 19*, 569–575.

Cohen, R. (1983). Students generate questions as an aid to reading comprehension. *The Reading Teacher, 36*, 770–775.

Conley, M.M.W. (1983). Increasing students' reading achievement via teacher inservice education. *The Reading Teacher, 36*, 804–808.

Dykstra, R. (1968). The effectiveness of code- and meaning-emphasis in beginning reading programs. *The Reading Teacher, 22*, 17–23.

Helfeldt, J.P., & Lalik, R. (1976). Reciprocal student-teacher questioning. *The Reading Teacher, 33*, 283–287.

Herrmann, B.A. (1988). Two approaches for helping poor readers become more strategic. *The Reading Teacher, 42*, 24–28.

Hunt, L.C., Jr. (1970). The effect of self-selection, interest, and motivation on independent, instructional, and frustrational levels. *The Reading Teacher, 24*, 146–151, 158.

Hollingsworth, P.M. (1970). An experiment with the impress method of teaching reading. *The Reading Teacher, 24*, 112–114, 187.

Hollingsworth, P.M. (1978). An experimental approach to the impress method of teaching reading. *The Reading Teacher, 31*, 624–627.

Labbo, L.D., & Teale, W. (1990). Cross-age reading: A strategy for helping poor readers. *The Reading Teacher, 43*, 362–369.

Mier, M. (1984). Comprehension monitoring in the elementary classroom. *The Reading Teacher, 37*, 770–774.

Nolte, R.Y., & Singer, H. (1985). Active comprehension: Teaching a process of reading comprehension and its effects on reading achievement. *The Reading Teacher, 39*, 24–31.

Reutzel, D.R. (1985). Story maps improve comprehension. *The Reading Teacher, 38*, 400–404.

Reutzel, D.R. (1986). Clozing in on comprehension: The Cloze story map. *The Reading Teacher, 39*, 524–528.

Samuels, S.J. (1979). The method of repeated readings. *The Reading Teacher, 32*, 403–408.

Shanahan, S., Wojciehowski, J., & Rubik, G. (1998). A celebration of reading: How our school read for one million minutes. *The Reading Teacher, 52*, 93–96.

Sinatra, R.C., Stahl-Gemake, J., & Berg, D.N. (1984). Improving reading comprehension of disabled readers through semantic mapping. *The Reading Teacher, 38*, 22–29.

Spiegel, D.L., & Fitzgerald, J. (1986). Improving reading comprehension through instruction about story parts. *The Reading Teacher, 39*, 676–682.

Topping, K. (1987). Paired reading: A powerful technique for parent use. *The Reading Teacher, 40*, 608–614.

Uttero, D.A. (1988). Activating comprehension through cooperative learning. *The Reading Teacher, 41*, 390–395.

Varnhagen, C.K., & Goldman, S.R. (1986). Improving comprehension: Causal instruction for learning handicapped learners. *The Reading Teacher, 39*, 896–904.

Wixson, K.K. (1983). Questions about a text: What you ask about is what children learn. *The Reading Teacher, 37*, 287–293.

Other *Reading Research Quarterly* Articles Related to Evidence-Based Reading Instruction

Baumann, J.F., Hoffman, J.V., Duffy-Hester, A.M., & Ro, J.M. (2000). The first R yesterday and today: U.S. elementary reading instruction practices reported by teachers and administrators. *Reading Research Quarterly, 35*, 338–377.

Block, C.C., Oakar, M., & Hurt, N. (2002). The expertise of literacy teachers: A continuum from preschool to grade 5. *Reading Research Quarterly, 37*, 178–206.

Reinking, D., & Watkins, J. (2000). A formative experiment investigating the use of multimedia book reviews to increase elementary students' independent. *Reading Research Quarterly, 35*, 383–419.

Shanahan, T., & Neuman, S.B. (1997). Literacy research that makes a difference. *Reading Research Quarterly, 32*, 636–647.

Van den Branden, K. (2000). Does negotiation of meaning promote reading comprehension? A study of multilingual primary school classes. *Reading Research Quarterly, 35*, 426–443.

International Reading Association Books Related to Evidence-Based Reading Instruction

Beginning Reading and Writing, Dorothy S. Strickland & Lesley Mandel Morrow, Editors (2000)

Children Achieving: Best Practices in Early Literacy, Susan B. Neuman & Kathleen A. Roskos, Editors (1998)

Distinguished Educators on Reading: Contributions That Have Shaped Effective Literacy Instruction, Nancy D. Padak et al., Editors (2000)

Reading Researchers in Search of Common Ground, Rona F. Flippo, Editor (2001)

Perspectives on Writing: Research, Theory, and Practice, Roselmina Indrisano & James R. Squire, Editors (2000)

Theoretical Models and Processes of Reading, Fourth Edition, Robert B. Ruddell, Martha Rapp Ruddell, & Harry Singer, Editors (1994)

What Research Has to Say About Reading Instruction, Third Edition, Alan E. Farstrup & S. Jay Samuels, Editors (2002)